Praise for *Blowout*

#1 *New York Times* bestseller

"An account of international intrigue, high finance, low characters, and outrageous legal and illegal acts that put the global economy and Western democracy at grave risk.... [Rachel Maddow] tells this tale deliberately and methodically, building her case not as a cable commentator, but as a Rhodes Scholar.... She displays a deep understanding of what makes Russia work in the age of Putin."

—*The Boston Globe*

"At its heart, this book is a tale of two countries, the United States and Russia, and how, as Maddow sees it—individually and together—they have been warped by a rapacious fossil fuel industry.... Fulminating comes easy to Rachel Maddow. What sets her apart from other serial fulminators is that she does it with facts—and sardonic wit."

—*The Washington Post*

"*Blowout* is a rollickingly well-written book, filled with fascinating, exciting and alarming stories about the impact of the oil and gas industry on the world today.... [It features] many colorful tales about villains, scoundrels and adventurers.... A brilliant description of many of the problems caused by our reliance on fossil fuels."

—*The New York Times Book Review*

"[Maddow] may be a popular, progressive news-and-commentary anchor on MSNBC, but it's not to be forgotten that she holds a doctorate in politics from Oxford and seems to devour whole libraries of data before breakfast each day.... Expect a tweetstorm as Maddow's indictment of a corrupt industry finds readers—and it deserves many."

—*Kirkus Reviews* (starred review)

"Known for her intense inquiries into complex subjects, Maddow brings her laser-like intuitiveness and keen and wily perception to Big Oil, that stalwart of global economics, and the shadowy nexus of commerce and politics. Maddow likes murky, the murkier the better, and her examination of the intricacies of off-shore drilling, transnational pipelines, and hydraulic fracking is as deep as the coveted wells themselves. . . . Like trailblazing journalists before her, Maddow exposes both the slapdash and sinister practices underlying geopolitics and energy policies and revels in peeling back the layers of malfeasance to stoke righteous outrage."

—*Booklist* (starred review)

"All fans of Maddow, and even her detractors, will learn something new from this highly readable yet impressively detailed book. Anyone interested in the covert deals that change the nature of the global environmental and political landscape will devour. A must-have for all collections."

—*Library Journal* (starred review)

"Radiates zing, intelligence, and black humor. Much like its author."

—*InStyle*

BLOWOUT

BLOWOUT

CORRUPTED DEMOCRACY,

ROGUE STATE RUSSIA, AND

THE RICHEST, MOST DESTRUCTIVE

INDUSTRY ON EARTH

RACHEL MADDOW

CROWN
NEW YORK

To the bots and trolls, all of you, with love.

CONTENTS

IN A SURREALIST LANDSCAPE

THE VERY IDEA OF IT WAS TOO IMPLAUSIBLE, TOO FANTASTICAL, to be believed; it was simply too outlandishly grand even for a grand opening. A visiting head of state, one of the most powerful men on the planet in the autumn of 2003, had announced his intention to be on hand to christen a tiny new franchise operation on the frowsy little corner of West 24th Street and Tenth Avenue in Manhattan.

The world potentate was in the middle of a three-day swing through New York City, on his way to a one-on-one summit with George W. Bush at the American presidential retreat, Camp David. He had spent the past few days in the august citadels of power, money, and meaning in New York; had taken private meetings with the president of France and the chancellor of Germany in his private suites at the Waldorf Astoria hotel; had delivered a widely anticipated address to the General Assembly of the United Nations; had fielded earnest questions about the benefits and the perils of democracy from scholars at the city's premier university; had bowed his head in prayer alongside religious leaders whose brethren had long ago been exiled from their shared home country; and had laid a bouquet of red carnations at a temporary memorial to the 343 New York City firefighters killed just two years earlier in the 9/11 attacks. The New York *Daily News* reporters thought they had detected an actual tear slide down the presidential cheek as he placed the floral remembrance for the dead American heroes. Now the world leader was going to veer off this power slalom to preside over the grand opening of a business with a few hundred square feet of retail space, valued in its recent purchase at $55,000?

As the hour of the scheduled grand opening in the increasingly gay New York neighborhood of Chelsea neared, he was meeting with two dozen captains of American industry in the cavernous banquet room of what might well be considered the Royal Palace of International Capitalism—the New York Stock Exchange. Heads of the largest companies in America were on hand; the CEO of the most profitable company in the history of the modern world, ExxonMobil, had flown in from Texas to be among the interlocutors. All of which appeared to please the guest of honor. "We have been surrounded by a very kind and warm atmosphere almost everywhere we have been in New York," was his opening message, as translated to the industrial barons through the elegant headset provided to each. "It is this direct contact that allows all of us—both politicians and entrepreneurs—to open new possibilities and spheres for wide cooperation."

Three miles north, meanwhile, at 24th Street and Tenth Avenue, as the security team began to shut down surrounding streets, shoo away the occasional Rollerblader, and tape off a makeshift pen for the growing press contingent, the store's attendants readjusted their new red shirts and ball caps. Among the curious onlookers at this unfolding scene, skepticism reigned. "Nobody thinks he will come," the store manager confided to one reporter. "We are telling people. They say, 'No way.'"

But then, at around two o'clock in the afternoon, there was a wail of sirens from the south, and a boxy Eastern European–style armored limousine tucked in among a phalanx of armored vehicles came into view. The small crowd of people who craned their necks and stared south toward the motorcade also noted the sudden appearance of the senior U.S. senator from the great state of New York, there to greet the arriving limousine. This was really gonna happen. The attendants and managers readjusted their shirts and ball caps one final time. The counterman checked again to make sure that the coffee was hot and the doughnuts were arrayed in comely fashion. By the time the honored ribbon cutter emerged from behind the steel curtain of armed and armored security and walked toward the gas pumps and cash registers, local reporters were already rehearsing their ledes. "In possibly the greatest show of political power ever to attend the grand opening of a gas station," the *New York Post* would offer, "Russian President Vladimir Putin showed up in Chelsea yesterday with Sen. Chuck Schumer to help inaugurate the first Russian-owned chain of petroleum stops in America."

The *Post*'s rival tabloid, the New York *Daily News,* countered with "Fill 'er up, Vlad," under the headline "No Fueling, That's Putin."

There was a hint of pride in Vladimir Putin's open, shoulder-swinging gait as he strode across the gas station lot to shake hands with the five nervous-looking attendants, who could now be officially counted among the ranks of Moscow-based OAO Lukoil's 120,000 employees. Their uniforms, President Putin must have noted, were snappy and vibrant and matched the rest of the station decor—power red! The day was overcast and the sky wan, but the nearby credit-card-ready gas pumps gleamed under lights recessed in the new high canopy built to shield customers from the vagaries of weather and to dispense retardant chemical foam in the event of a gasoline fire.

The franchisee of this station, Paramgit Kumar, was in his glory too, and all thanks to Lukoil, the largest and most profitable oil company in Russia, a country second only to Saudi Arabia in daily production of crude. Lukoil claimed more proven reserves of oil than any publicly traded company on earth and had taken up its position at the point of the flying wedge of Russia's entry onto the new world order's wide-open field of commerce. The corporation had emerged from the dank, state-run ruins of the Soviet Oil Ministry into the bright lights of free-market capitalism, a fact recently confirmed by the company's official listing on the London Stock Exchange. Another first for Russia! Share prices of Lukoil had risen from $3.54 to $24.55 in just four years. Revenues had jumped from $15.5 billion to more than $22 billion in the previous year alone. Western bankers had enthusiastically stuck their heads into the scrum for the chance to win enormous fees for trail-bossing Lukoil's $775 million public stock offering.

Lukoil had used a wee bit of its new Western-fed capitalization to acquire the moribund Getty Petroleum Marketing Inc., with its thirteen hundred gas station properties dotting the Eastern Seaboard of the United States. That made it the first Russian company to own an

American company listed on the New York Stock Exchange. And that meant that some of the Lukoil shine had fallen on Mr. Kumar. He had been one of the first operators to grab his new parent company's offer of a loan guarantee—at way-below-market financing—to upgrade his seedy little Getty station. "[My] station is a piece of junk," one fellow Getty operator complained. "My pumps are about fifty years old." The cash infusion allowed Kumar to upgrade his pumps, his flame-retardant canopy, his Kwik Farms minimart, and his color scheme. Power red! You could see it ten blocks away. So what if the Lukoil name was new to his customers and kind of foreign sounding. The makeover and rebrand meant he had it all over his nearest competitors—ExxonMobil, Hess, and Gaseteria. "There aren't too many gas stations in New York City that are new and attractive, so we stick out," Kumar would boast to a reporter from *Convenience Store News*. "Plus, now we have a convenience store as well, which brings in gas customers and customers just walking by on the street."

Schumer had to walk quickly to stay at the shoulder of the Russian president as the two men were escorted under the new canopy, past the giant flowerpots teeming with chrysanthemums, toward the convenience store tucked back in the corner of the lot, under the hulk of what used to be elevated train tracks. Putin kept his head bent away from Senator Schumer as he made his way toward the soda-pop-and-cigarette wiles of the Kwik Farms. The Russian president was instead listening intently to the gentleman on his right, a beefy executive in a dark suit, with a head of gray hair cropped tight and neat in the old Soviet military style. This was the CEO of Lukoil's worldwide operation, Vagit Alekperov, who had flown in from Moscow for the opening.

Alekperov was a welcome sight for Putin, a man he knew he could count on. There were other tycoons back in Moscow more able in the area of high finance, more schooled in the Western-style corporate governance that international investors now demanded, and more adventurous in developing and deploying expensive new technologies for extracting crude oil and natural gas from Russia's vast and waiting reserves. But there were risks in being too keen. Putin had seen too many Russian businessmen whose heads had been turned by the enormous financial possibilities in oil and gas, who had become eager to invite American and British oil majors in to develop the Russian fields. He worried men like that might accidentally give away the store. But Vladimir Putin did not worry about Vagit Alekperov, who had come up among the roughneck ranks in the Soviet oil fields in Azerbaijan, managed fields in western Siberia, and served as the youngest-ever deputy head of the Soviet Ministry of Energy when it was overseeing production of more barrels of crude per day than any country in the world, single-handedly meeting the U.S.S.R.'s daily energy needs, financing the Soviet government and its ruling Communist Party, and providing both energy and necessary cash to the worldwide span of Soviet satellites and friends.

By 2003, of course, the Soviet Union was no more, but Alekperov retained his sense of mission from the old superpower days. He was still a dedicated patriot. Russia's coat of arms enjoyed a place of pride on his office wall back in Moscow; a black-and-white headshot of Vladimir Putin was the lone photograph on his orderly titanium-and-glass desk. The imperatives of the Russian Federation and its president were never far from mind. The move into the retail gas market of the United States, for instance, was likely to be a losing financial proposition for Lukoil, but Alekperov understood that his duties as CEO of the country's largest oil company were not merely fiduciary. He understood the geopolitical and symbolic importance of this move into the American market, and he understood the need to support the aims of the Russian president. "It is impossible to divide the interests of a country and a company that works on its soil," Alekperov told the American reporter Peter Maass, who was working up a profile of the oil baron for *The New York Times Magazine*. "Our interests are the same. What's good for Russia is good for the company."

Alekperov had been on hand at the New York Stock Exchange just an hour before his arrival at the gas station and had heard Putin sing his song of Russian success to a handful of America's corporate luminaries. "In the first half of this year, in comparison with the equivalent period last year, the volume of GDP increased by 7 percent, industrial production by 6.9 percent, and investment by almost 12 percent," Putin told the group. Russia's economic growth topped world averages year after year, he boasted. "It must be noted that the results achieved are not just thanks to the favorable internal economic situation but also growing entrepreneurial and investment activity. These figures can be attributed to the structural reforms taking place in Russia and the general improvement of the business climate in the country." Putin went on to reiterate his recently announced goal of doubling Russia's GDP in the next decade.

"I am certain that the personnel, scientific-technical, and rich natural potential of the country, combined with new economic and civic freedom, should give us the desired result," Putin said. "I am certain that we have every justification to also expect a breakthrough in Russian-American business partnership."

The cornerstone for the construction of that international partnership was to be oil and gas. Which meant Russia's Lukoil beachhead on that unprepossessing corner in Manhattan was more than just a gas station. More, even, than a gas station with a Kwik Farms convenience store. Sometimes sharing coffee and Krispy Kreme doughnuts—"He ate a glazed," Schumer told reporters about Putin—can portend something bigger. Was this little chat and chew the time and place where the Cold War would commence its final, satisfying melt?

President Putin was there at the gas station in 2003 to convince all New Yorkers, and all Americans, that Russia could deliver stability and reliability at a time when America really needed that, or at least craved it. It had been just a few months since the U.S. military had toppled Saddam Hussein in Iraq, and Americans were becoming once again attuned to the danger of being too dependent on Middle East–dominated OPEC, which supplied nearly half of America's crude oil and seemed to be able to control prices at will. American consumers had watched helplessly at the end of August, in the waning weeks of summer vacation, as gas prices at the pump skyrocketed at the fastest rate in nearly fifty years. Los Angeles had absorbed a 30 percent hike; in Phoenix, it was 40 percent. American consumers were paying more than $2 a gallon for the first time ever.

There were other factors at play, but some Americans apprehended this price hike as an OPEC plot, payback for putting American boots on the ground in a sovereign state in the Middle East. The announcement that OPEC would cut production by nearly a million barrels a day—made just a few days before Putin's arrival at the Kwik Farms doughnut counter—seemed to confirm the fear. American gas prices were certain to keep going up, at least as long as OPEC had us on such a short leash. Thank God for Russia. Thank God for the honeypot of known oil reserves in western Siberia, not to mention the vast untapped reserves off Russia's Arctic shelf. Lukoil had five Arctic-ready, icebreaking oil tankers on order at that very moment—an investment of nearly $200 million. And Vladimir Putin had pronounced himself ready to provide America's new not–Middle Eastern fuel supply, indefinitely, in exchange for a little help with the much-needed modernization of the Russian oil sector.

There was already a plan afoot, worked out among the energy poohbahs of the Bush and Putin administrations. U.S. companies would help finance a new pipeline from the oil fields in western Siberia to the Russian port city of Murmansk, as well as new storage tanks there and improved deepwater facilities commodious enough for big tankers to maneuver in and out. The Russian military would give over some of its submarine berths to accommodate the big ships, and Russian oil companies would load up those oil tankers for shipment straight to the American market. Putin thought that Russia could be supplying 10 percent of U.S. oil imports before George W. Bush finished his second term in office. Maybe more. There was also talk of constructing a special new facility for exporting liquefied natural gas to America. "It's not just oil," Bush's deputy secretary of energy had said on a reconnaissance visit to Murmansk. "Natural gas is also going to be an important factor in our energy relations." Just two days before Putin arrived in New York, at the second annual U.S.-Russia energy summit in St. Petersburg, the U.S. energy secretary, Spencer Abraham, proclaimed that the United States was now prepared to "assist Russia as her role in the global energy market increases."

Even skeptical Russia watchers in America were tuning in to new possibilities. An ascendant American scholar of modern Russia—the future U.S. ambassador to Moscow Michael McFaul—was just beginning to take the measure of the new Russian president and had already warned of the risk that Putin would evolve into an autocrat who monopolized control of government and the economy behind the window dressing of democratic institutions. But despite long-range concerns, the week that Putin was in New York had McFaul feeling optimistic. He told the members of the U.S. House subcommittee charged with keeping an eye on Europe that the Russian president and his key deputies no longer seemed to view America as an implacable enemy bent on emasculating Russia. That old antagonistic perspective, McFaul said, is no longer "the dominant view among foreign policy elites [in Russia] and is most certainly not the orientation of Putin and his government." McFaul even went so far as to voice the possibility of the most felicitous of outcomes: "If Russia consolidates a liberal democracy at home, then I have no doubt that Russia will develop into a reliable and lasting ally of the United States in world affairs." And Putin might be just the man to do it; at the very least, he seemed to be embracing the idea of Western-style capitalism: "Since becoming president, Putin has done much to accelerate Russian economic reform."

Maybe that kind of optimism about Putin had been buoyed by the story that had run the previous week in *The New York Times* about Paul McCartney's recent visit to Moscow. The old Beatle, there to do a concert and film a television special called *Paul McCartney in Red Square,* had been summoned to a private audience with President Putin, who walked him into his inner sanctum, dismissed his interpreter, and carried on a conversation in rather serviceable English. "He was fun," McCartney told Bill Carter from the *Times.* "He said, 'I really know your music.' He agreed the Beatles had been a force for freedom." Putin even showed up in person for McCartney's Moscow concert—McCartney played a second iteration of "Back in the U.S.S.R." just for him, and the crowd didn't mind one bit.

The week after that heart-warmer ran in the *Times,* Putin, Alekperov, and Schumer stood inside the Kwik Farms amid the doughnuts and soda pop and potato chips, the heat lamp on the hot dogs radiating a gentle warmth against the old Cold War chill. They didn't linger too long; there was the press corps outside, after all, waiting for a statement. Yet when the three men walked out and settled in front of the fuel pumps to address reporters, Putin demurred and said nothing. That reticence was unexpected; this was a photo op and a press availability, wasn't it?

Putin's reserve that afternoon on Tenth Avenue might have had something to do with a brief but unsettling interaction at the New York Stock Exchange, just before his visit to the Lukoil station. The Russian president had been whisked into a side room for an audience with ExxonMobil's CEO, Lee Raymond, a meeting laid out in spectacular detail in Steve Coll's book *Private Empire*. Raymond, who seemed to believe that his position as head of the world's most profitable corporation made him approximately equal in power and stature to the president of the Russian Federation, appeared to have rattled Putin. Putin was aware that ExxonMobil had been negotiating to buy a 30 percent stake in Russia's most impressive up-and-coming privately held oil company, Yukos—a company that might one day challenge Lukoil as Russia's biggest producer of crude. What Putin did not fully appreciate before his talk with Raymond, however, was that ExxonMobil was in the habit of getting final say in all of its partnership ventures. In Coll's vivid sketch of the meeting at the stock exchange, Raymond asked for an assurance from Putin that ExxonMobil would one day be permitted to acquire a majority stake in Yukos. He more or less demanded it as a condition for moving forward. "I need to have an understanding of our ability to get to fifty-one percent," Raymond told Putin.

"That means if I want to have Yukos do something, I'm going to have to come and talk to you?" Putin asked.

"Yeah, that's not so awful," Raymond told him. "That's true in a lot of places in the world."

Coll detailed the aftermath of the meeting also: Raymond would report back to the home office in Texas that his meeting with Vladimir had gone swimmingly and that the ExxonMobil-Yukos deal was on track. Putin saw it differently. He had been offended by the American executive's arrogance. According to Leonard Coburn, a U.S. Department of Energy official who understood the enormous strategic importance of the Russian oil industry to the country itself, Putin had also been "a little scared." The Russian Federation president found himself in a bind. Without the weird parallel Soviet economic netherworld that had channeled and shielded Russia's oil and gas bounty, his country's economic future was in uncharted territory. The way things were going, the post-U.S.S.R. Russian economy would basically be entirely dependent on its oil and gas industry's ability to compete in the world market. By 2003, that meant Russian oil companies urgently needed both money and technology from the West to modernize and compete. It might have been dawning on Putin, under that bright red Lukoil canopy in New York in September 2003, that in allowing Russian businessmen—even patriotic Russian businessmen—to do business with ExxonMobil and BP and Chevron and Shell, he risked losing his iron grip on the industry that provided the lifeblood of the Russian state.

Whatever the cause, Putin chose not to employ that rather serviceable English for the enlightenment of the reporters outside the Kwik Farms. He stood silent and nodding, with a bloodless, pursed-lip smile on his face, while Vagit Alekperov offered the sort of brief, heavily accented, to-the-point statement that makes Americans think of the cartoon characters Boris and Natasha: "Through today's action, America will have a new source of energy." Senator Schumer was more voluble about the potential partnership symbolized by the Lukoil–Kwik Farms team, five of whom were standing just over Schumer's shoulder, red ball caps ablaze. Together, the senator suggested, Russia and America were going to take on the bully. "I hope it does cause problems for OPEC," Schumer said. "I hope OPEC is hurt by this so they don't have a stranglehold on the oil market anymore." Having spent about ten minutes on-site, Putin was then swept up into his armored motorcade, and he and his entourage sped off toward the summit at Camp David.

It was hard to tell just what the local civilians who had happened onto the scene made of the entire Lukoil grand-opening exercise. Some were distracted by the curtains in Putin's limo, one by a full-on machine gun he was sure he saw mounted in one of the SUVs in the Russian motorcade, others by the Russian president's physical stature. Putin was, well, surprisingly tiny. "Diminutive" was how the *New York Post* put it. And yet he struck one woman, even in his diminutiveness, as "rather totalitarian." Leave it to that paragon of workingman's New York, the taxi driver, to offer up the most clear-eyed and incisive take on the strange event. "I know nothing about [Putin]," the cabbie said idly, while filling up his tank at the new Russian-owned pumps. "If he's going to put the gas cheap, then I'm going to know about him."

We all know how it turned out, looking back from the vantage point of 2019. In the end, Vladimir Putin didn't ever put gas cheap. After a ten-year life, the once-celebrated Lukoil station at 24th Street and Tenth Avenue is no more. The property had a brief run as a public art installation called *Sheep Station*. "Set in a surrealist landscape amidst the existing industrial gas station architecture," the exhibition brochure explained, "the sheep symbolize [François-Xavier] Lalanne's mission to demystify art and capture its joie de vivre." Today, the lot is home to a glass-and-chrome luxury residential building with an art gallery on the ground floor. Twelve stories housing six $15-million-and-up condos. The condo complex is called the Getty. It skipped a generation, in other words; it was a Getty station before it was a Lukoil station before it was condos, but Lukoil has been wiped from public memory. Hopes for a world-changing American-Russian partnership—the canopy to protect us all from the vagaries of the international and political weather—have long since crumbled. As has the idea of Vladimir Putin as a force for global stability.

Turns out Putin made mistakes over the past fifteen years—big, fundamental, hard-to-reverse mistakes. That can happen when you try to build your country's future on the oil and gas industry. Putin's decisions stripped his country of its ability to compete fairly in the global economy or global politics and limited its strategic options to the unsavory list he and his apparatchiks are ticking down today. His efforts to restore Russia as a world-stage superpower no longer depend on capacity and know-how. They depend on cheating. Putin and his minions cheat at the financial markets. They cheat at the Olympics. They cheat at their own fake democracy. They cheat other people out of their democracies.

It's easy to look back on those strange days at the end of September 2003 and identify the warning signs about Putin and Russia that American policy makers missed. But it would be unfair to them and unfair to history to do so without recognizing that the way things turned out was not inevitable. There really was the spore of a bright new future in 2003. And it is certainly true that Russia itself had the resources and the capability to go in another direction. That things turned out as they did is a tragedy—a sprawling but explicable tragedy. And it is not Russia's alone.

I believe there is one narrative thread that stitches together the greater part of that tragedy—a thread that wraps its way around the globe: from Oklahoma and Texas and Washington, D.C., to London,

Kyiv, Siberia, Moscow, Equatorial Guinea, and the Alaskan Arctic; from the Arbuckle formation deep in the earth's crust to the icy surface of the Arctic seas; from a Malibu mansion stuffed with the world's largest collection of Michael Jackson memorabilia to a thousands-of-dollars-a-night luxury hotel in central London to a divorce court in Oklahoma City to a crappy office building offering its workers a "Free Power Supply!" in St. Petersburg, Russia. The saga involves, among other incidents, the purposeful detonation of a fifty-kiloton nuclear bomb eight thousand feet below the earth's surface (unsettlingly close to an I-70 exit ramp in Colorado); an international financial crisis; a twenty-eight-thousand-ton vessel dragging unmoored and unmanned onto the craggy coast of Alaska; tornadoes; the novelty of man-made earthquakes; murdered cows; and a third-grade public school teacher panhandling to provide school supplies for her students. Even an inept Russian spy ring ferreted out of suburban tract houses in New Jersey and Virginia. Even Russia's interference in the 2016 U.S. presidential election. Seems unlikely, but it all ties.

The motive force of all the action—its fuel as well as its engine—is the most consequential, the most lucrative, the most powerful, and the least-well-governed major industry in the history of mankind. Oil and gas. I do not propose to discount or minimize the powerful and positive effects the producers of our hydrocarbons have had on our own country and on the world at large. I like driving a pickup and heating my house as much as the next person, and the through line between energy and economic growth and development is as clear to me as an electric streetlight piercing the black night. But the political impact of the industry that brings us those things is also worth recognizing as a key ingredient in the global chaos and democratic downturn we're now living through.

I don't mean to be rude, but I also want to be clear: the oil and gas industry is essentially a big casino that can produce both power and triumphant great gobs of cash, often with little regard for merit. That equation invites gangsterism, extortion, thuggery, and the sorts of folks who enjoy these hobbies. Its practitioners have been lumbering across the globe of late, causing mindless damage and laying the groundwork for the global catastrophe that is the climate crisis, but also reordering short-term geopolitics in a strong-but-dumb survival contest that renders everything we think of as politics as just theater. It's worth understanding why. And why now.

In the past twenty years, a technology-driven accelerant has been poured onto the fires of an industry that was already pretty good at burning up whole national economies and hopes of democratic governance. One signal (and unplanned) consequence of this earth-shattering leap in oil and gas production is that it stranded Russia economically and strategically, in a way that has driven Russia's leaders to distraction—and beyond. With no option now to retreat within the controlled global order of Soviet satellite states, Russia's one essential industry today has to keep up even with the West, even with the democracies. Putin knows Russia can't do it alone, but it also won't do it together—not if it has to be on the West's terms. And so the West's terms must be changed. Behold the new world disorder. Behold the foreign trolls in your Facebook feed. At just the wrong time and in just the wrong place, the worst instincts and practices of the most powerful industry on earth mapped onto geopolitics in a way that didn't just stunt the prospects for success; it turned them monstrous and backward.

This book won't catalog the whole slimy slick that the oil and gas industry has left behind it all over the world. Think of it as more of a guided tour of some of the landmarks, like Oklahoma, and Equatorial Guinea, and Russia, of course. But naturally—gnash your teeth all you want, Vlad—it all starts right here in America. It's always America.

BLOWOUT

....

ONE

SPLENDOR AND FRAGRANCE

F YOU HAD TO POINT TO A BEGINNING, TO THE EXACT LOCATION OF the big bang from which American industrial and economic power began its astounding and sometimes reckless expansion, it would be at the end of a percussion-driven, blunt-force drill bit, lowered through a cast-iron pipe, powered by a six-horsepower steam engine, slamming down and down and down into the earth on a farm in northwest Pennsylvania. At a depth of sixty-nine and a half feet, the operators of the drill struck what they had been looking for, and on August 28, 1859, the crude yet sublime substance—"rock oil," as it was called at the time—presented itself on the earth's surface.

That discovery, like the big bang itself, is but a subatomic pinhole in space compared with all that has followed. Edwin Laurentine Drake and his hired man, "Uncle Billy" Smith, pulled the equivalent of maybe twenty forty-two-gallon barrels of crude oil from the ground on a good day. The inhabitants of our planet weren't exactly starving for more in 1859, or at least didn't yet know they were. The first commercially viable gas-powered engine, and the ensuing addiction, were still a few generations away.

Today's drillers produce an average of more than ninety *million* barrels of oil worldwide every day, and a lot of natural gas, too, which fuels cars, jets, freight trains, ocean liners, power plants, factories, and farm machinery, as well as the economies of republics, monarchies, and dictatorships around the globe. Nearly a hundred countries, representing six continents, are in the oil and gas game, and many have been in it for a century or more. But the United States got there first (Russia was a very distant second), and only the United States can lay claim to having shaped the industry's prevailing culture: the tools of its trade, its financing, its administration, its ethic, and its reach. "The organization of the great business of taking petroleum out of the earth, piping the oil over great distances, distilling and refining it, and distributing it in tank steamers, tank wagons, and cans all over the earth," the president emeritus of Harvard noted in 1915, "was an American invention."

In fact, it could be argued, the oil business as we know it today was the invention of one particular American, John D. Rockefeller. Rockefeller was there almost from the beginning. He created and husbanded the exemplar of the industry, Standard Oil, and along the way he helped to popularize the idea of America as the testing ground where the extravagant possibilities and the outsized benefits of free-market capitalism have been proven. Rockefeller, a junior partner in a Cleveland merchant commission house trading in grain, hay, meat, and miscellany when Edwin Drake made his strike in 1859, watched the oil business unfold up close. When he entered the field in 1863, at age twenty-three, he understood his best bet was to concentrate on refining the crude oil and to leave to others the rather messy and costly process of actually getting it out of the ground.

Within ten years, Rockefeller had managed to get control of nearly all of the oil refineries in Cleveland, which had established itself as the nation's main refining center. Rockefeller's new corporation, Standard Oil, shipped a million barrels of refined oil in a single year. By 1875, thanks to the fire sale that followed the first frightening financial panic and depression in industrialized America, Rockefeller had taken control of every major refining center in the country. "We were all in a sinking ship," he would later explain, "and we were trying to build a lifeboat to carry us all to shore. . . . The Standard was an angel of mercy, reaching down from the sky, and saying 'Get in the ark. Put in your old junk. We'll take the risks!'"

Standard Oil's main product at the time was kerosene, which proved a welcome innovation in illumination. It was efficient, effective, plentiful, and reasonably priced. The most widely used lighting oil at the time, which was struck from soft coal, was dirty; whale oil was hard to get (see *Moby-Dick*) and dwindling in supply; kerosene from petroleum—or rock oil—was just the thing to illuminate the clean, bright new future. "Rock oil emits a dainty light," promised the new industry. "The brightest and yet the cheapest in the world, a light fit for Kings and Royalists and not unsuitable for Republicans and Democrats." Farmers and city dwellers could afford to read well into the night. Factory owners could afford to keep their works open around the clock. Rockefeller's magic potion was a worldwide phenomenon; in 1875, before any European-based company was producing kerosene in bulk, 75 percent of the output from Rockefeller's American refineries was loaded up and shipped overseas. Cash flowed back across the Atlantic. Standard's production capacity grew year after year. The efficiencies that followed—economies of scale—allowed Rockefeller to cut the cost of refining by more than 85 percent and to cut the cost to the consumer by 70 percent. Demand swelled, and so did revenues.

Rockefeller's company, meanwhile, just kept eating would-be competitors. About 90 percent of America's crude flowed through Standard Oil by the end of the 1890s. The company had money and means to produce its own crude, and refine it, and get it shipped to market on its own (always favorable) terms. Standard was capable of controlling the price of oil and railroad freight rates and had cash in the bank to pay off the state and federal legislators who wrote laws governing the industry. "John D. and his colleagues regarded government regulators as nuisances to be bypassed wherever possible," says Rockefeller's estimable biographer, Ron Chernow. "He felt that politicians were basically parasites who would shake down businessmen. I mean, all of this bribery he saw as extortion; that is, the politicians shaking him down, rather than his paying off the politicians. . . . I think he regarded these payments really as a business expense."

Standard Oil eventually grew into "the largest business empire on earth," according to Chernow. "I don't know that the business world has ever seen an agglomeration of wealth and power on the scale of Standard Oil." This was the era of consolidation, of the Big Trust, which was nineteenth-century parlance for monopoly—the Sugar Trust, the Beef Trust, the Steel Trust, the Tobacco Trust, the Rope-and-Twine Trust. But the Rockefeller-controlled Oil Trust was the first, the biggest, the most powerful, and easily the most talked-about trust in the country. Rockefeller himself stood with Andrew Carnegie (steel), Philip Armour (meat products), and James Buchanan Duke (cigarettes) as the richest and most powerful commodity producers on the continent. They sat on mounds of private wealth unimaginable in the young republic at the time of Rockefeller's own birth. John D. died nearly fifty years before the debut of the *Forbes* 400, the annual listing of the wealthiest private individuals in the country. But when the editors of a book timed to coincide with the twenty-fifth-anniversary edition of that list made some calculations, they declared Rockefeller the richest single individual in the history of America. They figured his peak net worth at $305 billion (in 2006 dollars), which means that if John D. were to be magically reanimated today, with his peak fortune still intact, his personal wealth would roughly triple that of the whippersnapper who sat atop the *Forbes* list in 2019.

Millions of barrels of ink have been expended in trying to explain the reasons for Rockefeller's spectacular achievement, to reveal the cardinal (and perhaps replicable) tactic, to pinpoint the specific innate genius that made it all happen. Theories abound. Take, for instance, what could be called the Bung Theory. A bung is the stopper once used to seal up a barrel of oil, and Rockefeller's intense interest in this unromantic industrial cog, his keen watch on the monthly bung count, offers a tantalizing lead on the secret to his success. "Your March inventory showed 10,750 bungs on hand," Rockefeller once wrote to one of his foremen. "The report for April shows 20,000 new bungs bought, 24,000 bungs used, and 6,000 bungs on hand. What became of the other 750 bungs?" Maybe the key was pinching every penny! John D. Rockefeller wasted nothing, see, so he could push his costs down, undercut all competitors on price, and drive them out of the business, or at least into Standard Oil's angel of mercy ark.

Then there is the well-traveled Great Monster Theory. "Run, children, or Rockefeller'll get you," was a threat that could strike terror in the Pennsylvania oil patch in the late nineteenth century. The Great Monster Theory gained much currency in the popular mind after Ida Tarbell's remarkable series of investigative articles published in *McClure's Magazine* beginning in 1902, "The History of the Standard

Oil Company." Tarbell, who grew up in the patch, itemized the more than thirty years of Rockefeller's underhanded, corrupt, predatory behavior that constituted his effort to wipe the field of competitors. He was, in Tarbell's rendering, a rapacious and devious villain. Widows and orphans, beware. It didn't hurt that Rockefeller, aged sixty-three at the time of publication, looked ready to inhabit the villain role by then. He was already growing thin and pinched—and worse. "He suffered from something called alopecia. In 1901, he lost not only all the hair on his head; he lost all body hair," Chernow explains. "Ida Tarbell came along a year later, did this series portraying him as a monster. And since he was hairless and suddenly looked old—and ghoulish—his appearance seemed to ratify what she was saying in the series, so that the timing was particularly unfortunate for Rockefeller."

There is also the Man of His Times Theory. Rockefeller, this theory posits, was simply playing by the very loose set of rules of his day, just like everybody else was. The boundaries of capitalism and democracy in America were still being chalked, the rules of the game still being written. The prevailing ethic was best summed up by one of Rockefeller's early partners, Henry M. Flagler, who kept a copy of this little ditty on his desk: "Do unto others as they would do unto you—and do it first." The point of the free market was not to compete but to win. "The most serious charge that can be laid at [Standard's] door is that it has succeeded," wrote an oilman who felt compelled to sell out to Rockefeller in the 1880s or suffer the consequences. "It has outwitted its competitors who sought to play the same game but had not so thoroughly mastered the art. . . . In the business battle, the extremity of one is the opportunity of the other. . . . It is the rule of our competitive life that the time when the business rival is on the downward road—when creditors are pressing him hard, when banks are clamoring that he shall meet his paper, when the sheriff is threatening to close his doors— this is the opportunity for the other rival to strike the finishing blow and make merchandise out of the misery of his fellow-man." Rockefeller's eldest son and heir offered an exceedingly aromatic metaphor to justify this need to (occasionally, of course) rely on cutthroat tactics. "The American Beauty Rose can be produced in the splendor and fragrance which bring cheer to its beholder only by sacrificing the early buds which grow up around it," John D. junior sermonized. "This is not an evil tendency in business. It is merely the working-out of a law of nature and a law of God."

Rockefeller himself had a number of pet theories about his spectacular rise. A devout and puritanical Baptist, John D. was certain there was a higher being at work. "I believe the power to make money is a gift from God," he explained to one writer, "just as are the instincts for art, music, literature, the doctor's talent, the nurse's, yours—to be developed and used to the best of our ability for the good of mankind. Having been endowed with the gift I possess, I believe it is my duty to make money and still more money, and to use the money I make for the good of my fellow man according to the dictates of my conscience."

These various theories, and the many others in circulation, are not mutually exclusive. The whole truth of John D. Rockefeller is complicated and involves pieces of them all. But the rock-bottom fact on which everything else rests is actually quite simple: Standard Oil just kept turning out the finest product on the market, at the lowest price to the consumer. *Ka-ching!*

By the first decade of the twentieth century, Standard Oil was so powerful it was pretty much writing its own rules; neither the federal government nor the various state governments were capable of reining it in. Rockefeller and his corporation were, demonstrably, beyond governance—a situation that raised alarms in a democratic republic purportedly constituted of free men, dedicated to the idea of equality. To some, it seemed, well, un-American that this extraordinary bounty of natural resources—in all its "splendor and fragrance"—should be fenced off in someone's private preserve. In 1911, about forty years after Rockefeller embarked on his quest to dominate the oil business and about twenty years after he got there, the U.S. Supreme Court ruled that Standard Oil was running a conspiracy in restraint of trade that had attempted to monopolize the interstate oil industry. And had largely succeeded. In his majority opinion, Chief Justice Edward D. White wrote that it was clearly Standard's "intent and purpose to maintain the dominancy over the oil industry, not as a result of normal methods of industrial development, but by new means of combination which were resorted to in order that greater power might be added than would otherwise have arisen had normal methods been followed."

As a remedy, the Court ordered Standard to split itself into about three dozen distinct firms that would be forced to compete with one another. Rockefeller, who retained ownership in all the spin-offs, found this arrangement surprisingly salubrious. The separate companies *all* flourished. John D. wound up a richer man after the breakup than he was before. And even today, more than a hundred years later, the major non-state-run international oil companies we know best—ExxonMobil, Chevron, BP, Marathon—have their roots in Standard Oil and trace their ancestry directly back to Rockefeller. Standard DNA is shot through the oil industry, as are Standard's dominant traits: a penchant for pinching pennies, an eagerness to devour and expand, a mistrust and even hatred of government regulation, a vaguely delusional sense of higher calling, and a wary respect for innovation. Worth keeping these traits in mind, because they've gone on to shape the modern world. They still function as a character sketch—or maybe a psychological profile—of the richest, most powerful, and most destructive industry on the globe.

In the century or so since the Court-mandated breakup of Standard Oil, technological innovation has been the main agent of renewal in the industry and has created entirely new fortunes. Take, for example, the Koch family, famous for funding right-wing causes and politicians across the country. Koch Industries today is the second-largest privately held corporation in the United States, encompassing everything from commodities trading to cattle to paper pulp, but the corporation owes its honest-money beginnings to invention, to petroleum engineer Fred Koch's discovering a better and cheaper method for making gasoline from crude oil, back in the 1920s.

And consider the story of the field engineer in Texas who perfected a toothy rotary drill bit that dramatically improved the ability to drive through underground rock. He made himself a star in the oil patch. The Sharp-Hughes bit (advertised as "A Friend to the Driller") ultimately made that engineer's son, Howard Hughes Jr., the richest man in the world for a time.

And consider the story of Robert S. Kerr, who built Kerr-McGee and made his own fortune by proving that you could stick a drilling rig out in the water, beyond sight of land, and suck oil up through the sea-bed. "Spectacular Gulf of Mexico Discovery" screamed a headline in *Oil & Gas Journal* in 1947, when Robert S. Kerr made good. "Possible 100-Million Barrel Field—10 Miles at Sea."

Most of us laymen have only a vague understanding of the science of oil and natural gas. Our fuels of choice started as living organisms hundreds of millions of years ago (Sinclair's Dino logo notwithstand-ing, oil is not from dinosaurs). And then over time—a lot of time—all that eons-old organic matter got covered up, deep in the earth's geo-logic layers, packed into an intensely hot and pressurized cauldron, where it was all boiled down, remarkably, into the stew we modern creatures use to power our daily existence. Fossil fuels! The popular vision is of a vast worldwide web of subterranean lakes and caverns filled with oil and gas. Enterprising people figure out exactly where a big pocket is, stick giant industrial straws into the ground, suck it dry, and then move on to the next one. And the world is lit. Voilà.

But the truth is, there aren't really giant underground lakes or even puddles filled with Jurassic Juice. Most of the hydrocarbons we want are spread through layer upon layer of what looks like nearly imperme-able underground rock—in very tight little micro-crevices. The cap-ture of fossil fuels is less like sticking a straw into a Big Gulp schooner and gently drawing it out, and more like sticking that straw into a sponge and having at it. Try them both some time. It's not too tough to drain the Big Gulp, is it? The extraction from the sponge requires con-siderably more, well, brutish effort. Things could tend toward violent. And this understanding of the need for near-violent force has driven most of the successful (a.k.a. lucrative) innovations in the oil industry. Big technological advances are not made by PhDs in white lab coats. Innovation in the oil and gas industry is rarely about quantum me-chanics or higher math. Innovation in oil and gas is about brawn. So it stands to reason that the shale gas revolution of the early twenty-first century was made possible by a pair of innovations that relied largely on pure brute force. And, as you might expect, that amount of industrial-scale pushing and shoving can produce some magnificent collateral damage along the way.

TWO

THE GENIE

I T WAS AUGUST 1969, LESS THAN THREE WEEKS AFTER NEIL ARM-
strong put the first footprint on the moon. Americans were just getting used to thinking of the world as our oyster; now maybe the sky
and the stars were included too. And with Project Rulison in Garfield
County, Colorado, the public affairs office of the U.S. Atomic Energy
Commission signaled the start of yet another bold new adventure—
another U.S. taxpayer–backed world first. The press release detailed
the itinerary, from the D-day Minus Two instructions for the registration of official visitors at the Ramada Inn in nearby Grand Junction, to
the final luncheon, where "a preliminary post-detonation briefing is
planned." The thirty-six families who lived within a five-mile radius of
the blast site had already been advised to evacuate temporarily; they'd
be allowed back in after, as soon as everyone was sure it was all safe.
The state game commission had cautioned hunters and fishermen "not
to venture" into the area. The AEC had determined an optimal detonation time after consulting with local officials as to the normal daily
traffic patterns on the nearby railroad tracks and nearby I-70 and as to
the local school bus schedule. Sure, there would be hassles and headaches, and perhaps even a little property damage in the immediate
(and maybe even not so immediate) surroundings. But if this industrial experiment proved out, it would be another problem solved—
another big-thinking American triumph—thanks to the magic of
science.

The problem that Project Rulison was designed to solve was especially frustrating to Austral Oil Company, owner of the rights to the natural gas deep in the Mesaverde formation in Colorado's Rulison Field—natural gas it had been unable to get out of the ground. Austral knew there was plenty of gas at that site, but it was all locked up in an impermeable shale formation, and in 1969 nobody had found a workable method of sufficiently fracturing all that tight rock to loose the bounty within. Austral was sure it was sitting on about 8 *trillion* cubic feet of natural gas in the Rulison Field and that there was another 100 trillion cubic feet in the surrounding basin. The U.S. Bureau of Mines estimated that the Rocky Mountains held a total of 317 trillion cubic feet of natural gas, enough to fuel the entire country for twenty years! And much of it was on government-owned land. Royalty payments might swell the U.S. Treasury by as much as $4 billion, Project Rulison's cheerleaders noted, if somebody would only figure a way to get at all that gas. And time seemed to be of the essence. The world population was growing every year, and so was its energy consumption, especially here at home. The United States accounted for 6 percent of the earth's population in 1969 but consumed 35 percent of the total global energy output. "[Natural] gas, which is the cleanest of all fuels, is in short supply and growing more critical," explained an Austral executive. "Something must be done to make more gas available to the constantly increasing market."

Happily, Austral had a willing partner in this enterprise: the U.S. Atomic Energy Commission. Austral agreed to pony up about nine-tenths of the $6.5 million cost of the "exploration" project, and the AEC provided the sorts of things a private oil company in Houston could not, like uranium and plutonium and detonation fuses and special devices for measuring radioactive fallout. The Project Rulison guys were so sure this new fracking adventure would work they were already promoting it as America's next big technological leap even before they tried it: "Since our society is constantly clamoring for more nonpolluting energy, we advocate vigorous efforts to bring the new technology of nuclear stimulation to rapid commercialization." You read that right. Nuclear. Stimulation. Why go straight to the old derricks and drill bits when you have the option to start with an atomic bomb, to loosen everything up? Faster, tidier.

Late in that summer of 1969, the separate components of an atomic bomb were driven by "specially equipped government vans" to surface ground zero, a.k.a. the Austral wellhead in Rulison, about five miles off I-70. SGZ was already fenced off and under armed guard, courtesy of the private contractor Wackenhut Services Inc. But the project manager, in his wisdom, instituted an extra layer of security. "Final assembly of the explosive was accomplished under 'Buddy System' controls in the Wellhead Building in the fenced exclusion area," he detailed in his final report. "The 'Buddy System,' or two-man concept, was utilized for protection of the nuclear explosive upon arrival and until detonation." Sure, one guy might screw up or go nutty when faced with the responsibilities of handling a nuclear bomb, but that's what his buddy was there for. So, *two* guys, not one: that was the safety plan. Once the bomb was assembled, Austral became, for a brief interval, proud owner of a 1,250-pound, 43-kiloton nuclear weapon. A weapon nearly three times the power of the bomb that incinerated the interior of Hiroshima and killed nearly half of its 300,000 residents.

Important as it was to Austral and the rest of the oil and gas industry, the success of Project Rulison was perhaps just as important to the AEC and its Atoms for Peace initiative. Not long after the United States exploded its second nuclear bomb over another densely populated Japanese city in August 1945, putting a final destructive exclamation point on the World War II civilian death count, the AEC had launched its effort to keep the scientific momentum going, but hopefully in a less deadly direction. A number of the young physicists and chemists who had helped develop the weapons dropped on Japan felt some ethical pangs, even as they were assured the moral scorecard was all in their favor. Dropping the atomic bombs had saved millions of other lives that would have been lost had the war been prolonged, American politicians insisted. But the casualties in Japan continued to pile up in the weeks and months after the war as thousands more died from the effects of radiation poisoning. The general in charge of the U.S. nuclear weapons project sought to ease the national conscience, telling senators in November 1945 that victims of radiation exposure die "rather soon, and as I understand it from the doctors, without undue suffering. In fact, they say it is a very pleasant way to die." More than a dozen years after the bombings of Hiroshima and Nagasaki, the body count was still climbing. Long-term studies had confirmed that people exposed to high doses of radiation were dying from cancer at extraordinary rates. Survivors who had been nearest the blast zone were thirty times more likely to develop leukemia, according to a study done in the late 1950s.

By then, though, Atoms for Peace was in full swing in the United States, in terms of both discovery and publicity. American scientists and engineers had brought the world previously unimaginable nuclear devastation and human catastrophe, but now those same scientists and engineers were working toward nuclear applications in energy, medicine, agriculture, and transportation. All for the good. And America's most revered storyteller was on the case. In January 1957, *Walt Disney's Disneyland* television show devoted an entire hour to a Tomorrowland episode called "Our Friend the Atom." The story of the atom was like a "fairy tale," Disney's team explained. Specifically, the one where the fisherman casts his net and pulls up a bottle with a big scary genie inside. After Hiroshima and Nagasaki, "the atomic genie was freed, and his devastating force posed a fearful threat," the narrator explained. "We are like the fisherman. When he first beheld the frightful form of the genie, he too wished that he had never found the vessel. But our fable had a happy ending. The fisherman had his means of making a friend of his enemy. And fortunately, science has its way of doing the same thing. . . . It lies in our own hands to make wise use of the atomic treasures. Then the magic touch of the genie will spread throughout the world and he will grant the gifts of science to all mankind."

By 1969, with the Atomic Energy Commission spending more than half its budget on nonmilitary uses of nuclear power, the gifts were already beginning to move from the theoretical to the practical. A big one was the advent of nuclear reactors for producing electricity, which the head of the AEC, Glenn Seaborg, promised could stave off a coming crisis. "At the rate we are currently adding carbon dioxide to our atmosphere (six billion tons a year), within the next few decades the heat balance of that atmosphere could be altered enough to produce marked changes in the climate—changes which we might have no means of controlling even if by that time we have made great advances in our programs of weather modification," Dr. Seaborg told a commencement audience in San Diego. "I, for one, would prefer to continue to travel toward the equator for my warmer weather rather than run the risk of melting the polar ice and having some of our coastal areas disappear beneath a rising ocean." It was 1966 when he gave that speech.

The head of the AEC was touting the development of portable nuclear plants and nuclear power plant barges that could be towed to emergency sites after a tornado or an earthquake or a hurricane. The commission was also at work on a nuclear-powered deep submergence research vehicle to open what Seaborg called the "new frontier of inner space," which was actually the vast ocean depths, which might hold billions of tons of copper and gold and uranium. "When it comes to extracting and processing these and the many more valuable materials in the sea and the ocean floor," Seaborg promised in 1967, "the extensive use of nuclear power will probably become essential."

The AEC was also developing some nifty outer space technology, like rocket engines powered by a launchable nuclear reactor. The mini reactor—the size of your average office desk and able to produce more power than Hoover Dam—would provide the propulsion necessary for interplanetary travel. There was research into atomic-powered supersonic jets (New York to London in thirty minutes!), and trains, and even automobiles. Nuclear cars? Really? An atomic-powered merchant ship was already churning through the high seas. There were studies on how to use controlled doses of radiation to keep meat, fruits, and vegetables fresh. We might double the shelf life of everything from a porterhouse to a peach with just the right amount of radiation. We still do that, to this day, by the way. The FDA says it's especially effective for crustaceans and alfalfa sprouts. Look for the international symbol for irradiation, the Radura, on your local crawdad.

Project Rulison fell under a specialized subset of the Atoms for Peace program, a bold attempt to harness the power of atomic bombs for industrial purposes—not just atomic energy, but the actual weapons themselves. This operation was named after a passage of the Bible, Isaiah 2:4: "They shall beat their swords into plowshares, and their spears into pruning-hooks." (The AEC wisely chose Plowshares, and not Pruning Hooks, for the project name.) The famed nuclear physicist Edward Teller was a big champion of Plowshares, and especially the possibilities it presented for "geographical engineering." There were plans afoot in the early 1960s to use nuclear bombs for strip-mining, open pit mining, and quarrying; for redirecting the course of rivers and carving out giant man-made lakes; for a deepwater port in Alaska, a sea-level canal in Israel, even a new Panama canal. When you really opened your mind to the possibilities, what *couldn't* be done with nuclear bombs?

Dr. John Gofman, head of the Biomedical Division of one of the AEC's key labs, tried to pump the brakes. Even just nuclear testing had already introduced potentially harmful levels of radioiodine into the fresh milk supply in Utah. He wasn't at all comfortable with the Federal Radiation Council's fix for that problem, which was simply to recalibrate its own edict on what constituted an "acceptable health risk." The FRC, Gofman lamented, "solved it by announcing that the safe level of radioiodine in milk was three times higher than they thought." Gofman was acutely aware of the long-term effects of radiation. Two of his colleagues in a wartime weapons lab had died of leukemia, way too young. "In about 1965, I decided that I ought to talk at the Directors' meeting on the Panama Canal," Gofman explained in an oral history years later. "I said, 'The conclusion of our Biomedical Division is: The idea of digging the Panama Canal with hydrogen bombs is biological insanity.' Edward Teller was unhappy but nobody else said a word about it."

The AEC directors didn't do anything about it either. Gofman later explained that he and his Biomedical Division became known around the commission as "the Enemy Within." The AEC directors and scientists were more comfortable with the can-do thinking of the deputy chief of staff of radiological health at the U.S. Public Health Service. Dr. James Terrill told a symposium on public health and nuclear explosives, "The potential applications of atomic energy are many and varied indeed. . . . As meritorious as clean air, clean water, and clean food may be, the term 'clean' must be translated into criteria and standards." In other words, what was clean, really, and who could say?

In 1969, as Terrill was making those kinds of public statements, and despite Gofman's warnings against it, the nuclear excavation of a second Panama canal (or maybe a Nicaraguan canal?) really had become a serious discussion in the Under Secretaries Committee at the National Security Council in the White House. According to Seaborg, though, the thinking of the undersecretaries was that they should maybe execute a couple more nuclear test shots before giving any final go-ahead to start using nuclear bombs to cut a new hole clear across Central America. They were all watching Project Rulison, of course, to see how that turned out in Colorado. And so was President Richard Nixon, who explained his feelings to the AEC chief, Seaborg, just eight days into his first term in January 1969. "[President Nixon] said he has a special prejudice for this program—the way all people have special quirks and prejudices," Seaborg later wrote. "He thought this was something that should be accelerated."

Project Rulison had its naysayers out in Colorado, as you might expect. To effect the release of 317 trillion cubic feet of natural gas from the shale beds in the Rockies, one expert from the Colorado School of Mines told an audience at a public meeting, would require not just one big blast but more like thirteen thousand detonations of fifty-kiloton nuclear bombs. Nobody could really be certain how much radioactive effluent—people in Garfield County, Colorado, were becoming familiar with radioisotopes such as krypton-85 and tritium—would be floating in the natural gas, or left at the site once the gas was extracted. They weren't much calmed by an AEC spokesman who tried to explain away the relative dangers of radioactivity by comparing it to iodine. Of course you wouldn't drink it "straight from the bottle," but "one drop diluted in a glass of water is harmless . . . even kills germs."

A lawsuit filed by a concerned citizens' group delayed the Rulison blast until early September 1969. Weather delayed it another week, because AEC technicians worried that any radiation vented into the air by the explosion might be carried into population centers by high winds. And then, on top of everything, when D-day finally came, on September 10, 1969, there were protesters in the mountains near the blast site. When the Atomic Energy Commission spokesman had announced that the agency's abiding interest in public health and safety would forestall detonation if anybody was in the quarantine zone, local hippies and environmentalists had taken that as an invitation. Chester McQueary wrote about it twenty-five years later for *High Country News*. "We scattered over the mountain in twos and threes, so that we could not all be removed in one fell swoop by authorities," he wrote. "At 30 minutes before blast time, we set off smoke flares to confirm for AEC officials that we were still on the mountain and inside the quarantine zone. A blue, twin-rotor Air Force helicopter soon hovered fifty feet above the aspen clearing where Margaret Puls and I stood." McQueary says that although some of his fellow protesters were yanked off the mountain at gunpoint, that blue Air Force twin-rotor couldn't land easily on the steep slope where he and Puls had set up camp, and the chopper let them be. He told one interviewer that an airman on board flashed him a peace sign as the helicopter flew off.

The protesters had consulted a geologist who told them that when the detonation countdown started, they should get away from cliff faces that might fall or large trees or boulders that might bounce. They should prepare their own bodies for the blast as well. "We lay down positioned so our feet, knees, and arms would absorb the shock and motion," which basically means they got into push-up position, or the dreaded "plank." "Then a mighty WHUMP!" McQueary remembered, "and a long rumble moved through the earth, lifting us eight inches or more in the air. We felt aftershocks as we lay there looking at each other, grateful that we were still breathing and all in one piece. Seismic detectors at the National Earthquake Center in Golden registered 5.5 on the Richter scale."

The jarring seismic motion shook the liquid tanks at the nearby Union Carbide plant so badly that the chemical manufacturer had to shut down for three hours to unclog drains. A rock slide took out the Denver & Rio Grande Western Railroad's signal system, but it was quickly restored. Damage to local structures was what the Rulison project manager called "of a minor nature and center[ed] around cracked walls and ceiling plaster, cracked and broken chimney bricks, broken windows, lamps and the like."

The pre-shot estimates envisioned more than 400 damage claims, for which Austral had budgeted $200,000. But the big fears were not realized. The two nearby dams escaped uncracked. I-70 had not been damaged by rock slides. Austral did end up paying a total of $110,000 on 322 separate claims, including $124.50 to a "nonresident hunter" who had been miffed at being forced off the mountain on detonation day. The protesters who had been taken off the mountain by force were released without charges. "There have been no reports of injury to people or livestock," the AEC reported to Congress's Joint Committee on Atomic Energy.

The bomb was exploded 8,426 feet beneath the earth's surface, where it vaporized enough rock to open a 300-foot-high, 152-foot-wide cavern. The "fracture zone" radiated out 433 feet. The team had to wait a few months to allow the giant new cave to cool down and the detonation-produced radioactivity to decay a little. But it soon seemed apparent that our new friend, the atom, had performed an industrial miracle. That gas was stimulated! In 108 days of flow testing, according to the Project Rulison Manager's Report, the "volume is the equivalent of approximately 10 years of production from a conventionally stimulated well in the Rulison field." The report noted "very little flow restriction through the penetrated fractures, thus confirming that an effective path between the chimney and the reentry wellbore had been established." Mission accomplished! Almost.

Turned out there were two problems. First and most fundamentally, this new method of drilling-for-gas-by-atom-bomb left the gas itself enhanced by its nuclear experience. "Mildly radioactive" was how the scientists put it, contaminated with krypton-85 and tritium. But— here's the second problem—it was hard to say just how much tritium was in the gas (or at the blast site), because the machine the scientists had brought to measure krypton and tritium contamination, a machine referred to by the excellent acronym STALLKAT, didn't actually work. In the otherwise cheery 265-page Project Manager's Report on Rulison, this was the part where a little palpable sadness crept in. "Though certain drawbacks with STALLKAT were readily seen, not the least of which was a poor sensitivity to tritium, it was clearly the best available system." You go to the bomb site with the STALLKAT you have, not the STALLKAT you might want or wish to have at a later time.

The project manager noted that "some quite active tritium material fell near the base of the stack early in flaring" and that the bomb site also tended to get littered with tritium when it snowed. But nobody honestly knew how much tritium that little slice of Garfield County had just been saddled with, because the damn STALLKAT couldn't sniff it out. Under "Recommendations," the project manager was blunt: "The STALLKAT should not be used for monitoring tritium."

Now, from a public relations standpoint, the mystery of just how much radioactive contamination Project Rulison had burped up into Colorado was a problem that might have been overcome. Once they started to get reasonable measures of how much radioactivity was actually around, public health officials could always just raise the level of radioactivity that was considered safe for humans—problem solved. That's how it worked with the hot milk in Utah.

But for all its technological dynamism, the cost-benefit balance of the program was daunting. It was going to require more and bigger bombs to make bigger caverns and greatly expanded fields of fractured rock if nuclear stimulation was going to be commercially viable. And atomic bombs don't come cheap. The boys at the AEC retained their can-do attitude, buoyed by the country's accelerating energy demand and by President Nixon's quirks and prejudices. He wanted more natural gas, in a hurry, including the bombed kind. Nixon's 1971 report to Congress on energy issues included the promise of more "nuclear stimulation experiments which seek to produce natural gas from tight geologic formations." In 1973, the AEC tried again in Colorado, in Project Rio Blanco, where this time it was *three* thirty-three-kiloton nuclear bombs, detonated simultaneously, at three separate depths within 851 feet of one another. Radioactivity increased. Commercial prospects did not.

In all, these gas-happy experiments cost about $82 million. The accountants figured that at the assumed rate, even with costs coming down, even if they took that entire coveted 317 trillion cubic feet of natural gas, the best they could hope to recover was about 40 percent of the cash outlay.

And so died our nation's experiment in nuclear fracking, way back in 1973, after four glorious years of trying really, really hard.

Nuclear stimulation equipment was mothballed at just the moment when Americans were beginning to get good and jittery about the guarantee of an ample and never-ending supply of fuel sources. The dire prophecy of the geologist and futurist M. King Hubbert, who said that oil production would hit its apex in around 1970 and then begin a long despair-inducing decline, seemed to be coming true, at least domestically. "The era of low-cost energy is almost dead," lamented the U.S. secretary of commerce at the end of 1972. "Popeye is running out of cheap spinach." This realization was followed by OPEC's surprise 1973 embargo that nearly tripled the price of oil. Filling stations became places of actual rage. Gas shortages, gas lines, and gas rationing were things. Teenagers were called into middle school assemblies to hear apocalyptic messages about the energy crisis from earnest missionaries from the church of "Peak Oil." And natural gas was not going to save us in the 1970s, because there just wasn't enough of it around to buy.

The frigid winter of 1977 brought a state of emergency in New York, with Governor Hugh Carey ordering schools shut down for a week. Banks opened for only five hours a day, and in New York City the power companies shut off natural gas supplies to anybody with access to other fuels. Con Ed asked its customers to drop their thermostats to sixty-five degrees, while New Jersey's governor flat-out ordered the drop to sixty-five in all public buildings. General Electric just told its workers in the area to stay home. Columbus, Ohio, had it worse. The city closed 145 of its 172 public schools for an entire month, for want of natural gas to heat the classrooms. Local media stepped up for a "School Without Schools" program that drew nationwide attention: "The three major commercial television stations and several radio stations have canceled regularly scheduled programming for as much as six hours a day to provide teachers with 15-minute sessions of air time for class programs. These are buttressed by publication in the *Columbus Dispatch*, the city's morning daily paper, of at least two pages of school lessons and a schedule of the classes to be taught on television as well as other school-related activities in the city."

In 1978, the federal government set stratified price controls on natural gas; gas from old wells got the cheapest price, gas from new wells the highest. The idea was to try to goose producers into finding new gas, fast. But even with that new incentive, it was still blood from a stone. America just wasn't capable of producing enough natural gas to meet our immediate energy needs. So we had to be deliberate and cautious about how to use the limited supply that we had. The decisions we made about that in the 1970s would have consequences for generations to come. "Natural gas was in such short supply that Congress passed a law in 1978 that essentially outlawed the construction of new gas-fired power plants," noted *Wall Street Journal* reporter Russell Gold in his excellent 2014 book, *The Boom*. "By the time the law was repealed nine years later, the United States had built 81 gigawatts' worth of power plants that burned dirty, reliable chunks of fossilized carbon—about a quarter of all coal plants that were still in use more than thirty years later."

Even though the country all but gave up on natural gas in the shivering late 1970s, there were a number of people who still dreamed of that bonanza deep under the ground, who couldn't unhear the Bureau of Mines' estimate of hundreds of trillions of cubic feet of shale gas just waiting down there. Even after the Atomic Energy Commission's blasts-for-gas thing didn't work out, enthusiastic experimentation in fracking continued, subsidized by money appropriated by Congress. Private actors and public-private partnerships went back to the drawing board to puzzle out how to free shale gas or tight gas in an economically viable way. They no longer had nuclear bombs at their disposal, but they tested chemical explosives, cryogenic nitrogen that was supposed to freeze the rock until it cracked, and foamed carbon dioxide. The experiments got weird and arcane as people flung basically whatever was on hand at their local deposits of natural gas locked up in shale rock. Consider one emulsion laced with the popular British toast spread Marmite. Marmite is a gooey dark brown concoction made of yeast and vegetable extract; it's either delicious on buttered toast or the worst thing you could ever do to a perfectly fine piece of buttered toast, depending on whether you absolutely love it or absolutely hate it, which are the only two options. As for natural gas production, according to the petroleum industry trade publication *GEO ExPro*, the thinking was that maybe if you shot enough of the gustatorily polarizing yeasty goo underground in just the right conditions, it would fuel production of special bacteria, which in turn would excrete enough acid to break down the rock and release the natural gas. Worth a try! Marmite is today as delicious as ever—and it is still advertised as an elixir capable of improving heart health, brain health, sleep habits, and libido—but it did not work any subterranean fracking magic.

For all the far-flung experimentation, by the mid-1990s the basic idea of fracking was pretty straightforward: inject enough fluid into the rock, at high enough pressure, to open up some narrow escape pathways for the stuff you wanted to capture. What should be in the fluid? That was the gazillion-dollar question. Recipes for fracking fluid called for a lot of thickening agents, and a good bit of sand, and a handful of toxic chemicals like hydrochloric acid, and lots of other stuff, too. The mid-1990s-era fluid tended to be gel-based and viscous, so that it could deliver the sand, which was supposed to stay behind to work as a "proppant," that is, to keep the new micro-fractured passages in the hard shale propped open. Problem was, even after the gelatinous fluid was liquefied under intense subterranean heat, it remained gummy enough that it often stayed behind with the sand and blocked the newly cracked-open pathways so the gas couldn't get out. Everyone knew the basic goal and the basic problems with reaching it, but as late as 1997 nobody had found a way to improve on the basic formula. You could get gas out of the ground, but not enough to make it worth it. The majors, like Exxon and Mobil and Chevron, had given up serious efforts on fracking innovation, because it looked like the money invested was never going to return enough natural gas to pay off. They were busy hunting for new oil and gas overseas, like in Africa or Eastern Europe, where they could get it cheap and easy. So the field of fracking was left wide open to the independents in general, and one very determined independent in particular: George Phydias Mitchell.

If George Mitchell's life proved anything, it was that a man could map his own future and make his own luck. He was born on the Gulf of Mexico, in Galveston, Texas, in 1919, son of a Greek immigrant who had herded goats at the base of the rocky escarpment of Mount Artemisio. Savvas Paraskevopoulos, who changed his name to Mike Mitchell for ease of operation in the New World, raised his four children in a two-story brick building near downtown Galveston. The top floor was the domestic realm. The bottom housed the family-run laundry and shoeshine parlor. George learned early how to work hard, and he learned early that knowledge was key to his future. He studied petroleum engineering and geology at Texas A&M and took to heart advice from his department's most renowned academic: "If you want to go to work for a [major oil company], fine, you can drive around in a pretty good Chevrolet, but if you want to drive around in a Cadillac, you'd better go out on your own."

George P. Mitchell went out on his own. And one of his first big bets, as Russell Gold tells the story in *The Boom*, put him in that Cadillac. Mitchell had done his homework, combing through reams of drilling logs in a blueprint library in downtown Houston. He had developed a very educated "hunch" that there was a whole lot of natural gas not far beneath the surface of Wise County, northwest of Fort Worth. And he was right. His first gas well there hit. So did the next dozen. He cobbled together enough investors to lease five hundred square miles' worth of mineral rights. In the early 1950s, Mitchell and his partners produced enough natural gas that they were able to sign a contract to supply a nice percentage of the needs of the city of Chicago on an ongoing basis. He eventually bought up mineral rights on 300,000 acres outside Fort Worth and became the number one natural gas producer in Texas, which was the number one gas-producing state in the nation.

But for all that, Mitchell was pretty sure he was only playing at the edges of a much deeper reserve of natural gas. The gas he was sucking out of the ground was what had managed to find little escape routes and migrate up to low-pressure rock formations. The real mother lode, Mitchell was pretty certain, was in the Barnett Shale, a tight rock formation way down deep, five thousand to eight thousand feet underground. By the late 1990s, when all the major oil companies and government scientists had about given up on fracking in tight shale formations, Mitchell's decades-long interest in finding a way to get at the trapped gas had matured into something else entirely. "He has a mind that people often refer to as persistent," Mitchell's son Todd told Gold. "To me it is different than persistence. It was a form of obsession. He has a theme, and he would stick with it and stick with it."

Mitchell kept plugging away at fracking, against the better judgment of the rest of the industry, against his company's board of directors, and even against the company president he had hired. Because he was the majority owner of his own company, however, nobody could really stop him. And anyway, as Todd Mitchell would note, he "had a tendency to ignore obstacles." By 1997, though, George Mitchell must have been wondering if his long run of luck was finally coming to an end. The price of oil and gas was at a low ebb. Mitchell stocks were dropping down to near $10 a share, from a recent high of $35. A second wave of layoffs had pared the company from thirteen hundred employees to eight hundred. Natural gas production was falling, and Mitchell feared the company might soon lose its ability to fulfill its decades-old contractual obligations to Chicago.

But in the summer of 1998, a Hail Mary pass by a company engineer on the ground saved Mitchell's bacon. It started, as so many things do in the oil and gas industry, as an attempt to cut costs. The fracking gels Mitchell drillers were shooting into the Barnett Shale formation didn't come cheap, and company engineer Nick Steinsberger figured it might be worth trying a frack or two with a fluid made up mostly of water. Steinsberger's recipe for "slickwater" called for the same basic chemical additives; a hint of a lubricant used for face creams and contact lenses; a touch of gel made from the guar bean, which was grown in India; and sand. And water. Lots of water. Way more water than they had been using before. His supervisors gave him the go-ahead to try it on a handful of wells, but not much encouragement. One of them, according to Gold, "told him he would eat his diploma if the idea worked."

It took a few tries with the slickwater to get it right. Steinsberger learned it was necessary to add the sand slowly, most of it late in the injection process, and that it took a heck of a lot of water, like, say, 1.2 million gallons, and a heck of a lot of pressure to crack open microfissures in the steel-hard shale. But the results were promising. Even the most successful gel fracks hadn't shown much staying power. Gel-fracked wells might produce a million cubic feet of gas in the first days but then drop off pretty quickly. The culprit was that gummy gel that stayed behind, clogging the sand-propped passages in the shale. But the S. H. Griffin No. 4, fracked with slickwater fluid, was still producing almost 1.5 million cubic feet of gas per day in September 1998, ninety days after the initial frack. When Steinsberger checked thirty days later, there had been no appreciable decline. Slickwater turned out to be a cheap trick but a damn effective one. "This was the aha moment for us," Steinsberger later said. "It was our best well ever in the Barnett." George Mitchell was thrilled. The company started using the slickwater method on all its shale wells. And it kept working.

"The potential for shale gas was so big," said a newly hired Mitchell geologist who had been studying the Barnett Shale for years, "it made your head spin." That geologist, Kent Bowker, had been working at the oil giant Chevron, which at that moment was basically giving up on shale gas. Bowker later explained, "The handwriting was on the wall. . . . I probably would have gone to West Africa." Instead, he quit Chevron, stayed home in Houston, and went to work for George Mitchell, the one man who might appreciate the magnitude of what was possible in the shale fields. Bowker made the case to Mitchell and his management team that there was nearly 200 billion cubic feet of natural gas *in each square mile* of the Barnett Shale—four times what the most optimistic geologists at Mitchell had estimated. "This is huge," George Mitchell exclaimed. "This is the biggest secret in the history of the company." Mitchell and his management team agreed that the thing to do would be to buy the mineral rights on every square inch of land they could get at in the Barnett, but quietly, quietly, so as not to alert other companies about what they had in store.

Other companies, though, were not picking up what Mitchell was putting down. Skepticism reigned. Why would Mitchell Energy be able to crack the code that Exxon and Chevron and the other majors could not? Eighteen months after Mitchell's breakthrough, Devon Energy, out of Oklahoma City, passed on a chance to acquire Mitchell and its huge stockpile of mineral rights in the Barnett Shale. Devon's technical team had sized up the Mitchell operation, and at the beginning of 2000 it reported back to the bosses that slickwater fracking wasn't any great shakes. "We turned up our noses because we didn't think it would work," Devon's CEO, Larry Nichols, remembered.

But it was hard to ignore Mitchell's swelling production numbers over the next few years. Devon soon suspected that it had been wrong about Mitchell Energy and what it had to offer. In 2002, Nichols and his team at Devon plunked down $3.5 billion to acquire Mitchell, and Devon's resources and technical know-how turned out to be extraordinary value added. Devon engineers went to work and proved they could extract gas more efficiently, and more effectively, by combining

Mitchell's new technology with the relatively new and little-used technology of horizontal drilling. Horizontal drilling allowed well operators to drill straight down, make a right-angle turn at a chosen depth, and then tunnel out thousands of yards or even miles more. Drillers could frack all along the horizontal line, which increased the potential pay zone exponentially. But it also required more slickwater. A lot more slickwater. Devon often injected five times the amount of fracking fluid Steinsberger had used on his first successful well. The horizontal gambit worked—better than the company had hoped. By June 2002, the Devon Energy suits were satisfied that they would probably be drilling new wells in the Barnett Shale for the next fifteen years and expected to sextuple the number of wells in the area, to more than six thousand. Trillions of cubic feet of newly gettable gas suddenly seemed not so fanciful a prediction.

The combination of slickwatered hydraulic fracturing and horizontal drilling was the breakthrough the oil and gas industry had been chasing for years. And it wasn't merely an upheaval of potentially epic commercial proportions; it was a hinge on which modern history has turned. A new genie was out of the bottle. It's hard to say, even today, if that genie is a friend. But he has had effect. Hydraulic fracking and horizontal drilling have rewritten the whole global energy equation and the future of a whole bunch of countries with it. "It is one of the most extraordinarily important, disruptive, technologically driven changes in the history of energy," the global head of commodity research at Citigroup said of the fracking boom. "It was revolutionary for the U.S. economy and it was revolutionary geopolitically."

THREE

STOLEN GOODS

IF THERE WAS ANYBODY IN RUSSIA POISED AND POSITIONED TO TAKE advantage of the new innovations in oil and gas production in the first few years of the twenty-first century, it was Mikhail Khodorkovsky. Khodorkovsky had grown a moribund little conglomeration of Soviet-era oil producers into the most successful single oil company in the Russian Federation. That company, Yukos, had grown under his leadership into a corporation worth more than $30 billion and doubled its output in just four years. By 2002, Yukos accounted for nearly 20 percent of the crude oil produced in Russia. Khodorkovsky was at that moment the most celebrated Russian businessman in the West. His company was widely regarded as the most technologically advanced corporation in his home country and stamped with the imprimatur of Western financial gurus. U.S. ratings agencies deemed Yukos the most creditworthy non-state corporation in all Russia.

The story of Mikhail Khodorkovsky and Yukos also happens to be a spot-on barometer for the commercial and political atmosphere of Russia in the decades surrounding the collapse of the Soviet Union.

Khodorkovsky, born in 1963, was a bright and unflappable youngster with a preternatural facility for understanding the game of life as it presented itself and for playing to the shortest odds. He saw early that the best career berths in the Soviet Union were solid government jobs, where an ambitious and careful operator could move up through the ranks, acquire a series of bigger and more ornate apartments and nicer automobiles and luxury goods, maybe scoop up an increasing cut of the loot shaken loose by the officially sanctioned graft machine of the Soviet government. The ticket to that happy life was the unbroken demonstration of fealty to the Communist Party. So this son of apolitical and undistinguished working-class engineers dedicated his boyhood and young adulthood to proving himself an enthusiastic and standout member of the Communist Youth League. And he succeeded, winning an entry-level job tending his minuscule part of the lurching Soviet machinery.

Alas, just as his career in government was really getting under way in 1989, the Soviet Union began its slow-motion implosion. Khodorkovsky saw it happening and changed course on a dime. The boundaries of capitalism and democracy in Russia were still being chalked, the rules of the game still being written, but Khodorkovsky flew onto the field with abandon.

"It is time to stop living according to Lenin!" Khodorkovsky wrote in an essay right around his thirtieth birthday, as quoted by the author Masha Gessen. "Our guiding light is Profit, acquired in a strictly legal way. Our Lord is His Majesty, Money, for it is only He who can lead us to wealth as the norm in life."

Khodorkovsky didn't just sermonize about the pursuit of wealth; he practiced the life he preached, though in actual practice it wasn't always "strictly legal" and it wasn't always successful. He started a small café. It failed. He started a business importing personal computers. It foundered. He started a bank. That worked! He made his first millions trading international currencies and managing funds for the Russian government and kept piling them up, drafting in the exhilarating new wake of the first democratically elected president of Russia, Boris Yeltsin.

Boris Yeltsin had done what Mikhail Gorbachev had been unwilling to even suggest; he tore up the old U.S.S.R. at its foundation. Yeltsin presided over the dissolution of the Union of Soviet Socialist Republics, recognized the independence of those states, and let loose the U.S.S.R.'s various satellites throughout Eastern Europe and Asia. Yeltsin exiled the Communist Party and seized its loot; he stripped national government apparatchiks of their control of business and industry; and for the first time in Russian history, he set free the torrential power of free-market capitalism. In the first years of his presidency, Yeltsin sang the glories of "populist capitalism," insisting that Russian businesses needed "millions of owners, not a handful of millionaires." His boldness and his vision made him a heroic and popular figure among his fellow citizens deep into the 1990s, until his overnight decentralization of the economy began to get somebody-forgot-the-training-wheels wobbly.

The Russian experiment once again proved that early-stage capitalism is a poor vehicle for spreading benefits far and wide. Almost all of those millions of would-be owners treaded in choppy, uncharted, and shark-filled waters, most without a stock certificate to their names. They were still trying to get the hang of credit cards and checking accounts (which were mainly empty). The impatient Yeltsin, meanwhile, steamrolled the national legislature when it tried to slow his dismantling of long-running state monopolies. As with most blunt tactics, Yeltsin's steamrolling had unfortunate and unintended effects. By the time his drive for privatization was complete, a handful of ambitious and canny sharks—the oligarchs, as they came to be known—had won control of the major industries in various Yeltsin-sanctioned fire sales and rigged auctions. "The jewels of the former Soviet Union industry were sold in a corrupt fashion to a handful of well-connected men, forming the new Russian elite," wrote Dmitry Gololobov, who had been an attorney working for Russian banks and oil companies in the go-go Yeltsin years.

This handful of well-connected men hadn't just made themselves millionaires; they had made themselves billionaires. And very quickly. President Yeltsin allowed this decidedly un-populist national heist to run its course with a wink and a nod from the Russian state. "The Russian economy operated on a regime of insiderism, bribery, and coercion," in the words of the American reporter Peter Maass. And where political primacy makes fortunes and might makes right, much of the commercial life of the Russian Federation wound up as a criminal enterprise controlled in a kaleidoscope of partnerships among oligarchs variously connected to Russian politicians, and a rising class of Russian mobsters. "I would submit all of my wealth to legal scrutiny," confessed the top dog among Yeltsin-era oligarchs, Boris Berezovsky. "Except for the first million."

Yeltsin learned to look the other way, or to look the right way. When the Russian voters started to lose faith in their first-ever democratically elected leader—his program of privatization was becoming known as "grabification"—Yeltsin was able to tap the now very deep pockets of the oligarchs to secure reelection. Mikhail Khodorkovsky was among that handful of new rich guys who poured money into Boris Yeltsin's 1996 reelection campaign—when Yeltsin really needed the help—and he was rewarded for it. Khodorkovsky became a skilled practitioner of "grabification." He won his controlling stake in Yukos, an odd mash-up of rusty Soviet-era oil-producing companies, at a rigged government auction that was—handily—run by his own bank. And just in time, too, because when the creakily built Russian economy collapsed in 1998, Khodorkovsky's bank was among the casualties. His last asset standing turned out to be Yukos, which he used all manner of tricks, perhaps not all strictly legal, to hold on to. It seemed worth the effort. Khodorkovsky, a self-styled man of ideas, had a big idea for his last best asset.

Yukos could have toddled along for decades, like the government-controlled Lukoil and what was then the lesser stepchild, Rosneft, using inherited Soviet technology to slowly suck crude oil from fields in western Siberia and sell it on the world market. But Khodorkovsky had a little too much free time now that he had lost almost all of his other businesses. And a little too much intellectual curiosity. And a little too much ambition. He decided to see if he could accomplish what no other Russian businessman had ever successfully done: taking a "Soviet era hulk," as the Russian oil industry expert Thane Gustafson explained, "and turning it into a modern corporation."

Khodorkovsky began by rebuilding the corporate governance of Yukos. He made his company attractive to skeptical Western investors by committing to financial transparency and protections for minority shareholders. He established an independent board of directors, released financial statements worthy of the generally accepted accounting principles adopted by the U.S. Securities and Exchange Commission, invited outside auditors to review the books. Most important, he hired experienced and respected executives and managers from French and American oil companies to ensure all these new corporate policies were properly implemented. Then he brought on an unlikely new head of production, an Oklahoma-born oilman who had worked in the United States, Europe, and Africa.

Joe Mach pronounced himself thrilled to make the move to Yukos, and he wasn't coy about why he was willing to pull up stakes again and go to work in godforsaken Siberia. "It's the same reason Bonnie and Clyde robbed banks," he explained to an American newspaper reporter in 2001, after his first year in Russia. "This is where the oil is . . . not slim pickings like Oklahoma." Mach fairly salivated at the geologic wonder of his new stomping grounds. "Siberia is the simplest environment in the world," he would say. "The West Siberian landscape has not changed in 130 million years. . . . You can go a thousand kilometers; it's the same goddamned sand. All across, it's 18 percent porosity. The water saturation is very consistent. The other no-brainer is [that] the reservoir pressure is 4,500 pounds and the bubble point's 1,800. In other words, it's pure oil. Man, it doesn't get any simpler than that."

Problem was, in western Siberia, it had been too simple, for too long. Mach found it difficult to get a quick buy-in for Yukos's new ambitions from the thousands of Yukos drillers and production pros who had grown up in the Soviet system, where managers were always guarding against the mistake of making too many tractors too fast. There was no urgency about the numbers when Mach arrived at Yukos. There was urgency about maintaining full employment, preferably until the end of time. The governing idea in the Yukos-owned oil fields was to drill new wells constantly and milk even the lowest-producing wells for as long as possible. The roughnecks in western Siberia might not eat well, but they would eat for a lifetime. Stoicism and resignation were the dominant traits in the Russian oil fields. "We never expected anything good," a Yukos employee had once explained to Khodorkovsky. And if nothing good was coming, the priority would be to make sure that what little you had already never went away.

Joe Mach went in determined to explode the system, and along the way he introduced a gritty new form of Russo-American cultural exchange. He prowled the oil fields, demanding closure of the poorest-producing wells and insisting on employing new methods for the best. The old Russian hands did not much appreciate Mach's suggested drilling innovations, but they had grudging respect for his volcanic, Oklahoma-style profanity, which he insisted be accurately translated for his Russian auditors. The Siberian roughnecks gave as good as they got. "When Joe first arrived, our guys said, 'We know everything better than anybody,'" Khodorkovsky explained to a Russian newspaper in 2002. "But Joe says, 'Set the pump lower!' And they said, 'Go fuck yourself. [*Da poshel ty!*]' Because we knew that if you set the pump low in the well, it'd burn out. Joe insisted. So we lowered it, and it burned out. Another one, and it burned out too. Six pumps burned out, but Joe kept saying, 'Lower, lower goddamn it! One out of three will burn out, but the other two will work so well that you won't miss the third one.'"

Mach eventually prevailed. He shut down the weakest half of Yukos's fourteen thousand wells and lowered the proverbial pump in the rest, bringing U.S.-style cutthroat aggression and ingenuity to the Siberian steppes. He used the new and improved hydraulic fracking on the best remaining wells. "I jumped on that enhancement like a chicken on a June bug," Mach boasted to *The New York Times*. (Translation still pending.) Production at Yukos jumped more than 10 percent in Mach's first year on the job, and the company was soon producing a fifth of all the crude oil coming out of Russia.

By then, however, Khodorkovsky's status as a favored man in the Kremlin was no more. Because the presidency of Boris Yeltsin was no more. A career launched as a crusader against privilege and corruption devolved into, well, a life of privilege and corruption. Yeltsin proved in the end to be a very interested pig at the trough, amassing a tidy private fortune for himself, his wife, his daughters, and select friends. When he resigned on December 31, 1999, sitting at his desk with a festive tinsel-adorned Christmas tree behind him, he did so under threat of criminal prosecution while overseeing an economic implosion that dwarfed America's Great Depression of the 1930s. The Russian GDP had fallen by 40 percent. The government defaulted on its debt obligations. The ruble tanked. Russian banks verged on collapse. Inflation soared. Estimates were that an extra three million Russians a year were dying from hunger, neglect, and alcoholism. By the time Yeltsin went, only a handful of Russians was sorry to see him go.

Yeltsin did manage to install his own replacement on his way out of office: a little-known pol who appeared both willing and able to shield the Yeltsin family from criminal prosecution—forty-seven-year-old Vladimir Putin. A trained Soviet KGB operative then heading its successor outfit, the FSB, Putin had done the sitting Russian president the memorable favor of successfully derailing the criminal investigation into the Yeltsin clan. He did so by blackmailing Russia's prosecutor general with a fake sex tape. Putin made sure the grainy tape of an actor playing the prosecutor general and two prostitutes (playing themselves) was broadcast on Russian television. The poor quality of the video rendered it unconvincing, but Putin made an appearance at the TV studio that night to personally vouch for the tape's authenticity. His word sufficed. The prosecutor resigned, and the case against Yeltsin was abruptly closed. Yeltsin had rewarded the FSB boss's intrepidity by nominating him to be the next prime minister. So when Yeltsin stepped aside on the final day of the twentieth century, Vladimir Putin was the next man up for the Russian presidency. "It was like spin the bottle," said Strobe Talbott, who was monitoring the situation for the U.S. State Department, "and the bottle stopped spinning at Putin."

Putin was a different kind of cat from Yeltsin. He had not had his head turned by Western pols, or Western economists, or the color-splashed vision of Western plenty that had wowed Yeltsin on his visit to a supermarket in Houston in 1989. Putin was disgusted by Yeltsin's swoon over the free market and shamed by the public spectacle of Yeltsin's drunken reel down a path of certain national disaster. Putin had been educated in KGB school and was stewed in the dark arts and dark ethic of that estimable and potent Soviet institution. The sworn agents of the Soviet security forces were all about Soviet security or, now that there was no more Soviet, all about Russian security. They were practiced and practical-minded operatives. They were going to wipe away the embarrassment of the Yeltsin debacle, stabilize the moribund domestic economy, and, most important, reestablish Russia's sense of honor. "Putin's objective, and the objective of those who came to power with him," wrote the late Russia specialist Karen Dawisha, "was to restore the idea of Russia as a Great Power and a state worthy of and demanding respect in international affairs."

Putin and his security-minded retinue had learned a few tricks for exercising power after branching off from spying into politics to run Russia's second city, St. Petersburg, in the early 1990s. Like the Yeltsin-made oligarchs, they found that democracy and capitalism, harnessed just so, could still deliver personal benefits just like the old communist regime did. Putin's team installed and managed a vigorous kleptocracy from their offices at city hall. The citizens of St. Petersburg might suffer from want of food and electricity and decent wages, but Deputy Mayor Putin and his key aides made out splendidly. Putin and his chosen minions—the *siloviki*—controlled the economic and political life of the city (and began to amass real personal wealth) by working the seams between democratically elected officials, foreign investors, billionaire oligarchs, and organized crime bosses. Putin's St. Petersburg clan relied on graft, financial manipulation, and violence as needed. There was no government or civil institution powerful enough to check them. The courts and the legal system were not instruments of justice in *siloviki* hands but instruments of power, or *vlast*. "For my friends, everything; for my enemies, the law," the saying went. Putin and his *siloviki* carried these tools from St. Petersburg to Moscow in 1996 (at Yeltsin's invitation) and then into the office of the Russian presidency in 2000.

Putin showed a comfortingly calm, competent face to the world when first elected president. He spoke of what was required in Russia to guarantee democracy and prosperity for all and of national self-sufficiency. He promised to be a team player in world affairs. He had oil and gas to provide to the world market!

The Russian people got a less soothing picture of exactly what Putin meant to accomplish in the days leading up to his inauguration, when a leading liberal newspaper in Moscow published the secret *siloviki* manifesto *Reform of the Administration of the President of the Russian Federation*. The document was tidy, easy to understand, and uncommonly forthright. Control over the economy and politics would once again devolve to a central authority, that is, the president's office. The legislature of the Russian Federation, the Duma, would be rendered impotent, as would local governors, administrators, and politicians—no matter how seemingly friendly. Key media outlets would be bought and controlled by the Russian government, to help provide "active agitation and propaganda" in support of Putin, and to actively discredit and undermine any opposition to the same. Who would be in charge of the state's new modern adventure in securing permanent, unitary, unchallenged power? The institution Putin most trusted: the FSB. "All of the special and secret activities of the Directorate relating to counteracting the forces of opposition to the President," read the manifesto, "will be entirely in the hands and under the control of the special services."

The toughest nut for Putin to crack when he first took office was the question of the oligarchs Yeltsin left behind (and their powerful gangster counterparts). A few months into his new regime, President Putin called them all, including Khodorkovsky, to a meeting at Stalin's old dacha just outside Moscow, still outfitted with the desk and daybed from which Stalin dreamed up his Great Purge of enemies and elites. With that unsubtle setting as an ambient cue, Putin laid down the new law, or more precisely, the new balance of *vlast*. They could hold on to their ill-gotten gains, Putin told them, and operate as they had for the last decade, as long as they offered no opposition to the new regime in the Kremlin. If anybody in the room was unclear as to the purport of Putin's message that day, or the genuine feeling behind it, what soon happened to Mikhail Khodorkovsky ended all confusion. "Khodorkovsky didn't know the limits," said the chairman of Yukos's largest rival, Lukoil. "He didn't realize that when power went from Yeltsin to Putin, things had changed."

Khodorkovsky's cardinal sin against the Russian state was being overly successful and overly independent. While production capacity at Yukos had doubled in just four years, production at Russia's state-controlled oil companies like Lukoil and Rosneft edged up by barely a percent or two a year. Profits at Yukos soared, as did its valuation— from $320 million to $21 billion—as did Khodorkovsky's personal fortune. "One key discovery he made along the way is you don't get rich by selling oil," Thane Gustafson explained in a talk promoting his recent book, *Wheel of Fortune*. "You get rich by selling stock. He was going around to London and New York and convincing people [Yukos] is worth buying and increasing the capital value of the company. By 2003, Khodorkovsky is the richest man in Russia."

From the Western vantage point, Khodorkovsky's (and Yukos's) success was proof that free-market capitalism was still the bomb, whatever Yeltsin's fuckups, so powerful it could grow blue-ribbon winners

even in the wan, depleted soil of the former Soviet Union. Khodorkovsky's company had become the premier oil company in Russia because of its superior management, its financial transparency, its
commitment to technological innovation. Khodorkovsky and Yukos
had won on the merits. In May 2003, *The Wall Street Journal,* devoted
town crier of the free market, ran a loving profile of Khodorkovsky
pegged to his next venture. "Late last month, the 39-year-old Mr.
Khodorkovsky picked his new battle—one that promises to shake up
the world's $550 billion annual oil market. Unveiling a $13 billion deal
to acquire competitor Sibneft and create the world's sixth-largest publicly traded oil and gas producer, he pledged to turn Yukos into the first
Russian heavyweight in the global energy arena."

The story must have produced a series of spit takes among the *siloviki* manning the presidential offices of the Russian Federation. Putin
and his St. Petersburg clan were already wary of Khodorkovsky, and
this profile proved him, inarguably, a threat to national security, or at
least to *siloviki* security. The *Journal* reported that the crown prince of
Yukos had been invited to Houston by President George W. Bush, personally, to help map out a plan for greater cooperation between the
U.S. and the Russian oil industries; that Khodorkovsky had plans to
challenge state-controlled Gazprom's monopoly on exported natural
gas; that Khodorkovsky had plans to fund two anti-Putin political parties and might even be "considering" a run for the Russian presidency.
The *Journal* also recounted for an international audience the story of a
recent public meeting Putin had called with key Russian oil executives.
The colloquy, held at the Kremlin, was widely publicized and televised
across Russia. Khodorkovsky had used the platform to stand up and
ostentatiously challenge Putin and to accuse Putin's pet oil company,
Rosneft, of corruption. He had a PowerPoint presentation to back it up!
"To those who knew Putin," Masha Gessen would later write, "it was
clear from a characteristic smirk on his face that he was livid."

All this might have been forgiven, considering the extraordinary
tax revenue Yukos was adding to the Russian government till (as much
as 5 percent of the annual government take, according to Gessen), but
Putin believed by then that Khodorkovsky was also in the middle of
entering into a pact that was something near treason. It wasn't just the

noise about promoting anti-Putin political parties; it was worse: Putin learned he was negotiating the deal with Lee Raymond and Raymond's number two, Rex Tillerson, that would give ExxonMobil 30 percent of Yukos—a deal that might one day permit the American company to gain controlling ownership of the most able and impressive company in the single crucial industry in Russia. Russia might not have been a superpower anymore, it might not have had a first-world military or economy or anything else anymore, but by God Russia had oil. And now Russia was supposed to willingly give that up, too? The thought, to Vladimir Putin, must have been somewhere between nauseating and enraging. Khodorkovsky's great meritocratic free-market ride came to a screeching halt. *For my friends, everything; for my enemies, the law.*

Putin's henchmen arrested and jailed Khodorkovsky in October 2003; drew up a host of tax evasion, fraud, and embezzlement charges against him; ran sympathetic witnesses out of the country; and won multiple convictions. *Vlast.* Khodorkovsky was sentenced to nine years in prison, while Russian prosecutors were already drawing up new charges. The new Putin/*siloviki* axis, according to the former Yukos attorney turned London-based economics professor Dmitry Gololobov, "functions in two main directions: the control of all the profitable business and direct confiscation from those who are not loyal." Khodorkovsky's imprisonment and ruin were only an amuse-bouche. Putin meant to swallow all that Khodorkovsky had built, that big, beautiful, now $36 billion oil-producing enterprise—for Mother Russia. It was cute what Mikhail tried with selling pieces of Yukos to minority shareholders, adorable with the Western-style financial transparency. Free-market competition on fair terms was really a lovely idea. But not really Vladimir's type.

Team Putin began with a series of audits of Yukos in the weeks after Khodorkovsky's arrest. By the time the federation's tax accounting department was done, Yukos had received bills for back taxes—including interest and penalties—totaling $27.5 billion. This would have been a difficult bill to settle in the best of circumstances, but because Putin's government had also frozen the corporation's liquid assets and crippled its production operations, Yukos found it impossible to pay. Putin's Russian Federal Property Fund provided a solution, though. The fund auctioned off Yukos's key subsidiary, Yuganskneftegaz, which accounted for 60 percent of its annual oil production and an even greater percentage of its $36 billion valuation.

The auction, which took place on December 19, 2004, lasted in the neighborhood of six minutes. The winning bid was a highly discounted $9.3 billion. The only real surprise was the successful bidder, a corporation nobody in Moscow had ever heard of—the Baikalfinansgrup. When journalists got hold of the group's registration documents, they discovered Baikalfinans was just two weeks old and had been incorporated with an initial capitalization of $300. Its "offices" were above a vodka bar in a small building in the remote medieval town of Tver, three hours from Moscow. The address was claimed as corporate headquarters by 150 other companies, according to Masha Gessen, "none of which appeared to have any physical assets."

The mystery of how a $300 company housed above a saloon bought Russia's most capable oil company for $9.3 billion didn't last long. A few days after the auction, the state-owned oil company, Rosneft, tapped government funds to relieve the $9,300,000,300 Baikalfinansgrup of its single asset, Yuganskneftegaz. Rosneft, with a lot of help from Putin and a few other surprising sources, would sweep in the rest of Yukos's discounted assets over the next few years. "The acquisition of Yukos triples the size of Rosneft," Thane Gustafson explained, "and what had been a very minor and no-account company suddenly becomes the largest oil company in Russia."

It was flat-out state-sponsored theft of a legitimate company: the Kremlin just shoplifting a capitalist *something* that might have otherwise actually succeeded on its own merits. A shiv in the supposed meritocracy of capitalist competition. And it had a big Western helper. We can now appreciate just how important this help was, thanks to some serious reporting by a team of *Bloomberg* reporters. Here's what they turned up: Rosneft's greatest non-Putin abettor in its campaign to devour every last bone and feather of Yukos turned out to be the American investment banking titan Morgan Stanley. Morgan Stanley had been doing business out of its office in Moscow since 1994, when Boris Yeltsin was beginning to goose the pace of privatization. When other Western financial institutions fled Moscow as the Russian economy collapsed, Morgan Stanley held firm. It kept its Moscow office fully staffed and hired a Russian economist named Rair Simonyan to run it.

Simonyan's previous job was vice president of international investment for Rosneft. Among Morgan Stanley's crucial business operations in Moscow over the next five years was rescuing Rosneft from extinction.

When Rosneft began to gorge itself on Yukos in 2004, Morgan Stanley's loyalty and friendship finally started to pay real dividends. With more than half of Yukos in Rosneft's gaping maw, and the rest being crammed in as quickly as possible, Rosneft's boss Igor Sechin was ready to embark on some serious growth plans. He was tired of playing second fiddle to Lukoil. Sechin and Rosneft had Putin's blessing; he was head *silovik* among Putin's *siloviki* and would make sure Rosneft's success accrued to Putin's advantage. But the Russian state banks were a little thin on rubles circa 2005, so Sechin needed a lot of new investment from the West, which meant he needed help from the likes of Morgan Stanley.

Western investors were spooked by Putin's gangster move on Yukos, and for good reason. An international arbitration court at The Hague would eventually find that Putin's government had illegally confiscated tens of billions of dollars from Yukos and its shareholders. "It's always wrong to handle stolen goods," the international economist and former Russian Federation adviser Anders Åslund opined, "and Yukos was stolen goods." But Morgan Stanley exhibited few qualms. "Rosneft was perceived as a world-class company that deserves respect," the investment bank's CEO later explained. And it was always nice to be able to count on elite whataboutism from select Russian specialists at high-end American universities. "What was Morgan Stanley supposed to know at the time?" the New York University history professor Yanni Kotsonis told the reporters from *Bloomberg*. "We knew that Russia was corrupt, but that applies to virtually any country producing oil nowadays." Morgan Stanley ran Rosneft's traveling roadshow through boardrooms in London and New York, serving as a character witness for the Russian oil giant. Sure, Khodorkovsky was living in a cage, but that's because he was a crook. *Look, you can tell he's a crook, he's in a cage!*

The tour was so successful that Sechin hired the troupe's leader, a thirty-six-year-old American, to be Rosneft's chief financial officer and to oversee what the company hoped would be a record-setting sale of public stock on the London Stock Exchange. "Peter O'Brien is living proof that the Kremlin is not what it used to be," *Institutional Investor* wrote soon after his hiring. "Or, at least, that Vladimir Putin's lieutenants are trying to learn how to charm investors." Whatever O'Brien's own charms, and despite Morgan Stanley's energetic PR efforts, the initial public stock offering for Rosneft still faced headwinds from the West, from across the political spectrum. George Soros wrote an op-ed in the *Financial Times* about the dangers of investing in a company that would still be controlled by Putin's government: "Rosneft is an instrument of state that will always serve the political objectives of Russia in preference to the interests of the shareholders." Soros asserted that a successful IPO would legitimize the Yukos theft and, because Europe was so dependent on Russian oil and gas, increase Putin's ability to wreak havoc there.

When Vice President Dick Cheney started making essentially the same argument against the Rosneft IPO, it might have been the first time George Soros and Dick Cheney agreed on anything. But criticism from the unlikely Soros-Cheney alliance was about as effective as a painted-line speed bump, especially because—thanks to the smash and grab of most of Yukos—Rosneft would soon have oil reserves to match ExxonMobil, and the price of crude oil had doubled in less than five years and seemed headed toward $100 a barrel. "The world's most prestigious investment bankers, lawyers and accountants are lining up to embrace the Rosneft offering," the decorated business columnist Allan Sloan wrote in *Newsweek*. "But remember that financial markets (and financial professionals) are frequently blinded by money—and there's enough money here to blind anyone."

J. P. Morgan joined Morgan Stanley as one of the four joint global coordinators and book runners while Goldman Sachs signed on as a senior co–lead manager. To put it bluntly, Rosneft's IPO campaign ended up making the world complicit in Putin's theft of Yukos and spread the shame of it around the globe. The markets knew the Russian government had ripped off that company and framed its leader, flat out stealing billions from Yukos shareholders. But Morgan Stanley and the markets and the investors in those markets chose to look the other way because the potential payoff was too enticing.

Rosneft's IPO raised more than $10 billion in cash on the London market. When the news first hit, the IPO ranked as the sixth largest in world history, and analysts thought it might jump past AT&T Wireless's $10.6 billion take from 2000 when the final tallies were made. "Billions of dollars of investments are being made by major foreign partners," Putin crowed on hearing the results. "I think this is absolutely correct. I am happy."

Happy Putin could imagine the world lining up to pay respects at his doorstep, according to *The New York Times,* in spite of his gangster behavior and in spite of the fact that the Russian oil and gas industry he controlled was known for its "tumbledown" machinery and technological deficiencies. "President Vladimir V. Putin has elevated energy to a central position in Russia's foreign policy," the newspaper wrote in 2006, "giving Moscow influence and respect in world affairs not seen since the demise of the Soviet Union, as consuming nations court the Kremlin for access to ever scarcer energy."

Putin wanted more—more respect, more influence, more oil. And he got it with a little more help from his friends. In 2007, Morgan Stanley helped to arrange another round of financing that allowed Rosneft to hoover up the last of Yukos's remaining assets. A State Department cable that year recorded O'Brien, the Russians' young American front man, assuring a visiting U.S. undersecretary of state "that corporate governance at Rosneft and other major Russian companies, while not yet up to Western standards, has improved dramatically."

What Morgan Stanley won for all its efforts—aside from an estimated $360 million in fees in a ten-year span, according to the *Bloomberg* reporters—was the great goodwill of Vladimir Putin and Igor Sechin. The Russian president and his *siloviki* were learning to live with foreign mega-businesses such as Coca-Cola, General Electric, Toyota, and DaimlerChrysler doing business on Russia's sovereign soil. But the Kremlin's favorite American bank looked like a special case. Putin and Sechin privately feted Morgan Stanley's CEO, John Mack, at the presidential estate outside Moscow. When the longtime head of Morgan Stanley's Moscow office, Rair Simonyan, was presented with Russia's Order of Honor in recognition of his work on Rosneft's spectacular IPO, Mack was invited to attend the ceremony. Sechin also included Mack among the select for a dinner cruise down the Neva River that evening. "Sechin treated Mack well, and with respect," Simonyan later recalled, according to the *Bloomberg* reporters who uncovered the long, queasy history of Morgan Stanley in Russia.

Mack clearly understood the coins of the realm—loyalty and friendship—and just how important they were. He knew, for instance, that it would be good for business to make the long trip to Sochi, on the Russian coast of the Black Sea, to make nice at the annual International Investment Forum. CEOs from other American corporate giants were there to meet with Putin, in public, that day in Sochi. The Russian leader was respectful to each of them, but not particularly warm. "We would welcome the expansion of your company's activity in Russia," Putin told the head of a Texas-based investment group with a starter office in Moscow, "and hope that you will find new opportunities for investing your capitals and the capitals under management."

"We'll be happy if you expand your presence in the Russian market and cooperate with Russian partners, which will result in business development and technology exchange," he told GE's Jeffrey Immelt.

The way Putin addressed Mack was demonstrably different; the Morgan Stanley CEO had limboed deeply enough under the constraints of legal and financial decency to help build Putin his own major international oil concern, and that afforded Mack the warmth and special recognition due a loyal and respected friend. Praising Mack's $55 billion worth of deals in the federation's crucial energy industry, Putin said, "We hope that this work will continue for the benefit of both our partners and the Russian participants in these projects. For its part, the Russian Government will facilitate this business in every possible way." Then Putin went positively gooey. "I am tempted to recall one of our late poets, Okudzhava," Putin told Mack. "He was very popular, and remains so. He wrote once: 'Let us join our hands my dear friends. We won't get lost if we're together.'"

Mack didn't lose a beat. "Indeed," he answered, "we did not get lost because we joined hands."

FOUR

CHARLIE HUSTLE

FOR ALL THE ROUGHNECK CHARISMA AND BRUTE FORCE AND slapdash derring-do of the oil and gas industry, the central characters in its drama are often more the green-eyeshade types. There are a surprising number of accounting majors who really do end up right at the center of the action. With charisma of their own—in some cases, with quite a lot to spare.

Aubrey McClendon could still remember the exact moment he decided for sure on a career in oil and gas, he once told a reporter from *Rolling Stone*, while sharing a $400 bottle of French Bordeaux from his personal cellar in the private dining room at one of his own restaurants in Oklahoma City. He was in his final year at Duke University in 1981, he explained, skimming articles in *The Wall Street Journal* as any aspiring accountant would, when a particular story caught his eye. It was a tale of two regular-guy independent wildcatters without much capital who happened to choose just the right spot in the Anadarko Basin, near where Aubrey had grown up. The well became a gusher—was *maybe the biggest gusher in the history of the country,* Aubrey remembered. (It wasn't really, but that's how he remembered it.) "They sold their stake to Washington Gas and Light and got a $100 million check," he told the magazine writer. "I thought, 'These are two dudes who just drilled a well and it happened to hit.' So that really piqued my interest."

He was just past the age of fifty at the dinner that night, favored dark expensively tailored pin-striped suits and conservative-looking rimless spectacles. His shock of wavy hair had grayed all through. But there was a lot of Tom Sawyer still in Aubrey McClendon. Even with a serious journalist who might just check the facts, Aubrey was more likely to try to amuse and entertain, and even awe, than to accurately inform. Accuracy just never really captured the expansiveness of his vision, or the arc of a good story well told. Especially a story with Aubrey. It was doubtless a big part of his charm—and a big reason for his success—that people *wanted* to believe Aubrey. What he lacked in strict truthfulness, he made up for in boyish and enthusiastic sincerity.

The reality of McClendon's entry into oil and gas was maybe a bit more prosaic than the way he sometimes told it. He had actually grown up in the business, at a slight remove, but near enough to feel the pull of its centripetal force and to understand the power its storied practitioners could wield in the wider world.

Aubrey McClendon's great-uncle had been a founder of Kerr-McGee, one of the nation's premier Big Oil companies of mid-century America. Robert S. Kerr, a Southern Baptist farm boy from Ada, Oklahoma, had used the piles of cash he made in the oil business to swing open the door to politics. He was elected governor of Oklahoma for a single term in the 1940s and U.S. senator for three. Senator Kerr damn near bought himself the Democratic presidential nomination in 1952.

Even ten years after his death, Old Bulls in the Senate still regarded Kerr as one of the most compelling forces they had seen in that body. (His biographical entry on official U.S. government websites refers to him as "the Uncrowned King of the Senate.") What made him so effective was that he operated at a vital nexus of government and business. Senator Kerr was a consequential politician who served the interests of the most consequential industry in modern America. By the 1950s, oil and gas was the most able, most profitable, most outward-facing commercial enterprise in the most able and powerful and outward-facing country in the world. Like it or lump it, the oil and gas industry and the country had grown up together, in lockstep, and neither would have risen to its improbable heights without the other.

It didn't take much effort for Robert S. Kerr to leverage his seat in the Senate, his place in the pantheon of oil and gas titans, and his vast personal resources to defend and protect what he regarded as the well-earned prerogatives of America's signature industry. "I been meanin' tuh give you this for the past six months," Kerr would tell one of his colleagues on a trip in the subterranean railway that ran from the Senate office buildings to the Capitol, according to one young U.S. senator who liked to collect stories about earlier members. Then Kerr would hand over an envelope full of stock certificates for some recent oil venture. "I knew you'd want into this deal," he'd say. "It's a helluva deal. Just the kind you like. So I put you in for $3,000. Just call my secretary and arrange to give her a check." The stocks would generally be worth ten times the purchase price by the time Kerr got around to distributing them, which made it very easy to write that check.

The Senate mostly voted Kerr's way on oil and gas interests, especially when it came to preserving the decades-old breaks written into the tax code to encourage oil-field production. "We could have taken a 5 or 10 percent figure," an industry-friendly U.S. senator later said of the sweetheart tax relief passed back in the 1920s, "but we grabbed 27.5 percent because we were not only hogs but the odd figure made it appear as though it was scientifically arrived at." Special tax favors for oil and gas producers have been in force since Woodrow Wilson's first year in office and still stand today, seventeen presidential administrations later, as the longest-running welfare program in the nation's history. Credit goes in no small part to Senator Kerr and his political brethren, Democrats and Republicans both, representing oil-producing states from coast to coast.

The McClendon line was not a serious stakeholder in the Kerr oil empire, because Aubrey's grandfather had opted out in the early days. But Aubrey's father did enjoy the sort of solid-paying sinecure at Kerr-McGee (he spent a lot of time checking up on the company's filling stations in Oklahoma) that afforded young Aubrey an upper-middle-class private school upbringing beyond want and worry. So while he had borne witness to the bruising cycles of the oil and gas industry on the Oklahoma prairie, he could not have felt the pain of bust as acutely as the child of a roughneck or a tool pusher or a third-tier company geologist, whose family paychecks diminished or disappeared as the price per barrel dropped on the international market. And despite the *biggest gusher in history* yarn he sometimes spun, the reason Aubrey entered the business in 1981 was less dramatic in some of his tellings. "I never really grew up thinking I wanted to be in the oil and gas business," he explained in a less excited moment, "but by the time I graduated, that's where the best jobs were."

Whatever the truth of his genesis story, once he picked oil and gas, McClendon started where everybody with no geologic or technical expertise started—as a landman. "Landmen were always the stepchild of the industry," Aubrey once explained. "Geologists and engineers were the important guys—but it dawned on me pretty early that all their fancy ideas aren't worth very much if we don't have a lease. If you've got the lease and I don't, you win." The position played to his strengths; it required energy, enthusiasm, and a whiff of sincerity. Tom Sawyer would have been a landman. The best of them kept their ear to the street, so they could stay ahead of the next big drilling play, to know where the major producers would be sinking wells (and cash) next, so they could get there first, ahead of their competitors, and buy up the mineral rights while prices were still low. A landman had to persuade farmers and ranchers and townsfolk near a future play to sell him the mineral rights for a little cash up front and the promise of fabulous payouts to come. You had to be able to sell the future, and Aubrey could sell it. Aubrey did sell it.

In 1989, the not yet thirty-year-old Aubrey and his partner, another ambitious young landman named Tom Ward, made a move toward exploration and production, with an increasing focus on natural gas and new drilling technologies. Within just four years, the two friends turned a $50,000 investment into a public company valued at $25 million. They named the company Chesapeake Energy, which is a little weird for a company from Oklahoma, but Aubrey liked the sound of it, with its faint aroma of mid-Atlantic yachtsmanship. The two men rejected the simpler McClendon & Ward, Aubrey would later say, because in the not-unlikely circumstance that the business ended up in bankruptcy, they didn't want their names on the top line of the Chapter 11 filing.

By the time Chesapeake Energy went public in 1993, the industry was sliding into the doldrums. Sluggishness in the rise of oil and natural gas prices offered scant incentive to drill. But Aubrey liked to zig when everybody else zagged. While other independents slowed their roll, Chesapeake Energy bosses floored the accelerator: they borrowed enormous amounts of money, which saddled the company with an unhealthy load of debt, but they used that borrowed money to drill and drill and drill some more. Chesapeake would reward the brave. The company would take oil and gas out of the ground as rapidly as it could, Aubrey told business writers, and turn it into cold hard cash for bold investors.

This appetite for risk (and a run of reasonably steady commodity prices) enabled the company to double its production three years running and still pay out a nice dividend to its stockholders. "I'd call us the most successful energy company of the last ten years, if not the last twenty," Aubrey said in 1997. Chesapeake stock soared—right up to the moment prices cratered at the end of the 1990s. Chesapeake had taken on a billion dollars of debt by the dawn of the new century, the big notes due in seven years, and it looked as if all were lost if it didn't do something fast. The board was pushing to sell the company in a hurry and clear the debt. Aubrey, however, refused to be chastened, or to let fear get the better of him, or to acquiesce in a fire sale. He had by then got the idea that he could trust his own luck, and he was still scouting hard for the main chance when he took a meeting with a major electricity-producing company in San Jose, California. The Calpine bosses told Aubrey about their plan to stand up dozens of new gas-burning power plants to meet the Golden State's massive energy needs. This alone could increase gas consumption in the United States by 10 percent.

Demand for natural gas would not only trend up, Aubrey calculated, it would go through the roof; prices would jump. The expensive new Mitchell-led drilling technologies capable of loosing natural gas from previously hard-to-get-to shale formations would finally prove worth the cost. "I went away from that meeting saying, 'We got a chance,'" he said. Another man a billion dollars in the hole might shy from the table. Aubrey shoveled in his chips. Chesapeake Energy issued more stock and went on another borrowing spree, with hundreds of millions of dollars in help from Deutsche Bank, J. P. Morgan, and Lehman Brothers. From his office in Oklahoma City, Aubrey executed a spectacular landgrab in promising shale-producing regions in upstate New York, Pennsylvania, West Virginia, Arkansas, Louisiana, Texas, and right at home in Oklahoma.

The beauty of the shale play was that it didn't require real technical expertise to target the best place to sink a well. You just needed to own the mineral rights to as much land as possible. Once a well was bored down into the layers of shale deep below the earth's surface, the gas was, as a rule, generously distributed. Pretty much anywhere worked. With the increasingly common techniques of hydraulic fracturing and horizontal drilling, it was kind of hard to come up with a dry hole, or "bust a pick" as one of his competitors liked to say. This played to Aubrey's strengths.

"When the game changed," he would say, "and acquisition became the key to capturing the greatest values from the unconventional plays, I felt like I had a natural advantage over most [competitors] because I understood how to put together a very formidable Chesapeake land machine to 'capture the flag' in big plays." In just seven years—from 2000 to 2007—the company locked up drilling and mineral rights on more than ten million acres in the United States, equivalent to owning everything under a landmass the size of Maryland, with Connecticut tossed in, too.

By the beginning of 2008, with the price of natural gas coming back up and Aubrey's incredible success talking people into his ideas and plans, his bet on shale gas was paying off in a big way. Chesapeake had grown from a few hundred employees in 2000 to nearly seventy-six hundred. There were three thousand Chesapeake employees in Oklahoma City alone, all housed in a modern campus Aubrey commissioned and helped to design. His vision of an ideal, sprawling office park was still growing and taking shape and would eventually include more than twenty redbrick Georgian-style buildings, a fitness center offering yoga classes and free massages, upscale cafeterias, and a sixty-three-thousand-square-foot day-care center. "I have been focused on building a campus that is architecturally appealing and functions well on a human scale," he would explain to a local magazine writer. "I like to think of our company as being organic and fast moving, so we build horizontally. . . . I believe businesses succeed if people work together on a collegial level. I wanted to keep our buildings horizontal in scale to reflect our environment of teamwork versus hierarchy."

Fortune magazine named Chesapeake one of the country's one hundred best companies to work for in 2008, owing mainly to the personal care and largesse of Aubrey McClendon. Aubrey made a special point to get to know new hires at the regional headquarters in his gas-producing fields of tomorrow. He jetted into the dedication of a regional office in White County, Arkansas, in the second week of 2008 with a $100,000 check to fund science and engineering scholarships at nearby Harding University and a pledge to grow the new thirty-five-person field office by three or even four times in the coming months. "We want to be the best neighbors they've ever had," Aubrey told a reporter at the gathering of more than five hundred locals. "The people of this area are about to see an economic boom the likes of which they've never seen before."

Who didn't want to believe Aubrey? Who didn't want to be part of his adventure? Who didn't want to cash his checks? He was the most visible and the most prepossessing face of the country's remarkable shale gas boom, the revolution in extraction technology that was finally going to set us free—free from our withering and costly addiction to foreign oil; free from the galling cupidity of prices at the gasoline pump; free from our long, polluted romance with dirty coal. Forget Russia and Lukoil; natural gas right here at home was the future. Or at least the near future—a perfect bridge between America's oil-importing and dirty-coal past and the green-energy panacea of wind and solar that Democratic presidential candidates like Barack Obama and Hillary Clinton were touting that spring. Natural gas, Aubrey McClendon was telling anyone who would listen, is "ready to rescue our economy, enhance national security and reduce pollution. . . . By converting just 10 percent of our vehicles to Compressed Natural Gas, we can lower our use of foreign oil by nearly fifty billion dollars per year. So let's ask Washington to put those billions to work as incentives to build and buy CNG vehicles like the rest of the world enjoys, incentives for retailers to sell CNG, for drivers to convert their current cars and trucks to CNG, and to install home refueling units that connect to residential gas lines."

We're all in this together, producers *and* consumers, was Aubrey's personal campaign message, and he pushed it straight down the corporate chain of command, all the way to subcontractors working at far-off regional headquarters in Arkansas or Louisiana or Texas or up-

CHARLIE HUSTLE : 51

state New York or Towanda, Pennsylvania, smack in the middle of the Marcellus Shale boom. Landmen gathering mineral-rights leases on behalf of Chesapeake Energy were showing up on doorsteps all over Pennsylvania to ply landowners with the lure of royalty packages that would likely pay out for thirty years, not to mention the chance to do their small part for national security. "He told us there was natural gas in the shale rock a mile down, and they had a new way to drill for it that was minimally invasive and would cause very little damage to our land," one dairy farmer told the *Rolling Stone* writer Jeff Goodell of the Chesapeake landman who secured her signature on a mineral lease. "He said it was a patriotic thing to do, that natural gas would help America gain energy independence."

Chesapeake Energy was making a big public show of doing its part, patriot-wise. The company was the Charlie Hustle of the natural gas world, drilling anywhere and everywhere: under a suburban country club's manicured lawns, a university's parking lot, an airport's runways and terminals, and right next to schools and day-care centers. *Fortune* magazine figured Chesapeake's drilling activity was double its nearest domestic competitor in the field of natural gas. "We're doing things that nobody else in the world is doing; drilling wells that other people wouldn't have," Aubrey boasted to his team at the Oklahoma City headquarters in March 2008, with a reporter from *Fortune* looking on to record the remarks for the wider public. "We've made discoveries that other people would never have found. When I wake up in the morning I'm ready to go because I get to work for a company that drilled more rock than anybody else on earth." This last brag was not strictly accurate; Aubrey did top the U.S. charts, but it's a big oil- and gas-producing planet out there, and Chesapeake wasn't anywhere close to the top. Still, the *Fortune* reporter seemed to accept this little exaggeration as just another case of Aubrey being Aubrey. His enthusiasm was off the leash again, running well ahead of his accomplishment. But, hey, who's to say he wouldn't catch up!

Chesapeake had the wind in its sails like never before. Natural gas was generating 20 percent of America's electricity—nearly twice what it was ten years earlier. More than four thousand miles of new pipeline was under construction in 2008, capable of transmitting almost fifty billon cubic feet of natural gas every day. "[This] could be completely transformative for our country," Aubrey McClendon exclaimed. "The plumbing is being built right now!"

Natural gas prices had already climbed from $2 and change per million BTUs (British thermal units) at the beginning of 2000, when Aubrey began putting all his chips on gas, to nearly $8 at the beginning of 2008. In the next six months, the price nearly doubled, nestling in just shy of $14 on July 3, 2008. Chesapeake stock rode the brisk and increasing winds up and up and up, from $38 a share in February 2008 to almost $70 in July. And even when the stock was performing its most dizzying climb, when the valuation began looking cartoonishly high to energy analysts, Aubrey remained bullish. He kept borrowing more and more money, personally, to buy more and more Chesapeake stock. By that summer of 2008, he had amassed more than thirty million shares for himself.

And, boy, did he look good on paper! Aubrey McClendon had increased his personal wealth nearly 50 percent in a single year, to $3 billion, which had jumped him almost a hundred places, to number 134 on the Forbes 400 list of wealthiest Americans. (He stood ten spots ahead of David Rockefeller Sr., who had long ago traded in most of his inherited oil company stock for a steadier portfolio of assets heavy in real estate and French impressionist paintings.) *Forbes* noted that Aubrey McClendon was one of 38 men and women on the list whose fortunes were made in the oil and gas business—a cohort whose combined net worth in 2008 ran to about $162 billion. Which meant Aubrey and these other 37 individuals could have shoved their collective fortunes into very conservative interest-bearing financial instruments and covered the entire annual spending of the state government of Oklahoma to the end of time. Aubrey, meanwhile, insisted wealth was not how he judged success. "I just plug away, hope for the best, and let everybody else keep score," he told a friendly local reporter. "Billionaire is a word that probably has more meaning to other people than it does to me."

They did love Aubrey in his hometown. He wasn't the only billionaire in Oklahoma City, but he was its most visible and most rah-rah citizen. He didn't make his fortune and then relocate to Tulsa or Dallas or Houston. He was OKC through and through. The locals knew him on sight: he looked like Archie Manning's long-lost younger brother, with the insouciant, unkempt shock of wavy hair, the soft unthreatening drawl, and the slightly doughy features that all belied a flinty, hard-edged need to win. Stories about Aubrey traveled second- and third- and fourth-hand. Somebody saw Aubrey and his wife, Katie, an heiress to the Whirlpool fortune, sneaking champagne into the local movie theater. Somebody saw Aubrey riding around downtown on a motor-cycle powered by natural gas. They heard he had ordered ties emblazoned with tiny drilling rigs. And had insisted that the investment bankers visiting from back east sample one of his many restaurants' famous duck-fat fries. He joked to friends and reporters about him and his Oklahoma redneck buddies pulling a fast one on the entire leadership suite of the City of Seattle. And bragged that when the governor of Connecticut accused Chesapeake Energy of "fleecing" her citizens by manipulating the price of natural gas, he flat out called her a liar. The suits at places like ExxonMobil might be willing to turn the other cheek, but Aubrey was going to defend the honor of his own. "You tell me—and when you tell me, you're also saying to all our employees—that we did something wrong," he said to a roomful of his Chesapeake co-workers, "I'm gonna come out swinging and fighting."

Then, too, there were the stories about his money and his stuff. Like how Aubrey had accumulated a multimillion-dollar, 100,000-bottle wine collection—not because he was a great connoisseur, but because he fancied himself a great investor. He started to collect, he told a reporter from *Forbes,* "with the idea that wine was an underowned and underpriced asset class, especially in China and other emerging countries. . . . As for favorites, I really don't have any. I like some very inexpensive wines and I like some high-end wines. I guess my favorite though would be a small St. Emilion wine called Clos Dubreuil, which in full disclosure, I own about 50% of, and plan to give you a bottle of it if allowed." (The reporter accepted and rated it "incredible.")

There were countless stories in the local papers about Aubrey spreading his wealth. "Asking me what to do with extra cash is like asking a fraternity boy what to do with the beer," he told a reporter from a trade paper. If he stopped in at Irma's Burger Shack, just across the street from his offices, and saw the place was empty, he'd hand out $100 tips to everyone on the job that night. The McClendons had given

$1 million to shore up the Red Cross in the aftermath of Hurricane Katrina and pledged more than $10 million to their alma mater, Duke University. But their biggest giving was close to home. In May 2008, Aubrey and Katie announced a $12.5 million gift to the University of Oklahoma to fund student housing, academics, and athletics. Five days later, they heralded an investment of $35 million in a new cancer treatment center specializing in a more targeted, less damaging form of radiation therapy. "I have every reason to believe ProCure will become the gold standard for providing proton therapy to treat cancer in this country," he gushed.

Aubrey's spending was infectious. He led the funding of a sleek new $3.5 million boathouse and training center on the recently restored and renamed Oklahoma River, which drew the U.S. Olympic Committee to the onetime drainage ditch to run the trials in sprint canoe/kayak for the 2008 Beijing Games. And wouldn't you know it, Chesapeake's biggest competitor in the shale gas play, Devon Energy, announced plans to build a $10 million boathouse right next door. When Chesapeake embarked on an expansion of its corporate campus, along with a big commercial development nearby, Devon Energy again went Aubrey one better. In March 2008, Devon's chairman and CEO, Larry Nichols, heralded his own company's plans to build a thirty-seven-story, million-square-foot, $350 million office tower in the heart of downtown Oklahoma City. By late spring, with gas prices on their dizzying upward trajectory and Devon's workforce still growing, the building specs were expanding. "Those numbers are no longer good numbers," Nichols said. When Devon Energy finally unveiled the scale models that August, the tower-to-be was now a fifty-four-story, 1.8-million-square-foot, $750 million behemoth. "We want to create a building that adds to [the city's] momentum," Nichols said. "A building that says to the rest of the world that Oklahoma City is an exciting, dynamic, vibrant place to be."

Construction cranes sprouted on the Oklahoma City horizon like oil derricks. A Dell computer office complex was already up and running, and an American Indian Cultural Center was rising on the riverfront. Residents of Oklahoma City had got to believing their own press: fourth on the list of best cities for commuters, according to *Forbes*, seventh cleanest, nineteenth best for job seekers. And the coup de grâce: the most recession-proof city in America. This seemed a mighty tall stretch for a city whose economy was built on the always-fickle boom-and-bust oil and gas industry. But, well, who didn't want to believe? Who didn't want to be part of this adventure?

Aubrey-ness seems to have fired up the entire city and urged it forward. "The coxswain is the one who steers the boat, the inspiration," one of his many local acolytes said of him. "If you have a good coxswain, you can win the race even if you don't have athletes as good as those in the other boats. And Aubrey was our coxswain.... There were naysayers, not that they were critical, but it was hard for them to imagine. But Aubrey got it. For him, no dream was too big." Aubrey McClendon truly believed he could change the future, one of his friends would say of him. And the thing he had already changed in 2008 was his hometown's idea of itself.

FIVE

···

THUNDER UP!

OKLAHOMA CITY'S LONG-STANDING HABIT HAD BEEN TO SEE itself through the eyes of outsiders, and it was not a healthy habit. The lyrics to the famous Broadway musical notwithstanding, the residents of Oklahoma City knew that in the popular imagination of the nation, "Oklahoma" rarely brought to mind wavin' wheat, or corn as high as an elephant's eye, or meadows bathed in bright golden haze. "Oklahoma" was more likely to conjure a black-and-white world of want and woe, of underfed domestic refugees fleeing a dusty hellscape. "It's burned in everybody's mind, that 'Grapes of Wrath' image," lamented an aspiring young architect to *The Oklahoman* in the spring of 2008. The most hard-hearted Americans regarded residents of OKC as the descendants of folks who lacked the gumption to git up and git to California seventy years earlier. It was an unfair and uninformed opinion, but that didn't make the reputation any less tough to live with or to live down. "We kind of inherently knew that the rest of America did not consider us a place worth talking about, living in, visiting, and doing business in," Oklahoma City's current mayor, David Holt, explained to an out-of-town reporter. "For a long time, people were sort of embarrassed if you were to run into your cousin on the east coast. You would have instinctively sort of bad-mouthed your own city, and that would have been part of the deal of living here."

But even facing these cultural headwinds, Oklahoma Citians had been trying, by God, for a couple of generations at least, to get themselves some national respect. And naturally, OKC's big-city ambitions sparkled to life in the effulgence of its oil and gas industry. The first big move came in the early 1960s, at the tail end of a long and insistent postwar oil boom, when city fathers had the cash on hand to entice a renowned architect to come to Oklahoma City and give it a full-on makeover. I. M. Pei had already pulled off the Mile High Center in Denver and had hired on to perform similar urban renewal projects in Boston, Washington, D.C., Philadelphia, and New York. He agreed to make Oklahoma City another of the big jewels in his crown. Maybe the biggest. The Pei Plan, when approved by the city council in 1965, was bold in vision and in promise. Much of downtown Oklahoma City's stodgy, low-slung, redbrick history would be wiped away and replaced with a new convention center, office towers, residential buildings, wide avenues, parks, gardens, and lakes. "Perhaps a monorail in the future," boasted the promotional material. The urban landscape included a public park modeled on the Danish amusement park that had inspired Walt Disney's famous Disneyland. And the entire development was to be anchored, of course, by a million-square-foot shopping mall called the Galleria.

The bulldozers, dynamite shooters, and wrecking crews got right to work. The Urban Renewal Authority's hired contractors razed nearly 450 downtown buildings to make way for Pei's grand plan. Private property owners got caught up in the fever too, taking down another 75 buildings merely on their own recognizance. "They were in a rush to create something shiny and new," one local newsman remarked. Creation proved much more difficult than destruction. A dozen years in, the forest fire of urban renewal had somewhat arbitrarily wiped away much of the old growth. Venerable and well-regarded structures like the thirty-story Biltmore Hotel, the old Overholser Opera House, the Mercantile Building, the terra-cotta Baum Building (Oklahoma City's architectural paean to the Doge's Palace in Venice), and three major department stores were gone. But not much new growth had sprouted in its place. Revenue to fund the big reimagining of downtown—and to fund everything else—had dried up as the oil and gas industry suffered a series of long, slow downward turns, eased only a little by the occasional, too short mini-boom. While the powers at the

Oklahoma City Urban Renewal Authority *had* been able to fund and produce a short booster film with a snappy new theme song—"Listen to the wind that rushes by you, listen to the magic in the air, that's the sound of people working hand in hand . . . growing with pride, growing with love, bringing lots of things that we've been dreaming of"— the authority had not been able to produce many actual buildings. There was an expanding new hospital complex and a spectacularly ugly theater center building. There was also the beginning of a massive parking structure for servicing the hordes drawn to the Galleria shopping mall. Unfortunately, there was no Galleria shopping mall.

The most ardent downtown boosters stayed strong through the 1970s and into the first years of the 1980s, while hopes of finally realizing the Pei Plan rose and fell with the price of oil and the fortunes of the city's dominant industry. But then, in 1982, the industry, as one local oilman put it, "just ran over a cliff one night." The price of oil fell sharply and stayed down. It bottomed out near $10 a barrel in the summer of 1986. Six in ten energy-related jobs in Oklahoma disappeared in just a few years. One in five banks had gone under by the end of the decade. Annual bankruptcies in the state quadrupled. The state's tax revenues from oil production—which had accounted for more than 30 percent of Oklahoma's total revenues—fell by half. And Oklahoma City took the worst of it. Seven of the capital city's ten biggest banks folded. More than a third of the offices in its downtown were empty. The Pei Plan, long on life support, was pronounced dead in 1988.

OKC gumption did not die with it. GOD GRANT US ANOTHER BOOM, read a popular bumper sticker at the time, AND THE WISDOM NOT TO PISS IT AWAY. In 1990–1991, town leaders engaged in a spirited fight against bigger cities like Indianapolis, Denver, and Louisville in the twenty-one-month bidding war for United Airlines' billion-dollar maintenance center. The new facility promised sixty-three hundred jobs (minimum $45,000 per annum, claimed United) and a whiff of big-city cachet. OKC's mayor, Ron Norick, figured his team spent more than two thousand hours per person working to woo the country's second-largest airline—nights, Saturdays, Sundays after church—and it showed. "[United] said Oklahoma City was by far the best prepared, well organized, the most professional, the most courteous, the most responsive," Norick said, when the final announcement was made in

October 1991. But that was cold comfort. Indianapolis had won the day.

"The big enchilada was lost," Norick admitted, and it hurt. Salt in that wound was the story that went around about the explanation Mayor Norick got from the CEO of United Airlines about what went wrong with the OKC bid. What could the city have done better? the mayor wanted to know. The United CEO, according to the talk of the town, said the mayor and his team had done everything right, but it was never going to be enough. "I just couldn't imagine making my employees live in OKC," the United boss had reportedly said. *Making them?* Whether it was absolutely true or not, the story seemed to line up with Oklahoma City's bad old habits and long-standing inferiority complex.

Norick himself didn't confirm the story. "We have nothing to be ashamed about," he told reporters. "We did an excellent job."

Norick did his due diligence after the United loss; he flew to Indianapolis, got in a rental car and drove straight into downtown. "I said shoot, I know why they got that United plant," he explained in a 2009 interview for the Voices of Oklahoma oral history project. "I mean this is a live city. I mean there's people on the street, and there were restaurants and hotels and a Convention facility and all this stuff. . . . [Indianapolis] had everything. It had Major League sports and they've had some big NCAA sporting events. . . . It didn't take but about thirty minutes driving downtown and I said, 'Wow, now I've got it. Now I've got it.'"

Norick went to the drawing board when he got home and came up with a new plan to make OKC a worthy opponent in the next competition with the nation's biggest cities. Then he went to work to convince the residents of Oklahoma City they were capable of competing, if they would just put their money where their hearts were. *If you build it, they will come.* Norick's new proposal called for a new indoor sports arena, a minor-league ballpark, a canal, and a public library, along with major overhauls of the convention center and the civic center. And the citizenry backed him. Voters passed a $350 million tax hike to fund this new attempt at downtown renewal at the end of 1993, which meant the ground was just being broken on the early projects when Oklahoma City absorbed its next devastating blow.

On the morning of April 19, 1995, less than a mile from the sites of the proposed new sports arena and library, and for no good reason on earth, an embittered racist, right-wing nutball named Timothy McVeigh detonated a Ryder truck filled with explosives in front of the Alfred P. Murrah Federal Building. The force of the blast, which was reportedly felt thirty miles away, ripped the face off the Murrah building, and damaged or destroyed more than three hundred nearby structures. Nearly seven hundred innocent people were injured that day, and 168 killed. Among the dead were children who had just been dropped off at the building's second-floor day-care center. Oklahoma City was suddenly notorious, home to the worst terrorist attack, to that point, in U.S. history. "We know this is making national news across the United States," a local anchor noted in her report that morning as bodies were being pulled from the rubble.

The effect in Oklahoma City itself was almost impossible to overstate. Two hundred thousand people attended at least one funeral of a bombing victim, and three of every four locals volunteered or gave money in support of devastated survivors. The city took down the remains of the Murrah building, then sanctified and memorialized the grounds.

Aubrey McClendon was among the first major donors to the Oklahoma City National Memorial, and a dozen years after the bombing he and his wife were still donating hundreds of thousands of dollars toward its maintenance and expansion. It stands today as one of the most thoughtful and arresting memorials on American soil. But while that spot will forever stand still, Oklahoma City truly transformed around it. The urban gem so many had hoped for, for so long, finally started to shimmer up out of the prairie. More than $3 billion has been plowed into downtown development since the bombing. Mayor Norick's entire urban renewal scheme was accomplished, and then some. "The bombings galvanized the average person to realize that the city needed to make a statement," said Governor Frank Keating. "There was a sense of pride and optimism and faith that bordered on the spiritual."

The subsequent rise of OKC had doubtless been aided by the renewal of civic pride. And optimism. And faith bordering on the spiritual. But to be honest, what really made it happen, finally, after decades of false starts, was the shale gas boom Aubrey had foreseen back in

2000—the shale gas boom he'd been selling the heck out of for years thereafter. Just like Aubrey, Oklahoma City was riding the wave. By 2008, Oklahoma-based energy companies accounted for something near a tenth of all the natural gas produced in the United States. And the price of natural gas meant those producers were minting money. Oklahoma City's two biggest, Chesapeake and Devon, scooped up $25 billion in gross revenues in that one year alone. By 2008, the new boom had finally made the dusty little oil and cattle town on the prairie, according to the headline in its glossiest upscale magazine, a "Major League City."

Oklahoma Citians could mark the time, to the day, when their city actually gained entry into the Urban Pantheon. "When I look over our history I think there are two birthdays," Oklahoma City's mayor, David Holt, likes to say. "One is the day we were created on April 22, 1889, and the second date is when we moved into the first tier of American cities. That's the day the Thunder took the court." That is the day, Holt went on, "our descendants will mark all our history as either before or afterwards. It is never going to be the same again. . . . People have this pride in our city now and they take it for granted that we are now part of American pop culture. To feel relevant living here and people knowing where OKC is. That if one of the most famous people on the planet, Kevin Durant, can live here, then obviously it's an important place in America and the world."

That a six-foot-nine-inch-tall teenager named Kevin Durant was "one of the most famous people on the planet" in the spring of 2008 is a disputable assertion. But Durant was unquestionably full of promise, and he could draw a crowd—a *paying* crowd. The skinny, smooth-shooting small forward had won college basketball's most coveted national player of the year awards and the NBA Rookie of the Year award in back-to-back seasons. His twenty-points-a-game average as an NBA rookie had been one of the few bright spots in the Seattle Supersonics' dismal 2007–2008 campaign, and as any basketball aficionado could see, he just kept getting better. Durant scored forty-two points and grabbed thirteen rebounds in the Supersonics' final game of that season, a rare victory for a team that won less than a quarter of its games that year. Three days later, on the thirteenth anniversary of the Murrah building bombing, residents of Oklahoma City woke to the news that the NBA owners had voted 28–2 in favor of moving Durant and all the other Seattle Supersonics players to Oklahoma City. There was a hurdle or two to overcome, like a pending legal dispute between the new owners and the City of Seattle, but it seemed like a done deal. A local news reporter captured the man-on-the-street reaction that summed up the tenor of public sentiment in OKC: "I'm freaking excited about it!"

It felt like a miracle. "The odds of Oklahoma City getting an NBA team in the beginning were incredible," said David Holt, recalling the story of how Oklahoma City's then mayor first tried to sell the NBA commissioner on the idea of a franchise in the middle of Oklahoma. It was 2005, and the mayor could point to the growing population, the booming economy (OKC-based companies owned the natural gas industry!), the glass and steel and brick and mortar revitalization of downtown, and most of all the brand-new nineteen-thousand-seat arena just waiting for the coming of a professional sports team. *Any* professional sports team. The NBA commissioner, David Stern, was open to the mayor's sales pitch, and polite. He did not rub the mayor's face in the less inviting facts on the ground. Oklahoma City was the nation's forty-fifth-biggest television market, for instance, on a par with Greenville, South Carolina, and Grand Rapids, Michigan, and Harrisburg, Pennsylvania. The city's recent history was not so very uplifting. "We had allowed ourselves to be branded by our tragedies," the mayor admitted. "If you said 'Oklahoma City,' chances are the next word out of your mouth was 'bombing.'" And the longer history offered little to brag about. The entire state of Oklahoma, let alone Oklahoma City, had never fielded a team in one of the four major U.S. sports leagues—the NFL, the NBA, Major League Baseball, or the NHL. Stern suggested OKC might want to start with training wheels, so to speak, in the smallest and least competitive league. He told the mayor as he ushered him out of his New York office, "I see an NHL team in your future."

OKC finally caught a break when tragedy struck another city—when relentless and damaging floodwaters following Hurricane Katrina disgorged the NBA's New Orleans Hornets from their home arena. Stern agreed to let Oklahoma City host the Hornets' home games until the New Orleans Arena was put back to rights. In Oklahoma City, turns out, the Hornets drew better than eighteen thousand fans per game for two full seasons, thirty-five hundred more than the team had drawn in New Orleans. The Hornets moved back to the Big Easy two years later, just the same, and that might have been Oklahoma City's final brief brush with the NBA, if it wasn't for Aubrey McClendon and a few of his friends. Buoyed by the success of the Hornets, eight Oklahoma City business titans went out in the summer of 2006 and bought themselves the Seattle Supersonics. Aubrey and his partners—each of whom had profited more or less enormously from the shale gas boom—forked over $350 million to seal the deal. "The same amount of money that was put into [the downtown improvement project] by the people of OKC," David Holt once noted, "was put into a team by four guys and their friends."

The lead dog in the owners' group, Clay Bennett, did what NBA brass expected of him. He made what seemed like sincere pronouncements about keeping the Supersonics at home in Seattle if the voters there would just approve tax-backed, public funding for a new arena. (The Sonics played in the NBA's smallest venue.) But while Seattle caviled and the other owners took care to say what they were supposed to say, Aubrey McClendon, in his enthusiasm, spoke a little too much truth in Oklahoma. "We didn't buy the team to keep it in Seattle; we hoped to come here," he told a reporter from Oklahoma. "We know it's a little more difficult financially here in Oklahoma City, but we think it's great for the community and if we could break even we'd be thrilled." Seattle cried foul. Bennett had to scramble. *Thanks, Aubrey.* He insisted to the NBA that he and his friends really were committed to making a good-faith effort to keep the team in Seattle, despite anything you might have read otherwise in Oklahoma City's *Journal Record*. The NBA fined Aubrey $250,000 for his extreme candor. He apologized for speaking out of turn, without the blessing of his fellow owners, but he never walked it back. When forced to explain himself, under oath, in a later legal battle with the City of Seattle, Aubrey went into full-on aw-shucks Tom Sawyer mode: "It's like me saying the sky is green. You know, sometimes you say things that you don't know why you say it."

But that was just for show, or maybe to shave some money off the final judgment. Aubrey knew exactly why he had said it. He was speaking to Oklahoma Citians and to them alone, plugging the local cause, and it worked exceedingly well. While Seattle voters blocked any effort to cough up public money to keep the Supersonics, Oklahoma City voters easily approved a one-cent local sales tax to raise more than $120 million to fund upgrades on the six-year-old downtown sports arena and to build a brand-new practice facility worthy of NBA talent like Kevin Durant. By the summer of 2008, once the lawsuit had wrapped and Seattle was paid off, the miracle had come to pass. Oklahoma City got its first major-league franchise.

Aubrey and the other owners were already auditioning team nicknames: the Barons, the Bison, the Energy, the Wind, the Marshalls (yes, "Marshalls" with two *l*'s. Who knows). Around Labor Day 2008, with the first preseason game just weeks away, the team finally unveiled its choice: the Thunder. Season tickets sold out in just five days, and the team hit its NBA-mandated target of annual merchandise sales in a single month. Downtown Oklahoma City was awash in Thunder red, Thunder blue, and Thunder orange. OKC was ready to Thunder Up!

Locals were nearing the state of civic nirvana. "The NBA adventure we've been on is the biggest thing to happen in modern Oklahoma City history," its mayor said that summer. "The NBA validates all the efforts that have gone in to create this Golden Age we've entered into. We knew we'd arrived, but until the NBA came in, the rest of the country might not have known it."

The state's governor was just as excited. "We'll be on *SportsCenter*," he exclaimed, "every night!"

Journalists from across the country were already making their way through the Will Rogers World Airport that summer. Sportswriters, business writers, cultural writers, even travel writers. Oklahoma City had become a destination. "Booming with Oil and a New Exuberance," read one headline in *The New York Times*, whose writer really couldn't be blamed for missing the distinction between oil and natural gas. He was mighty busy with the fifty-five-foot-tall blown-glass Chihuly at the new art museum, the etymology of the word "denim" (it's French!), and the custom-made goods at Shorty's Caboy Hattery—"the only hat that will stay on your head in Oklahoma wind." Reporters from back east were still likely as not to lead their stories with the *Grapes of Wrath* Okie trope, but at least OKC had the wherewithal to fight back, now that it had been imbued with that certain Aubrey-ness. That young local architect who had worried about the indelibility of Oklahoma's dust bowl image walked a reporter from *The Oklahoman* through proposed designs for the city's new Oz-like convention center. The plans included a sloping roofline for directing rainwater into a sunken courtyard spanned by glass bridges. "It would be lush, with an ivy screen that stretches from the bottom of the courtyard to the top of the roof," she explained. "We would be encouraging images that are opposite of the stereotypical Dust Bowl Oklahoma."

But a funny thing happened on the way to the first big NBA tip-off in Oklahoma City. The price of natural gas on the commodities market started to fall again—and fast. Chesapeake stock fell with it, losing nearly half its value in just two months. And its debt load was starting to look less like a case of bold financial buccaneering and more like a threat to the company's survival. The same week he and his NBA partners christened their team the Thunder, Aubrey was selling hard at the Lehman Brothers CEO Energy Conference. This little mini-slump, Aubrey assured the money crowd there, just meant investors could buy into Chesapeake at a discount now. Whatever the temporary vagaries of commodity pricing, shale gas was the future, and no company in the country was better positioned to win that future than Chesapeake. Aubrey pointed to the half a million acres Chesapeake had secured in the newly discovered Haynesville Shale formation in Louisiana and Texas. That field would one day be the largest gas-producing field in the country and the fourth largest in the entire world, Aubrey insisted, and Chesapeake had already captured that flag. Haynesville contained 800 *trillion* cubic feet of natural gas, Aubrey assured the investors at the Lehman Brothers conference, and they were going to be able to recover about a third of it, which meant Chesapeake's proven reserves were going to swell by more than twenty times.

Call what happened next bad timing—of the epic proportion kind. And you couldn't blame Aubrey, though you could kind of blame the firm that hosted that energy conference. A week after the conference,

Lehman Brothers shares plunged 45 percent in a single day. Two days later, when investors began to understand for certain that the seemingly unshakable 158-year-old private bank was sitting on a very porous foundation built of too many worthless subprime mortgages, Lehman shares plunged by another 40 percent. Turns out Lehman had a debt and leverage habit that might have embarrassed even Aubrey. Four days after that, with nobody to make a rescue, the firm declared bankruptcy. The news dragged the Dow Jones Industrial Average down nearly 5 percent, which loosed the worst financial panic in nearly a century. Lehman was clearly not going to be a one-off.

Oklahoma City, having finally been declared a Major League American City, was getting a lesson in taking the good with the bad. Local media ran with an Associated Press wire story reporting gloating statements made by hard-line anti-American potentates and clerics in the Middle East. "[Americans] are oppressors, and systems based on oppression and unrighteous positions will not endure," the Iranian president, Mahmoud Ahmadinejad, spouted.

"God has responded to the supplications of an oppressed people," a popular Lebanese sheikh declared. "It is the curse that hits every arrogant power."

Chesapeake stock fell with the rest, by 60 percent in less than three weeks, settling at a whopping 75 percent off its highs just a few months earlier. Aubrey got somewhat mauled in the churn, but most of the damage was self-inflicted. Many of the thirty-three million shares of Chesapeake he had pocketed over the years had been bought in the recent run-up, most of them with borrowed money. At the beginning of October, just days before the first-ever Thunder tip-off, he found himself unable to meet his gargantuan margin calls and was forced to sell about 95 percent of his Chesapeake stock to cover. He had lost two-thirds of his wealth in a matter of weeks, and that stark fact was reported in business sections of newspapers across the country.

But did Aubrey cower or hide his face? He did not. When the Thunder took the court in Oklahoma City for the first time ever, on October 14, 2008, Aubrey McClendon—19 percent owner of his hometown's NBA franchise—was front and center, in Thunder colors, cheering with the rest of his city. He'd taken hits before, and he would come back better than ever. So what if he had lost 95 percent of his stake in his own company? "My confidence in Chesapeake remains undiminished," he said, "and I look forward to rebuilding my ownership position in the company in the months and years ahead."

Thunder Up!

Less than a month after his embarrassing stock sell-off, he closed a much-needed, long-term deal with Norway's StatoilHydro. The joint venture agreement delivered Chesapeake more than 21 billion Norwegian kroner, or $3 billion, of operating cash—and the wherewithal to drill another fifteen thousand or so horizontal wells over the next two decades. Aubrey picked up extra assistance from an old Duke fraternity brother who helped him market a sleek new financial vehicle called volumetric production payments. The VPP buyer got a piece of a well's future production, while Chesapeake got the cash to pay for drilling it in the first place.

Didn't matter to Aubrey that natural gas storage tanks were already filled to bursting in the summer of 2009. Or that the price of natural gas was through the floor, which meant it didn't actually pay to drill wells just then. He had ramped down Chesapeake's drilling activity a bit, but he was still thinking full steam ahead, playing the long game, even willing to shift his politics to protect the future of natural gas, the future of Oklahoma City, and, most dear to his heart, the future of Chesapeake Energy.

Aubrey had been a big donor to the grotesque and preposterous right-wing Swift Boat campaign that kneecapped Democrat John Kerry in the 2004 election and helped reelect those two former practitioners in oil and gas, George W. Bush and Dick Cheney. (Cheney had been heading up Halliburton, one of the world's largest oil service companies, when he selected himself to be Bush's running mate.) But in 2009, after Democrats had taken back power in Washington, Aubrey wanted it known that he had voted for Barack Obama. Because the country needed an inspirational leader! And Aubrey could help the new president realize his campaign promise of protecting the environment. Natural gas was the better alternative to "filthy" coal, remember, the perfect bridge to a bright, clean, wind-and-solar renewable energy world. "I really don't want to be labeled a Democrat or a Republican," Aubrey told a reporter. "I'm just an American with an idea."

He showed up at every NBA game for the next year, and he showed up for work at his Chesapeake office. When the fallout from the financial disaster, which would soon be known as the Great Recession, dragged the price of natural gas below $3 in the summer of 2009, to a level that made it nearly impossible to drill for profit in the short term, Aubrey did not show fear. This was what he had signed up for when he got into oil and gas, right? This was the casino, and a man had to accept the fact that sometimes the wheel was going to turn against him. Aubrey had made his bet on shale gas. He was still up a billion or so on that bet, and he meant to emerge from the downturn an even bigger winner. He was still touting a two-hundred-year supply of clean, affordable energy. Natural gas would free the country from the ravages of "dirty coal" and from its costly addiction to foreign (read Middle Eastern) oil. It promised national prosperity and national security. "A better, brighter and more prosperous future awaits us," Aubrey chirped to potential investors in 2009, "if we pursue the full potential of natural gas."

Who didn't want to believe?

SIX

REX SHRUGGED

THE BLAST OF ARCTIC COLD MOVING INTO OKLAHOMA CITY FROM the north on December 14, 2009, could not dampen the spirits of Aubrey McClendon. The Thunder, in their second season in Oklahoma City, already looked like playoff contenders. They were certainly winning more often than they were losing. The financial markets appeared to have found some solid footing. The Dow Jones ticked up by 0.3 percent that day, capping a long, slow climb from its post-crash bottom, to reach a level not seen since the full-on financial dive fourteen months earlier. Best of all, Chesapeake Energy stock jumped nearly 6 percent that day, back to a respectable $24 and change. The spectacular single-day pop had little to do with Chesapeake or its charismatic CEO; it had everything to do with the standing of natural gas.

That day, Rex Tillerson, head of ExxonMobil, the biggest of the Big Dogs in the Energy Kennel, the CEO who had banked a $45 billion net profit for his shareholders the previous year, tops in reported corporate history—anytime, anywhere—gave his seal of approval to Aubrey and the rest of the shale players. After years of waving off shale gas as a domain for minor leaguers, Tillerson was tipping his cap and joining the game. "Natural gas is well-suited to meet that growing power generation demand, both from the standpoint of its lower environmental impact, but also its capital efficiency and its flexibility," Tillerson said that day, when announcing that ExxonMobil, in its biggest deal of the new century, had just agreed to shell out more than $30 billion to buy a company called XTO Energy.

XTO was a mirror image of Chesapeake Energy, only with a level of debt that made for a more prepossessing balance sheet. Like Aubrey, the company's co-founder Bob Simpson had been an early believer in natural gas and an early adopter of hydraulic fracturing and horizontal drilling. Simpson had grown his company profits from just under $200 million in 2002 to nearly $2 billion in 2008. Like Chesapeake, Simpson's company had serious landholdings and had completed wells in almost all of the major shale plays across the country, from New York to Pennsylvania to Oklahoma and in Simpson's home state of Texas. XTO was actually operating wells right next to the ExxonMobil headquarters in Irving, Texas. Simpson's company, it appeared, had what Rex Tillerson lacked, and therefore coveted: the tool kit, the skills, and the know-how to extract natural gas from the stingiest of rock formations.

Exxon itself had done some early research and development in horizontal drilling and hydraulic fracturing back in the 1990s but found the process time-consuming, expensive, and risky. And anyway, the company was really thinking more, well, globally. Exxon was very busy using its gargantuan financial resources to exploit exciting new areas that had opened up when the Cold War thawed, like the Arctic waters off the coast of Russia, or the rich continental shelf in the Gulf of Guinea. Tillerson's predecessor, Lee Raymond, had long ago shut down the company's efforts to unlock unconventional gas beneath American soil. To Raymond, natural gas was somehow, and not just literally but figuratively, beneath an oil giant like ExxonMobil. Hell, ExxonMobil couldn't even do anything with a good portion of the natural gas it captured as a matter of course at its oil wells around the world. This was *gas,* which couldn't be loaded up and shipped off in a tanker. What was Exxon going to do? Build a pipeline from Equatorial Guinea to Peoria? The stranded gas was often just flared off, literally burned away.

Raymond never second-guessed himself on his decision to bail on natural gas, even after advances in horizontal drilling and hydraulic fracturing began to spur big rises in production and consumption. In 2003, around the same time he was unwittingly terrorizing Vladimir

Putin about buying Yukos, Raymond asserted that natural gas production had likely peaked, and if America became too dependent on gas, it would suffer terrible consequences to come. Two years later, the U.S. Department of Energy begged to differ. The continental United States alone, according to the experts, had sufficient natural gas reserves to get the country pretty well into the twenty-second century. By 2009, the department was forecasting that U.S. shale gas would one day provide half the country's energy production.

So now that the shale gas boom had well and truly hit, ExxonMobil had some catching up to do, and it was a good thing Tillerson had a spare $30 billion sitting around to get it done. Rex knew he would have to pay a premium for XTO, 25 percent above the company's stock price, but what choice did he have? ExxonMobil had been late to the party and had to accept the consequences. Tillerson paid top dollar for expertise ExxonMobil simply lacked. The company paid Bob Simpson, personally, $84 million to walk out the door and not come back, but Tillerson insisted that all the other XTO management and technical talent stick around. XTO would continue to do what it did best, operating as its own separate unit inside Tillerson's domain, drilling for shale gas. And ExxonMobil would continue to do what it did best; it would take all that XTO expertise global. "The world's economy has a voracious appetite for energy," Tillerson told *Fortune*, "so thank God we can do this."

Rex Tillerson had been at Exxon since his graduation from the civil engineering program at the University of Texas in 1975 and was, by the end of the century, a fully realized creature of the corporation's business, intellectual, and ethical culture. He was a key player in Exxon's 1999 merger with Mobil, which reunited two of the entities carved out of Standard Oil in 1911. The petro-marriage of the century produced the largest oil company in the world not owned by a national government—and the most profitable. Tillerson believed deeply in Exxon's overriding mission, which was to maximize shareholder profits, and he believed deeply in Exxon's secondary mission, which was to bring the world's most vital commodity to market. He maintained a vigilant watch for any forces that could threaten either endeavor.

Tillerson had already managed projects all over the world, from the United States to Africa to the Middle East to Russia, and had taken the measure of various forms of governments and governors. Monarchies and dictatorships clearly presented certain political problems for the subjects of those countries, but from Exxon's perspective—or for any foreign company wanting to do large-scale work on someone else's sovereign soil—it was hard to argue with the fact that they could also offer much appreciated certainty and control, at least as long as the monarch or strongman stayed in power. If ExxonMobil needed something in, say, Equatorial Guinea, it knew exactly where to go to get it—which was to say from the good offices of the country's president for life, the autocrat Teodoro Obiang Nguema Mbasogo. The president for life might have his own quirks and his odd desires, but for a company like Exxon his office was at least one-stop shopping: there was no one else you needed to talk to. Real democracies, where competing ideas and ideologies and other would-be could-be leaders were in a constant tug-of-war that could never be finally won—a mercurial electorate actually swaying outcomes and policies and national preferences back and forth—that was a neat trick for people-powered governance. But it wasn't necessarily ideal for those concerned with maintaining the steady flow of oil and progress and profit. Big oil development projects can take decades and billions of dollars in up-front investment. If the control of government and the relevant laws and regulations and tax structures start shifting around inside that time frame, that isn't a first-choice environment for this kind of business. Rex just didn't find doing business in democratically governed countries all that appealing, and that included his own. "What I find interesting about the U.S. relative to other countries is in most every other country where we operate, people really like us," Tillerson said to the reporter Brian O'Keefe at *Fortune*. "They're really glad we're there. And governments really like us. And it's not just Exxon Mobil. They admire our industry because of what we can do. They almost are in awe of what we're able to do."

Sufficiently awed and hopefully impressionable governments—that was so nice in all these little countries on the other side of the globe, why couldn't ExxonMobil have that everywhere? His favorite book, Tillerson had told the readers of *Scouting* magazine, was Ayn Rand's

Atlas Shrugged, that bible of bright, contrarian high school sopho-
mores and adult free-market zealots, in which slug-brained bureaucrats and politicians are the obstacles blocking the exalted few
individuals of drive and genius who are the only real heroes who can
be counted on to power world progress, if they could only be allowed
to operate unfettered by the small, the meek, the uninformed, the uncertain. Tillerson, à la Rand, chafed at anyone who thought they had
some good reason why Exxon should slow down or alter its course.
Anyone operating outside his industry, in his reckoning, was operating
without sufficient knowledge to offer constructive criticisms or solutions. His biggest challenge in leading ExxonMobil, he confided in his
Scouting magazine interview, was to "communicate to the public and
policymakers the complexities of the energy business in ways that help
them better understand some of the issues involved and why things are
how they are." He once told his fellow oilmen at a Houston conference,
"You can be afraid of a lot of things that you don't understand."

When Rex Tillerson ascended to the top of ExxonMobil in 2006, at
age fifty-three, after more than thirty years at the company, he was
crawling atop a juggernaut. ExxonMobil had booked all-time world-
record earnings in each of the three years prior to Tillerson's installation as chairman and chief executive officer. Its gross revenues the year
he took over were approximately equivalent to the gross domestic
product of Sweden, Switzerland, Indonesia, or Saudi Arabia. And CEO
Tillerson had scant cause to worry about malign interference from the
political classes, even on his tricky home shores. Like all U.S. oil producers, ExxonMobil (and its investors) continued to enjoy the sorts of
subsidies and incentives that had been in the tax codes for almost a
century. This kept its annual tax bills low—at times, almost unbeliev-
ably low—no matter how high its profits.

Both houses of the U.S. Congress, and all the relevant committee
chairmanships, were in the hands of industry-friendly Republicans
when Tillerson took over in 2006. The White House was manned by
George W. Bush, who had started his career, in the footsteps of his father, as a landman in the Texas oil business. George W. had entered the
oil fields at an inopportune time, so his early career was much more
bust than boom before he left the oil bidness for baseball and politics.
As president, the younger Bush did give his fellow oilmen a little fright

in 2005, when ExxonMobil and other companies were booking gargantuan profits, largely because the price of oil—along with the price of gasoline at the pump—was on the rise. "With $55 [a barrel] oil, we don't need incentives for oil and gas companies to explore," the president told a group of newspaper publishers that spring. Bush's policy team that year stunned the oil and gas industry by broaching the possibility of a reduction or repeal of the hallowed oil depletion allowance and of new tax breaks that would instead encourage the development of woo-woo hippie renewable energy sources like wind and solar. This sent a serious shiver down the spines of oil industry execs, until President Bush thought better of it. Or was talked out of it. He not only backed off a proposed repeal of the oil depletion allowance; he ultimately signed on to Congress's decision to expand it.

But that mostly cuddly, only occasionally and briefly scary, political environment for the oil business began to change, as luck would have it, soon after Rex Tillerson took hold of the corporate reins. The Democrats won back both the House and the Senate in 2006, and then ahead of the 2008 presidential race a charismatic young first-term senator began using the oil industry in general (and ExxonMobil in particular) to great political advantage in his unlikely journey toward the White House. One of the few pieces of legislation Barack Obama introduced in his brief, four-year stay in the Senate was the inelegantly named Oil Subsidy Elimination for New Strategies on Energy Act. Senator Obama's Oil Sense Act took big bites out of the oil depletion allowance and introduced some environment-friendly regulatory hurdles to offshore drilling in Alaska and the Gulf of Mexico, and to "unconventional" natural gas and petroleum operations (a.k.a. horizontal drilling and hydraulic fracturing). The legislation did not gain a single cosponsor, and it died without getting so much as a hearing in the Senate Finance Committee. But it put Obama on record against what many Americans were beginning to see as the industry's well-lubricated free ride.

Candidate Obama got more traction on that issue out on the campaign trail than he did in the Senate, largely because ExxonMobil presented a very easy target. Gas prices jumped to a record high in the long hot summer of 2008, to more than $4 a gallon, while Obama was battling for the presidency with the Republican nominee, John McCain. Would-be vacationers were doing the math and were not happy with the results. Hundreds of extra dollars would have to be set aside just to make the drive to Disney World, or the Grand Canyon, or Yellowstone. Obama had done his own calculations and saw he could tie Rex Tillerson's record profits at ExxonMobil, like an albatross, around John McCain's neck. "At a time when we're fighting two wars, when millions of Americans can't afford medical bills or their tuition bills, when we're paying more than $4 a gallon for gas, the man who rails against government spending wants to spend $1.2 billion on a tax break for ExxonMobil," Obama began saying at rallies across the country. "That isn't just irresponsible. It's outrageous."

These theatrics were annoying to Tillerson but not tremendously concerning—that is, not until Obama's surprisingly decisive victory helped sweep into office the largest Democratic majority in the House in sixteen years and the largest Democratic majority in the Senate in thirty-two years. Democrats had gained fifty-six seats in the House and fourteen seats in the Senate in just two election cycles. ExxonMobil, it was noted by the new majority, had spent heavily in the failed effort to keep friendly Republicans in power. Doggone democracy had thrown Exxon a nasty curveball.

But Tillerson and his ExxonMobil team hadn't failed entirely to anticipate the trouble ahead. They knew how to hedge. Back in 2006, when the Democrats were starting to achieve liftoff, the head of ExxonMobil's in-house Washington lobbying office had acknowledged, "We need a conversation with Democrats." That conversation ended up costing, and plenty. ExxonMobil quadrupled its lobbying budget from $7.3 million in 2005 to around $28 million in both 2008 and 2009. At the tail end of 2009, heading into Obama's second year in office, it was still too early to say just what ExxonMobil was getting for its millions. The company was chiefly playing defense when it came to public policy. There were plenty of threats afoot in the halls of Congress: a rollback of the (by now politically toxic) tax breaks for the oil and gas industry; a windfall profits tax to clip the energy companies whenever oil and gas prices went way high; limits to offshore drilling; tougher standards for carbon emissions; and a cap-and-trade program designed to reduce the amount of greenhouse gases released into the environment and to force major carbon producers to pay a heavy price for the right to continue doing damage.

On climate change and global warming, Tillerson had taken a much more diplomatic line than his predecessor, who had led a campaign of flat-out denial. The Tillerson regime at ExxonMobil was willing to admit that global warming was a dangerous phenomenon *and* that it might be caused in some unknowable portion by man-made activities, like, for instance, burning fuel that spewed carbon dioxide into the air and the oceans. "Let's continue to support the scientific investigation of what is one of the most complicated areas of science that people are studying today, and that is climate," Tillerson pronounced shortly after he took over. But what sounded like moderation turned out to be an effort to run out the clock while ExxonMobil hoped for a new and less alarmist Congress. The climate models, he kept saying, are "inconclusive." This was "a risk-management problem," Tillerson would say. And he liked to remind folks that risk management was ExxonMobil's stock-in-trade. There was nobody better—so long as the company's bottom line was the final judgment.

Turns out Tillerson's 2009 purchase of the shale gas player XTO Energy presented an entirely new front on which ExxonMobil would have to push back against the Democratic majority in Congress. A certain amount of toxic evidence was beginning to bubble up to the surface, suggesting potential environmental hazards inherent in the very technologies—hydraulic fracturing and horizontal drilling—that had combined to make recovery of tight gas and tight oil commercially viable. The Bush-era EPA had concluded a multiyear study back in 2004 and pronounced fracking safe and sound, good to go, then left it to the states to write the regulations as they saw fit. But now it was the Obama administration and a new guard on Capitol Hill. This Congress authorized and funded a fresh new EPA study on the risks to groundwater and drinking water. There was also legislation in both the House and the Senate to end a Bush-era Clean Water Act exemption and require fracking operations to disclose the ingredients—including all chemi-

cals and carcinogens—of the slickwater they were shooting at subterranean rock by the hundreds of millions of gallons.

And now that the mammoth ExxonMobil was finally lumbering
into the field of shale gas, the U.S. Congress was eager to hear from Rex
Tillerson on this very subject. There was an interesting little piece of
the ExxonMobil-XTO agreement that had got into the news. "The proposed deal with XTO," wire services reported, "is contingent on Congress not passing laws that would make hydraulic fracturing 'illegal or
commercially impracticable,' according to contract language filed by
Exxon with the Securities and Exchange Commission."

The chairman of the House Subcommittee on Energy and Environment summoned Tillerson and XTO Energy's chairman, Bob Simpson, to share their thoughts on the merger and on the future of shale
gas. "Remember the old commercial—'When E. F. Hutton talks, people listen?'" Chairman Edward Markey said in opening the hearing,
on January 20, 2010. "Well it is no secret that I disagree with ExxonMobil on many aspects of energy policy. But when America's biggest company makes a big move in the energy sector, policy makers
need to listen and understand what it means. . . . This merger heralds a
fundamental long-term shift in U.S. energy markets and one that deserves our close attention."

There were twenty-one Democrats on Chairman Markey's subcommittee, only a few of whom had ever enjoyed the benefit of financial support from ExxonMobil's prodigious PAC, and only ten surefire
industry-friendly Republicans. But if Rex Tillerson anticipated a rough
morning-to-midday session, he didn't show it as he sat, unperturbed,
listening to Chairman Markey's opening statement. He didn't confer
with aides or riffle through his prep notes, but kept his attention focused on Markey. He had the sort of steely self-possession that could
not be bought, even with a compensation package worth $27 million a
year, which Tillerson currently claimed. His face was unlined, still a bit
tan even in winter, and jowly in the subtle and pleasant way that suggests the absence of menace; every Dry Look strand of Tillerson's thick
graying hair, swept elegantly back off his forehead, remained in its
place. He sat silent, next to Bob Simpson, listening to eighteen separate
long-winded opening statements from committee members. Tillerson

didn't fidget. He didn't occupy himself by taking faux notes. He didn't look away from his about-to-be inquisitors. And when it was his turn to speak, his voice remained mellifluous and measured, like he was talking to schoolchildren, trying to, you know, explain "the complexities of the energy business in ways that help them better understand some of the issues involved and why things are how they are." If the Boy Scouts started a course in unflappability, Eagle Scout Rex Tillerson would have to find more room on his sash for a new merit badge.

Turns out, that January hearing was mostly a cheerleading session for him and his new merger. The chief concern of the subcommittee at large was energy independence—getting America to stop importing oil and gas from unsavory foreign countries—and even the Democrats seemed perfectly willing to overlook a lot, given how much this fracking and horizontal drilling was doing to move the country toward that long-sought and elusive goal. "We love having [XTO] in Pennsylvania," offered a Democratic congressman from Pittsburgh. "We want to get that gas out of the ground. We are all for doing that." Everybody was pretty much in agreement that a federal mandate requiring operators to disclose the recipe of fracking fluids was fine, so long as no secret recipe was shared with competitors. But past that, very little time was spent drilling down on the potential hazards of hydraulic fracturing.

When questions of safety did occasionally arise, Tillerson asserted that oil and gas producers had employed hydraulic fracturing in more than a million wells in the previous decades, "and there is not one reported case of a freshwater aquifer ever having been contaminated." Nobody challenged him. A congressman from North Carolina quoted Obama's new secretary of energy, a Nobel Prize–winning physicist, who said he believed fracking for tight gas held extraordinary promise. There were potential dangers, and a hundred different ways to screw it up, but as Secretary Steven Chu had said, "if it can be extracted in an environmentally safe way, then why would you want to ban it?" Rex agreed! "You have hundreds to thousands of feet of rock strata between the freshwater and the hydrocarbon-bearing shale, then you have multiple layers of steel casing as well," he explained to the subcommittee. "So it is a risk that we know how to manage." Nobody challenged him.

Tillerson's compatriot, XTO's chairman, Bob Simpson, told the committee he had faith "in the wisdom of Congress collectively, the greater wisdom, that [fracking] will continue because it is safe and the consequence of not being able to do it for our economy is too grave." And then Tillerson reminded the committee that if stringent regulations on fracking were adopted, the added costs could make drilling prohibitively expensive and kill off the great national march toward energy independence, just as it was finally within reach. "Without hydraulic fracturing the gas that is locked in the shale rock stays locked. It just stays there," he said. "If you remove hydraulic fracturing as one of the key enabling technologies, this resource can no longer be recovered." And this, Tillerson added, would cost jobs, right now, in the middle of a recession, when the country could least afford it. "All of the job growth we have talked about would pretty well come to a halt," he said, "because you wouldn't drill the wells anymore if you couldn't fracture them." Nobody challenged him on that either.

The colloquy devolved into an opportunity for Democrats to put themselves firmly on the record—for energy independence. One Colorado Democrat wanted it known that she had offered a bill to disclose the recipe of fracking fluids injected into the ground, but even that was accompanied by the congresswoman's firm declaration: "I have absolutely no intention of outlawing fracking. In fact, I think fracking is important to get a lot of these reserves out of the ground." The general consensus was that the industry had always been at its most productive when it was allowed to police itself; the company's bottom line would suffer if anything went wrong, and what could be a more effective deterrent than that! "Clearly it is a risk that we have to manage," Tillerson said of fracking, "and the expectation is that we manage it well."

The most colorful defense of the industry's commitment to safety was offered by Representative Steve Scalise, a newbie from Louisiana's First Congressional District, which stretches from inland Folsom out into the Gulf of Mexico. Scalise wasn't even an official member of this particular subcommittee, but he got himself into the room just the same, and in front of the cameras. Left-wing pols and environmentalists were simply behind the curve as always, Scalise implied. Unaware of the spectacular advances being made in drilling technology and safety. "It gets lost in the shuffle a lot," he said in a lead-up to a question for Tillerson. "People talk as if the technologies of twenty years ago were still being employed. You know, I like to tell my colleagues that the best place to go fishing in the Gulf of Mexico is next to an oil rig because, number one, with the environmental safeguards that are in place, it is one of the best habitats for fish. They love congregating and thriving in that area. And the fishing captains know that because that is where they take people to go fishing. And you will catch some really good fish and some of the best eating you are going to find right there next to the oil rig."

Food for thought, anyway.

SEVEN

A RISK MANAGEMENT PROBLEM

THE SKY WAS A SLATE GRAY AND THE CLOUDS HUNG LOW ON THE morning of April 19, 2010, as one of ExxonMobil's nine corporate jets, Rex Tillerson aboard, made its gentle descent into Houston. The runway was still wet with overnight rain when the Gulfstream touched down and the CEO of the single most profitable corporation in the world settled into a car to be whisked to the Hilton Americas-Houston, where he was to be feted by nearly a thousand banqueters. The annual Jones Award from the World Affairs Council of Greater Houston honored "an individual who—in the spirit of Jesse H. and Mary Gibbs Jones—has contributed to the international life of our city." This was a hometown award all the way through, almost always given to a Houston business titan, never mind the caveats or asterisks. Its 2000 honoree, the criminally indicted and glut-shamed Kenneth Lay, of Enron, has never been struck from the council's list of past recipients.

The temperature was still down in the sixties, unusually cool for April in east Texas, as Tillerson rode into downtown. By the time the Cornish game hens were plated, though, the sun had begun to peek through in the sky. The world was brightening. This happy uptick in weather matched the general disposition of Rex Tillerson and his ExxonMobil team that spring. There were plenty of dark clouds still out there—the eighteen-month recession was still a rolling threat of foreclosure, job loss, and drained retirement accounts for a sizable portion of the American population—but the sun was beginning to pop through. West Texas Intermediate crude was a long way from its $145-a-barrel high before the financial meltdown, but it had climbed from all the way down near $30 in the last week of 2008 to $81.52 on that cool April Monday. ExxonMobil was about to report a net profit of more than $6 billion in the first quarter of 2010, up 38 percent over the previous year.

The U.S. Securities and Exchange Commission and its international equivalent, the Netherlands Competition Authority, had also both given the green light to Tillerson's proposed merger with XTO, which would soon make ExxonMobil not just one of the great oil companies on earth but America's largest producer of natural gas. And XTO's technology could travel anywhere. The company had plans to exploit shale deposits in central Europe and Canada and the Middle East.

Tillerson was, in fact, using ExxonMobil's extraordinary cash reserves to fine effect all over the world. He was kick-starting multibillion-dollar projects in Ghana and Papua New Guinea (within reach of the giant Asia markets), expanding his already enormous drilling operations in Nigeria and Equatorial Guinea, putting on line a fourth liquefied natural gas plant in Qatar (the nation of Qatar being the current *world* leader in LNG production/exports, but watch out!). Team Tillerson had also just outbid Russia's Lukoil and the China National Petroleum Corporation to win a foothold in an Iraqi oil field believed to hold nearly ten billion barrels.

Sure, a corporation the size of ExxonMobil, with hundreds of far-flung subsidiaries, was going to have a few headaches and publicity hiccups, as well as a few nicks and cuts to its shareholders: a guilty plea and $600,000 in fines and fees for violating the Migratory Bird Treaty Act by whacking a total of eighty-five feathered beings (members all of protected species); a $32.2 million payout to settle allegations it had cheated the federal government and Indian tribes out of royalty payments; $17.5 million to avoid defending against a claim that it had, as the Justice Department alleged in a press release three days before Tillerson's trip to Houston, "illegally discharged hundreds of tons of volatile organic compounds into the air each year from the bulk gasoline terminals on Cabras Island in Guam and in the Lower Base area of Saipan." But that was just the cost of doing business in an industry locked in a violent daily battle with Mother Nature. To Exxon, those were minor setbacks, easily dwarfed by all the great news the company was fixing to report to its shareholders. After nearly two decades of frustrating and profitless effort, Rex Tillerson believed he was about to land his White Whale. He was nearing unprecedented new agreements in Russia, the country that held tens of billions of barrels of proven oil reserves, along with more gas reserves than any in the world, and a country that badly needed the expertise and technology (XTO!) that ExxonMobil could provide.

So Tillerson, sporting a surprisingly unconservative royal blue shantung suit, and a soft yellow silk tie, was feeling mighty okay when he stepped to the podium in the Lanier Grand Ballroom at the Hilton Americas-Houston. The title of his speech was "The Future of Energy," but this being a civic award, Tillerson, who was known at corporate headquarters as the Eagle Scout, took some time to expound on the idea of citizenship. "We have a long record of going beyond our primary responsibility of delivering the energy that benefits our consumers, shareholders and business partners," said Tillerson. "As a company and as individuals, the men and women of ExxonMobil are dedicated to being good corporate citizens wherever we operate. We believe this ideal is so integral to our long-term success that we have built it into our business model and our corporate governance. In other words, we believe our commitment to citizenship is fundamental to our year-to-year success as a company."

Rex's team had all its oars in the water, he wanted it known that day, and ExxonMobil was pulling hard to get the country out of the hideous recession. "Leaders in government and in business agree that we face an urgent need to revitalize our economy and spur job creation," he told the upscale Hilton crowd, whose needs were rather less urgent than those of the great unwashed. "To achieve these goals, we must unleash the extraordinary power of private citizens to seize new opportunities in free markets. . . . If the private sector knows that government will stay the course and resist the temptation to over-regulate, it can invest with confidence." He cautioned a few times that day about the perils of overregulation: "Often the policy changes that are most damaging to entrepreneurs and innovation flow from a fundamental mistrust in the private sector."

Despite the unmistakable *don't tread on me* theme of his remarks, Tillerson "was willing to throw the Democratic president a bone," wrote *The Houston Chronicle*. "When it comes to energy policy, which Tillerson said is still lacking, '[President Obama] is about as good as anybody else has been.'" A reporter from *Offshore Engineer* quoted him saying, "The president is trying to understand [energy], and he is trying to make some steps which, in his view, are very well intended." Aww, nice president, he's trying.

Tillerson's signature composure and button-down élan—the Tao of Rex—were sorely tested in the weeks that followed that happy Houston gala. Less than forty-eight hours after the luncheon, Tillerson woke to the news that a drilling rig in the Gulf of Mexico, forty miles offshore—not far from Representative Steve Scalise's excellent rig-side fishing waters—had suffered what a Coast Guard spokesman termed a "catastrophic" explosion. The pictures that day were ugly and compelling. They showed emergency boats surrounding the Deepwater Horizon and waging what looked like an unwinnable battle against the fire raging from the deck of the rig. Black smoke billowed up hundreds of yards above the water and took flight on the wind.

The casualty news was grim. Seventeen of the 126 workers had been medevacked off the rig with injuries, a few in critical condition. Eleven workers were still missing and assumed (correctly, it would transpire) to have been killed in the explosion. "We are deeply saddened by this event," was the first statement from a spokesman for the company that owned the drilling rig. "Our thoughts and prayers are with the crew members of the Deepwater Horizon and their families." It was the sort of boilerplate statement Tillerson would recognize from his own corporation's releases. When workers died in explosions or flash fires or security breaches at ExxonMobil drilling rigs or refineries or pipeline facilities—from Beaumont, Texas, to Southampton, England, to Singapore to Papua New Guinea—the corporation, according to its spokesperson, was always and inevitably "deeply saddened." That phrase, along with others such as "this was clearly an accident and we are working to respond to the immediate needs" and "we comply with all applicable laws and regulations," was right there in the preferred pre-drafted press release language available for quick deployment by the ExxonMobil public relations team.

At least Deepwater Horizon was operated not by ExxonMobil but by one of its chief rivals, British Petroleum, or BP. The other silver lining for Tillerson—as well as for the industry at large—was that the damage appeared, in the first few days anyway, to be contained. There was a theoretical possibility that the rig itself would eventually sink to the bottom of the seabed, 5,000 feet below, dumping into the Gulf of Mexico its own 700,000 gallons of diesel fuel. But that didn't seem to be the way this was going. And, also, the integrity of the 18,360 feet of cement-encased well pipes, which extended more than 13,000 feet beneath the seabed, did not appear to have been breached. "We are only seeing minor sheening on the water," the Coast Guard commander on scene said that first day. "We do not see a major spill emanating from this incident." A BP vice president seconded that assessment: "If there is any pollution, we believe it is minor pollution because most of the oil and gas is burning." The director of an industry-friendly petroleum institute at the University of Texas sought to allay any (likely irrational) public fear. "They've built safety into the operations," he said, "because they know that if you have a fire on an isolated rig that's out in the Gulf, you have a real issue."

But as the Deepwater Horizon continued to burn and then listed dangerously out over the Gulf of Mexico, BP and the rig's owner, Transocean, and the drilling services company Halliburton started to seem flummoxed. The whole truth of the matter would only rise to the surface slowly, over the next few weeks and months and even years. Although Transocean asserted that the company had simply been carrying out the routine final steps of putting the well on line, with "no indication of any problem" right up to the moment of the explosion, the truth was that warning signs had been blaring for days before the explosion, and BP, Transocean, and Halliburton had all been cavalier and sloppy. The piping from the Deepwater Horizon ran down 5,067 feet to the seafloor, and then 13,300 feet through hard rock to the pay zone. There are enormous pressures at that depth, which must be carefully monitored and controlled in order to avoid a "kick," which is the unwanted and uncontrolled flow of oil and gas into the well. A serious kick, if not contained, can shoot flammable oil and gas back up toward the rig. Worst case, such a blowout leads to an explosion. Drillers take pains to build in multiple fail-safes to guard against this sort of disaster. The last and most important is the blowout preventer, which in the case of Deepwater Horizon sat on the seafloor, between the 13,300 feet of subterranean piping and the 5,000 feet of riser leading up through seawater to the rig. The blowout preventer, which is operated by electrical and hydraulic power, is designed with a couple of nifty safety features. It can seal up the pipes with rams or rubber devices, like a stopper, or, as a last resort, it is equipped with a pair of sharp metal blades that cut the drill pipe and shut the well.

But, according to the federal investigators, most everything that could have gone wrong on the Deepwater Horizon did go wrong. Halliburton had used crappy cement to seal the well bore. The crew was a bit blasé about monitoring and controlling the pressure in the days leading up to the blowout. And once oil and gas kicked all the way up to the rig itself, the blowout preventer's stoppers and pipe cutters failed. Differentials in pressures caused the piping (also crappy) to buckle, and the flammable oil and gas just kept racing up into the rig until it exploded. The first explosion on the rig shut off all electrical and hydraulic power to the blowout preventer. Fortunately, those last-resort blades have two separate backup battery systems that will trigger the cutting of the pipes. Unfortunately, both were mis-wired. Fortunately, one was so ham-handedly mis-wired that it actually made a cut. Unfortunately, the crappy piping was already so buckled that it was only partially cut.

The U.S. government's final assessment of the cause of the blowout was damning to all involved. BP, Transocean, and Halliburton had cut corners to save both time and money, increasing the chance of catastrophe. "It is an inherently risky business given the enormous pressures and geologic uncertainties present in the formations where oil and gas are found," the National Commission on the BP Deepwater Horizon Oil Spill said in its final report. "Notwithstanding those inherent risks, the accident of April 20 was avoidable. It resulted from clear mistakes made in the first instance by BP, Halliburton, and Transocean, and by government officials who, relying too much on industry's assertions of the safety of their operations, failed to create and apply a program of regulatory oversight that would have properly minimized the risks of deepwater drilling." In other words, it takes a village to make a disaster this big. This wasn't one screwup by one bad employee or even one bad company; this was a whole industry screwup, and—maybe worse than that—a government that screwed up by deferring to that industry.

Here's the crux of the matter. Oil and gas companies do the kind of risky, capital-intensive work that the average Joe, the average mom-and-pop business, even the average country, doesn't do for itself. In so doing, they can make a spectacular pile of money, but they can also make a tremendous amount of mess. And ruin. And even catastrophic, polluting apocalypse, when they really put their shoulder into it. But they are also big enough and hold enough sway that even big powerful governments tend to defer to them when it comes to how to best police their behavior. What could you, in Congress, possibly know about oil that Rex Tillerson doesn't? How could you, with your lily-livered environmental worry beads, think to weigh in on what might go wrong when pumping oil up through five thousand feet of one of the richest fisheries on earth? The oil industry is fairly capable when it comes to extracting resources; it's very capable when it comes to lobbying against any and all bothersome rules that might constrain it; but it's not that capable of anything else. It's ridiculously *in*capable of cleaning up after itself, for example.

Had the damage done by the initial Deepwater Horizon explosion been capped at eleven dead, seventeen wounded, and an unwanted but "minor sheening on the water," that damning report—and a few cursory updates to offshore drilling regulations—would likely have been the last anybody ever heard of the event. But it didn't work out that way. By the time the Deepwater Horizon rig did disappear below the surface of the Gulf, about thirty-six hours after the first explosion, aerial photography revealed an oil slick five miles long. Two days later, the Coast Guard commander admitted that the last line of defense, the blowout preventer, had failed and was probably useless, that as much as a thousand barrels of oil per day were leaking from the well, and that nobody was entirely sure how to make it stop. BP began preparations to drill a relief well to connect to the blown-out well, plug it, and stop that thousand-barrel-a-day spew, but admitted it would take months to complete. A few days later, a National Oceanic and Atmospheric Administration scientist raised the estimate of the spill from a thousand barrels a day to five thousand. Residents of the Gulf Coast states braced for impact as the oil slick on the surface continued to spread toward marshes and wetlands. The Coast Guard, for the first time in history, trotted out the designation of a "Spill of National Significance" to describe the seriousness of the unfolding catastrophe.

The intensity of the concern was not matched by the intensity of the cleanup effort. BP simply didn't have the tools to do much. No oil company did; that's not what they do. BP did have a bang-up 580-page response plan prepared by an outside consultant that asserted its ability to tackle a spill of maximum magnitude, like 250,000 barrels per day. The BP plan claimed the company had access to equipment and means to capture 491,721 barrels per day and storage equipment for 299,066 barrels (such specificity!). Problem was, in the actual event, it couldn't even handle the estimated 5,000. It tried everything in its ridiculously meager arsenal. The company paid for controlled burns on the ever-widening oil slick, then began pouring dispersants onto the surface water. By the middle of May, BP had applied more than 300,000 gallons of dispersant, compared with the 5,500 gallons Exxon had applied following its horrifying national-record spill in Alaska in 1989.

Cleanup workers in the Gulf began complaining of nausea and other side effects from prolonged exposure to the dispersants, but they were reassured the fluids were not toxic, even while BP refused to divulge the chemical recipe. The dispersants "are actually less toxic than detergent soap which you would flush down your sink every day," Rex Tillerson would later explain. Which was not necessarily true, but was much more helpful to the industry cause than statements from BP's CEO, Tony Hayward, who was just beginning a short career as his company's one-man public relations wrecking crew. "The Gulf of Mexico is a very big ocean," Hayward explained in his Etonian British accent. "The amount of volume of oil and dispersant we are putting into it is tiny in relation to the total water volume."

Bad enough that these dispersants might possibly be adding to the environmental damage as opposed to subtracting from it. Worse than that, the dispersants didn't work. In fact, nothing seemed to work. And nobody had any real answers to either of the vital questions: How do we stop the oil leak? How do we clean up what has leaked?

The five Minerals Management Service employees stationed at the command center in Houston were not equipped to provide any real guidance or assistance to the BP engineers trying to find answers to these two central questions. It was, said one MMS factotum in a burst of honesty, like "standing in a hurricane." Oil executives from other companies, like Rex Tillerson, kept their distance from the entire affair, even when the Obama administration first started making noise about a moratorium on offshore drilling. The governor of Texas, praise be, came out swinging in defense of oil and gas. "I hope we don't see a knee-jerk reaction across this country that says we're going to shut down drilling in the Gulf of Mexico, because the cost to this country will be staggering," Rick Perry said as the oil slick spread and made its first landfall. "From time to time there are going to be things that occur that are acts of God that cannot be prevented." God didn't fail to properly cement that drill pipe, it should be noted, but alas, God would be blamed.

Five days after Rick Perry blamed God, an attempt to corral the leaking oil by placing a massive ninety-eight-ton containment dome on the well failed. Advice came in from around the globe after that; one Russian newspaper suggested detonating a nuclear bomb deep in the well. (This method was said to have worked in a couple of unfortunate but rarely talked-about offshore spills in the Soviet era.) BP and the Coast Guard Command passed on that particular plowshare, but they did execute a "junk shot," which involved rifling golf balls and rubber tires into the wellhead.

Didn't work.

Next they tried an operation called "top kill," which sounded to the *Tonight Show* host, Jay Leno, like a "bad Steven Seagal movie." BP's Hayward, however, confidently said there was a 60 to 70 percent chance this new method would stop the flow once and for all. Engineers pumped 100,000 barrels of mud per day into the five-thousand-foot riser for three days and spiced the action with an occasional junk shot of more golf balls and rubber tires and, who knows, maybe even a Crock-Pot and a Chuck Taylor Converse tennis shoe or two.

Didn't work.

The number of booms and skimmers available was not enough to stop the spread of the oil, and soon the little tar balls that first reached land were followed by big toxic oil slicks. Pictures of seabirds covered beak to talon in brown sludge, unable to take flight and suffocating to death, became a staple of the daily newsfeed. The only things that actually seemed to do much good were the absorbent pads, which the cleanup workers called "paper towels." That's certainly what they looked like, and that's essentially what they were: flat sheets of material made from the same kind of stuff that's inside disposable diapers, either shoved into a long thin link-sausage casing of a boom or just used by hand, to sop up the oil. A 580-page plan had been developed and adopted by all the major oil companies over the twenty years since the *Exxon Valdez* spill, and still the best cleanup tool they had at their disposal was diaper filling. Honestly. The most profitable corporations in the history of corporations. And the only thing their two-decade brainstorm produced was fancier paper towels.

At the end of May, after more than five weeks of unmitigated ongoing disaster, the Obama administration instituted a six-month deepwater drilling moratorium, which shut down thirty-three current drilling operations in the Gulf of Mexico. By June 2, 2010, the administration had closed more than a third of the federal fishing zone in the Gulf because of the spill.

By then, it was clear the math just wasn't adding up. BP had rigged up a two-prong system capable of capturing or burning off something near twenty-five thousand barrels per day; if five thousand barrels a day were leaking, the size of the disaster should have been not only contained by then but drastically shrinking every day. And yet it was only getting worse. Somehow, the twenty-five-thousand-barrel-a-day effort was not enough to keep up with the daily flow from the leaking well.

By the time Rex Tillerson and four other Big Oil bosses were summoned to appear before Chairman Ed Markey's subcommittee in early June, estimates of daily leakage had been revised up from five thousand barrels per day to as much as forty thousand per day. This back-of-the-envelope estimate was still far short of the true flow—which would be something nearer sixty-five thousand barrels per day at its worst, for a total of nearly five million barrels dumped into the sea.

"The most difficult challenge confronting the whole industry at this point," Tillerson told reporters who buttonholed him after a shareholder meeting not long after he was summoned to Washington, "is regaining the confidence and trust of the public, the American people, and regaining the confidence and trust of the government regulators and the people who oversee our activities out there." How paper towels fit into that plan, he did not say.

Composure and patience were at a premium in the House subcommittee hearing on June 15, 2010. Rex Tillerson had to sit through an hour and twenty minutes of long opening statements by angry and disappointed and frustrated and nervous and embittered congresspeople. Tillerson was appearing with the heads of BP's North American operations, Shell's North American operations, and CEOs from Chevron and ConocoPhillips. The worst of the criticism was directed at the BP prez, who was instructed at various points to apologize, or resign, or consider committing hara-kiri. But Tillerson took plenty of heat. In fact, he got Chairman Markey's first question out of the box: "Mr. Tillerson, like BP, on page 11-6 of your plan, ExxonMobil's Gulf of Mexico oil spill response plan lists *walruses* under sensitive biological and human resources. As I am sure you know, there aren't any walruses in the Gulf of Mexico; and there have not been for 3 million years. How can ExxonMobil have walruses in their response plan for the Gulf of Mexico?"

"Congressman Markey," Tillerson began obfuscating while at times somewhat nervously twirling a paper clip, "those response plans incorporate a number of broad-based studies, marine mammal studies, many of which are part of the EIS and EIA statements that are put together by the MMS; and much of the response plan and what is contained in it is prescribed by regulation, including the models that are used to project different scenarios for oil spills; and many of the statements and representations that are in the plans—"

"These are *regional* oil spill response plans," Markey said, cutting him off. "How can walruses be in a response plan for the Gulf of Mexico? This is a regional response plan that the company has put together."

Tillerson conceded the point: it *was* embarrassing that walruses were included. To Exxon. Not the walruses. But he tried to defend the inclusion of one Dr. Lutz, an expert in marine mammal biology, who was cited in the report as a reliable expert and a resource for technical support in case of an offshore spill. Lutz had died four years before the ExxonMobil response plan was filed.

"The fact that Dr. Lutz died in 2005 does not mean his work and the importance of his work died with him," Rex argued, twiddling that paper clip.

"I appreciate that," Markey said. "It just seems to me that when you include Dr. Lutz's phone number in your plan for a response that you have not taken this responsibility seriously."

Tillerson, to his credit, took the shot and kept his calm. He used most of his time to testify to ExxonMobil's long history of safe practices and excellent environmental stewardship and to point out how this BP event, awful as it was, was a one-off. "This incident represents a dramatic departure from the industry norm in deepwater drilling," he said. "We are eager to learn what occurred at this well that did not occur at the other 14,000 deepwater wells that have been successfully drilled around the world." He allowed that deepwater drilling was a risky proposition and a delicate science, but he made sure that everybody tuning in to the hearing that day understood that this was a BP problem, specifically; ExxonMobil would never have allowed this to happen in the first place. "We would not have drilled the well the way they did," Tillerson said. The testifying execs from Chevron, Shell, and ConocoPhillips agreed, but none piled on BP like Rex. "We would have run a liner, a tie-back liner," Tillerson explained. "We would have used a different cement formulation. We would have tested for cement integrity before we circulated the kill-weight mud out. We would have had the locking seal ring at the casing hanger before proceeding. And leading up to all of that, though, there was clearly—and this is just based on what has publicly been made available—there were clearly a lot of indications or problems with this well going on for some period of time leading up to the final loss of control. And why those—why— how those were dealt with and why they weren't dealt with differently I don't know."

Even when one of the Democrats on the subcommittee lambasted him for other walrus and dead-scientist embarrassments in ExxonMobil's disaster response plan, like devoting forty pages to media strategy and only nine pages on contingencies for oil removal, Rex Tillerson kept up his merit-badge level of calm. "We are not well equipped to handle [major spills]," Tillerson explained. "And we've never represented anything different than that. That's why the emphasis is always on preventing these things from occurring, because when they happen, we're not very well equipped to deal with them. And that's just a fact of the enormity of what we're dealing with."

We're not very well equipped to deal with major spills. But no one else is either. How can your industry be the only entity on earth capable of causing a giant tanker spill or a blown-out deep-sea oil rig or a pipeline leak or a bomb-train oil railcar explosion, and not also be the entity responsible for coming up with ways to respond to that kind of problem? If not you, who?

After more than four hours of back-and-forth with this Democrat-run committee, after taking a few direct shots particularly from Chairman Markey, Tillerson must still have felt as if he'd dodged one particular bullet: nobody said a thing about Africa. Just ten days after the Deepwater Horizon explosion, an aging ExxonMobil pipeline in the Gulf of Guinea, near a series of coastal villages in Nigeria, had ruptured. The breach was not discovered right away and not halted for a full week, according to *The Guardian.* The newspaper's man on the scene had just reported that almost a million gallons of oil (or twenty-five thousand barrels) leaked into the delta in those seven days. ExxonMobil insisted the spillage was only a small fraction of that figure, but this did little to placate the people who depended on those waters for their livelihood. "We can't see where to fish," one local man told a reporter. "Oil is in the sea." And this was not an uncommon experience in Nigeria. A 2006 study found that an average of 11 million gallons of oil per year, or 546 million gallons over the preceding fifty years, had leaked into the Niger delta. That's one *Exxon Valdez*–sized disaster every year, and the government there didn't even require the oil producers to have paper towels on hand. But this being in far-off Nigeria, the news had not yet washed up on U.S. shores. At least not to the extent that anyone in Congress was ready to bug Exxon about it.

Since Rex Tillerson never had to answer to any of that, he had a clean pass to talk about how ExxonMobil continued to be "dedicated to being good corporate citizens wherever we operate." The top of his pre-drafted opening statement sort of said everything about his performance that day. "As someone who has spent his entire career in the energy industry, it truly is deeply saddening to see the loss of life, the damage to environmentally sensitive areas, the effect on the economic livelihoods, and the loss of the public trust in the energy industry that has resulted." Truly. Deeply. Saddening.

EIGHT

POSTER BOY

MORE THAN ANYTHING ELSE, TEODORIN NGUEMA OBIANG Mangue wanted a simple white cotton glove bejeweled with clear Swarovski Lochrose crystal beads. Actually, you could say, he *needed* it—along with other apt and related accessories. Sometimes, when a guy is really truly down in the dumps, a garden-variety shopping spree is insufficient to improve the mood. Sometimes, those happy frissons that attend the purchase of hundreds of thousands of dollars' worth of sartorial splendors from Versace, and Dolce & Gabbana, and Gucci, or a sleek Nor-Tech speedboat (top speed 100 miles per hour), or a $2 million Bugatti Veyron (top speed 250 miles per hour) cannot cut through the torpor of melancholy. In June 2010, Teodorin, who was turning forty-one that month, was suffering that kind of a pall.

A dogged journalist named Ken Silverstein and a slew of federal investigators were already beginning to reveal the extent of Teodorin's psychic doldrums. The army of staff on hand to serve the heir apparent to the presidency of Equatorial Guinea (Teodorin's father had held that office for more than thirty years by 2010) would describe to them a man whose daily habits and schedule suggested a very definite lack of mission, or purpose. The boss rarely emerged from the bedroom suite of his $30 million mansion in Malibu before late afternoon and often required a bowl of shark fin soup from Hop Li Seafood Restaurant to take the edge off his hangover. Teodorin spent the waning hours of daylight playing video games, watching movies, or noodling around on Facebook. He was more likely that summer to stay home and allow a regular staff driver to escort one of his girlfriends to the shops on Rodeo Drive in Beverly Hills. Teodorin set limits for each of them, but he liked to be seen by his paramours as a generous man. So even when he wasn't there with his valise a-bulge with bank-fresh shrink-wrapped $100 bills, his driver was often in possession of a Nike shoebox full of cash—and able to make good on up to $80,000 worth of purchases in a single outing.

There had been a time a few years back when Teodorin would spend real business hours at his hip-hop label, TNO Entertainment, trying to launch the next big act. But after every artist in the meager TNO Entertainment lineup flopped, Teodorin had lost interest. He had also once enjoyed spending the afternoon and early evening riding roller coasters at a nearby amusement park, but these days Six Flags Magic Mountain was ready to close its gates by the time Teodorin got himself out the front door of his Malibu mansion.

He even seemed to staff a little less enthusiastic about entertaining at home. The annual "Nguema Summer Bash" had been a notable Malibu party a few years earlier, with beautiful people from the entertainment world sashaying around the edges of his fifteen-thousand-square-foot mansion to find the best spot for ogling the skyline of downtown Los Angeles and no expense spared on the comestibles or the rented eye candy prowling in cages. "The food was great, the drinks were better than great, the house, the view, the DJ, the *white tiger* were all SO COOL!" one of the attorneys who was helping Teodorin move millions of dollars of suspicious money through the U.S. banking system wrote to him after the 2007 bash. But the summer of 2010 seemed different, and the staff wasn't sure if the Summer Bash would happen at all.

Teodorin would usually leave his house only after it was already dark, his security "chase team" on his tail, in whatever luxury ride he might choose. He had his pick of a fleet—Ferraris, Bentleys, Rolls-Royces, Lamborghinis, and Maybachs. "I'm wearing the blue shoes," he would say to one of his drivers, "so get me the blue Rolls." After a bit of pre-gaming in a rented suite at Raffles L'Ermitage, Teodorin would head out to the clubs, where he would spend thousands on champagne for would-be actresses and models draped with titles like "Playmate of the Month, October 2009." At the end of the night, if he was in a particularly surly mood, Teodorin might grab the wheel of the car from his professional driver and leave the chase team to earn their keep by chasing their drunken charge west on the Pacific Coast Highway and then up winding roads toward his estate, running red lights, speeding around hairpin turns. "Like a maniac" as his minders would describe it.

None of it seemed to make him much happier that summer.

It had been, to be sure, a pretty rough year for Teodorin—which kicked off on his birthday near the end of June 2009 with the sad, premature death of the King of Pop, Michael Jackson, whom Teodorin had just been trying to get to know through Jackson's sister Janet and his brother Jermaine. Word among the L.A. celebrity-watching crowd was that Teodorin had offered the family his Rolls-Royce Phantom for Michael's funeral but was distraught at losing the chance at a real friendship with the world music icon—the Gloved One. Teodorin's monthlong trip to Maui a few months later was something of a disappointment, too. He flew across the Pacific in his private Gulfstream V, which was trailed by a separate charter jet carrying his security team, drivers, household staff, and two chefs. Then he took up residence in a $7,000-a-night villa and installed his factotums, along with what Silverstein called a "revolving cast of escorts," at a mansion perched on the beach. Four of his favorite cars—Bugatti, Ferrari, Lamborghini, and Rolls-Royce—along with three motorcycles, were shipped over and garaged nearby to be at his disposal 24/7. Alas, his Nor-Tech 5000 speedboat had been banged up in a fall off a trailer en route to Maui and did not arrive until the final week of the stay.

The much-anticipated first ride on the repaired speedboat was further delayed while staff arranged for the proper fuel—at $600 a barrel—to be shipped over from Oahu. And the first fifteen-minute speedboat ride off Maui turned out, sadly, to also be the only one of the trip. The damage the boat had suffered in transit was apparently not properly fixed and Teodorin's half-million-dollar nautical toy capsized and sank just a few hours after that first brief jaunt. He spent a part of the few final days of the trip watching as a helicopter and a number of trucks retrieved the soggy Nor-Tech from the Pacific Ocean.

Things just got worse after he returned from that bust of a trip,

thanks largely to the intrepid journalist Silverstein, who had been rooting around the Obiang family for nearly a decade. In November 2009,
Silverstein published a long investigative piece on the *Harper's* website
revealing the existence of a multiyear federal investigation into Teodorin's finances. The burning question of the U.S. government inquiry
was this: How could a man whose position as Equatorial Guinea's minister of agriculture and forestry paid him about $60,000 a year move
$75 million through U.S. banks in order to buy a sixteen-acre Malibu
estate with a swimming pool, tennis courts, and a four-hole golf course,
a $38.5 million private jet, and an armada of cars insured at a value of
$10 million? "It is suspected that a large portion of [Teodorin] Nguema
Obiang's assets have originated from extortion, theft of public funds,
or other corrupt conduct," read a Justice Department memorandum
Silverstein had got hold of.

The taproots of those plunderable public funds were the wells Western majors had planted off the coast of Equatorial Guinea. This was oil
money. Spigoted into the Obiang accounts by Marathon, Hess, and Rex
Tillerson's ExxonMobil, among others.

Silverstein augmented this reportage on Teodorin by contributing
to a thirty-two-page four-color pamphlet published that same month
by Global Witness, titled "The Secret Life of a Shopaholic." Silverstein
added some *People* magazine-ish detail to Teodorin's spending sprees,
like the time he rented a three-hundred-foot private yacht for $680,000
"in an effort to woo the rapper Eve." The pamphlet went on to explain
the simultaneous decline in the fortunes of the overwhelming majority
of Teodorin's fellow Equatoguineans in the years since American oil
companies had discovered more than a billion barrels of oil reserves
just off their coast. "Between 1993 and 2007," the Global Witness report read, "annual government oil revenues shot up from $2.1 million
to $3.9 billion." No typo. That's $2.1 million to $3.9 *billion*. The gross
domestic product of the country had increased by about 8,400 percent
in those years. "Equatorial Guinea now enjoys per capita income of
about $37,200, one of the highest in the world," the Global Witness
report continued. "Yet 77 percent of the population lives in poverty, 35
percent die before the age of 40, and 57 percent lack access to safe water.
Between 1990 and 2007 the infant mortality rate actually rose from 10

percent to 12 percent." If a country's GDP is going up by multiple-thousand percent, wouldn't you expect its infant mortality rate to *drop*?

In February 2010, the U.S. Senate's Permanent Subcommittee on Investigations released its own 323-page bipartisan report titled "Keeping Foreign Corruption Out of the United States: Four Case Histories." The case study on Equatorial Guinea ran nearly a hundred pages, focusing entirely on Teodorin. This was the third headline-grabbing Senate investigation featuring Equatorial Guinea in five years, following on 2004's "Money Laundering and Foreign Corruption: Enforcement and Effectiveness of the Patriot Act," and 2008's "The Petroleum and Poverty Paradox: Assessing U.S. and International Community Efforts to Fight the Resource Curse." By the beginning of 2010, Teodorin—"an unstable, reckless idiot," according to one U.S. intelligence official—had become the poster boy for a phenomenon known as Dutch Disease, the Paradox of Plenty, or, most widely among academic circles, the Resource Curse.

By any name, the phenomenon is simple and demonstrable. The discovery of oil, you'd think, would be a *Beverly Hillbillies*-style windfall for any country. *Next thing you know, Old Jed's a millionaire*—swimming pools, movie stars, the whole thing. But what actually happens is that many if not most countries that discover oil end up poorer and in worse shape specifically because they've found themselves in possession of that remarkably remunerative tradable commodity. Here's how it reads in academia: "Proponents of oil-led development believe that countries lucky enough to have 'black gold' can base their development on this resource. . . . To the contrary . . . countries dependent on oil as their major resource for development are characterized by exceptionally poor governance and high corruption . . . often devastating economic, health and environmental consequences at the local level, and high incidences of conflict and war. In sum, countries that depend on oil for their livelihood eventually become among the most economically troubled, the most authoritarian, and the most conflict-ridden in the world."

The basic problem is that oil doesn't happily coexist with other industries upon which you might build a reasonably stable national economy. That's true in the third world, the first world, and even in the world in between, e.g. Russia. It creates such large, up-front, sweat-free gains for connected elites that no one wants to do anything else but chase the oil jackpot. And as oil crowds out other industries, the profits don't ever seem to end up redounding to the nation at large. Extracting oil takes a lot of up-front capital investment, but that expensive initial, physical investment doesn't create anything utile for any other purpose. The technology and infrastructure of pumping oil and gas out of the ground don't transfer usefully to any other follow-on industry. Worse, oil infrastructure is often environmentally destructive, which thereby screws up other economically productive things that could be done with that same land.

Oil extraction is much more capital-intensive than it is labor-intensive—which means it doesn't produce a lot of lasting jobs. But in the end, it does produce big revenues when it's sold on the global market. That sets the stage for grand-scale corruption of the political class: people who can maneuver themselves into getting a cut of that sale price of oil will find themselves quickly rich, whether or not they actually expend any effort to pump the stuff out of the ground. Political elites that can get themselves in the catbird seat when it comes to oil revenues will have every reason to curry favor with the oil companies doing the drilling, and every reason to fight anyone else who might take political power and thereby edge in on the financial teat they've stuck themselves to. Even with less rapacious political elites, there's still the baseline problem that oil is a tradable commodity subject to wild international winds; with big swings in the price of oil, any effort at long-term, sane budgeting and investment for the population's basic needs is impossible in a country newly dependent on oil revenues for its cash.

It's not an inescapable curse; countries with oil do okay if they've got strong small-d democratic institutions that won't buckle under pressure and are capable of responding to citizens' needs and desires. But in countries that lack strong, legitimate democratic governance, the discovery of oil generally leads to more trouble and more inequality. Back in 2002, around the time that Equatorial Guinea was being identified as a key potential supplier of U.S. oil imports, Dr. Terry Karl, the American professor at the vanguard of these studies, explained to a group of government officials and oil executives, "Without intervention of some sort," they should expect "a reduction of the welfare of people in oil exporting countries. It will provoke violence and unrest. It will lead to the violation of rights. It will lead to the destruction of the environment. It will buffer authoritarian rule."

Karl would sometimes tell people the story of how she began the study that led to her first book, *The Paradox of Plenty:* "A long time ago when I was looking for a dissertation topic, I went down to Venezuela to interview the founder of OPEC, a man named Juan Pablo Pérez Alfonzo, and I asked him some questions about the founding of OPEC. . . .

"And he said to me, 'Teresita, you know, you're such a bright young person. Why are you studying OPEC? Why don't you see what oil is doing to us, the oil exporters?'

"And I said, 'What do you mean?'

"And he said, 'Oil is the excrement of the devil.'"

So began Dr. Karl's decades of study into why the citizens in big oil-producing countries such as Venezuela and Angola and Iraq live in hot messes, while some others, such as Norway and the United States, do well. Professor Karl remained neutral on the properties of the commodity itself. "Oil in itself means nothing," she would say. "It's just a black viscous liquid." But it was hard to forget the OPEC founder's words, or those of a former minister of oil for Saudi Arabia, a country that had, on paper, financially benefited from its vast oil reserves more than any other on the globe. "All in all," Sheikh Ahmed Zaki Yamani, whose position made him one of the most powerful men on earth, had told Professor Karl, "I wish we'd discovered water."

Equatorial Guinea was hardly the first country to fall under the spell of the Resource Curse, but the stark lifestyle contrast between Teodorin and the mass of Equatoguineans made for compelling new fieldwork. Teodorin's primary residence was the oceanside estate in Malibu, but he also spent a few months a year surrounded by his $22 million worth of artwork (including paintings by Degas, Gauguin, and Renoir) at his $100 million six-story mansion on L'Avenue Foch in Paris's 16th arrondissement. And a little time at his modest $7 million property in Cape Town, South Africa. Resource Curse scholars could comb through the recent Senate report for highlights of Teodorin's spending in the previous five years: $330,173.96 for a Lamborghini Roadster (one of his three dozen luxury cars), $102,053.29 for home security, $82,900 for furnishings, $58,500 for a Bang & Olufsen home theater (installation included), $3,221.31 for a portable car wash machine, and—are they dishwasher safe?—$1,734.17 for *two* wineglasses. Two. These expenditures hardly seemed beyond the family budget considering that Teodorin's father, President Teodoro Obiang Nguema Mbasogo, ranked eighth on *Forbes* magazine's list of the wealthiest world leaders. He was just ahead of Queen Elizabeth II. This was public record after all.

What wasn't a matter of public record at the time was that Teodorin had signed a contract for the construction of his most extraordinary and costly toy, what promised to be the world's second-largest yacht. The Russian oligarch Roman Abramovich's *Eclipse* would still dwarf Teodorin's floating palace, but the $380 million price tag would far outstrip the total annual spending of his father's government on education and welfare programs in Equatorial Guinea. And it showed. Peter Maass, the journalist who had profiled the head of Russia's Lukoil, went on assignment in Equatorial Guinea more than a decade into the country's oil bonanza and returned with a grim report: "Nearly half of all children under five are malnourished. Even major cities lack clean water and basic sanitation. . . . The main hospital is a place for dying, not healing. The wards are dingy rooms with soiled mattresses and no medical equipment except for a couple of IV drips."

Equatorial Guinea's president, Obiang the Elder, had paid no real electoral price for the accelerating degradation of living standards alongside the astronomical growth of state revenue. Teodorin's father had just won a fourth term, with a little more than 95 percent of the vote. But Professor Karl's prediction that this sort of oil boom would provoke violence and unrest was dead-on. President Obiang, whatever his political prowess, was prey to insecurities and always on the lookout for the next coup. The entirety of his armed forces—army, navy, and air force—was only about 1,500 men, poorly trained and untrustworthy in his eyes. The president's chosen personal guard was, instead, a cadre of 350 soldiers hired from Morocco, armed with the latest in

German assault rifles. But the increasing necessity of safeguarding all the new oil production facilities was well beyond the capacity of the Equatoguinean military and President Obiang's rented security guard.

That recognized fact had attracted an American mercenary firm led by a group of retired Pentagon officers. "The greatest corporate assemblage of military expertise in the world," the mercenary's publicity team claimed. In February 2010, Military Professional Resources Initiative—which had been acting as the Equatoguinean Coast Guard off and on for about a decade—was surreptitiously awarded a new $250 million contract to provide added assistance to the Obiang administration. The contract, as explained by one defense industry trade publication, was to "establish a network of surveillance sites and operation centers at different points along the country's coast to protect against piracy and other maritime concerns that exist in the region." The deal had to be approved by the U.S. government. And it was. Because, as President Obama's State Department explained, it was "consistent with our foreign policy goal of ensuring maritime security in the Gulf of Guinea."

Even with the increased sense of security that comes with American-trained firepower, President Obiang continued to live by that old saw: keep your enemies close. And by his own corollary to that old saw: and under guard. Many of his political opponents over the years had ended up in Black Beach prison, an interrogation and detention center just a few miles down the road from the presidential palace. The happenings at Black Beach included stringing up prisoners "like a marlin at the weight scale," waterboarding, electric shocks to the genitals, isolation, routine beatings, and starvation, according to an American economist working in the country early in Obiang's reign. The leaders of one failed coup were reportedly handcuffed around the clock, deprived of food, drink, sleep, and medical attention, and beaten relentlessly for ten days straight—until one tight-mouthed conspirator died of a heart attack.

In 2010, around the same time the United States granted the new license to the corporate mercenaries at MPRI, the State Department also itemized President Obiang's activities in its annual report on human rights: "increased reports of unlawful killings by security forces; government-sanctioned kidnappings; systematic torture of prisoners and detainees by security forces . . . arbitrary arrest, detention, and incommunicado detention . . . judicial corruption and lack of due process; restrictions on the right to privacy; restrictions on freedom of speech and of the press; restrictions on the rights of assembly, association and movement; . . . violence and discrimination against women; suspected trafficking in persons; discrimination against ethnic minorities; and restrictions on labor rights."

That said, the State Department assured reporter Ken Silverstein separately, the MPRI contract "includes an important human rights component and anti-trafficking provision and we believe this training is a strong tool for tangible improvement in human rights and transparency." Yes, let's definitely invest our hopes in improving human rights and transparency in Equatorial Guinea to a contract with an armed mercenary group. Why not? Sounds bulletproof.

Whether training in human rights and proper penal practices was high on President Obiang's list of priorities was hard to say, but he was certainly motivated to up his public relations game in the United States. In 2010, the government of Equatorial Guinea signed a million-dollar-a-year contract with Lanny Davis, an old Friend of Bill Clinton turned lobbyist (the Dems were back in power), to "promote Obiang's interests in the United States." At press events designed to reintroduce President Obiang and smooth his global image, Davis tried humor—"I've kidded him he'd do better to win with 51 percent than 98 percent"—and pathos—"[President Obiang] feels very vulnerable, without any friends." Aaaaah, sad. Obiang also hired Qorvis Communications, an up-and-coming public relations firm specializing in lipstick-on-a-pig operations for unsavory dictators and potentates around the world, like helping the Saudi royal family clean up all that bad press after 9/11.

Qorvis didn't have a lot to work with where Obiang's reputation was concerned. There was a little sound bite from a 2006 event in Washington where then secretary of state Condoleezza Rice called President Obiang "a good friend." There was the photo Obiang and his favorite, er, senior wife managed to get with President and Mrs. Obama in a receiving line at the Metropolitan Museum of Art in September 2009. There was also a recent State Department cable noting, inexplicably, President Obiang's "mellowing, benign leadership." The Qorvis flacks could maybe point out Teodoro Obiang's exemplary tennis game, his valiant ongoing battle with prostate issues, his $3 million donation to fund the UNESCO–Obiang Nguema Mbasogo International Prize for Research in the Life Sciences, and his new public promise to begin investing more of his country's oil revenue in the general welfare of his people.

When a pair of young aces from Qorvis sat down with Ken Silverstein in the summer of 2010 to make the case for President Obiang, they insisted the talk of human rights abuses was greatly exaggerated. The capital city of Malabo was as safe a place as you'd want to visit, they suggested, in a head-spinning non sequitur. "We could walk around at night and talk with people and no one interfered with us," Qorvis's Matthew J. Lauer told Silverstein over cocktails at a downtown Washington bar. "No one is saying there are no problems, but it's not North Korea." You play the hand you're dealt. If *It's Not North Korea* is one of your best cards, play it.

The Shopaholic Son of President Obiang was also tough to explain or excuse, but since Teodorin was reportedly paying Qorvis an added $55,000 a month to polish his own personal reputation in the wake of the recent bad press, they played his hand too. The Qorvis fellows reminded Silverstein that Teodorin's lifestyle was similar to that of dozens of other public officials and scions from oil-rich countries such as Nigeria and Saudi Arabia. As the pitch went, Teodorin was being "unfairly singled out." Qorvis reminded Silverstein that Teodorin was still a young man sowing his wild oats—kind of like George W. Bush before he got serious about life and governance. President-in-waiting Teodorin, Qorvis execs assured Silverstein in the summer of 2010, "is at the point where he's thinking about his legacy."

Actually, what Teodorin was mostly thinking about just then were his upcoming plans for serious, high-end retail therapy, which took some special doing in the summer of 2010. Having been tagged by U.S. financial regulators as a Politically Exposed Person from a notoriously corrupt country, Teodorin had to take extra precautions. He employed a special agent to do his bidding anonymously. "Please make sure that [Minister Obiang's] name does not appear anywhere," the intermediary explained to Julien's Auctions. "He should be invisible." Then Teodorin, wearing this cloak of invisibility, executed an enthusiastic shopping spree at three separate live celebrity-memorabilia auctions. Before 2010 was over, Teodorin had made winning bids on millions of dollars' worth of things his lost would-be friend, the King of Pop himself, had touched, worn, or maybe at least gazed upon. Among the items Teodorin bought for his personal amusement were sculptures and porcelain figurines from Michael Jackson's Neverland Ranch, a Jackson 5 gold record ($1,500), a bag signed by Jackson and Paul McCartney ($3,000), a football signed by Jackson and Troy Aikman ($4,000), Jackson's gold record for "Beat It" ($10,000), Jackson's personal MTV Moonman ($50,000), a pair of Jackson's crystal-studded socks ($80,000), four of Jackson's fedoras—one of them signed and two of them "stage worn" ($187,500)—a basketball signed by Jackson and Michael Jordan ($245,000), and the coup de grâce, the Rosebud of the lot: that Swarovski Lochrose crystal-covered glove worn by Mr. Jackson on his 1987 Bad tour ($275,000). He won them all!

When the first invoices from Julien's Auctions arrived in Malibu, Teodorin instructed they be returned to sender and revised to reflect the billing party and address as one Amadeo Oluy, Malabo, Equatorial Guinea, a.k.a. *definitely* not Teodorin. The payment of $1,398,062.50 to settle the bill from the first auction was promptly paid from a bank account in Equatorial Guinea. The total of Teodorin's 2010 Julien's Auctions bill, it is worth noting, would have covered the living expenses of about thirty-three hundred of his fellow countrymen for a year, given the fact that three-quarters of the population of Equatoguineans lived on $2 a day, just as they had five years earlier, and ten years earlier, and even twenty years earlier, when their vast and valuable oil and gas reserves were still tucked away, unknown and unrealized, well below the ocean floor.

NINE

PRACTICAL REALITIES

EQUATORIAL GUINEA'S MAIN LANDMASS IS A LITTLE SQUARE THE size of Vermont on the west coast of Africa, just north of the equator, that looks to have been carved out of the larger nation of Gabon. The national capital, Malabo, is actually on Bioko Island, which is about the size of Maui and sits 150 miles across the Gulf of Guinea from the country's biggest mainland coastal city.

Equatorial Guinea won its independence from Spain in 1968 and thereafter found itself at the tender mercies of the extended Obiang family. Francisco Macías Nguema, the country's first president, guarded his new position with a fierce and lethal jealousy. His security team is estimated to have killed or driven away more than a third of the country's citizenry during his eleven-year reign. President Macías, who billed himself as the "Leader of Steel," the "Implacable Apostle of Freedom," and "Divine Miracle" (and "woe be to anyone who snickered on hearing it," remarked one foreign diplomat), made examples of some of his political opponents by having them crucified in public view. Macías was also notorious for a mass murder of his political foes in a soccer stadium, in which the public address system blared the song "Those Were the Days" to drown out the dying screams of the victims. The CIA's *World Factbook* is typically terse on the subject: in the eleven years after independence, Equatorial Guinea's first autocratic ruler "virtually destroyed all of the country's political, economic, and social institutions."

Teodorin Obiang's father, Teodoro, served out most of those years at the pleasure of his uncle, President Macías. Among other things, Lieutenant Colonel Obiang had been in charge of the notorious Black Beach prison and its torture-happy "Black Beach Parties." One German publication described Lieutenant Colonel Obiang's cruelty thus: "Prodded with red-hot iron bars, prisoners were forced to dance around a fire for hours singing songs of praise" to President Macías, a.k.a. the Leader of Steel.

In 1979, Lieutenant Colonel Obiang ran a bloody coup against his uncle and took over the presidency for himself. President Obiang has operated since, according to international consensus anyway, as a less malevolent figure than Mr. Divine Miracle, but force and terror still have reigned. In 1994, when John Bennett, the American ambassador in Malabo, called out President Obiang on his ugly human rights record, the diplomat received a very distinct reply from Obiang's crew, tossed at the ambassador from a moving car: "You will go to America as a corpse." The Obiang regime started tailing Bennett around the capital and officially accused the ambassador of employing witchcraft against President Obiang. The Clinton administration hastily pulled up diplomatic stakes and closed the U.S. embassy in Malabo. On his way out of town, in his farewell address, Bennett named the Obiang regime's top torturers, one by one.

But neither Obiang nor the handful of international oil companies already operating in Equatorial Guinea were much concerned. One oil executive had already screamed at Bennett, as the ambassador remembered it, for "making it difficult for his company to do business." By the early 1990s, Western oil companies were ramping up production at the Zafiro oil field off the country's coast. With or without any "political, economic, and social institutions," tiny Equatorial Guinea was about to take a cannonball leap into the international commodities market.

Whatever the challenges were that President Obiang found so insurmountable when it came to providing potable water or education or roads or basic democracy to his citizens, he found all the authority and organization he needed to make it easy for oil producers to do business in his country. There was a very clear path to winning the right to drill off the coast of Equatorial Guinea, and it ran right through the Presidential Palace in Malabo. "In a place like Equatorial Guinea," that longtime industry watcher, Ken Silverstein, explained in an interview with *Mother Jones* magazine, "it's whoever figures out how to give the president and his inner circle the most money, gets the contract."

And that is how the black gold, the excrement of the devil, the natural resources—whatever you want to call it—the giant pots of oil under the seabed in Equatorial Guinea ended up producing giant pots of money for the Obiang family. Start with an already ruthless dictator divorced from international norms and unmoved by opprobrium for his human rights record. Now add oil company bribes and oil revenues to make that dictator suddenly wildly wealthy, with billions of dollars' worth of new incentives to not just hold on to power but hold on to every single lever of power in the country, to ensure the continued flow of oil revenue directly to and through him, with no political competitors horning in on the action. And bingo, the God-given resources of an entire nation become the private wealth of one family.

From the oil companies' perspective, that kind of arrangement is no muss, no fuss: if all decisions on oil development are made by the president, all the bribing is a one-stop shopping experience. There was no government body in Equatorial Guinea capable of checking Teodoro Obiang, or even questioning him. And he did not feel a compelling need to press Western oil companies for good deals on behalf of his citizenry; it's not as if he were looking to fund universal pre-K. Where the ministers in most oil-producing countries in Africa might demand anywhere from 50 to 90 percent of a foreign company's locally generated revenue, Obiang was happy to settle for a third, or a quarter, or even 15 percent. Equatorial Guinea has "by far the most generous tax and profit-sharing provisions in the region," according to a 1999 report from the International Monetary Fund.

Despite the "going home as a corpse" threat to the allegedly witchy last U.S. ambassador, President Obiang ended up being especially friendly to representatives of American business. And he had even more reason to be after the 9/11 attacks, when the United States— which produced a bit fewer than six million barrels of oil a day in 2001 and consumed a little more than nineteen million—was suddenly parched for imports from anywhere that was not the Middle East. This was the time, remember, when the Bush administration started wooing President Putin with promises to build Siberian pipelines and other infrastructure so the United States could buy more oil from Russia. Latin America might be good for more. And Africa, too, was a big, barely tapped newcomer on the horizon.

"It's occurred to all of us that our traditional sources of oil are not as secure as we once thought they were," Congressman Ed Royce (R-Calif.) explained to a symposium of oil executives, U.S. government officials, academics, and envoys from several African countries four months after 9/11, in January 2002. "Oil is where you find it. Oil companies cannot always invest in democratically governed countries. It would be ideal if it could be guaranteed that the head of an African country where a U.S. oil company invested was, in fact, an advocate of democracy and always respected human rights. Unfortunately, that is not a realistic expectation."

His colleague Congressman William Jefferson (D-La.) concurred, but he saw possibility: "While there may be strivings and failings in Africa over democracy, in the Middle East there's not even talk of it. Talk about democracy does not even part the lips of those who are in charge in those countries. So in Africa there's at least a chance for the kinds of things we talk about here: rule of law, for transparency. There's a chance for us to overcome some of the issues of bad governance through democratic influences." Jefferson's personal democratic influence would include soliciting hundreds of thousands of dollars' worth of bribes from companies seeking to do business in Africa; $90,000 cash was discovered wrapped in aluminum foil in the congressman's icebox. That most notorious case of freezer burn in national history would ultimately send Congressman Jefferson to federal prison for five years.

Just two weeks after that January 2002 African oil colloquy, a group of fifty men and women, including investors, oil company executives, and a handful of State Department officials, hosted President Obiang at a luncheon at the Army and Navy Club in Washington. This was a far cry from his visit to Washington a year earlier, when Obiang had found it difficult to get an audience with an assistant secretary of agriculture. At the club that day, according to contemporaneous reporting by Silverstein, one oil executive raised a toast to the future of Equatorial Guinea. "It will be the Kuwait of Africa," he said. "It's a fabulous country." Another presented Obiang with a wooden letter box and then thanked the officials from the State Department for "pressing" their bosses to reopen the U.S. embassy in Malabo. President Obiang knew what was expected of him that day. He told the gathering that he hoped for an even larger and more energetic presence of American oil companies in his country, and he rolled out the welcome mat for businessmen and investors from the oil-hungry United States. "We can promise American companies," he said, "that their investments are guaranteed."

The floodgates opened after the general bargain was struck. "The United States wouldn't openly criticize the regime," as the authors of a Pulitzer Center study would succinctly put it, "and the regime guaranteed the U.S. oil industry near-exclusive access to the country's national oil reserves." Every Saturday morning, a Houston Express flight arrived in Malabo (nonstop from Texas!), carrying a new cadre of oil workers. The gated and guarded residential areas, whose amenities included company-provided water, electricity, and cell phone service, swelled with Americans. The roughnecks drove their trucks over to local bars like La Bamba and Shangri-La where they could buy Budweiser or Michelob or Coors, just like back home. Equatorial Guinea's Independence Day parades suddenly featured lines of American flags and a host of banners and placards festooned with the names and trademarks of Halliburton, Chevron, Marathon, and ExxonMobil.

The country's annual oil production nearly quadrupled in just five years. ExxonMobil was the biggest player in the Equatoguinean offshore oil game by far; its take from Equatorial Guinea grew to represent nearly 10 percent of ExxonMobil's total production worldwide. In thanks, and in return, CEO Tillerson and ExxonMobil made sure President Obiang, his family, and his cabinet were well compensated. Very well.

What happened to the money after ExxonMobil wrote the checks was not of particular concern to anybody at the company. "We are private investors," said an Exxon spokesman in 2005, "and it is not our role to tell governments how to spend their money." What the execs at ExxonMobil did know, and did bear in mind at all times, was that Obiang owned the tollbooth all oil companies had to go through in Equatorial Guinea. But it was the only tollbooth, and his price was not particularly onerous, given the amount of money they were sucking up onto those offshore platforms. Why look that gift horse in the mouth? "Their concern is getting oil out of the ground with as little trouble as possible," Frank Ruddy, who had been an attorney for Exxon in the 1970s and ambassador to Equatorial Guinea in the 1980s, told Silverstein. "Their first priority is not going to be that there is a democratic government. That's not their business. And it shouldn't be."

But somebody was, thankfully, following that money. Most of it was flowing into Riggs Bank, headquartered right around the corner from the White House in Washington. President Obiang's other favored son, Gabriel, would sometimes explain that the State Department recommended the bank as a safe spot to keep the money. "We wanted to make sure," Gabriel told Peter Maass, "that American companies feel comfortable."

Well, Riggs certainly felt comfortable. At one point, the bank was holding as much as $700 million in various accounts controlled by Obiang, his handpicked government officials, and family members like Gabriel and Teodorin. The primary account, into which ExxonMobil, Marathon, Hess, and others deposited their royalty payments, was controlled by President Obiang himself. The source of other deposits was not always easy to trace. On two separate occasions, the Riggs Bank vice president managing the Equatoguinean accounts hied himself to the country's embassy a mile away, where he received suitcases full of $3 million in shrink-wrapped $100 bills, and then hauled the sixty-pound package back to the Riggs bank vault. "Where is this money coming from?" another Riggs vice president wrote to colleagues. "Oil—black gold—Texas tea!"

A U.S. Senate investigation, sparked largely by Silverstein's early reporting, uncovered some financial transactions that looked to be uncomfortably close to the boundaries of the Foreign Corrupt Practices Act, a 1977 law that makes it illegal for Americans doing business abroad to bribe officials of other countries. ExxonMobil was by no means the only oil company that faced these kinds of accusations at the time, but the firm did stand out among its peers for what appeared to be its remarkably generous application of emoluments. According to the Senate investigation and follow-up reporting, ExxonMobil cut President Obiang in on an oil-distribution joint venture that enriched him by about $640,000 on a $2,300 investment; the company paid Obiang's senior wife at least $365,000 in questionable rental fees; it paid Obiang's brother about $700,000 for security (an ExxonMobil spokesman explained to Senate investigators the company was pretty sure this was "market rate"); it paid Obiang's interior minister $236,160 on a labor contract and the minister of agriculture $45,000 for a rental house. ExxonMobil was unable (or maybe unwilling) to promptly deliver to the committee the complete list of payments made to Equatoguinean officials or Obiang family members. There were, after all, five hundred separate "contracts" to comb through. "The business arrangements we've entered into have been entirely commercial," Andrew Swiger, ExxonMobil executive vice president, explained to a roomful of senators at a public hearing. "They are a function of completing the work that we are there to do, which is to develop the country's petroleum resources and, through that and our work in the community, make Equatorial Guinea a better place."

Answereth Senator Carl Levin to that statement: "Make it what?"

"I know you're all in a competitive business," Levin said. "But I've got to tell you, I don't see any fundamental difference between dealing with Obiang and dealing with Saddam Hussein."

Riggs Bank took the big bullet, or more like the bunker buster. The venerable old financial institution that had dated from the President Andrew Jackson era and took a measure of credit for funding the Mexican-American War, the construction of the Capitol dome, and the purchase of Alaska is no more. After paying enormous fines in the aftermath of the Equatorial Guinea bribery, corruption, and money-laundering investigation, it was sold on the cheap. The once glorious forty-two-thousand-square-foot marble Riggs Bank building (constructed in 1902, when Teddy Roosevelt was president, with regal Ionic columns and a view of the White House) was bought just a few years ago by the family foundation of the junk-bond felon Michael Milken and will soon be part of a conference center and a museum dedicated to, you guessed it, finance and entrepreneurship.

The Senate's final 2004 report on the Riggs Bank money-laundering episode did oh-so-gently rebuke ExxonMobil and its brethren: "Oil companies operating in Equatorial Guinea may have contributed to corrupt practices in that country." But even with the scandal and the implosion of Riggs Bank, five years later, things were still pretty much business as usual in Equatorial Guinea. President Obiang continued to hold power and control the money. And, the shopaholic president-in-waiting had refused to trim his sails. "Lesser kleptocrats might have turned tail and fled," Ken Silverstein wrote, "but not Teodorin. He employed two lawyers to set up [new] shell companies and associated bank accounts that he controlled but on which his name never appeared."

And while Teodorin luxuriated in Michael Jackson's fedoras and socks and crystal-sequined glove and porcelain figurines, ExxonMobil kept on doing what it had to do to keep the oil pumping out of the Gulf of Guinea. The world's most profitable corporation was still at pains to, as Rex Tillerson would say, "communicate to the public and policymakers the complexities of the energy business in ways that help them better understand some of the issues involved and why things are how they are."

When Human Rights Watch asked for comment on business practices in Equatorial Guinea in 2009, the other oil companies were quite circumspect. They explained their "rigorous Foreign Corrupt Practices Act compliance program" and their well-circulated Business Conduct and Ethics Code and their "highest standards of ethical conduct" and their "compliance with the letter of and spirit of applicable laws in the countries where we operate." ExxonMobil, like the man at the helm of the corporation, was merit-badge calm and happy to explain in greater detail exactly *why things are the way they are*. "The practical realities of doing business in developing countries are challenging," Kenneth P. Cohen, vice president of public affairs, wrote to Human Rights Watch. "Equatorial Guinea, like many developing nations, has a limited number of local businesses and a small population of educated citizens. As a result, there is a small community of government officials and business owners. Not unexpectedly, many of those persons are connected by a network of social and family relations. Many businesses have some family relations with a government official, and virtually all government officials have some business interests of their own, or through a close relative. . . .

"While we can assure you that ExxonMobil and its affiliate in EG take the utmost care to conduct our operations in a legal, ethical and above board manner, for competitive reasons, we do not provide the details of our business activities."

We do not provide the details of our business activities—sort of says it all. By 2010, that oft-repeated phrase (see ExxonMobil public relations team template) represented almost a century's worth of standard operating procedure for Big Oil. "Oil," after all, "is where you find it." Sometimes American corporations had to make deals with unsavory sorts to get at it, sure, but remember, even with domestic energy production on the rise in 2010 (thank you, fracking), the United States still needed to import about half of the crude oil it consumed. The oil companies could always make the claim, with that actual fact as evidence, that they were doing it . . . for us.

Everywhere they operate on earth, oil and gas companies are incentivized to push as far as they can on extraction (that's how they make their money) and to escape negative consequences caused by that extraction. That's the basic math that produces their profit, their market share, their stock price, and the happiness of their shareholders. Because oil and gas are found all over the freaking place, though, oil and gas companies need a rudimentary foreign policy to maximize shareholder happiness by maximizing their ability to produce their product. And it turns out, rationally and understandably, the foreign policy priorities of the oil and gas industry are stability, access, control, simplicity. Countries may come and go, but oil and gas companies need to think bigger than that: they make big expensive investments that cost a ton up front, and they need to be assured they'll be able to collect the promised payoff after all that work and expense. So, the longer the relevant foreign ruler is in power, the better. And if the local autocrat is happily on the payroll, no one's going to bother anyone about cleaning up any mess that oil production might cause in his country. And if any of the citizens of that country do step out of line and make a fuss, the ruling family (and its well-paid paramilitary forces and its expensive PR firms) will take care of that, too. And everyone else will look the other way.

That global system of anti-governance driven by Western energy companies—that corporate shadow foreign policy—persists year in and year out, as American presidencies come and go. But occasionally, its costs become too much to ignore. By 2009, two important American politicians had decided that the costs of looking the other way in Equatorial Guinea were too high. Senator Richard Lugar (R-Ind.) and Senator Ben Cardin (D-Md.) did not appear at a glance to have a lot in common. Lugar was a six-term senator and former Rhodes scholar with the calm demeanor of an old-school midwestern patrician; Cardin was a first termer, grandson of Russian Jewish immigrants, graduate of a state law school, who had a gait and cadence earned on the streets of Baltimore. They were both, however, increasingly fed up with the status quo, especially after Lugar's staff finished a long investigation that resulted in a 125-page Senate Foreign Relations report titled "The Petroleum and Poverty Paradox: Assessing U.S. and International Community Efforts to Fight the Resource Curse." The "excrement of the devil" part was only implied.

As Lugar wrote in an introductory letter to the report, "Too often, oil money that should go to a nation's poor ends up in the pockets of the rich, or it may be squandered on the trappings of power and massive showcase projects instead of being invested productively and actively." The Resource Curse, Lugar noted, "affects us as well as producing countries. It exacerbates global poverty which can be a seedbed for terrorism, it dulls the effect of our foreign assistance, it empowers autocrats and dictators, and it can crimp world petroleum supplies by breeding instability." Lugar's study took the measure of oil-rich, governance-challenged countries in Africa, Asia, Europe, Latin America, and the Middle East. His solution was elegant and straightforward: transparency. Companies operating in extractive industries (from oil to diamonds) needed to provide the details of their business activities in foreign nations. And the countries needed to be more open about reporting what money came into state accounts and how it was spent. "When oil revenue in a producing country can be easily tracked," Lugar wrote, "that nation's elite are more likely to use revenues for the vital needs of their citizens and less likely to squander newfound wealth for self-aggrandizing projects."

Lugar then introduced the Energy Security Through Transparency Act. The legislation required companies in the extractive industries to make an annual report of all payments they made to foreign governments for the purpose of "commercial development of oil, natural gas, and minerals." Cardin signed on as lead co-sponsor. "This was a bipartisan bill," Cardin later explained. "[Senator Lugar's] interest in this was solely because he believes in transparency and he believes in good governance." Cardin believed that transparency would improve the bang we got for our foreign aid bucks and act as a hedge against corruption. "The United States spends the most on soldiers and weapons than any country in the world," Cardin said. "If we had less corruption in the world, we would need a smaller budget on soldiers and weapons."

The legislation eventually got a dozen more co-sponsors—Republican, Democrat, and independent. But it did not make it out of the Banking Committee before the end-of-the-year recess. So Lugar and Cardin cleverly got it attached as an amendment to a legislative juggernaut of 2010, the Dodd-Frank Wall Street Reform and Consumer Protection Act, which was the administration's best effort to curtail the financial shenanigans that had led to the epic near collapse of the world economy just before Obama's election.

Cardin's public explanation for putting what became known as Section 1504 in the Wall Street bill was "so investors can make intelligent decisions based upon the information on the companies they're being asked to invest in." And yes, that was a bit of a fig leaf, but it also made sense. "Look at the squandered resources," an investment industry trade group spokesman said at an event with Cardin. "Our interest as investors is to gain access to data, hard data, hard numbers . . . to evaluate risk. That's the business that we're in. And there are hardly any more acute sources of risk in the extractives industry globally, than those connected with corruption around revenue payment. So there's this, for us, coincidental, but happy coincidence here, a convergence of interests with civil society."

The co-founder of Global Witness, a group that had been pushing for transparency for a decade, liked that Section 1504 put the onus on both government *and* business. "It takes two to tango," Simon Taylor said. "We're stuck in this world with despotic leadership and lack of good governance and somehow companies fly above the fray. . . . The entire structure, the modus operandi of those companies in certain places, in certain corrupt places, is to be involved in illicit transfers of funds. Whether they're illegal or not is a different matter."

As Dodd-Frank raced toward passage in 2010, no amount of lobbying from the big oil companies could unhorse the Section 1504 rider. Law firms serving the industry began preparing client alerts explaining that it might soon be time to set up systems to track all payments to foreign governments and foreign officials—even if there were five hundred contracts to sort through in a little place like Equatorial Guinea. Beyond that, the lawyers warned, new SEC rules regarding Section 1504 might require the reports to be posted online, *available to the public*. "Affected companies," Hunton & Williams attorneys would counsel, if the legislation passed, "should thus begin preparing for any potential public relations issues that may arise out of the public disclosure of payments of the type contemplated by Dodd-Frank."

Positively disgusted by that prospect, Rex Tillerson decided it was time to act. ExxonMobil had been dispatching its lobbyists over to Capitol Hill to argue against this legislation since Lugar's bill was first introduced, and continued after the Lugar-Cardin measure became Section 1504 of Dodd-Frank. But the damn thing was still alive. So one day in early 2010, in between picking up awards in Houston, dealing with the Deepwater Horizon fallout, and trying to close deals with the oil tsar Igor Sechin for big new joint ventures with Russia, Rex Tillerson finally decided to just do it himself. He flew to Washington and got himself a one-on-one meeting with the architect of Section 1504, Senator Richard Lugar.

One of Lugar's key staff members on the Senate Foreign Relations Committee, Jay Branegan, could tell that quashing this little transparency movement meant a lot to Tillerson. "He was the only CEO to come in to lobby personally," Branegan later told a reporter. Tillerson tried to explain to Lugar that forcing American companies to report all these foreign payments, and divulge specific dollar amounts, would disadvantage ExxonMobil in its competition against oil companies from other countries. And somebody at that meeting would remember in vivid detail that when Lugar said he wasn't going to stand down on Section 1504, the ExxonMobil CEO did something altogether unexpected and uncharacteristic. Rex Tillerson lost his cool. "He got red-faced angry," that person told *The New Yorker*'s Dexter Filkins in 2017. Tillerson denied this, but Filkins's source was adamant. "He lifted out of his chair in anger. My impression was that he was not used to people with different views."

Another thing still remembered long after that meeting was this: "[Tillerson] listed a number of his and the industry's objections to the bill," Branegan told a reporter, "including that it would harm Exxon's relations with Russia."

TEN

WHO DOES THAT?

ARQUETTE ROAD IN MONTCLAIR, NEW JERSEY, WAS THE SORT of suburban tree-lined street designed to discourage unwanted bustle and traffic. The road itself was just a third of a mile long, a slow arc of unlined pavement neatly edged with Belgian block, ending in a tight little circle of a cul-de-sac. Which meant Marquette Road led to nowhere—unless, of course, you lived in one of the three dozen mid-century colonial/split-level houses on the street. If that were the case, then Marquette Road led home, and happily so. The street was always quiet. The sidewalks straight and mostly smooth. The houses were set back from the road at a respectful remove, so the yards were ample, and each was diligently mowed and landscaped after the American middle-class fashion, with easy-to-maintain plants and shrubs and bushes you could pick up on a Saturday or Sunday at the Home Depot a convenient few miles away, just the other side of the Garden State Parkway.

Not much unexpected happened on Marquette Road, which was the way everybody there seemed to prefer it. The same cars pulled in and out at regular hours most workdays, the same people walked their dogs (on leash) up and down the sidewalk, the same children came bounding down the block every afternoon on the way home from the school bus stop just around the corner. When somebody new moved in, it didn't take long for an ad hoc Welcome Wagon to come knockin' with some wine, or flowers, or sundry genial offers. *We have a teenager who babysits!* And it didn't take long to become familiar with the daily rhythms of the new residents. Take the Murphy family, who had moved into the boxy beige 1950s-era four-bedroom colonial ($481,000, anybody could look it up on Zillow) in August 2008, just when a new school year was about to kick off. The Murphys seemed like something of a cliché in the New York suburbs: solidly middle-class, middle-aged professionals willing to give up the easier commute for an extra bedroom or two, a real yard, and, of course, the promise of good schools for their two young daughters. Probably the house was a stretch for the Murphys, financially, the way things looked. After almost two years in Montclair, the couple still hadn't traded up for something better than their twelve-year-old Honda Civic.

Richard Murphy was a stay-at-home dad. He wasn't what you'd call outgoing or friendly, but he was polite and seemed like a man who could be counted on. He escorted his two daughters, Katie and Lisa, to the bus stop every morning and saw them off the big yellow school bus in the afternoons. He knew his way around a hamburger grill, mowed his own lawn, and favored Coors Light. His wife, Cynthia, was clearly the breadwinner. She took the DeCamp commuter bus number 66 into Port Authority every weekday morning and went to her office at a financial services company down near Wall Street, where she spent most of her time doling out tax and investment advice to high-end clients. And this was New York, so "high-end" also meant well connected in business and political circles. Cynthia Murphy was already gaining a reputation among her small group of friends on Marquette Road for her wide-ranging and thoroughgoing competencies. She had just earned her MBA from Columbia University but knew her way around the kitchen. "Oh, I had your lemon squares at the block party," Cynthia exclaimed to one neighbor. "I wanted to get the recipe." And she knew her way around the garden, too. Mrs. Murphy was a wizard with hydrangeas.

The budding star of the family, however, was Katie Murphy, aged eleven. She could be seen, often with her sister in tow, riding down the block on her blue bicycle, her blond pigtails athwart in the wind. Or chalking out princess stories on the sidewalk. Or manning her lemonade stand. Or stopping to make a fuss over her neighbor's dog, the extra-fluffy keeshond. Katie had been a distinguished participant, maybe *the* distinguished participant, at her recent fifth-grade gradua-tion ceremony. "I was just struck at how accomplished she was," an-other parent later told reporters, after the whole unlikely story of the Murphys began to emerge. "They called her up to the stage and said, 'Stay right here. You're getting more awards.'"

It was right around the time of Katie Murphy's impressive fifth-grade graduation in June 2010 that Marquette Road began to take on a slightly different aspect. And you didn't have to be a nosey parker to suss it out. Something was amiss. The traffic patterns were different for starters. A number of unfamiliar cars parked up and down the street. One driver sat in a parked sedan down near the cul-de-sac for an hour and a half or more, which was a damn sight longer than any car service guy would wait around for a tardy client who had a reservation for a ride to Newark Airport. Gas company trucks were digging up the street, too, though nobody on the block had smelled gas and nobody had called the company, as far as anyone knew. There was also a smat-tering of people the neighbors had never seen strolling up and down Marquette Road, walking unfamiliar dogs. And then, all of a sudden, the last Sunday in June, the street was crawling with black Ford LTDs. Who drives a Ford LTD, in 2010?

The arrests themselves happened in a hurry. The FBI and whatever other law enforcement agents were involved descended on 31 Mar-quette Road with all deliberate efficiency, because they knew Richard and Cynthia Murphy were at home for the taking. So was their younger daughter, nine-year-old Lisa. There was, however, a little glitch. Katie wasn't there. She arrived home a few hours after the raid commenced, entirely unaware of the unfolding kerfuffle, carrying an animal bal-loon party favor from the birthday shindig she had just attended. Fam-ily friends escorted Katie and Lisa out of their house later that same evening. The teenage girl next door described the scene for one of the many reporters who would shortly arrive on Marquette Road. She said the young girls were in a state of obvious confusion and fear when they walked out the front door of the house, carrying backpacks and "clutching pillows." The neighbor girl also described watching Richard and Cynthia Murphy being taken from the house, in handcuffs. No doubt headed for jail. Cynthia remained composed even as she was paraded out past her hydrangeas and all the gawkers. "[She] was like, 'OK, I know exactly what this is and I am not saying anything,'" the neighbor remembered, "'I have pride.'"

The Murphys were not the only suspects rolled up in what turned out to be the capper of a ten-year-long FBI counterintelligence investigation. This was a full-on sleeper cell spy ring. The captured co-conspirators numbered ten, all with similarly nondescript aliases and covers: Don Heathfield and his wife, Tracey Foley, were Canadians who had moved to Boston about ten years earlier with their two sons. Heathfield had a master's degree from Harvard's Kennedy School of Government and worked as an international consultant specializing in leadership and management; Foley worked in real estate. Juan Lázaro was a citizen of Peru who occasionally taught a college course in Latin American politics and lived in Yonkers with his wife, Vicky Peláez, a firebrand columnist for a Spanish-language newspaper. Their seventeen-year-old son was already gaining a reputation as a classical concert pianist in the making. Michael Zottoli and his wife, Patricia Mills, both had business degrees from the University of Washington in Seattle and had recently moved with their two toddlers across the country to the Washington, D.C., suburbs in hopes of landing jobs in or around the federal government. Mikhail Semenko was also living in the D.C. suburbs and working at a travel agency. Just twenty-eight years old, Semenko had recently completed a master's degree in international relations/Asian studies and an internship at the World Affairs Councils of America in Washington. He also had a bang-up LinkedIn page, which to this day still reads, "Highly creative and analytical professional with recent education and diverse experience involving development assistance, meeting and event planning, partnership building, and high-level client relations. Natural leader and communicator with in-depth knowledge of government policy research."

The co-conspirator who captured the greatest portion of the media attention in the days following the dragnet was the youngest and the most attractive of the suspects, Anna Chapman. Cynthia Murphy's businesslike competency, her prize hydrangeas, and her lemon squares were no match in the press for Chapman's flaming auburn hair and youthful allure, which netted the twenty-eight-year-old a week's worth of covers and headlines—"Double-0 Heaven"—in the always editorially tumescent *New York Post*. The "leggy redhead" was billed as a modern seductress worthy of Mata Hari. Her ex-husband back in London, Alex Chapman, fanned the flames by sharing with the sleaziest tabloid then on record, *News of the World,* racy photos of Anna and tales of sex romps involving nipple clamps and whips. "Anna was great in bed and she knew exactly what to do," said the jilted ex-husband. "She was awesome." A subsequent boyfriend and sugar daddy in London told other reporters he "was very, very shocked to see this news." He said it never crossed his mind she was a spy.

The same could be said by any of the Murphys' friends and neighbors on Marquette Road. *It never crossed my mind they were spies.* But the neighbors watched the whirlwind postarrest legal proceedings and began to understand something quite extraordinary had transpired right there on their sleepy little road. "Sometimes," one of the elders on the block told a New York reporter, "things make sense to you after the fact."

The ten defendants were arraigned in federal district court, charged with money laundering and conspiring to act as unregistered agents of a foreign government. All but one was held without bail. The final disposition didn't take long. The Murphys and their co-defendants were back in court less than two weeks later to plead guilty to the charges. The federal judge in Manhattan, at the urging of the U.S. Department of Justice, sentenced the defendants to time served—eleven days so far—and ordered them deported. "The agreement we reached today," Attorney General Eric Holder announced, "provides a successful resolution for the United States and its interests."

The media tracked the Boeing 767 carrying the Murphys and the others to a remote runway at the main airport in Vienna, Austria, where it rendezvoused with a second plane. The two aircraft idled nose to tail on the tarmac for a little more than an hour, while a secure bus shuttled in between, swapping out the ten "foreign agents" arrested in America for four soon-to-be imports to the West—a spies-for-spies trade between Moscow and Washington, a full-blooded Cold War throwback.

Less than three hours after taking off from Vienna, the Russian Yakovlev Yak-42 jet touched down in Moscow. The Murphys and their co-conspirators were home again, back in Russia after almost twenty years in the United States for some of them. They were received in general triumph, which included a ceremony a few months later at the Kremlin, where the Russian president, Dmitry Medvedev, presented the "talented adventurers" with special award citations. Prime Minister (and soon-to-be president again) Vladimir Putin promised "a bright and happy future" back home in the motherland for them all. The bosses in the Russian intelligence service took the celebrated secret agents on a victory tour, which reportedly culminated at Putin's villa on the Black Sea. Anna Chapman later told acquaintances that the former KGB agent Vladimir Putin gave her a ride into the deepest lake in the world, Lake Baikal, in his personal submarine.

According to press reports out of Russia anyway, most of the "Illegals" settled into the "bright and happy future" they were promised. (Only the Murphys disappeared into oblivion.) Mikhail Semenko went to work in the Moscow office of the same travel agency he had worked for in the suburbs of Washington, D.C. He didn't even have to update his LinkedIn page. Natalya Pereverzeva, armed with her business degree from the University of Washington, became an adviser on international projects to the CEO of Russia's powerful oil pipeline company, Transneft. The most impressive of the new professional assignments went to Donald Heathfield, a.k.a. Andrey Bezrukov, who had compiled the finest record of *almost* accomplishment among the spy team. Not long after he and the other Illegals completed their weird Putin-led Victory Tour, Bezrukov was awarded a job at the jewel in the crown of Russia's state-controlled corporations, Rosneft, which would shortly surpass ExxonMobil in pure size and breadth. The appointment was made, it was reported in the Russian press, "as per orders from above."

But nobody made out like Anna Chapman, that auburn-haired, latter-day Mata Hari. She landed a job as "adviser" to a Russian investment bank specializing in high tech and aerospace, with no fixed office hours and, consequently, free rein to exploit her Kremlin-powered celebrity to its fullest. Anna appeared on the cover of the Russian edition of *Maxim* wearing lingerie and holding a Beretta pistol. She launched a fashion line, a perfume, a poker app, and a weekly television show called *Secrets of the World with Anna Chapman*. She drove a sleek black

Porsche Cayenne, frequented high-profile nightclubs in Moscow, and drew hordes of paparazzi at movie premieres.

Ms. Chapman even tweeted a marriage proposal to Moscow ensconced American defector Edward Snowden a few years back, and she maintains a Western-friendly social media profile. Her Twitter feed quotes Winston Churchill, Albert Einstein, the Dalai Lama, Oscar Wilde, and John Stuart Mill: "There are many truths of which the full meaning cannot be realized until personal experience has brought it home." And she remains, above all, a loyal and patriotic Russian who briefly led the Young Guard of Putin's United Russia political party. "Anna is Putin's girl," one Kremlin watcher told *Politico* reporter Brett Forrest.

The way the Illegals' story was told inside Russia, this ten-person cell of deep-cover spies had done extraordinary work in the United States, uncovering a trove of useful intelligence while successfully pulling the wool over the eyes of the CIA and the FBI. "Nobody [in Russia] thinks [they] were a failure," Andrei Soldatov, a Moscow-born journalist who specializes in Russian security services, explained to Forrest a little more than a year after the return of the spies. "It's a victory. Because it shows we can still compete with America. We are a great power. We can do everything we want to do."

Russia's great "victory" was not conceded here in the United States. The spies were caught, right, and without much trouble. And yet their story made for a fantastic tale. The saga of these deep-cover agents, spooling out in official legal filings and news accounts, offered tantalizing hints of intrigue, and peril, and old-school spycraft at work. The senior of the key suspects had been trained by the old Soviet KGB; the younger by the KGB's Russian successor in foreign intelligence, the SVR. But these were not your garden-variety agents; the ten Russians captured in the United States in 2010 were modern inheritors of a long and storied history of Russian Illegals. Among spies, Illegals are a special breed of cat—long known for their "sophistication and flair," as one Russian counterintelligence expert put it—assiduously prepared for long years on foreign assignment, pretending not to be Russians at all.

At the beginning of their careers, they had received training in the language and culture of the country they would inhabit. They were taught the basics of identifying and communicating with their fellow travelers: how to execute a brush pass; how to nonverbally signal danger to a comrade; how to send radiograms; how to cipher and decipher coded messages; and more recently, in the age of the internet, how to join a temporary wireless network or operate software to pull encrypted data off innocuous-looking public websites. Once trained, Illegals were shipped off on assignments around the world, including to the United States, often as married couples, armed with legends—stolen identities and invented backstories—to work the long game. They did not gather foreign intelligence while safely under the guise of factotums at Russian embassies and consulates and trade missions, working in broad daylight, with the promise of diplomatic immunity if they were caught in acts of espionage. They instead lived like locals. *As* locals. They moved into American communities and made friends, went to graduate school and made new friends, got jobs and made new friends, had children and made new friends.

The newest generation still operated as their predecessors had in the early days of Soviet spydom: switching on and off multiple taxis, buses, and subways to shake real or perceived surveillance; exercising discretion in all ways (their cars, by official edict, should not be pricier or nicer than those of "embassy workers who are of equal or higher rank than the station chief"); and being constantly on guard against slipups that might get them reassigned to some godforsaken outpost in Siberia or demoted to a job in "internal security," where they would end up spying on Moscow dentist offices or St. Petersburg tennis clubs. Most of all, they waited for and followed the coded instructions from SVR's Directorate S, whose chief ran the 2010 version of Russia's nontraditional espionage program. "Try to single out tidbits unknown publicly but revealed in private by sources close to State department, Government, major think tanks," was the routine order from on high, as detailed in the U.S. Justice Department's federal criminal complaint.

Their assignments in the United States were actually pretty cushy during the first decade after the breakup of the Soviet Union. While their countrymen back in Russia fought for their economic survival, the Murphys and the Heathfields and the Zottolis lived in the land of plenty, with money to pay exorbitant graduate school tuitions and without a lot of heat from their bosses back at Moscow Center. Instructions from Directorate S were spotty, and general, and not particularly urgent right up to the early years of the twenty-first century, just after Vladimir Putin took over the Russian presidency.

Putin was happy to allow the United States to pony up for oil pipelines and tanker-friendly deepwater ports in Russia. He was more than thrilled to have the bankers at Morgan Stanley shake the Western money tree on behalf of Russian companies and quick to boast of the world-beating economic growth that foreign investment engendered in Russia. But the old KGB man would never let go of his suspicion of the United States of America and its insatiable hunger for more. And it wasn't just paranoia; it was worry borne out of legitimate weakness. Would Wall Street bankers horn in on the claptrap Russian industry that produced the nation's one economic advantage? Would the United States somehow threaten Russia's increasing dominance in Europe's oil and gas markets? Even after the Cold War thaw, by Putin's reckoning, the American government still seemed committed to eating away at Russia's already-depleted global standing. America still had an appetite that grew as it was fed. So President Vlad was going to be keeping tabs. And the Illegals rather suddenly found themselves on an uncomfortably tight, and short, leash.

As Putin consolidated his hold on power in Russia, Directorate S prodded its agents in America to widen their circles of unwitting informants and acquaintances who might prove susceptible to blackmail. "Your relationship with 'Parrot' looks very promising as a valid source of info from US power circles," read a radiogram in 2007. "To start working with him professionally we need all available details on his background, current position, habits, contacts, opportunities. . . . Agree with your proposal to keep relations with 'Cat' but watch him."

By 2009, as Russia and the United States were just beginning to negotiate a breakthrough treaty to reduce their respective stockpiles of nuclear weapons, Directorate S was increasingly intrigued by Cynthia Murphy's ongoing contact with a New York venture capitalist named Alan Patricof. Patricof, who had fallen into Cynthia Murphy's lap as a client of the financial services company she worked for, was not just a major donor to the Democratic Party but the finance chairman of Hillary Clinton's first Senate campaign and a key fund-raiser for her presidential campaign in 2008. He and Clinton were friends! Perhaps even close confidants. Which meant, as far as the SVR bosses in Moscow were concerned, Mr. Patricof should be able to provide inside dope on the new secretary of state and the inner workings of the Obama administration. "Try to build up little by little relations with him moving beyond just [work] framework," instructed Directorate S. "Maybe he can provide [Cynthia Murphy] with remarks re US foreign policy, 'rumors' about White House internal 'kitchen,' invite her to venues, etc. . . . In short, consider carefully all options in regard to [financier]."

For all the ways it hit the fundamentals of a shiny-cover airport bookstore spy novel, the real story of these new Illegals had to have been unsettling to an old spymaster like Vladimir Putin. To an American audience, sure, the arrests in the summer of 2010 exposed something right at the overlap of exciting and ridiculous—dead drops, fake accents, and code words, oh my. But it could only be funny if you didn't think much was at stake; for the Russians, this was their best effort. And the excruciating ineptitude of what were supposed to be the Kremlin's elite spies was now on display for a world audience. The evidence was irrefutable: the Russians were losing their edge even in the arenas where they once enjoyed their most trumpeted victories. While Mrs. Patricof might have had cause to worry about what sorts of "options" were considered and deployed in the attempt to entice her seventy-five-year-old husband into deeper relations, nothing suggested that the White House's famed "internal kitchen" was ever in danger of a serious breach. The Illegals had gleaned, well, pretty much nothing they couldn't have gotten reading their local newspapers. Putin's best spies in America seem to have never really had their heart in the mission. *The New Yorker*'s Keith Gessen, a Russian-born American journalist and novelist who came to the United States when he was six years old, found the entire episode "sad and touching. . . . Sad because, according to the F.B.I. affidavit, the information requested by the Russian government ('Moscow Center,' as it's called) is so mundane, and some of it merely trade secrets, unbefitting a mighty state and redolent too of the central planning that once turned the U.S.S.R. into an economic basket case. Touching because the other information they are said to have sought—American plans for fighting terrorism; American plans for Iran; Obama's hopes for last summer's summit in Moscow—seems to dance around the real issue. Like a kid in the presence of his new crush, asking, 'Do you like movies?,' 'What's your favorite color?,' Russia really wanted to ask America: What do you think of me?"

The Illegals operation was not merely sad and touching; it was also dated. The spies were still using invisible ink, for God's sake. "If the accusations prove to be true," noted *Time* magazine, "the biggest lesson from this entire episode may be that real-life spies today act just like fictional spies from the 1980s." Yeah, only less like John Le Carré characters and more like the ones in the movie with Chevy Chase and Dan Aykroyd. Despite the public boasts about their heroic victory in Moscow, the Illegals were demonstrably bumbling, even slipshod. The group was under close and constant surveillance for nearly *ten* years, with footage and photographs and audio recordings to prove it. Their countersurveillance efforts had bordered on gross negligence. Their homes were searched and their cars tagged with GPS trackers, and the Illegals never knew. The best of the spies, Heathfield/Bezrukov, was for years kept under the watchful and unseen eye of the U.S. lead agent Peter Strzok—the G-man later torched by the Trump administration and congressional Republicans for his role in investigating the Russia scandal surrounding the U.S. 2016 presidential election. The Illegals had repeated contact with FBI agents posing as fellow Russians. "Are you ready for this [next] step?" one undercover agent asked Anna Chapman. "Shit," she replied, "of course." Then she unwittingly handed over her laptop to the American undercover agent, and then she bought a burner phone and a Tracfone calling card, and then she dumped the receipt into a public trash can where it was fished out by the FBI. Double-0 Heaven indeed.

Almost all of the SVR spies exhibited stunning deficiencies in both tradecraft and general attitude. Richard Murphy was an exemplary nincompoop on each count. There was a reason Cynthia Murphy was bringing home the bacon and Richard was a stay-at-home dad. To begin with, and maybe this was just the dark Tolstoyan Russian in him, he was an incessant whiner. "They don't understand what we go through over here," Murphy liked to say. At a 2002 meeting at a restaurant in Sunnyside, Queens, he spent an hour complaining to a Russian agent sent to give him money. "Well," said the other Russian, while handing him a black bag containing $40,000, "I'm so happy I'm not *your* handler."

At one point, near the end of the operation, the directorate seemed worried that Richard Murphy might go walkabout, especially after he suggested putting the house on Marquette Road in his own (fake) name. "From our perspective, purchase of the house was solely a natural progression of our prolonged stay here," Comrade Murphy tried to explain to his bosses. "It was a convenient way to solve the housing issue, plus to 'do as the Romans do' in a society that values home ownership."

The answer from Directorate S was an emphatic *nyet:* "Your education, bank accounts, car, house—all these serve one goal: fulfill your main mission . . . to search and develop ties in policymaking circles in US and send intels to [Moscow Center]."

Murphy was assigned simple tasks only, like handoffs of backpacks or gym bags with other Russian Illegals. To his credit, Murphy could be counted on to remember the code phrases for identification: "Excuse me, could we have met in Malta in 1999?"

"Yes indeed," was the correct reply, "I was in La Valletta, but in 2000."

He was, however, not great on details—such as knowing there is more than one entrance at the southwest corner of Central Park. "We might have, ah, have different place in mind," he apologized after one botched attempt at a meeting. And he was apparently not great at identifying his fellow Russians, which made for a few uncomfortable incidents, like when he walked up to one benighted soul beneath the metallic globe sculpture at Columbus Circle in New York City and unleashed his code phrase: "Uncle Paul loves you."

The man did not return the agreed-upon retort—"It is wonderful to be Santa Claus in May"—but instead looked at Murphy like he was crazy, until Murphy and his backpack went off in search of his real contact.

Richard Murphy fell well short in "sophistication and flair" and also in flat-out competence. When the FBI executed a clandestine search of the Murphys' New Jersey apartment in 2005, they were quickly able to access Richard's computer address book, the websites he had visited, and the images he had downloaded. He apparently hadn't bothered to clear his browser history. In an open book near Murphy's computer was a page with the notation "alt control e" followed by a string of twenty-seven characters, which turned out to be the password that unlocked a software program that allowed the FBI to access readable text files sent from Directorate S in downloadable images.

The FBI detailed all this in its criminal affidavit, along with a recap of an embarrassing 2004 conversation captured on tape at the Murphys' residence. Anybody who wishes to read between the lines of the FBI's clinical recitation will detect some rather aggressive spousal hectoring couched as career advice: "CYNTHIA MURPHY advised her husband that he should improve his information-collection efforts. CYNTHIA MURPHY explained to RICHARD MURPHY that he would not be able to work at the top echelons of certain parts of the United States government—the State Department, for example. CYNTHIA MURPHY suggested that RICHARD MURPHY should therefore approach people who have access to important venues (the White House, for example) to which he could not reasonably expect to himself gain direct personal access." *He could not reasonably expect to himself gain direct personal access.* Ouch, Spy-Boy.

Over and above his numerous tactical missteps, Richard Murphy just didn't seem committed to his mission or his craft. After nearly twenty years in the United States, not much of America had rubbed off on him. "I was always puzzled by the inconsistency between a completely American name and a completely Russian behavior," said a professor of international affairs who had been Murphy's faculty adviser at the New School in New York for three years. Professor Nina Khrushcheva, the great-granddaughter of former Soviet premier Nikita Khrushchev, had no problem spotting Russians, even when they were trying to hide their true identities. Richard Murphy was barely even trying. "He had a thick Russian accent and an incredibly unhappy Russian personality," she said. "I knew he wasn't American. I knew it was very odd." Or as one of Richard Murphy's Marquette Road neighbors told a reporter a few days after the arrest, as the tumblers were beginning to fall into place, "It *was* suspicious that he had a Russian accent and an Irish last name. Who does that? . . . He must have been the worst spy ever."

ELEVEN

THE OTHER 1 PERCENT

THE OKLAHOMA CITY METROPOLITAN AREA COULD BE A WEIRD and occasionally exciting place, with or without the civic exertions recently employed to try to vault the region onto the roster of America's major cities. In 2009, for example, there was the unveiling in Norman of a life-sized bronze depicting a nude Angelina Jolie breast-feeding her twins. The naked-Angelina sculptor had previously been best known for his graphic yet strangely romantic depiction of Britney Spears giving birth on a bearskin rug, on all fours. Also in 2009, the state's Democratic governor, Brad Henry, proclaimed the Flaming Lips' song "Do You Realize??" from the album *Yoshimi Battles the Pink Robots* to be Oklahoma's official rock song: "You realize the sun doesn't go down / It's just an illusion caused by the world spinning round." The move was not without its detractors: in the legislative debate over the song's designation, the Republican lawmaker Mike Reynolds complained that members of the Flaming Lips—proud Oklahomans though they may be—had an unfortunate reputation for using foul language in public. "Their lips *ought* to be on fire," Reynolds said.

But for all of the mildly controversial glories of Oklahoma's homegrown strain of deliberate weirdness, starting round about 2010, things went weird in an altogether different way. There was, for instance, the bump in misdemeanor criminal activity around brand-name fast-food and retail outlets. In March 2010, a twenty-year-old woman, upset and confused about payment procedures at the McDonald's drive-thru window, and maybe upset and confused about life in general, exited her car, climbed through the service window, and began "knocking milkshakes off the counter," according to the arrest report. Then, in July, a woman dressed in black, sporting a blond wig, gloves, and with "underwear over her face held in place with yellow paperclips," according to local media accounts, pried open an unmanned drive-thru window at a second and unrelated McDonald's and absconded with an unspecified amount of cash. "I've seen a wide variety of crime over the last thirty years," said the local police chief, "but this particular case is one of the strangest, based on her method of operation and weird disguise."

Just three weeks later, the owner of a Sinclair gas station near the University of Oklahoma took his young grandson for their daily drive past the seven-hundred-pound green fiberglass rendering of Dino the dinosaur that fronted the establishment. And got a rude awakening. "We came around and [Dino's] head was sawed off," the chagrined proprietor, Jerry Masters, told reporters, while police dusted the area for fingerprints. Then, too, the 2010 election was like no other in recent Oklahoma history and seemed to portend a very different kind of political future for the state. The slow, decade-long changeover from Democratic control of state government toward complete Republican control took a final hard lurch that November. The state's Republicans won a thirty-two-to-sixteen advantage in the state senate, and a whopping seventy-to-thirty-one advantage in the state house. The Republican gubernatorial candidate, Mary Fallin, who had wrapped herself in the Tea Party's "Don't Tread on Me" banner, cruised to a twenty-point victory over Brad Henry's lieutenant governor and would-be Democratic successor.

But for all the shake-ups and oddities of 2010, the strangest and most telling one was what entered Sooner lexicon as the "earthquake swarm."

Earthquakes were not unknown in Oklahoma, but they were extraordinarily rare. In the three decades since the state entered the modern era of seismic activity monitoring, the Oklahoma Geological Survey had recorded a grand total of around forty earthquakes above 3.0 on the Richter scale. A little more than one a year. But in 2010 some seismic switch had apparently flipped. Monitoring devices in Oklahoma recorded more than twenty 3.0-magnitude quakes in the first half of the year alone. Draw a circle with a fifty-mile radius around Oklahoma City, and a very large percentage of the people inside it had felt a temblor or two. "Shook the windows and shook the house," a woman who had felt six separate tremors in the previous few months told a reporter from local KOTV at Shuff's Main Street Grill in Jones, just northeast of downtown OKC. "Horses taking off running, and dogs running off the porch. It's kind of that magnitude, y'know."

The locals had worked up a number of theories as to the cause of what KOTV calculated as a *10,000 percent* jump in the number of felt earthquakes. "A bunch of gophers," joked one man at Shuff's. "The only theory that I have," said his wife, "is that it's a Biblical statement." The more widely held suspicion in the community was that the earthquake swarm was a by-product of the enormous increase in hydraulic fracking in the area. Oil and gas drillers were pumping close to fifty million barrels of water deep into the earth's crust every month in 2010. Most of the toxic water that flowed back up in the production process, drillers injected back into the ground for permanent storage. That had to have consequences, right? It at least was the obvious question. So the KOTV reporter went for an expert take to Austin Holland, the geophysicist/seismologist who was in charge of a small team of Oklahoma Geological Survey technicians monitoring earthquake activity across the state. The reporter put it to Holland directly: Did the data suggest that the enormous spike in earthquakes was tied to the enormous spike in hydraulic fracking? "I just can't make the connection," the state seismologist said. "There just doesn't seem to be a link, and it's the easy answer. Everyone wants to pin it on the oil activities, but it just doesn't seem to be there yet."

Austin Holland was a restrained, not overly demonstrative man, so you wouldn't be able to tell from his matter-of-fact responses to the growing number of inquiries about the swarm, but the truth was he was kind of excited. Still in his thirties, Holland had just parachuted into the ideal spot for a scientific inquiry into the phenomenon of induced seismic activity, a.k.a. man-made earthquakes. Oklahoma in 2010 was about as close as a geophysicist could get to a controlled experiment, and Holland meant to keep gathering and collating seismic activity data, along with whatever data oil and gas producers were willing to give him about the deep underground disposal of hundreds of millions of gallons of flowback water and wastewater and production water. He was hoping to be able to form some real hypotheses, based on hard evidence, about exactly what effect all that hydraulic fracturing and all that extra underground water might have on nearby fault zones. He was about to start living the geophysicist dream.

Austin Holland had three consuming interests growing up—the outdoors, science, and computing. When he wasn't in school, or working to save money for college, or working toward his own Eagle Scout badge, he was out backpacking or rock climbing in the Grand Tetons and Yellowstone National Park, which were just a few hours' drive from his hometown of Idaho Falls. The beauty, and the breadth, and the sheer power of the natural world left him both awestruck and eager to understand it. His parents encouraged his outdoor hobbies, just as they encouraged his keen academic interests. They went to bat for their son at Idaho Falls High School when he needed special permission to take an extra science class. They let him take on extracurricular work as a computer programmer with the school district. They cheered when he built a gas chromatograph that won him the Eastern Idaho science fair. Even arranged for him to travel to Montana Tech for a monthlong mineral education program sponsored by the National Science Foundation. By the time he enrolled in college, eighteen-year-old Austin Holland was confident that his professional future was in the sciences. And he proved himself talented and able enough to snare a series of summer internships and then a full year's postbaccalaureate fellowship at the seismic monitoring program at the Idaho National Laboratory. Holland's fellowship included some memorable work concerning the town of Challis, an unprepossessing little burg that happened to fall within a geologic region called the intermountain seismic belt.

Challis had a long and storied history of measurable earthquake activity. A magnitude 7.3 quake had hit near Challis in 1983, and during his Idaho fellowship just a dozen years later Austin Holland could climb right up to a spot where he was able to see and touch the vast scar left behind. "What happens is that when the earthquake ruptures, the mountains go up and the valley goes down," he explained in a 2017 deposition for a civil suit. "And then that way, you're actually stretching and extending the crust and creating new earth. In this case it was only, you know, a few feet of horizontal new earth, but the mountains I think went up approximately 14 feet."

Earthquakes continued to be a constant around Challis, so there was plenty to keep Holland busy at the monitoring station. The budding scientist was captivated. "When I started my undergrad I wanted to be a geological engineer [the sort that scouts the deep earth for the best places for oil companies to drill], and that was partly because my dad said they make more money than geologists," he would say. "And maybe they still do, and I probably should have chosen to be a geological engineer in that regard. But I fell in love with seismology."

By the time Holland arrived in Oklahoma in 2010, fifteen years after his seismic epiphany, big and weird things were happening there. Oklahoma was taking what Holland called "a significant departure from [its] historical naturally occurring background seismicity rate," and the National Science Foundation was installing new seismic monitors at forty locations around the state. People were already talking about the possibility that these new earthquakes were man-made and perhaps caused by the oil and gas industry's current enthusiasm for fracking. The implication of that theory, of course, was that the earthquakes could be stopped. If mankind could turn them on, couldn't we turn them off, too? "From the moment I got into Oklahoma, that was one of the questions I was asked to examine," Holland said. "That was the question everybody wanted answers to."

From the outside, this looked like an opportunity for Austin Holland to do what he had dreamed of: gather reams of new live data, make deep scientific inquiry, and publish important and maybe groundbreaking findings in the field of triggered seismicity. From the outside, you could say, Holland looked like a man who had a chance to make a name for himself. But he was not the type to get carried away. Austin Holland remained, as always, governed by professional and personal humility, a prisoner to his long training in the scientific method. He was always mindful of what he did not know. Always cautious. Always aware that there was much more than a single variable at play in the fault zones deep beneath his feet. "When you're a geologist you can't control your experiments because you can't see inside the earth," he explained in his deposition. "We can't control properties inside the earth."

So while the running total of 3.0-magnitude-plus earthquakes in Oklahoma climbed near forty in his first year on the job, Holland kept his head down and gathered his scientific string. He eschewed drama and headlines even in the immediate heady wake of a 5.1-magnitude quake that erupted near enough that it shook his office on the University of Oklahoma campus. Nearby residents were less calm. Locals described the experience of that October 13, 2010, quake as a feeling akin to a tractor trailer or a trash truck crashing headlong into their house, or a 747 landing next door. How exactly somebody knows what a 747 landing next door would actually feel like is hard to say, but the use of the image does speak to the frightening novelty of the sensation they experienced. Some said the rumbling lasted for a full and harrowing thirty seconds. "That sucker it rattled my whole house," said a man who lived within a mile of the epicenter. "It literally shook the whole thing." The quake had knocked one do-it-yourselfer off his ladder and landed him in the emergency room with a broken ankle. And he had been on the *other* side of Oklahoma City, a dozen miles away. The tremors had reportedly been felt nearly seven hundred miles from the quake, in Brentwood, Tennessee.

The public service button on the Oklahoma Geological Survey website—"Ask a Seismologist"—lit up like Christmas that day, and the next, and the next, as little aftershocks rippled through the surrounding area. Holland was also fielding press inquiries from all over the country. When the science editor of the website *Boing Boing* called for comment, Holland was patient, straightforward, and plainspoken. He explained the tectonics of Oklahoma, where "the North American Plate has been pulled apart and where old plates fused together." He explained the difference between California's renowned faults and Oklahoma's, where the rocks are older, smoother around the edges, and stronger: "Here in central U.S., the energy from an earthquake gets radiated much further than in California, because the rock the seismic waves travel through is more solid. It's just like how sound carries faster and louder through metal, than through wood or Styrofoam."

He suggested that history proved an even bigger quake was not out of the question. But Oklahoma's lone—and much overworked—official seismologist was still not willing or able to isolate any particular cause for the recent swarm. What was it now, a 20,000 percent increase over the historic average? "We don't know for certain what triggers peak years," Holland said, when the *Boing Boing* science editor asked if the boom in fracking was the culprit. "The research is still in its infancy. I just started here in January. . . . The jury is still out, I'd say. Until I can prove with good science that it's the case, my assumption is that this is natural seismicity. Earthquakes have happened naturally here in the past. It doesn't have to have an outside cause."

By the time of the Oklahoma quake outbreak in 2010, Aubrey McClendon—the closest thing America had to a public face of the national frack-fest—might have suspected his natural gas revolution was built on shaky ground. Aubrey was happy to explain, though, that if you looked at it from the proper perspective, everything was peachy. He had weathered the financial storm, and his personal net worth was on the rise again. The company he had founded and continued to lead stood as a behemoth among America's natural gas suppliers. That year, it ranked number two in average daily domestic production. Only Rex Tillerson's ExxonMobil (thank you, XTO merger) was loosing more natural gas from the earth. Chesapeake had forty-six thousand wells (87 percent of its product was natural gas) and owned mineral rights on properties in twenty-three different states, from New York and Pennsylvania, to Arkansas and Louisiana and Oklahoma and Texas, to Colorado and Utah and Wyoming. And Aubrey was on another buying spree in the spring of 2010, executing one of the biggest landgrabs in the state of Michigan—figuring to shell out about $400 million for mineral rights on 450,000 acres. When one of his subcontractors there praised McClendon as "the most successful Landman in the world," Aubrey emailed him back immediately: "That is the nicest title anyone has ever given me."

The Michigan play was a typically daring McClendon move. Chesapeake's balance sheets weren't ideal just then. The selling price of natural gas had fallen to around $4 per million BTUs, well off its 2008 precrash high of nearly $14 per, and there was a bit of a glut in supply.

Chesapeake was barely able to break even. But Aubrey was still bullish on natural gas. And he prided himself on being able to locate surprising new veins of financing to keep Chesapeake's land acquisition and drilling operations humming, even in the most challenging times. Especially in the most challenging times. Just a few days before the 5.1 earthquake hit outside Norman, for example, the government-owned China National Offshore Oil Corporation agreed to pay Chesapeake $1.1 billion for a one-third stake in Aubrey's enormous shale play in south Texas. China further agreed to fork over another $1.1 billion to help pay for Chesapeake's enormous drilling costs in the region. Aubrey insisted that it was a win-win: the energy-hungry China tapped a new source for fueling its rapidly expanding economy; Chesapeake would be able to speed the pace of its drilling operations in south Texas, which would create more jobs, and ensure "payment of very significant local, state and federal taxes." Increased production would move the United States of America that much closer to everyone's favorite important-sounding national-security-ish industry buzz phrase: "energy independence." Never mind the awkwardness that in this case it was being funded by the Chinese.

Aubrey McClendon, at the end of 2010, looked like the Oklahoma City version of A Man in Full. He was that rare modern figure who inhabited a world that was largely his own creation. The eleven-thousand-square-foot French château-style mansion he built in the premier Oklahoma City neighborhood of Nichols Hills—his estate included a sweeping lawn, conspicuous gardens, a swimming pool, and a lit clay tennis court—was an easy four-minute drive to the fifty-acre campus of Chesapeake Energy. Aubrey had built that too, and was still adding on. On the way to the office, he could pass the Chesapeake-owned site that would soon house a thirty-five-thousand-square-foot Whole Foods. High end. High fiber. Aubrey had persuaded the Whole Foods team to locate the largest "natural and organic" supermarket in the state within walking distance of his offices. The new store, according to the local media, was to be constructed in line with Whole Foods' recent pledge to reduce its energy consumption and carbon emissions by 25 percent. It was green, just like Aubrey McClendon, who gave to the Sierra Club by the millions. "The area around Chesapeake's distinctive and beautiful campus," the CEO of Whole Foods explained to reporters in Oklahoma City, "combined with Aubrey's vision to create an eco-friendly, aesthetically beautiful and people-pleasing environment caught our attention." The coming of Whole Foods, McClendon boasted, "signifies a major step forward in our vision to create the most vibrant and dynamic urban environment for our employees and neighbors. . . . We are taking the retail, entertainment and business environment to a new level."

Around the Chesapeake offices, CEO McClendon had a reputation for focus bordering on obsessive. He didn't just worry over details on where to drill, or where to seek financing, or how to sell the bigger Chesapeake story. He weighed in on the colors of the latest corporate logo. He wanted a green stroke above the company name, to "visibly communicate the company's commitment to the environment." Aubrey weighed in on color schemes for company hallways and brochures, the proper spacing between the redbud trees on the Chesapeake campus, the proper snack choices for its cafeterias, the proper use of commas in company press releases. "I make hundreds of decisions every day," he told his architect. "I've gotten pretty good at it. And I think I hit 90 percent of them right."

This extraordinary batting average was apparently not lost on the Chesapeake board of directors, which had recently approved a generous new five-year contract for the company founder and CEO. His $975,000 base salary was augmented with a number of special perks and incentives. He was not likely to receive the $77 million annual bonus he had pocketed in precrash 2008 anytime soon. But he was doing fine, thank you very much—on his way, with stock options, to a $21 million take in 2010. And that didn't count the $3 million worth of administrative support services Chesapeake gifted him for the various personal enterprises he was running on the side: real estate, restaurants, wine, catering, investments in oil and gas drilling operations, and, most implausibly, a $200 million hedge fund that operated out of a building on the Chesapeake campus. Whether McClendon took advantage of the teeth whitening or Botox injections available at the company's health and fitness center was not disclosed in proxy filings.

Another lovely perk was the unlimited travel on Chesapeake-leased jets the board afforded Aubrey, his family, and his friends. Didn't matter if the travel was for business or just for fun. This kindness, according to the language of his employment contract, was extended to ensure his "safety, security and efficiency," and Aubrey was obviously serious about his safety, security, and efficiency. As well as his comfort and his general welfare. The flight logs later turned up by some excellent reporting by Reuters showed exactly how Aubrey (and friends) really made the most of it, including about seventy-five personal trips in 2010 alone, all on the company dime. In June, he and his two sons flew a Gulfstream G550 direct from Oklahoma City to Amsterdam, where Aubrey gave a speech at an energy conference, then took a two-week European vacation that ended with a direct flight from Paris to Oklahoma City. There were flights to New York, Mexico, the Cayman Islands. Aubrey hosted five local rowers for a one-day jaunt to San Diego.

The McClendons owned plenty of far-flung vacation homes that required air travel: the $6 million house in Minnesota, on a lake where Aubrey's mother had summered since she was a little girl; the $10 million house on Lake Michigan, right at the mouth of the Kalamazoo River; the refurbished $20 million estate on eight acres in the priciest enclave in Bermuda, just down the road from Michael Bloomberg, Ross Perot, and Silvio "Bunga Bunga" Berlusconi. The island estate had a luxurious main house and three extra cottages, all designed and sited, according to Aubrey's builder, to follow "classic Bermudian architecture using local materials and maximizing the legendary views." On one happy occasion, a Chesapeake jet flew nine of Mrs. McClendon's girlfriends to Bermuda to enjoy the sun and sand and those legendary views. Chesapeake, as per Aubrey's employment contract, footed the entire bill, even though Aubrey did not make the trip.

All in all, life was good for Aubrey McClendon, despite the gathering publicity storm surrounding fracking. A new round of questions and media attention had flared following a measurable seismic event not far from the Dallas/Fort Worth airport, near a Chesapeake drilling site. Quakes had started there just a few weeks after Chesapeake began injecting fracking wastewater at the site, and then mysteriously stopped once Chesapeake shut down the well. Aubrey didn't see much need to coddle people over the issue, though; the company's statement on the matter was blunt: "In every state where we operate . . . we isolate and safely dispose of any saltwater produced during the drilling process." Never mind that rumbling in the distance.

The typical drilling and well completion process at a Chesapeake shale gas site in Pennsylvania or West Virginia or Louisiana or Texas or right at home in Oklahoma in the first decade of the twenty-first century was the product of those twin technological innovations, horizontal drilling and hydraulic fracturing. Here's how it goes: The first crew comes in and prunes, hacks, and bulldozes away all trees and vegetation, then shoves the earth around to make a level spot for the drill pad and all the roadways and draining areas required. Dump trucks haul in thousands of tons of rock and gravel to form the foundation of a drill pad. The rig is then delivered and assembled, and the team drills down through maybe six or eight thousand feet of rock, well below the water table, where the richest shale deposits await.

Then the tip of the drill bit at the bottom of the hole is rotated ninety degrees, give or take, by a powerful armature so that the well bore can be extended through the rock, horizontally, for a mile or more. This gives a single horizontal well a pay zone, which constitutes the area from which oil and gas can be extracted, of more than five thousand feet—a pay zone fifty or a hundred or even five hundred times that of a traditional vertical well. And a driller can choose a number of different vectors on which to extend the well, thus increasing the pay zone even more. Or turn the drill bit to chase the promising rock formations suggested by underground 3-D imaging technologies. For safety, the length of the wellbore is cased with carbon steel pipes and poured cement, all to protect the freshwater aquifers near the surface from contamination. Because nobody wants what goes through those pipes to end up in our drinking water.

Then technicians snake perforating guns down and through the well to a desired location and set off a charge powerful enough to crack open fissures in the very new casing and the very old surrounding rock. The perforating process is followed by the injection of slickwater down through the well bore. This cocktail of water, sand, and chemicals, with a hint of gels, foams, and maybe even bean paste, is mixed and stirred on the surface and then pumped in at pressures of up to nine thousand pounds per square inch, which is about thirty times the force needed to shoot water from a fire hose to the top of a thirty-story building. Powerful enough to crack open more micro-fissures in the tight and stingy shale and loosen up all that previously impossible-to-capture oil and gas. The final steps are repeated over and over (explode and inject, rinse and repeat) along the length of the horizontal portion of the well. The process might take four or five weeks in all, and the cost is about three times that of a traditional vertical well. But once completed, after all the happy new egresses for oil and gas have been hammered and propped open, these wells produce, and for a long while. But then, there's the water, too.

In the beginning, there is the slickwater, that chemically contaminated cocktail of water-based liquid, which drillers like Chesapeake shoot by the millions of barrels deep into the ground to shake free natural gas deposits. Once the well starts producing the desired hydrocarbons, millions of barrels of water come up too. That's called flowback water, and it has all the same contaminants as the slickwater, along with additional salt deposits and something called naturally occurring radioactive material, often known by its acronym, I kid you not, NORM. Cheers! At least everyone knows its name. Much of that flowback water is brand new to the surface, having resided deep in the underground rock, undisturbed, for eons. This "produced" water is up to five times more salty than seawater and can contain chemicals, radium-226, radon-222, uranium-238, methane, and crude oil. Some of the flowback is stored in tanks and recycled for subsequent fracking ventures; some is shot through cement-encased well bores deep enough under the earth's surface so as to make it theoretically impossible to contaminate the aquifers. Some is trucked off to some other disposal site or holding tank.

But this is not an entirely closed system (what is, really?), and the various waters can sometimes get away from the operators. Soil and water tests near fracking sites often turn up an unfortunate amount of dangerous chemicals and radioactive material. And that's not awesome for a rapidly expanding industrial process, even in the abstract, but the nature of the American oil and gas business has meant that modern fracking operations are often sited uncomfortably near residences and pastureland, increasing the chances for human and animal exposure to any dangerous waters mishandled by drilling operators.

For a study called "Impacts of Gas Drilling on Human and Animal

Health," veterinarian Michelle Bamberger and professor of molecular medicine Robert Oswald documented the experience of two neighboring families just south of Pittsburgh whose homes were surrounded by twenty-five separate drilling sites. What had been visited on them in 2009 and 2010 was truly awful. Both families noted pets dropping dead two or three days after they drank from open puddles in the street. When one family's purebred boxer gave birth to fifteen pups, the entire litter was born with either complete or partial absence of fur. Seven were stillborn and the eight others were dead within a day. That family's perfectly healthy American quarter horse suffered "an acute onset of anorexia, malaise, rapid weight loss and mild incoordination." Within a week, the horse was "unable to rise" and soon had to be put down. "Blood and clinical chemistry parameters indicated acute liver failure due to toxicity," the scientists would report. "The [family's] veterinarian suspected heavy metal poisoning." Unfortunately, nobody performed a toxicology test to find out.

Their neighbors were also suffering from ongoing health issues, issues not confined to the household's animal population. One teenager in that house (identified in the study as Home B) was in the middle of a long series of bouts of fatigue, sore throats, delirium, and abdominal pains so severe he had to be treated with morphine. Yes, morphine. When the boy's pediatrician got wind of the early demise of a number of neighborhood quadrupeds, it got him to thinking. He did a toxicology test on the thirteen-year-old, David, and found the cause of the illness to be arsenic poisoning. He "gradually recovered," Bamberger and Oswald would write in their study, "after losing one year of school."

Ongoing toxicology screenings and urine tests on both families revealed exposure to the chemical benzene, which was apparently floating around in the air on their properties. The members of both families continued to suffer fatigue, headaches, nosebleeds, rashes, nausea, vomiting, diarrhea, and difficulty smelling and hearing. David, now fourteen, "also had difficulty breathing," according to the study, "and again had to be taken out of school." Drilling operations in the area, meanwhile, did not shut down, or even slow. Hey, in the quest for American energy independence, maybe a few of us have to take one for the team—line up your pets, line up your eighth graders.

Tests done in November 2010 on the springs and wells that supplied the two families with water turned up about what you'd expect. Their water was laced with ethylene glycol, propylene glycol, ethanol, butanol, and propanol, otherwise known as a set of chemical additives used in fracking fluids. Turns out there were unexpected rips and tears in the lining of a nearby operator's aboveground wastewater impoundment, which had allowed all those ugly chemicals to seep into nearby springs and wells and then into human blood systems.

To be fair, nobody—and least of all the drillers—*wanted* this to happen. Or did it on purpose. And this was the common public excuse offered up for the dozens and hundreds of similar fuckups around that time. To err is human. "If people are involved," said the king of the frackers, Aubrey McClendon himself, "accidents are going to happen. Planes crash, trucks crash, cars crash. It happens. We will have an incident or two." Okay, that definitely works for an incident or two. But the sheer volume of extraordinary happenings—one Pennsylvania woman's well exploded on New Year's Eve 2008—certainly hinted at the enormity of the industry's reckless disregard. Ineffectual wastewater impoundment liners allowed flowback water to leak into pastures and ponds. Fracking fluids dripped out of old pipes or poured out of tanks through defective valves. Truck drivers sped off from drill sites without plugging their intake valves, spewing highly poisonous water onto every road they drove down, for miles and miles.

One of the most dramatic and reckless accidents happened at a Chesapeake-owned drilling site in northwest Louisiana's Caddo Parish. From the beginning, nearby citizens complained about the usual things with regard to Chesapeake's operations in Caddo Parish: the noise, the floodlights on the drill pads that were often on all through the night, the constant parade of trucks carrying water to and from their well sites.

But then mid-afternoon on April 28, 2009, folks in the southern part of the parish, down by the town of Spring Ridge, noticed cows in serious distress in the pasture about 150 feet from a Chesapeake drill pad. Some of the cattle were already dead; others were described as "foaming at the mouth," "bleeding from the tongue," and "bellowing." They were undoubtedly in agony, so it was a small mercy that they expired quickly. All told, seventeen cows died in a matter of hours. Their only mistake, apparently, had been drinking from water puddles in their own pasture—just as they always had. A few of the local civilians were understandably incensed when they saw what was happening. One called the Louisiana Department of Environmental Quality, the state police, the local sheriff's office, and Homeland Security.

The guys from Chesapeake and its on-site operator, Schlumberger, meanwhile, were taking it all in stride. They really didn't know what was happening, they said that day. But they hadn't done *nothing*. They called the home office when they first learned the cows were dropping dead and then started collecting surface water samples. They called in the owner of the bovine decedents and suggested maybe he should fence off the offending water puddles so he didn't lose any more stock. They called in more Chesapeake personnel to "evaluate the situation" and summoned their hired environmental consultant to take more water samples for in-house study. They did not call the sheriff's office, as they were required by law to do. So they were kind of surprised when the deputies showed up in hazmat suits and took charge of the scene. It was around nine o'clock that night when they finally got around to calling the Department of Environmental Quality's Hotline service to report a "potential release" of hazardous fluids. Locals didn't think there was anything "potential" about it. Two claimed to have seen a yellowish-green substance spewing into the air at the drill site. Kind of smelled like antifreeze. But Louisiana DEQ regional manager, Otis Randle, who was running the test on the nearby groundwater the next day, said he didn't see yellow or green. "What we ran into today was milky white in color," he told reporters from the local Shreveport *Times*. If only someone had turned up with some Pantone color chips.

More than twenty-four hours after the spill, according to *The Times*, Chesapeake and Schlumberger were still maintaining that they had no evidence of a chemical release at the drill site. "Nobody is owning up to it," said Randle.

News of the episode in Caddo Parish might have made it up the chain to Chesapeake's CEO, Aubrey McClendon. He wasn't hard to reach, even when he was in Bermuda with the corporate jet. But Aubrey kept mum. In fact, it was almost two months before anybody from Chesapeake owned up to a spill. "During a routine well stimulation/ formation fracturing operation by Schlumberger for Chesapeake, it was observed that a portion of the mixed 'frac' fluids, composed of over 99 percent freshwater, leaked from vessels and/or piping onto the well pad," a company spokesman wrote in a belated report filed with the State of Louisiana seven weeks after the bovine die-off. The company's own study of the water and soil in question concluded that after the leak some of Schlumberger's "products" had probably hopped a ride in recent storm water runoff into the adjacent pasture. Blame it on the rain.

The operators had not initially reported the spill, Chesapeake claimed, because it was too small to meet the definition of a "reportable quantity" under state and federal law. And remember, after all, this was 99 percent freshwater. But think about that claim for a second. If it's true—and who's to say that it's not—it's the kind of thing that might reasonably keep you up at night, if you lived anywhere near Caddo Parish. The 99 percent argument would mean the other 1 percent—the 1 percent that the drillers are not required to disclose to the public— must be pretty freaking toxic if it was enough to kill off seventeen healthy fifteen-hundred-pound beings in a matter of hours, or even minutes, after ingestion. This was decidedly not the "natural and organic" "people-pleasing environment" "eco-friendly" vibe Aubrey McClendon wanted to project with that new green swoosh in the logo.

Aubrey had to know what was coming in the fall of 2010, when he agreed to sit down with Lesley Stahl for a long segment about fracking on television's popular investigative news program *60 Minutes*. But he was sure he had a story to tell, or sell. These new technologies weren't perfect. And they were, after all, merely instruments in the hands of fallible human beings. But horizontal drilling and hydraulic fracturing had made the United States of America the world leader in the production of natural gas, which he still insisted was the cleanest bridge to a renewable energy future. Were we really going to screw that up, just because of a bunch of Nervous Nelly negative press coverage? CEO McClendon came out of the gate with a flourish on the show. "In the last few years, we've discovered the equivalent of two Saudi Arabias of oil in the form of natural gas in the United States," he told Stahl. "Not one, but two." He used his fingers to do the count, to make sure it registered.

"Wait," Stahl asked, "we have twice as much natural gas in this country, is what you're saying, than they have oil in Saudi Arabia?"

"I'm trying to very clearly say exactly that."

The 60 Minutes report was an on-the-one-hand-on-the-other-hand dance. The fracking boom was creating fabulous wealth. But the gargantuan drill sites, the noise, the tumult, the dangerous chemically laced frackwater, were wreaking havoc on local populations. But the actual fracking was happening miles underground, safely below the aquifers that supply our water. But the industry had already proven itself "cavalier" and "irresponsible." Just look at the Deepwater Horizon debacle. Drill pads were now right next door to homes and farms. And the industry's accidents and outright regulatory violations were piling up—into the thousands.

"Part of the fracturing process involves you pouring down some pretty nasty chemicals," Stahl put it to McClendon. "What happens if they spill all over the place?"

"Okay, let's define nasty chemicals," Aubrey countered. "Nasty chemicals are underneath your sink. The reality is, you don't drink Drano for a reason, but you have Drano in your house. If you want to define them as nasty, go ahead."

Stahl cut him off. "There are nasty chemicals that affect your liver, that cause cancer, that shut down your system."

"You don't want to drink frack fluid," McClendon answered. "If you take away nothing from this interview . . ."

Okay, America. Note to self: Do not drink frack fluid. Good advice. Someone tell the cows. And the neighbors.

Stahl ended up giving Aubrey what amounted to the final word. "If you use natural gas, America can establish independence from OPEC and can put Americans back to work," he said, as always, exceedingly patriotic. "We can lower our carbon emissions, and we can begin to improve the economy as well by not exporting a billion dollars a day of American wealth. The greatest wealth transfer in human history takes place every day. And it doesn't have to."

Interesting side note. At the moment the 60 Minutes segment was airing, toxic wastewater was cascading out of a valve that had been left open on a twenty-one-thousand-gallon storage tank at a drilling site outside a nondescript and out-of-the-way little township in north-central Pennsylvania. The tank—connected by pipe to five other tanks—was owned by ExxonMobil/XTO, which had already earned a place in the top-ten safety violators among drillers in Pennsylvania, averaging near one violation per well. This XTO-owned leaking waste-water, which contained many of the requisite dangerous fracking substances (chloride, bromide, barium, and the always notable strontium, which has a habit of leeching calcium from healthy human bones, making them not healthy at all), was seeping into a freshwater spring and a nearby tributary of Sugar Run Creek. And had been for a while. The tank had been leaking, undiscovered, for a month or more. Thousands of gallons of sick-making liquid, and more to come. Nobody from the company seemed to be paying attention, and no one was making them pay attention, either. At the time, see, the Pennsylvania Department of Environmental Protection had only thirty-seven inspectors available to monitor 64,939 active wells. That's less than one inspector for every 1,750 wells, so there was no telling when somebody would finally notice that one open valve, and shut off the toxic flow.

TWELVE

ULTRAHAZARDOUS ACTIVITY

O N SEPTEMBER 21, 2011, A CONSTRUCTION CRANE HOISTED A pine tree and an American flag high above downtown Oklahoma City. This was a topping-out ceremony, a tradition in the building trades. Hundreds of construction workers and hundreds more onlookers watched as the evergreen ascended 845 feet, up beyond the floors where the crews had already attached the glass skin to the rising fifty-story Devon Energy Center. "This is not just a building for Devon," the company's CEO, Larry Nichols, told the construction workers that day. "You are transforming the landscape of a city." The Devon structure was the tallest building in Oklahoma City by far, 345 feet taller than the runner-up, Chase Tower. Devon's new tower dwarfed the handsome art deco skyscrapers built in the 1930s, during Oklahoma City's first big boom, and it dwarfed the brutalist concrete-happy cubes that rose in the postwar oil boom, too. Devon's sleek new corporate headquarters was thoroughly modern and built in no small part on the foundation of Barnett Shale.

Like Aubrey's Chesapeake, Devon Energy was crushing it in 2011. Reports of poisoned water, dead cattle, sickened schoolchildren, and earthquake swarms aside, the shale gas revolution was a juggernaut.

Devon still claimed the lion's share of the gas wells in the Barnett, thank you, George P. Mitchell, and that field was roaring. Production of natural gas there had increased from around 100 million cubic feet per day to more than 3 billion per day. The number of wells had jumped from about three thousand back when Devon acquired Mitchell Energy to more than fourteen thousand. That one field—the Barnett—was producing nearly 10 percent of the nation's burgeoning natural gas supply; drillers had already sucked more than 10 trillion cubic feet from the ground. But the innovations built to slurp gas out of Barnett Shale turned out to work on shale everywhere; the combination of horizontal drilling and slickwater fracking had unlocked previously trapped fortunes all over the country. Turns out there was plenty of shale gas (and shale oil) to be got in North Dakota and Pennsylvania and New York and West Virginia and Louisiana and Arkansas and right down the road from the Devon Energy Center in Oklahoma, if you were willing to spend the money. And it had seemed worth it to spend the money; the first few years of the twenty-first century saw all-time-high market prices for natural gas.

When the lead dog in the American energy sector, ExxonMobil, abandoned its previous diffidence and finally decided to go all in on gas in the middle of 2011, Wall Street stood and applauded. The day Exxon announced a deal to increase its lease holdings in the Marcellus Shale in New York, Pennsylvania, and West Virginia to more than 300,000 acres, its stock price popped a full percent, completing a rise of 32 percent in the year since it had acquired the natural gas producer XTO.

More wells were being fracked in the United States than ever before in 2011, and almost six in ten new wells were horizontal. It had been less than one in ten a decade earlier. America muscled past Russia to become the largest producer of natural gas in the world, and the timing couldn't have been better. The Wall Street–induced Great Recession had thrown the American economy into free fall, but the fracking-driven energy boom was like an unexpected net appearing underneath a doomed trapeze artist, mid-tragedy. Renewable energy might turn out to be an important legacy for Obama and Biden in the long run . . . but in the short run, the shale gas revolution was crucial.

In 2011, the energy experts at a respectable nonprofit organization called the Potential Gas Committee positively kvelled over the spectacular domestic natural gas production data. The committee's experts, backed by research from the Colorado School of Mines, figured there was a total available future supply of 2,170 trillion cubic feet of natural gas under American soil, which would last ... well, as long as we wanted it to last. What's a thousand trillion, anyway? Let alone two of them? Somebody in the Obama administration glommed on to that good-news report and tucked it into drafts of the president's final State of the Union address before his reelection effort in 2012. "This country needs an all-out, all-of-the-above strategy that develops every available source of American energy," Barack Obama told an applauding Congress, Democrats *and* Republicans. "We have a supply of natural gas that can last America nearly 100 years. And my administration will take every possible action to safely develop this energy."

Safely. That was the issue. "Can [shale gas] be produced safely, while protecting water supplies and the environment?" read a print ad ExxonMobil placed in big-city newspapers and national magazines ahead of all those State of the Union standing ovations. "The answer is yes. . . . Detailed procedures are used to manage air quality and to reuse or responsibly dispose of water. We are continuing to work with the industry to develop best practices for the safe handling of produced water." *Best practices:* by this point, a phrase to send a shiver down your spine. Many of the fifteen million Americans who lived within a mile of a fracked well knew up close and personal that sometimes "best" wasn't even all that good when it came to the industry's practices. The oceans of hazardous industry-made slickwater, flowback water, and production water weren't just sloshing in and out of America's subterranean depths; they were doing real damage to people living on the surface. Folks in Bradford County, Pennsylvania, were just then suffering through another blunder by Aubrey McClendon's Chesapeake, after an equipment failure during a drilling operation caused about ten thousand gallons of fracking fluid to spew unchecked. At least the Chesapeake team sounded the alarm on this one. Seven nearby families were immediately evacuated from the area as the slickwater seeped into nearby pastureland and a small farm pond and then into a tributary of Towanda Creek, which had been a fine place to fish for trout, right up until that afternoon.

Later tests exposed dangerous levels of contamination in a number of residential water wells. One unfortunate homeowner got a letter from Pennsylvania's woefully understaffed Department of Environmental Protection, dated June 28, 2011, ten weeks after the spill. "The analytical data collected by the Department reveals that several compounds were found above the Department's drinking water standards," it read. "Strontium was found at 14.2 [parts per million] and the EPA health advisory level is 4 ppm." The DEP recommended the homeowner's water "be treated prior to consumption." Prior to consumption . . . ten weeks earlier, when the spill had happened. Time machine not included.

Seems unlikely that the residents of Bradford County apprehended this latest release of Chesapeake fracking fluid as a rarity or took much solace from ExxonMobil's national advertising blitz. Especially not given the recent statistics in their own neighborhood, where drillers had rung up an average of three safety violations for every four wells drilled in the previous year.

And how about Chesapeake's CEO, Aubrey McClendon, was he suitably abashed? He was not. His guys hadn't even killed any cows this time. Aubrey still insisted fracking, done right, was "100 percent" safe. He still insisted that his drillers properly cased and cemented their wells and properly disposed of flowback water. He still insisted the industry could police itself and trumpeted dire warnings about the effects of adding new safety standards. "Overreaching federal regulations can also be used to simply create roadblocks to development," he told a friendly writer from *Forbes* magazine a few months after the Bradford County spill. "More roadblocks to develop natural gas simply mean higher natural gas prices and more imported oil and more coal burned, all of which have very negative impacts on the American people. What is our critics' plan for addressing those outcomes? The reality is they don't have a plan. They are just modern day Luddites. In the future, we will simply continue doing what we are doing today, which is constantly improving and perfecting our techniques throughout the industry. By relentlessly pursuing best practices across the industry, we'll continuously improve all that we do." Best practices.

Except that the industry did not relentlessly pursue improved "best practices" concerning safety, ever. Even old George Mitchell, who had become known as the Father of Modern Fracking, could see that. Mitchell joined with the former New York mayor and current environmentalist Michael Bloomberg to make a public plea for increased regulation in the summer of 2012. "The rapid expansion of fracking has invited legitimate concerns about its impact on water, air and climate," Mitchell and Bloomberg wrote. "Concerns that industry has attempted to gloss over." Privately, according to the *New Yorker* writer Lawrence Wright, Mitchell was less diplomatic. "These damn cowboys will wreck the world in order to get an extra one per cent" of profit, Mitchell told one of his sons-in-law. "You got to sit on 'em."

Having spent sixty years in the business, Mitchell well understood the chief imperative of the oil and gas industry. There was no great mystery to it: extract valuable parts of the earth *from* the earth, and sell it for private profit—as much private profit as possible. John D. Rockefeller's manic insistence on keeping costs at a minimum remains the overriding ethic of modern fossil fuel producers. Which means they care a lot about how efficiently they can get the most product out of the ground but not necessarily about what they leave behind. Dead cows, dead quarter horses, stillborn puppies, and human beings imbibing radioactive effluent or suffering nosebleeds, vomiting, diarrhea, and difficulty seeing, hearing, or breathing may be unhappy outcomes, but they're not a core issue for the core business. Minimizing damage done to the environment and the local human population has never been a critical variable in the oil and gas equation. Historically speaking, in America as in the rest of the world, it's proven more cost-effective for oil and gas drillers to grease the political classes with cash and favors in order to persuade them to let producers escape the hard work of minimizing that damage. The submission of government officials has kept the cost of complying with health and safety regulations comfortably low. Very little has been asked of the oil and gas industry, and very little expected. It's no great wonder that BP's feckless attempt at controlling and cleaning up the largest oil spill in the history of mankind depended largely on paper towels. Why would it be better prepared? These *were* "best practices," according to the industry. The public officials whose job it is to safeguard the general health and welfare of all of us didn't demand anything more.

Stands to reason, then, that the sudden ubiquity of fracking in the first decade of the twenty-first century occasioned no equivalent leap in safety demands from federal, state, or local governments. And consequently, safety occasioned no great concern on the part of the operators, even as fracking operations and drill sites spread out into communities large and small, all over the country. Heedlessness, like business operations, proved scalable. Drilling teams in DeSoto Parish, Louisiana, sparked an explosion that reportedly caused gas, sand, and frack fluid to shoot a thousand feet in the air, killed one worker on the rig, and required the evacuation of everybody within two miles. Operators from North Dakota to Pennsylvania to Texas to Louisiana hired waste disposal flunkies who left spigots open on their trucks and dumped poisonous wastewater onto highways, or tossed radioactive "filter socks" into landfills, Indian reservations, municipal garbage cans, abandoned gas stations, and open ditches alongside state highways or county roads. And why not? Who was going to sit on 'em?

"Best practices" is industry speak that's meant to imply persistent improvement. But things only improve over time if there's pressure—and in business, it's always economic pressure—to actually get better. In the oil and gas business, the only real economic pressure over time has been to increase production and reduce costs. The capacity to clean stuff up when it goes wrong or to stop bad environmental and health consequences downstream has been a more esoteric matter. Just look at the pace of innovation in the industry when it comes to drilling and producing more oil and more gas from ever more dangerous places, compared with its innovation on cleanup. Bottled water, paper towels, stray boom here and there—a 1967 oil and gas environmental disaster looks exactly like a 2019 oil and gas environmental disaster for a reason. The only difference is that now everyone signs more waivers of their rights.

And, honestly, when the industry *did* do everything right—*according to best practices*—there were even bigger problems to deal with. Even when everything went right, it went wrong.

To hear Austin Holland tell it, it was not a big surprise when his cell phone started ringing a little after two o'clock in the morning of November 5, 2011. Almost two years on the job, and life wasn't getting any easier for the head seismologist at the Oklahoma Geological Survey. Holland was working as much as eighty hours a week then, trying to keep up with the cascade of data from the cascade of seismic events in Oklahoma. The state was on track for sixty, maybe seventy, magnitude 3.0 or greater earthquakes that year, almost double the already incredible number in 2010. And it seemed to Holland as if they all occurred on the weekend or in the middle of the night. So it figured there was a reporter calling him at two o'clock in the morning on November 5. Actually it was reporter after reporter after reporter. They all wanted a comment on the new earthquake out in Prague, fifty miles due east of that little pine tree planted atop the Devon Energy Center. Holland got out of bed and drove straight over to his office on the University of Oklahoma campus, where he could field calls and do his work without disturbing his wife's sleep. The "Ask a Seismologist" button on the OGS website was still lit up at dawn, with desperate entreaties from folks in and around Prague. "That may have been an ill-informed button," Holland later said, drily.

By the middle of the morning, the head seismologist had left his office and taken the sixty-mile drive over to the epicenter of what had been a magnitude 4.8 earthquake, nearly one hundred times the size of a magnitude 3.0 event. Holland stayed busy in Prague supervising the installation of portable seismic monitoring equipment needed to measure aftershocks, and having a look at the damage done to buildings and homes. "There [was] a really impressive shearing of a chimney at one residence where we ended up putting a seismic station where basically the entire top of the chimney was detached from the base of the chimney, and it was only being held by the stovepipe," he still remembered, more than five years later.

Holland was back home just before eleven o'clock that night, bone tired from the excitement and activity of the day, when he felt a new rumble. This was followed by another round of media calls, more urgent than the night before. The number of "Ask the Seismologist" clicks was off the charts. Turns out the magnitude 4.8 earthquake in Prague had just been a foreshock. The town was hit, only twenty-one hours later, by an earthquake twenty times stronger. At magnitude 5.7, it registered as the most powerful earthquake ever recorded in Oklahoma, stronger even than the seismic pop caused by the explosion of that forty-three-kiloton nuclear bomb under Rulison, Colorado. More than sixty thousand people, in fourteen different states, reported in to the U.S. Geological Survey's "Did You Feel It?" website. Yes, they did feel the Prague quake—as far away as St. Louis and Dallas and Milwaukee.

In Prague itself, Lincoln County's emergency manager spent the night assessing damage in the dark. He could make out a boulder that had rolled onto one roadway, buckling in three separate sections of Highway 62, a number of cracked foundations, and a chimney or two collapsed into rubble. "It was," the emergency manager told reporters, "a pretty ornery little earthquake." There was more than a million dollars' worth of property damage, all told, including the collapse of a turret on a building twenty miles from the epicenter. More than thirty aftershocks rippled through Lincoln County in the next ten hours, ten of them greater than magnitude 3.0.

Austin Holland had a pretty clear notion about a likely cause of the single most powerful earthquake in Oklahoma history. Oil and gas frackers in the state were pumping, month after month, fifty million barrels of flowback water thousands of feet underground into permanent disposal wells, increasing pressure and stress near ancient fault lines. "That pressure acts as a lubricant," Holland explained, but only years later. "It's not actually the water itself, but the pressure, and the best way to think about that is an air hockey table" and the way those pucks and paddles slide around and smack into each other more easily when the air is blowing than when the table is unplugged. The big magnitude 5.7 boomer had occurred in the vicinity of the Wilzetta fault, and as seismic monitors would soon show, the tip of the initial rupture plane was within 650 feet of an active injection well. There were another 180 active injection wells in that one Oklahoma county.

Humans had already proven themselves capable of inducing seismicity, and it didn't require a nuclear blast. Back in the 1960s, technicians at the Rocky Mountain Arsenal chemical weapons manufacturing center thought they had come up with a novel hazmat disposal system: over the course of five years, they had simply injected 165 million gallons of hazardous liquid waste deep underground. That genius move triggered a seismic swarm topped off by a 5.3-magnitude earthquake near Denver. The weaponeers halted the injections immediately. "The U.S. Army Corps of Engineers and the U.S. Geological Survey (USGS) determined that a deep, hazardous waste disposal well at the Rocky Mountain Arsenal was causing significant seismic events in the vicinity of Denver, Colorado," was the very tardy admission embedded in an Environmental Protection Agency study a quarter century later.

Holland did not bring up the Rocky Mountain Arsenal debacle in his public statements in the aftermath of the Prague earthquake. He remained, as always, honor-bound by the requirements of good science. He would not speculate about a specific event without hard facts. "We know that this is an old fault, now reactivated, interacting with the North American plate and generating pressure," he told reporters. "What we can do is use and learn from these instruments so we can make decisions for the future." Oklahoma's head seismologist didn't yet have the data to *prove* the cause of the Prague earthquake swarm was wastewater injection. And he wasn't even sure if his duties included the issuance of public warnings. "The primary role of the Oklahoma Geological Survey was to help the state understand its natural resources and appropriately exploit those natural resources," Holland explained in a sworn deposition for a civil suit concerning the Prague earthquakes. The OGS "has nothing about protecting the population of Oklahoma in its mission statement—well, I guess maybe loosely."

There does appear to be some leeway in the state constitution's vaguely worded charter of the Oklahoma Geological Survey. But "consideration of such other scientific and economic questions as, in the judgment of the Survey shall be deemed of value to the people" was a phrase that offered little real guidance. And a lot of political and legal cover for public officials who chose to look the other way. Holland's state overseers were not keen to cross swords with the real powers in Oklahoma, which were oil- and gas-producing titans like Aubrey McClendon at Chesapeake and Larry Nichols at Devon and Harold Hamm at Continental Resources.

And so, in March 2013, Austin Holland's bosses at OGS produced an official statement on the state's recent, destructive, and unprecedented earthquake activity: "The interpretation that best fits current data is that the Prague Earthquake Sequence was the result of natural causes."

Austin Holland knew better. "It's given me heartburn ever since this statement was made," he later admitted. It's true that Holland, at that time, was unable to say for certain what was the cause of the largest earthquake in the history of the state. He was still gathering data. But he did know by then that the chances of the earthquake being "naturally occurring"—as the statement said—were very small. He at least knew for sure that that interpretation most definitely did *not* fit current data.

There would come a time when Austin Holland would no longer hold his tongue about the dangers posed by the best practices of the fracking industry. "So like if you're handling explosives," he explained several years later, when he was no longer in Oklahoma. "Now most of the time when people are handling explosives, nothing happens. Right? But there's a chance that something can go wrong, and it carries extra risk. And I think the scientific community would agree that wastewater injection deep within the earth . . . is an ultrahazardous activity. Because you can't control the risk."

THIRTEEN

A SIGNIFICANT STRATEGIC STEP

LOOKING DOWN FROM ABOVE, AS ONE APPROACHED THE CITY OF Sochi by air at the end of the summer of 2011, a bright new future appeared to be a-sparkle. Sleek new structures were shimmering into view on the eastern edge of the Black Sea as the Russian Federation geared up to host the next Winter Olympics. The sun glinted off glass panels being fastened into place on the outside of the Iceberg Skating Palace, the Adler Arena speed-skating venue, and the Bolshoy Ice Dome. It lit the new steel frame of the forty-five-thousand-seat state-of-the-art stadium under construction. Winning the rights to host the 2014 Games had been, in itself, a major feather in the federation's *ushanka*. (Assuming a fur cap can sport a feather.) The victory represented a momentous step in Russia's fitful post-Soviet reentry onto the international stage. Russia's political leaders meant to use the opportunity to remind the world of their country's long history as a cultural and commercial power—and to prove that its cultural and commercial future was just as sparkly. The Russian economy was growing at more than 4 percent a year in August 2011, thanks in no small part to an acceleration in foreign investment. Ninety billion dollars of new foreign money had flowed into the country in the previous month alone, triple what it had been that same month a year earlier. And the greatest boast the Russians could make at the end of that summer was that the single most profitable private company in the

West wanted a piece of the action. The Russian government had chosen Sochi as the optimal spot to make this happy fact known to the world.

Rex Tillerson, CEO of that exalted Western corporate behemoth, was alert to the Russian leadership's keen desire for recognition and celebration, so he made a point to be there personally in Sochi on August 30, 2011. Loyalty and friendship were the coins of the Russian realm. So Tillerson clearly understood his presence at the ceremony announcing a spectacular and unprecedented new partnership between the biggest oil company in America and the biggest oil company in Russia would generate a nice little fund of goodwill. And Tillerson reckoned he would have to bank a lot of goodwill to keep this unlikely deal on track for the years—decades, actually—it would take to reap the biggest possible rewards. There was a lot of risk in this deal; Tillerson's trip to Sochi was all about risk management.

CEO Tillerson could afford to take some big chances in the middle of 2011. He had a lot of irons in the fire for ExxonMobil just then, and most of them were hot. Industry analysts heralded "a return toward the boom days that preceded the financial collapse in 2008." By almost any measure in 2011, the company was outperforming every other non-state-run oil and gas producer on the planet. Tillerson and team had just reported a free and clear take of $21.3 billion in the first half of 2011, which put them within reach of the all-time world record for annual corporate profits. ExxonMobil stock had risen 45 percent in thirteen months, nearly double the rise in the stock exchange indexes *and* crude oil prices. The corporation's oil production numbers were up 10 percent in a single year, and its production of natural gas was up almost 25 percent. The management team had expanded ExxonMobil's footprint all over the United States, buying access to millions of acres of shale gas deposits in Pennsylvania, in Arkansas, in Louisiana, and at shale gas ground zero, the Barnett formation in Texas, whose bounty spread right to the doorstep of ExxonMobil's corporate headquarters in Irving. Add to that, Tillerson's engineers had recently won the trust of the Regulation and Enforcement department of the Bureau of Ocean Energy Management, which had just approved ExxonMobil's application to restart drilling operations in the Gulf of Mexico. The BOEMRE bosses were happy to discover that the ExxonMobil proposal "complies with the rigorous new safety standards implemented in the wake of Deepwater Horizon."

Even so, domestic production was but a small trickle in the great ExxonMobil oil and gas flood. Team Tillerson was on the prowl all over the world, and not just where they had a long history of work—like Qatar and the Gulf of Guinea off the western coast of Africa. The company had announced the discovery of a new oil field in the East Java province of Indonesia; negotiated a deal with a Chinese company to "jointly assess shale gas potential" in Sichuan province; and fracked its first shale gas wells in Poland, a country that promised more recoverable shale gas than any other sovereignty in Europe.

But all of that glorious news paled against the gleaming possibilities that presented themselves in Russia. No other spot on earth could equal the allure of Eurasia's hydrocarbon honeypot. The actual quantity of oil and gas beneath Russian soil was a closely held state secret, but what was known tantalized oil and gas execs around the world. Russia already produced close to 15 percent of the world's oil, and that was with the same rusty technologies employed by Soviet-era drillers. There were reliable reports that Russia held more natural gas underground than any other country on earth—as much as a quarter of the entire world supply. But it was hard to know for sure how much oil and gas might be sequestered deep in the tight shale formations of western Siberia, or how much might be just offshore, on the continental shelf—on the edge of the Black Sea to the south, or the Sea of Okhotsk to the east, or most intriguing of all, in the Kara Sea to the north, in the Arctic Ocean.

ExxonMobil's soon-to-be partner, Rosneft, the state-controlled oil company that owned the rights to drill the Russian continental shelf, had concluded that there were at least 36 billion barrels of oil in the Kara Sea alone. Add in the natural gas there, and the number rose to 110 billion barrels of oil equivalents. That was a potential game changer for Tillerson—quadruple the amount of ExxonMobil's current reserves, *worldwide*. So it didn't take a genius to know the trip to Sochi to massage the fragile Russian ego was a must.

. . .

State-controlled Russian television cameras were on hand in Sochi to record the signing of the new strategic alliance between ExxonMobil and Rosneft. The agreement, which called for an immediate investment of $3.2 billion to develop the oil and gas in the Kara Sea, was heralded as a partnership of equals, each of whom brought something of real value to the table. Rosneft offered its "unique resource base" (all that oil and gas off Russia's Arctic coast) and ExxonMobil its "unique technology" (a track record of at least trying to tackle the obstacles of offshore drilling in the Arctic). One Russian official in Sochi complimented Exxon on the fact that its platforms in Canada "can sustain an impact from a one-ton iceberg."

When Tillerson spoke for ExxonMobil at the signing ceremony, his flat, Texas-twang corporate-speak belied his actual and very real enthusiasm. "This large-scale partnership represents a significant strategic step," he droned. "This agreement takes our relationship to a new level and will create substantial value for both companies." The most compelling spokesman on the Russian side was not a Rosneft executive but a Russian government official. Vladimir Putin, prime minister of the Russian Federation, as well as its former and soon-to-be-again president, did not hide his enthusiasm for this new partnership. He showed particular pride in the fact that the deal gave Rosneft a stake in ExxonMobil wells working the Gulf of Mexico and Canada, and promised enormous amounts of money for further exploration and drilling projects in Russia. He expected the first $3.2 billion to be a minuscule percentage of future spending. "Including funding for development, infrastructure and new construction, the amount of investment could reach 500 billion dollars," Putin said, and then paused for a moment to let that sink in. "The scale of the investment is very large. It's scary to utter such huge figures." When have you ever heard Putin describe something—anything—as "scary"?

Putin's closing remarks were music to Rex Tillerson's ears and signaled that all his hard work over the previous months on this deal was already paying dividends. Tillerson had been in talks with one of Putin's key consiglieri, Igor Sechin, who had been not only Putin's handpicked head of the government's energy policy but also Putin's handpicked chairman of the board of Rosneft. What Tillerson needed most from Sechin was an assurance that the Russian government would reward ExxonMobil's expertise and its investment by applying a de minimis tax burden to its profits and a de minimis regulatory regime to its operations. That important request—it seemed to Tillerson that day in Sochi—had been received on high. "The Russian government," Putin said, "will support your efforts to ensure the success of your business in Russia." Those words portended many happy days to come for Tillerson and suggested the twenty-hour flight to the resort town on the Black Sea had been well worth the effort.

There were still plenty of details to work out, but the partnership agreement with Rosneft put Tillerson within reach of a bounty he had been chasing for more than fifteen years. While George Mitchell and his engineers were trying to unlock the secrets of hydraulic fracturing, Tillerson had been trying to unlock the secrets of doing business (always risky) in post-Soviet Russia. By the time he showed up at Sochi in the summer of 2011, Tillerson appeared confident he was putting ExxonMobil's money on the right horse, in the right way, at the right time: he was all in on Vladimir Putin. The 2012 Russian elections were just six months away, and Putin appeared eager to shove aside his protégé and chosen presidential placeholder, Dmitry Medvedev. The oil deal celebration at Sochi was meant to send a strong signal of Putin's control to the Russian electorate, and to the rest of the world. Which it did. "Putin demonstrated he is firmly in charge and ready to remain Russia's paramount leader by securing the deal with Exxon," read a next-day analysis by Reuters.

"If ExxonMobil had tried to make the deal with Medvedev, nothing would have happened," an analyst at Russia's Center for Current Politics opined. "Even if they had got something with Medvedev, the deal could have collapsed at any time, whereas Putin will be the guarantor." If anybody had doubts about that, some breaking news in Moscow quickly became a powerful piece of corroborating evidence. The day after the deal was signed—that very next morning—armed Russian bailiffs executed a raid on the Moscow offices of ExxonMobil's rival BP, which had been relying perhaps too heavily on the wrong horses in Russia to help it complete its own partnership deal with Rosneft. The Russian authorities peremptorily ordered all employees out of the BP offices and gathered up evidence to be used in an 87-billion-ruble lawsuit filed by supposedly disgruntled Kremlin-friendly TNK-BP stake-holders.

The raid was the sort of strong-arm tactic much in vogue in Vladimir Putin's Russia, and not particularly surprising to Westerners doing business there. In fact, it is a testament to the powerful enticement of Russia's oil and gas reserves that BP still even had offices and employees in Moscow in 2011. The company's highest-ranking executive in the city—Bob Dudley—had been compelled to flee Russia three years earlier, following months of menacing personal harassment and legal threats. Internal State Department cables later published by WikiLeaks showed that U.S. officials feared for his safety at the time and felt they couldn't guarantee his protection. There were even credible reports, which Dudley still refuses to confirm, that he was being slowly, progressively poisoned in Moscow. But according to BP's chief antagonists in Russia, the British oil major had only itself to blame. "BP," one explained, "is apparently poor at analyzing political situations."

Rex Tillerson had been "analyzing" the action in Russia for a long time by then, since way back in 1997, when he was the corporate vice president put in charge of Exxon's fledgling business in Russia. Tillerson's read, by the summer of 2011, went like this: success in Russia depended almost exclusively on making nice with Vladimir Putin. Like President Teodoro Obiang in Equatorial Guinea, Putin alone had the power to make most of Exxon's dreams come true in Russia.

By the time Tillerson left Sochi in 2011 after having put his personal imprimatur on what could be the biggest deal of his life—of Putin's life, of anyone's life—he had to know that this performative international handshake was not merely ceremonial; it was the vital determinant of whether a real business partnership was possible in Russia. You get Putin's buy-in on the deal, or there is no deal, period.

Let us join our hands my dear friends. We won't get lost if we're together.

FOURTEEN

TRUST

A S REX TILLERSON FIXED HIS DESIGNS ON WHAT RUSSIA COULD
do for ExxonMobil, and what ExxonMobil could do for Russia, he knew there was at least one other Russian hand he would have to grasp to get there. That hand was connected to the very sturdy arm of the man who ruled the Russian energy industry on behalf of Vladimir Putin: Igor Ivanovich Sechin. This was not a comfortable undertaking. Sechin's firm grip of a handshake, like Sechin himself, suggested a range of contradictory inclinations: from the capacity for true friendship and loyalty, to the capability of inflicting both menace and outright injury. Sechin, just past the age of fifty, was a startling figure to behold in person: a once skinny boy, now grown plump and round in the face, with beady but piercing slate-blue eyes, a billboard-sized forehead, a prominent nose that missed being noble by a pretty wide margin, and a mouth that rested in a perpetual frown. Just as well. When Sechin did smile, he looked like a fairy-tale ogre who had just swallowed a small tasty child. By the beginning of 2012, when Tillerson's relationship with Sechin was beginning to take on international import, he could read through a decade's worth of Sechin profiles produced by journalists and government operatives in the West and in Russia and still come to no settled conclusion as to the manner of man with whom he was doing business.

The earliest reporting on Sechin began around 2000, when he stepped into the role as key deputy to newly elected President Putin.

Biographical details of the forty-year-old apparatchik were thin. The Russian media offered only vague reports of Sechin's early career as a linguist for the KGB. He specialized in French, Spanish, and Portuguese and did stints as a translator in Mozambique and Angola in the 1980s. According to a widely circulated allegation by the security firm Stratfor, Sechin's assignments were not confined to translation or to Africa. He was, Stratfor said, "the USSR's point man for weapons smuggling to much of Latin America and the Middle East." After the collapse of the Soviet Union, Sechin returned to his hometown of St. Petersburg and leaned on a network of security-minded former KGB colleagues for help in monetizing the sundry professional skills he had acquired.

He settled on a job with the former KGB hand and then deputy mayor Vladimir Putin, quickly gleaned that his new mentor prized loyalty above all else, and set to proving himself a faithful and indispensable servant. "He treated Putin as a god before Putin was a god," the head of the Russia-based National Energy Security Fund would explain. Sechin took pains to demonstrate a canine-level obedience to Putin, always doing more than what was asked of him—from carrying Putin's duffel bags and briefcase to providing muscle sufficient for his boss's personal protection. Putin and his family took note. When Putin's wife and daughter were involved in a car crash in 1993 and unable to reach Vladimir, Mrs. Putin summoned Igor Ivanovich Sechin instead. He proved himself once again.

Mrs. Putin's hubby was more or less running St. Petersburg by then and profiting enormously from his position. The deputy mayor, for one instance, cut a side deal with the city that made him and his friends the dominant gasoline suppliers in all St. Petersburg. As Putin rose in power and possessions, Sechin rose to leader of the *siloviki,* a master among Putin's myrmidons. "It's no secret," the Russian mathematician and political analyst Andrey Piontkovskiy has written, "that Putin's political philosophy and favorite concepts—managed democracy, administrative vertical, dictatorship of law, a 'control' shot to the back of the head, etc.—are close to this group."

When Putin headed off to Moscow in 1996 to work in the Yeltsin administration, Sechin accompanied his boss. "I liked Sechin," Putin wrote as a matter of obvious fact in his autobiography. "He asked to go along. I took him." Four years later, fate would have it, Sechin found himself deputy chief of staff to the president of the Russian Federation, his good friend Vladimir Putin. "I somehow unexpectedly ended up in the Kremlin," he told a reporter in a rare interview in 2010. "There is a special feeling here that this place is holy and deeply significant. There is a very good aura here."

Sechin might have been Putin's closest confidant, and his number one loyalist, but he was a nobody to the Kremlin watchers in Russia's newly free press in 2000. "When he first arrived in Moscow no one took him seriously," says the well-connected commentator Stanislav Belkovsky. Sechin used his relative anonymity to great advantage. While Putin evolved into a more public and more charismatic leader, Sechin lurked out of sight, but always nearby. Sechin acted as the president's jealous sentry and, when needed, his enthusiastic attack dog. And he did it from deep in the shadows. "During Putin's first presidential stint, the joke doing the rounds in Moscow was that Sechin didn't actually exist," a reporter from *The Guardian* wrote. "US diplomats mischievously suggested he was a sort of urban myth, a bogeyman invented by the Kremlin to instil fear." Sechin was called, at various times in his early career in Moscow, "the Gray Cardinal of the Kremlin," "Darth Vader," and simply "the scariest man on Earth." Said one former U.S. Defense Department official who specializes in Russia, "Sechin is one of the most brutal, cynical, thuggish figures in all the Kremlin. He is like Putin, only Putin can turn on the charm."

Sechin never made a peep to improve his reputation or defend his honor in those early years. He was chiefly concerned with Putin's honor, and with the Kremlin's honor, and with Russia's honor. By those measures, he judged his stint in the Russian Federation's Office of the President an incontrovertible success. When Vladimir Putin was forced to step away from the presidency in 2008 (the Russian constitution provided that nobody could serve more than two consecutive terms), Sechin and the rest of the *siloviki* took enormous pride in the fact that while in office they had rescued the motherland from Yeltsin's disastrous economic debacle. "Tumbling into the abyss, post-Soviet society grasped at the security services for support and clung to them for dear life," one of Sechin's cohorts wrote in an op-ed for a leading Moscow newspaper in 2007, near the end of Putin's second term. "We saved the country from falling over the edge. This imparts meaning to the Putin era and historical merit to the Russian president."

Sechin was counted a key player in that save. He was also an emblem of that save. The success of the Putin era as exemplified by Igor Sechin depended less on genius and wisdom than on pitiless drive and sheer grit. Throughout his eight years of service in the president's office, Sechin was often first in and last to leave. "No one else in the administration, for instance, took the time to accompany the president to the airport and meet him there on his return, but Sechin did," the Russian author Mikhail Zygar writes in *All the Kremlin's Men.* "Insiders say that Sechin is like a cyborg. He can go without sleep for days on end and works standing up; it's even said he cured himself of cancer."

Just a few years into the first term, Putin chose Sechin—a man with exactly zero experience in the oil industry—to take on a second post in addition to serving as deputy chief of staff to the president: Sechin would now also be chairman of the board of Rosneft, the largest state-controlled oil company in the most lucrative and strategic of all Russia's industrial sectors. Part of Putin's thinking in appointing his *silovik* chieftain to run the state's best remaining oil asset, according to some after-the-fact analysis in *The Economist,* was Sechin's "willingness to inflict pain on opponents." That willingness, or perhaps natural proclivity, was the guiding principle of Sechin's run at Rosneft. With an assist from all those very capable American and British and German and French bankers, he managed to devour almost every last bit of Russia's only technologically capable oil company, Yukos (pause briefly to smile, Igor). He also convinced Putin that their old nemesis, Yukos's boss, Mikhail Khodorkovsky, should rot in jail. He was well rewarded for this energetic smash-and-grab reverse privatization. In 2008, when Putin moved over to the prime minister's office to bide his time until the next presidential election, he made Sechin the deputy prime minister in charge of the energy industry for the entire country.

This promotion required some changes in Sechin's public profile. The energy sector was the most outward facing of all of Russia's commercial enterprises. So, for the first time in his career, Igor Sechin was forced into the limelight. An array of Western governments and media outlets took the opportunity to update and flesh out their Sechin entries in their always-evolving Kremlinologies. The U.S. State Department authored an extensive internal report in 2008 titled "Bringing Sechin into Focus." The preponderance of evidence from confidential informants inside Russia was not complimentary to Sechin. "Lacks a moral center . . . does not use his power for good . . . maintains a business empire protected by Putin, and run using bribes, fear and *kompromat*." One operator in the Russian oil business insisted the deputy prime minister had piled up a fortune of $14 billion while in office at the Kremlin. A former deputy energy minister posited that Sechin was in over his head in his new job: "The long-term game is not Sechin's strong suit." The same critic would later append this statement with a more evocative conclusion. Sechin's is "not a comprehensive strategy, but rather the spontaneous action of a carnivore, of a crocodile. He sees something and attacks."

But Sechin was no longer lurking as some mysterious figure in the background. He was out there now, known around the globe. *Forbes* magazine had ranked him the world's forty-second most powerful human, one place ahead of President Medvedev (pause briefly to smile, Igor). *Time* was reserving a place for him on its annual list of the world's hundred most influential people. The editors could not see the logic of placing him among the Pioneers, Leaders, Icons, or Artists. They instead listed him as a Titan, alongside the music mogul Jay-Z, the television producer Shonda Rhimes, LeBron James, the Facebook executive Sheryl Sandberg, the fashion designer Michael Kors, and the inventor/entrepreneur Elon Musk. "Among the members of Russian President Vladimir Putin's inner circle, Igor Sechin has always been known as 'the expansionist,'" his profile read. "While others have been happy skimming profits, Sechin was always about conquest." Sechin's clever and remarkably potent ace-in-the-hole method of conquest was more finely spelled out in Mikhail Zygar's *All the Kremlin's Men* than it could be in *Time:* "He immediately manages to get criminal proceedings started against any potential partner as a backup, as well as to facilitate the negotiating process."

As Sechin spent more and more time among Western financiers and oil executives—and their legions of corporate communications professionals—he started to see the value in tailoring his personal narrative. Alongside his well-earned "scariest man on Earth" rep, he started to build a counter-story—a more salubrious Igor, signs of whom began appearing in the press around 2012. It was almost enough to launch a creditable dating profile: *Igor Ivanovich Sechin. Fifty-two. Very smart. Incredibly hardworking. Exceptionally courteous. Holder of advanced degree in economics. Drink of choice: orange juice. Favorite pastime: hunting. Also enjoys making sausages out of big game animals he shoots himself, riding motorcycles, spending time on his yacht, listening to jazz. "The most important thing in jazz, as in real life, is improvisation," says Igor.* Swipe right, honey.

The updated portrait of Sechin included enough pointillist dollops that, if you squinted just right, showed a humble and soft-spoken self-made man who had not forgotten where he came from. He and his twin sister, it was reported, were raised in St. Petersburg by a single mother who worked on the line at a metals factory to make ends meet—and those ends rarely met. The fridge and the cupboards in the Sechin household were often bare. "He was interested in money and a career for money from the beginning to exit this nightmare," one of his classmates told reporters. She described Igor as a skinny and shy youth, entirely unexceptional, except in his determination to study long, hard hours to make up for his middling intelligence. Even when Sechin attained real wealth—he was reputed to make around $25 million a year as chairman of Rosneft—he didn't flaunt it. "I don't know what he would do with the money," remarked an American banker who worked on deals with Sechin. "The guy is always in the office, morning to night." Sechin was lauded for preferring the efficiencies of a crowded minibus to the luxuries of a limousine and for his small-*d* democratic tendencies. "Sechin's courtesy," read a U.S. State Department cable that was leaked at the end of 2010, "is especially evident when dealing with helpers to whom many others in Russia's elite would barely give a passing glance—doormen, drivers, guards, etc."

Turns out, Sechin was possessed of certain charms after all, if you looked hard enough for them. Leaving aside Igor's whole menace vibe, Rex Tillerson was charmed on a number of fronts. First off, clearly and unavoidably, Tillerson was charmed by the fact that Sechin was the gatekeeper to the finest semi-available oil and gas properties in the entire world. But at a personal level, Tillerson appreciated that Sechin let it be known that he respected Tillerson for his toughness and his staying power. The Texan hadn't allowed ExxonMobil to be bullied in early partnership deals in Russia as executives from Shell and BP had been. "Exxon, because they're so big, they have this swagger," a former American diplomat in Russia explained to the *New Yorker* writer Dexter Filkins years later. "They told the Russians, Fuck you. And the Russians backed off." Another Western oil executive who worked for years in Russia told Filkins, "Sechin wants to be the next Rex Tillerson. The head of the world's biggest oil company."

Most charming of all to Tillerson was Sechin's ability to pull the right levers inside the Kremlin. What Tillerson needed most was an assurance from Sechin that if ExxonMobil and Rosneft went ahead with the Arctic offshore drilling scheme in the Kara Sea, the Russian government would not get greedy and try to confiscate all the profits through taxation or trumped-up lawsuits. Sechin had already persuaded Putin to make public his promise that the Kremlin would help ExxonMobil succeed in Russia, which Putin had done that August day in Sochi. Six months later, in March 2012, Tillerson was still pushing Sechin to persuade Putin to keep taxes on ExxonMobil low and steady.

Tillerson could be pretty sure Sechin had Putin's trust, because Sechin was always diligent in making sure Putin knew he was trustworthy. Asked by a reporter from Reuters if he had any interest in running for president of the Russian Federation in 2012, Sechin at first laughed it off. "I have never heard a more interesting question," he said. "At least not from the realms of fairy tales and fantasy." But Sechin thought better of that flip answer after the interview concluded. He wanted it on the record—with no winks and no nods, no possible misinterpretation of light humor—that he would never, under any circumstances, challenge Vladimir Putin. "The question proves so sensitive," Reuters reported, "that his spokesman calls back hours later asking to suggest another response on a possible Sechin presidential candidature: 'This is not possible for objective and subjective reasons.'"

This was the sort of talk that gave a businessman like Tillerson confidence in his new friend Igor Sechin. If faithful-to-a-fault Sechin was the one making the tax case on behalf of ExxonMobil, Putin would listen. "Sechin is not just Putin's sounding board," a member of Putin's first cabinet once explained. "Sechin is part of his brain cells."

FIFTEEN

THE HANDSOME HERO

I T SEEMED ALL BUT CERTAIN THAT PUTIN WAS GOING TO BE CLIMB-
ing back into the Russian presidency at the beginning of 2012, with
the loyal and dependable Igor Sechin at his side. Putin's role in the
restoration of Russian honor—as measured by the macroeconomic
numbers, which he loved to cite—was a big factor in his reelection
campaign. The country had weathered the worldwide storm of the
Great Recession and righted itself. It looked to be headed for a spot in
the top-five world's largest national economies. The country's GDP was
growing at better than 5 percent a year again; the gargantuan foreign
debt Putin had inherited from Yeltsin had been reduced to negligible.
All the happy economic indicators were driven largely by a single industry: energy. Oil and gas, Igor Sechin was proud to say, remained
"the locomotive of the Russian economy."

Russian drillers had pushed daily production past the Soviet-era
benchmark of ten million barrels of oil for the first time ever. Russia
was exporting more oil and gas than any country except Saudi Arabia. And much of the cash take flowed right back into the Kremlin.
The two most important energy companies in Russia were once again
state owned: Sechin's crocodile act had grown Rosneft from a fourth-
rate company accounting for about 4 percent of Russia's crude production to a behemoth producing close to half of it. And that would
continue to be his modus operandi. Any Russian oil venture that
showed any technological promise or any promising assets, Igor ate it.

And so, ever-larger Rosneft, along with Gazprom—the state-owned entity that enjoyed a near monopoly in natural gas—became ATMs for the Putin government.

Now, do not think this cash windfall wafted down from the heavens and alighted upon the Russian population. While the median household in the oil exporter Norway enjoyed an income of more than $50,000, and Saudi Arabia about $25,000, the median household income in Russia was less than $12,000. Oil exporters such as Algeria, Venezuela, Qatar, Kuwait, and of course Saudi Arabia held back enough crude that their citizens at least got fuel at rock-bottom prices. Russians received no such break. And even if a Russian could afford an entire tank of full-price petrol, the state of the roads made driving dicey. A trip on any of the major thoroughfares connecting Moscow's international airport to downtown was an obstacle course of potholes, some of them, according to the writer Peter Podkopaev, "large enough to dislodge wheels from vehicles." Neither did those glorious energy export revenues fill the pockets of the minority shareholders of Rosneft and Gazprom.

But this was the game plan for oil and gas all along. Putin and Sechin had never seen the country's most valuable natural resources as a tool for swelling Russian household income or the bank accounts of their investors. The possibilities inherent in democracy and capitalism had not exactly captured the imaginations of these two modern Russian leaders. "[Sechin's] doctoral dissertation in 1998 on oil transport networks drips with contempt for market forces," *The Economist* explained in a profile of Russia's oil tsar. "Whereas market economies evaluate projects based on expected returns on investment, Mr. Sechin praised the Soviet nuclear-weapons and space programmes, which he said operated on a different principle: 'at any price necessary.'"

Putin and Sechin believed their energy industry was about restoring Russian honor, about winning prestige in the eyes of the world, à la the cosmonautical Soviet space program or the Soviet nuclear arsenal. Most of all they were convinced they could use all that Russian oil and gas, à la nuclear warheads and ICBMs, for power and leverage in advancing Putin's foreign policy aims. Russian oil and gas would be treated as the property of the president, and they could and would be weaponized to serve the president's purposes. By the time Putin was regaining the presidency in 2012, this stealth weapons program was well under way; it was mature, even. Trace it back to his first term, back in 2005, when President Putin glommed on to a new foreign policy strategy proposed by his chief economic aide titled "Energy Superpower."

Putin had seen the value in this plan right away and acted on it. At a state visit in Berlin in September 2005, he persuaded the German chancellor, Gerhard Schröder, to sign on to a partnership to build a new 750-mile pipeline under the Baltic Sea to carry Gazprom gas into Germany. Gazprom would then take large ownership stakes in the new Nord Stream pipeline and new storage facilities across Europe. The European Commission nodded in approval of Nord Stream, especially after proposals to extend the pipeline into the Netherlands, Britain, Sweden, and Finland. News of the deal came as a relief to Western Europe, where natural gas reserves were dwindling so fast there was fear they'd be entirely depleted in five years. Europeans desperately wanted and needed that plentiful Russian gas to heat their homes and run their factories.

On New Year's Day 2006, Putin offered Europe a little demonstration of just how vital was his proposed new pipeline and just how desperate things could get if it went unbuilt. That day, as the frigid season was setting in across Europe, Gazprom made sudden drastic cuts in its supply of gas into Ukraine, which at that time held the only extant pipelines from Russia into the rest of Europe. Ukraine predictably siphoned off the gas it needed from the supply transiting through its landscape into other European countries. Gas deliveries into Austria dropped by a third the next day; gas deliveries to Hungary fell by 40 percent on the day following. Slovakia, also down 40 percent, declared a national emergency. Industrial output in Bulgaria and Romania ground to a stop. While these and other European nations shivered in panic, the Russians pointed the finger at Ukraine for stealing the natural gas bound for them, and insisted Gazprom customers could not rely on Ukraine to play fair with EU-bound gas. By the time the Russians made peace with Ukraine and turned the spigot back on, the new Nord Stream (which bypassed the allegedly pilfering Ukrainians entirely) was the talk of Europe.

When Russia hosted the G8 summit in St. Petersburg six months later, Putin's government chose as its theme international energy security. Russian representatives used the summit to offer the West a deal. It ran like this: We Russians are tired of your constant carping about our human rights and free speech violations. Let's just put all that to the side and have a proper business relationship. We'll be your energy supplier. In fact, we will guarantee enough energy for every house and factory in Europe. You'll never have to worry about that again. All you have to do is pay us for the fuel and stop with the moralizing. Sounded like a pretty fair trade at the time. Much of Europe signed on the dotted line, waving away concerns that it essentially made the Continent beholden to Russia for its productivity as a region on earth.

By the time the Nord Stream project broke ground in 2010, Team Putin had proposed a second and longer pipeline, South Stream, which would carry gas from Russia across the Black Sea and then as far as Austria and Italy. As he had done with Chancellor Schröder of Germany, who became the chairman of the shareholders committee of Nord Stream after he lost his government job to Angela Merkel, Putin cut Prime Minister Silvio Berlusconi and his favorite Italian energy company into the South Stream deal. "Schroeder and Berlusconi were firmly ensconced as Putin's new friends after the fallout with [U.S. president George W.] Bush and [British prime minister Tony] Blair," Mikhail Zygar wrote in *All the Kremlin's Men*. "Putin found it so much easier to deal with these two European cynics, and the feeling was mutual." Berlusconi, in particular, was a role model for Putin according to Zygar: The Italian prime minister "had used his business empire to win elections and then used politics to further enrich his business. That made Berlusconi a natural ally of Putin's. Neither man ever criticized or found fault with the other."

Nord Stream had been on line for almost six months in March 2012, when Putin won a third presidential term. Russia was supplying the European Union 40 percent of its natural gas imports while cutting Ukraine out of the deal. Gazprom supplied every single cubic meter of imported natural gas up the line to EU members Bulgaria, Slovenia, Slovakia, Latvia, Estonia, and Finland. It supplied about a third of Germany's natural gas imports (as well as a third of its oil imports). Add to that, Russia had completed a new pipeline for pumping oil into China, the country with the fastest-growing economy and the fastest-growing energy needs on the planet. Meanwhile, construction on the South Stream project was about to commence, adding Austria and Italy to Gazprom's soon-to-be-satisfied-but-wary customers.

To discerning eyes in 2012, a map of the two pipelines transiting much of the continent appeared, as Zygar puts it, "like a pair of giant pincers with which Russia would squeeze Europe." With Gazprom as his instrument for natural gas, and Rosneft the same for oil, this was just the sort of global hydrocarbon leverage Putin had long desired. And it came just at the moment Rosneft was in the process of overtaking ExxonMobil as the world's biggest publicly traded oil company. Sechin's baby was producing more crude oil than all of China's energy companies, market analysts pointed out, and double that of Nigeria's.

"Rosneft has grown dramatically in the last ten years. Not by chance, but because Rosneft is Vladimir Putin's vehicle to reassert state ownership over a fair chunk of Russia's oil fields," *Forbes* reported just after the company choked down BP's choice Russia assets. BP ended up with a 20 percent stake in Rosneft after the strong-arm takeover of TNK-BP, which made the firm deeply and literally interested in the success of Russia's signature industry. Even BP's (maybe poisoned) Bob Dudley had been welcomed back into the fold, now that he would be pulling for Rosneft as a minority partner. "We are glad that BP has made a decision to remain one of the biggest investors in the Russian economy," Putin said, "thus admitting vast prospects of Russia's oil and gas industry and Rosneft's big potential."

So Putin's whole Energy Superpower strategy was working.

Except that it wasn't. And not just because BP was a pretty homely dance partner in the wake of the Deepwater Horizon debacle.

There were more substantial problems in 2012, and almost all of them of Putin's making. Gazprom, for instance, wasn't really able to keep up with all the new European demand, because its production capabilities, uh, sucked. It's not as if Gazprom grew big because it deserved it, or because it was good at what it did; it wasn't, at a fundamental level. The company hadn't invested in new technologies, because as a state-sanctioned monopoly propped up by the Russian government and therefore free from competition, it really hadn't needed to. "Gazprom is what one would expect of a state-owned monopoly sitting atop huge wealth—inefficient, politically driven, and corrupt," was the U.S.

State Department's assessment. Dig deep enough in the company accounting ledgers and you'd find that Gazprom lost about $40 billion a year to corruption and waste. That's a loss nearly equal to its annual profits.

Industry watchers gave Gazprom no points for having diversified its portfolio by adding a large Russian media company. A media company? Why was the state gas company buying TV stations? Well, why not? Gazprom was better understood not as an energy company but as a big battering ram President Putin used to get stuff he wanted. So yes, inefficient, money-bleeding, crappy Gazprom owned a television station and a bunch of other media properties, but only because Putin had arranged it in order to silence one of the few remaining critical voices in the Russian press. Vladimir used his security forces to arrest and to intimidate the critic who owned the media company, and then he used Gazprom as the piggy bank to buy the company at a steep jailhouse discount. Independent television journalism in Russia was thus dealt another blow, and Putin would instead have another reliable mouthpiece for the Kremlin's party line.

For pure waste, though, little in the Gazprom history measured up to the Nord Stream gambit. "We're spending money like hell," said Managing Director Matthias Warnig, an old pal of Putin's from their spy days. Nord Stream was a pipeline project that was built from both sides at once—from Russia and from Germany. Same pipeline, same materials, same building standards. But the Russian side of the construction project (led by the Rotenberg brothers of St. Petersburg, and remember them) cost three times as much, per mile of pipeline, as the German side did. That money was not going into the pension and health fund of the Russian pipe fitters' union; it went into the pockets of Putin and his pals. The founder of *Grant's Interest Rate Observer,* James Grant, sized up Gazprom and rated it, simply, "the worst managed company on the planet." Congratulations, citizens of Russia, that's the hash your government managed to make of the globe's biggest supplies of natural gas.

On the oil side, the Energy Superpower strategy posed even bigger problems. Putin had been gangstering up the Russian oil industry for years. Eschewing competition that might encourage innovation and meritocratic success, Putin instead just smashed and grabbed any homegrown enterprises that proved resourceful or entrepreneurial or attractive to legitimate investors—goodbye, Yukos. He harassed foreign interlopers, too. He invented a dubious environmental violation bill of attainder, to force Shell Oil to hand over controlling interest to Gazprom in a $20 billion project in the far east of Russia. The consequences for Russia could be overlooked when oil prices remained high, but the rotten core problem was pretty clear to anybody who was paying close attention. Like Thane Gustafson, for instance, who had just finished his book about the Russian energy industry, *Wheel of Fortune*. Putin and the Russians "have essentially been coasting on the assets inherited from the Soviet Union," Gustafson explained in talks promoting his book back in 2012. "Virtually all of Russian oil comes from fields that were already known in Soviet times. There have been very few new discoveries that are producing today. The drama of this situation is that the inheritance is now starting to run down. . . . Russian oil experts are saying to Putin, 'Mr. President, if you do not address this problem you're going to be having a decline in production after 2015.'"

The possibility of a true reckoning was all the more ominous because Russia had no other dynamic commercial enterprise to fall back on. "Russia took home only 0.2 percent of the 1.3 million overseas patents awarded since 2000 by the U.S. Patent and Trademark Office, lagging behind the state of Alabama in total annual awards," Karen Dawisha wrote in *Putin's Kleptocracy*. Oil and gas was the whole ball game in Russia; energy exports accounted for more than half of its government revenue in 2012. "We're talking about addiction," Gustafson said at the time. There was still plenty of oil and gas underfoot in Russia. But it was in the tight shale formations, or offshore in the Arctic seas, and it was going to be both difficult and expensive to get. "Bottom line is Russia is not running out of oil, but it's running out of cheap oil," explained Gustafson. "That looks pretty bleak. . . . Putin's in trouble. . . . It's curtains for Pauline. But wait. Here comes the hero. Here comes the handsome hero."

The personification of that handsome hero, a former Boy Scout and University of Texas Longhorn Marching Band drum section leader turned ExxonMobil CEO, came to call at a private residence on the outskirts of Moscow on April 16, 2012. When Igor Sechin ushered Rex Tillerson into the palatial mansion built by the Soviet leader Georgy

Malenkov, the current occupant, Vladimir Putin, greeted him as a most welcome visitor—perhaps even a savior. He was there to shake on the new details of the expanded partnership he and Igor Sechin had been working out since the promising Sochi visit seven months earlier.

Aside from being the possessor of impressive (and very valuable) technological prowess—or so it was said—Tillerson had shown himself a savvy strategist, both in business and in geopolitics. Why was Exxon (under Tillerson) welcomed with a bear hug when Shell and BP and even Exxon (before Tillerson) had all been roared at and given such a hard time? Well, for one, Tillerson was not making boneheaded Lee Raymond–esque demands about getting majority control of Rosneft; Rex made clear—in word and in deed—that he was fine with Putin staying in charge; he just wanted to be a good minority partner. He also seemed dialed in to the foreign policy game afoot in Russia. Since Tillerson's visit to Sochi the previous summer, ExxonMobil had reportedly throttled down its efforts to tap natural gas in Poland. Poland becoming its own natural gas supplier—let alone an exporter to rival Russia—was a positively disgusting idea to Putin. ExxonMobil shutting off that possibility—and indeed declaring it "not commercially viable"—was a fine hostess gift for Tillerson's Russian excursion. "ExxonMobil's failed shale-gas wells in Poland," a reporter for *Bloomberg* had written, "may hobble the nation's effort to become one of the world's major energy resources and dismantle Russia's dominance of Eastern European natural-gas markets."

Credentialed news photographers were there to record the moment Tillerson joined hands with President-elect Putin in one of the drawing rooms of the Malenkov mansion in mid-April 2012. Inauguration Day in Moscow was three weeks away. Putin wanted the world to take heed of the contours and the ambitions of the ExxonMobil-Rosneft megadeal, especially the fact that ExxonMobil was giving as well as it was getting. Rosneft received 30 percent stakes in a handful of ExxonMobil's projects in North America, from Alberta, Canada, to the Gulf of Mexico. In exchange, ExxonMobil was getting a crack at unlocking all that hard-to-get oil and gas in the tight formations in Siberia, in the Black Sea, and, most important and most difficult, in the Arctic waters of the Kara Sea. The up-front costs would be enormous. The project could be on line for more than twenty years. Total spending might well run into the hundreds of billions. But the risk seemed manageable to Tillerson. Everyone involved—everyone—understood that Putin would be in charge, indefinitely. Obiang-like. Unchallenged. And Putin would deliver on that promise to remake the federal tax structure of the Russian Federation to accommodate the desires of the oil majors. The mineral extraction tax on the Black Sea properties was to be capped at 10 percent and on the Kara Sea at just 5 percent. Most crucially, Putin offered a guarantee that this tax structure would remain in force for a minimum of fifteen years *after* the project began to produce oil and gas "on an industrial scale."

Putin stood over Tillerson's right shoulder as the Texan affixed his name to the agreement. When the ink was dry, the two men raised a glass of champagne and toasted the future. This was "an historic day for ExxonMobil and Rosneft," Tillerson told Putin.

Two days later, Tillerson and Igor Sechin took part in a videoconference to sell the deal to analysts who gathered at the St. Regis hotel in New York. Sechin was uncharacteristically rhapsodic in his presentation. The announcement of the deal alone, Sechin said, had added $7 billion to the combined value of the two companies. Points for vision! "Experts say that this project, in terms of its ambitions, exceeds sending man into outer space or flying to the moon," he crowed.

Reuters summed up the news like this: "The deal is likely to prove transformational for Exxon."

Pause briefly to smile, Rex.

SIXTEEN

THIS AIN'T NO DISCO

THE OIL AND NATURAL GAS STASHES NORTH OF THE ARCTIC CIR-cle, according to the U.S. Geological Survey's first-ever publicly available assessment of the area in 2008, "account for about 22 percent of the undiscovered, technically recoverable resources in the world. The Arctic accounts for about 13 percent of the world's undis-covered oil, 30 percent of the undiscovered natural gas, and 20 percent of the undiscovered natural gas liquids." A lot of that potential hydro-carbon haul—maybe most of it—resided in Russian territory. But it wasn't going to be easy to get, or to deliver to world markets. Not with-out a lot of help.

What the Russians brought to the oil and gas game north of the Arctic Circle in 2012 was sheer brute force. Which was much needed. Almost any maritime operation in the Arctic promised a punishing battle against the harshest nature can offer. The Northern Sea Route from Murmansk, Russia (up near the northern coast of Finland), through the Barents Sea, the Kara Sea, the East Siberian Sea, the Chuk-chi Sea, and out through the Bering Strait was navigable only a few months a year because of ice. The increasing ice melt caused by climate change was easing the way, but even in the annual midsummer-to-early-autumn thaw, passage required massive self-propelled sea plows to clear a path in places. Russia had done the hard work to solve this problem back in the last innings of the Soviet era, having started con-struction on four separate nuclear-powered icebreakers. When completed, two of the ships had not one but two nuclear reactors on board. These were ships of hulk and ingenuity—able to cut through layers of ice eight feet deep at a speed of ten knots, equipped with a superstructure that included commodious living quarters, recreation areas, and an enormous indoor winter garden for providing fresh vegetables to the crew. Anywhere. Anytime.

A quarter century later, those four Soviet-era seafaring plows were still in operation and formed the backbone of the most able and impressive fleet of icebreakers in the world. No other country had the maritime brawn to match. The U.S. government, by comparison, had constructed only two serviceable heavy icebreakers back in the 1970s. And then pretty much stopped. The U.S. Coast Guard's *Polar Star,* already well past its thirty-year life expectancy, was wheezing away on a refurbished but highly suspect electrical system; its sister ship, *Polar Sea,* was sitting lifeless at its home berth in Seattle. The *Polar Sea* had been dead towed there in 2010 after five of its six engines failed. The finest repair and modernization experts at Vigor Marine had been unable to bring her back to life. The ship's main continuing utility was in allowing its parts to be cannibalized to maybe keep the dying *Polar Star* afloat a bit longer.

Americans like to think the dueling-superpower thing ended conclusively with the Cold War, with the United States now the undisputed winner in every conceivable matchup between the two countries. But in ice water? Turns out Russia still ruled. In 2011, a tanker chartered by Russia, the *STI Heritage,* made the quickest Northern Sea Route run of that year—just eight days—with two nuclear-powered, fresh-vegetable-producing icebreakers clearing the way. Russian-escorted tankers filled with tens of thousands of tons of iron, jet fuel, and gas condensate had made the Arctic transit more than thirty times that year. The Russian Federation was already writing big checks to manufacture four even larger and more powerful icebreakers to lead the fleet. Three of them double-reactor nuclear. Which meant the Russians would be able to plow out to offshore Arctic drilling sites and to deliver crude oil and liquid natural gas from that icy domain to almost any country in the world, for years to come.

But here was the problem: despite its unrivaled ice-busting prowess, Russia didn't bring much to the actual offshore drilling operations in the frozen north. Russian companies, for instance, offered little in the way of useful drilling rigs or equipment of any kind—not even basics like subsea wellheads. In 2012, having made Russia's economy and its power in the world almost entirely dependent on oil and gas, Putin faced a serious conundrum: his ability to maintain Russia's place as an "energy superpower" depended almost entirely on availing himself of the expertise and technology of major Western oil companies. Russia had oil companies, sure, but they were gangster economy creations, and not one of them was technically or even financially competent. To do something difficult when it came to oil and gas production, Putin's pet crocodile Igor Sechin was going to be no help. It would have to be ExxonMobil. BP. Chevron. Shell.

They all wanted in, of course. The potential profits were ginormous. But success in the Russian Arctic would require overcoming two very difficult challenges. First, some Western oil major would have to figure out the proper care and feeding of Vladimir Putin, given the desperately high stakes of oil and gas for his presidency. Look at the ashes of Yukos; look at the chewed-up remains that Putin and Sechin spit out from what used to be BP's "joint venture" in the country. This was going to be a delicate thing. What Western company would be willing to put itself in service to the Russian government, in service to Putin? Whose shareholders, whose home country, would stand for it? Which executives could stomach making that kind of arrangement?

And then there was the second difficult prospect for this potential partnership. No one much liked to talk about it. But, um, were the Western oil majors actually capable of drilling up in the Arctic? They said they were, but could they really do it? Good news for President Putin in 2012, he was about to get a true measure of the West's state-of-the-art Arctic offshore drilling operation. Such as it was.

Royal Dutch Shell in particular was an operation worth watching that spring. The company owned more offshore drilling leases in the Beaufort and Chukchi Seas off the northern coast of Alaska than anyone, having paid $2.1 billion for the rights to drill there back in 2008. By the beginning of 2010, the company had invested close to $4 billion in its

Arctic exploration program and was champing at the bit to start drilling.

But as Shell's permits were wending through the final approval process that year, the epically disastrous Deepwater Horizon blowout in the Gulf of Mexico prompted Obama's Department of the Interior to hit pause on all offshore drilling applications. The president of Shell scrambled to keep hope alive. "I want to acknowledge the tragedy of the Gulf of Mexico blowout and oil spill. I commend the Department of Interior (DOI) for its role in coordinating the unprecedented joint industry-government response effort." The letter was sent to a key DOI official less than three weeks into the unfolding disaster, while tens of thousands of barrels of oil were spilling into the Gulf of Mexico each day. The spewing was just getting started, but Shell's president, Marvin E. Odum, wanted it front of mind at Interior that his company was still "committed to undertaking a safe and environmentally responsible exploration program in the Chukchi Sea and Beaufort Sea *in 2010.*" Hint, hint, tick tock. He reminded the deciders at Interior that the waters in Alaska were much shallower than in the Gulf of Mexico; that his wells in Alaska would not be drilled nearly as deep as Deepwater Horizon; that Shell would have another rig on-site to quickly drill a relief well in the case of a blowout. They'd have plenty of dispersants on hand, too, and most crucially a "pre-fabricated" and "pre-staged" containment dome in waters nearby. "We have already begun to enhance our operational excellence in light of [the Deepwater Horizon] incident and we will continuously make adjustments as new learnings are revealed."

But the prolonged drama of Deepwater Horizon—nearly five months to seal the well for good, and only after almost five million barrels of oil flooded into the Gulf of Mexico—was too much to overcome. Shell had to cool its operationally excellent jets while the 2010 and then the 2011 drilling seasons passed. Since it couldn't drill during that time, Shell focused its operational excellence instead on its paperwork, which—it must be said—was demonstrably enhanced during that time-out.

The drilling application Shell filed for the 2012 season was its finest ever. The Oil Spill Response Plan alone ran more than four hundred pages and incorporated the latest in best practices, thanks to all those Deepwater Horizon learnings. Relief wells and government-approved dispersants were all the rage. Shell had them. Containment dome was a must. Shell had it. And the Obama administration seemed to be buying what Shell was selling. Secretary of the Interior Ken Salazar noted in public statements that the seas in the Arctic drilling region were, in fact, much shallower than in the Gulf of Mexico and that he trusted Shell professionals when they said they could trap and contain all but about 10 percent of any spill. "I believe there will not be an oil spill," Salazar said in 2012. "If there is, I think the response capability is there to arrest the problem very quickly and minimize damage." Shell's capabilities, Interior insisted, had been borne out by drills, inspections, and "tabletop exercises." It was left unsaid whether these "tabletop exercises" involved scale models of the industry's only proven oil spill cleanup tool, which was still basically just paper towels.

Stands to reason that there would be some magical thinking going on in 2012. There was a president who needed reelecting, which every armchair political scientist knew would be made more difficult if American commuters and vacationers were screaming mad about the highest gasoline prices in history. Obama had hit the GOP on high gas prices, and to great effect, in the 2008 campaign season. But the high price of gas in 2012 was on Obama's watch. And in 2012, it was worse even than the previous summer's record highs. The Obama administration was careful not to invoke "Drill, baby, drill," but it was not going to be seen standing in the way of *any* new energy sources. Not in an election year. Wind, solar, the spoils of fracking, Arctic oil and gas, it was all on the tabletop. "Alaska's energy resources—onshore and offshore, conventional and renewable—hold great promise and economic opportunity for the people of Alaska and across the nation," said Salazar.

Still, the Obamanauts were cautious and kept invoking their insistence that good science rule decisions. Official permission for Shell to drill in federal waters in the Alaskan Arctic rolled out slowly in the first months of 2012 and was in no way final. There were a lot of contingencies to the approval, like making sure all the components of Shell's promised oil spill response program were available on-site. Shell bosses appeared confident they could pull it off. Hell, with crude oil prices back up over $100 a barrel, the company was actually increasing its ambitions in the Arctic. Shell filed updated plans to drill four wells in the Beaufort Sea off Alaska's remote north shore, and another six in the little-explored Chukchi Sea just west of Beaufort.

But time was of the essence. Even factoring in increasing ice melt caused by climate change, there was still a very narrow window of reasonable weather north of the Arctic Circle. Encroaching ice would close off safe operations around November 1. The Department of the Interior's newfound caution, meanwhile, narrowed Shell's window for drilling even further. The company would need to finish up drilling about five weeks before that date, Interior insisted, so that any oil spill response could be performed in open water, before the seas froze over. The Coast Guard's moribund *Polar Sea* was not going to be coming to anybody's rescue. That meant Shell had to cease drilling "into known hydrocarbon zones" by September 24. The company could noodle around out there until about Halloween, but not anywhere it might hit oil or gas. This was a race, and it loomed as an epic test of man against nature. Shell pronounced itself ready for the task.

When the first of Shell's twenty-one-vessel flotilla pulled out of Puget Sound and headed north for Alaska in the last week of June 2012, Seattle's seagoing community looked on with excitement and pride. "I think there will be huge opportunities for seafarers out here," said Carl Ellis, assistant dean of the Seattle Maritime Academy. "The industry in the Gulf is finally coming back, and we're going to see the same thing in a microcosm in the Arctic." The prized ornaments of the fleet were two fresh-painted blue and white drillships, both of which had been refurbished by the pros at Vigor. Shell could certainly have afforded to build brand-new, state-of-the-art drillships for this mighty endeavor. But it chose to go the more, shall we say, economical route. Why spend extra money to protect a $4 billion investment? In a region that might produce oil and gas for forty or fifty years? Let's go with *used*. But let's really trick 'em out. Vigor had spent nearly a year upgrading Shell's cone-shaped, 266-foot-by-230-foot *Kulluk*. The company had retrofitted all the *Kulluk*'s waste systems, for instance, to ensure that there would be exactly zero discharge of liquids from the rig into the pristine

Arctic seas. No oil, no diesel fuel, no sewage, no sink water. No nothing. "Everything down to the smallest detail is centered on protecting the environment," Vigor's senior director of ship repair said as the fleet motored away. "Ensuring safety at all levels was our primary focus." The Vigor company website boasted, "Even the blue and white paint scheme was chosen to accommodate the preferences of whales." This was news on a few fronts. Not the least that whales had color preferences. The *Kulluk* was also newly equipped with what *Marine Log* magazine called a "bird avoidance system," though it is hard to imagine how exactly this gargantuan, buoy-like rig—a propeller-less, twenty-eight-thousand-ton mobile offshore drilling unit—could make a controlled feint around an eagle or two. Still, it did sound good. Bang-up paperwork.

The second drillship in the Alaska-bound flotilla was the *Discoverer,* which Shell had contracted from the Noble Corporation. Unlike the *Kulluk,* which had to be towed north by an ice-class tugboat, the *Discoverer* cruised out to sea on its own power. The *Discoverer* was a kind of maritime version of the Little Engine That Could. Known affectionately by its 124-person crew as "the Disco," the vessel was an underdog with an unprepossessing backstory—and by nautical standards, a pretty long one. The Disco was the second-oldest drillship at sea. The vessel was built in Japan in 1966 and launched as the *Matsushiro Maru;* it began life as a bulk carrier with the unromantic duty of hauling wood from North America to Asia. Converted into a drillship in New Orleans way back in 1976, by 2010 the Disco seemed to be limping toward the salvage yard (and—spoiler alert!—it would be there soon). It did sport a handsome, newly installed main drill rig at midships that year, but everything else on board was dicey. A second mate who served briefly on the Disco in 2010 was horrified at its condition. "Parts of it below decks looked like Swiss cheese," she wrote. "NOT good!" The main engine wouldn't start, and it was so old the ship's mechanics were hard-pressed to find replacement parts. If you turned on the fire pump, it spit water into a giant maw that formed a "swimming pool" that rose from the bilge to the main deck. Nobody seemed to know exactly why, or to be much concerned about it, according to the second mate. She resigned her post after just three weeks.

But Shell had faith in the Disco. In 2011, in anticipation of its upcoming Arctic adventure, Shell dispatched the creaky, forty-five-year-old ship on a shakedown operation in the relatively calm waters off the coast of New Zealand. It shook down, all right. It just didn't shake down too good. A quick series of modest New Zealand storms that April knocked the Disco cockeyed. Its anchor lines snapped. Some of its drilling equipment dislodged and sank to the ocean floor. "The veteran drillship was so badly damaged," wrote a reporter from the *Taranaki Daily News* as he looked at the idle vessel all lit up in the waters just beyond the port, "that it will be unable to return to drilling operations any time soon." Noble and Shell kept the faith, though, and were determined to make the Disco seaworthy once again. Even Arctic seaworthy. They hired Vigor Marine to make it so. But then came the fricking superheroes.

On the day before the Disco was due to head from Taranaki to Vigor's shipyard in Seattle in February 2012, eight environmental activists—including Lucy Lawless, the actress who played Xena, Warrior Princess—managed to sneak aboard and scale the 175-foot-high drilling tower, festooning it with banners reading "Stop Shell" and "SaveTheArctic." The activists refused to come down off the tower. They had brought food enough for a week. Environmentalists, as a rule, try to eat light. Taranaki police boarded the ship to effect arrests, but the protesters told the local gendarmes they were not going anywhere. Xena and her fellow eco-warriors said they had a moral obligation to keep the Disco from its next appointment. "Deep-sea oil drilling is bad enough, but venturing into the Arctic, one of the most magical places on the planet, is going too far," Lawless told the gathered press. "I don't want my kids to grow up in a world without these extraordinary places intact."

The protesters did eventually disembark, but the to-do made the Disco almost a week late in getting to its rejuvenation berth at Vigor Marine in Seattle, at a time when every day counted. Vigor had already assembled a team of more than five hundred to hasten the upgrades necessary to make the Disco ready for drilling the Alaskan Arctic. The crew scrambled to complete its work, which would generally take six months. They got it done in just ten weeks. The ship was newly winterized, its hull reinforced to do battle with Arctic ice. The long-in-the-tooth vessel now had six engines that not only started but were equipped with twenty-foot-high catalytic converter equivalents that made the Disco's carbon emissions somewhere between negligible and nonexistent. And all the work was completed on time! "It is impossible to overstate the pride Vigor Marine teams have felt working on these critical rigs," a company spokesman reiterated as the flotilla disappeared over the horizon and churned north toward its great Arctic challenge.

The Noble *Discoverer* was clearly feeling its oats on the trip to Alaska; it left the *Kulluk* and its tugboat in its wake. On July 7, the Disco pulled in to Dutch Harbor, a little port town near the midpoint of the Aleutian Islands, which jut like a tail into the Bering Sea. Other vessels in its little fleet were still churning slowly up the North American coast, probably a week away from the Alaskan port. Shell decided to wait up for the rest of the team; it would anchor the Disco at Dutch Harbor until it was time to make the thousand-mile trip farther north, through the Bering Strait, to its drilling grounds in the Chukchi Sea. But it didn't take long for things to go wobbly. One late afternoon, a few days into the Disco's stay at Dutch Harbor, the Arctic winds kicked up to thirty-five miles per hour and got the better of the ship. "We received a report at about 5:18 p.m. that the anchor let go and they were traveling toward shore," a rather laconic Coast Guard spokeswoman later explained. The Disco reeled aimlessly and out of control for nearly half a mile that night before it ran aground on a remote little spit of land called Hog Island. When first light came up the next morning, it looked bad. But Shell got out ahead of the news and insisted the vessel had not actually grounded but "stopped very near the coast," maybe 175 yards from shore. By the next afternoon, the company had towed the drillship back to its original mooring position and a dive-team inspection confirmed that no damage was done to the hull or any other part of the ship. However, Disco pride did not escape the incident unwounded. Locals and environmentalists (they seemed to be everywhere the Disco went) had already posted online a series of morning-after photos of the worse-for-wear drillship, resting slightly atilt in the soft sand bed at what actually looked to be only about twenty feet from shore.

A week later, still in Dutch Harbor, the Disco began vomiting oily bilgewater from its holding tank into the bay, coating the waters nearby with an unsightly sheen. The Disco's storage tanks were proving unequal to the amount of effluent produced by the ship, even after the crew made secret modifications to what one regulator genteelly called its "decanting system." "Noble devised a makeshift barrel and pump system to discharge water that had entered the vessel's engine room machinery spaces directly overboard without processing it through the required pollution prevention equipment as required by law," a federal inquiry found. "Noble failed to notify the Coast Guard about this system, and took steps to actively hide the fact that it was being used." But this finding came only much later, long after Shell tied up its operations for the season. Back in July it seemed like maybe the Disco was just getting used to the choppy Alaska seas, and a little green around the gills.

Three weeks after the unfortunate *we swear we didn't run aground* incident, the Disco and the *Kulluk* and most of the rest of the Shell fleet were all still lying low in Dutch Harbor, more than a thousand miles away from the drill sites in the Beaufort and Chukchi Seas. A small commercial icebreaker and a couple of other ships were at the two sites, making early preparations, but it was becoming evident that Shell's paperwork excellence had outrun its operational excellence by a long shot. Even at that late date, the linchpin of Shell's four-hundred-plus-page Oil Spill Response Plan, the *Arctic Challenger*—tasked with hauling the dispersants and the big paper towels and the crucial and promised containment dome to Shell's Arctic drilling sites—was back in Bellingham, Washington, just north of Seattle, still on the maritime operating table. Superior Energy Services was having a hell of a time converting the ship into a certifiable, ice-class oil spill response vessel. Like the Disco, the *Arctic Challenger*—a vintage 1976 barge—had grown a bit flabby over its long life, and understandably so. It had been inactive for the previous ten years. Superior was working overtime to upgrade the ship's electrical system, its fire safety system, and its entire piping system, among other things, to gain the required Coast Guard certification.

After conferring with the Coast Guard, local reporters suggested that those prospects didn't look great: "As of August 4, about 400 items still needed to be completed, inspected or reviewed." Even as the Disco and the *Kulluk* and the tugs and icebreakers loitered in Alaska, watching the days tick by on the calendar, neither the *Challenger* nor the containment dome it was to carry was ready to take the in-water tests required before the Coast Guard could certify the ship for Arctic duty. "The opportunity to drill exploratory wells this year in Alaska's Arctic is rapidly diminishing," was the lede of a McClatchy wire story on August 14, 2012, "and it's a situation of Shell's own making, Interior Secretary Ken Salazar told reporters." Salazar, who was on a personal visit to the drill sites in the far north of Alaska, sounded a little peeved. "The waters in the Chukchi around the so-called Burger find are in fact already open," he said. "So it's not a matter of ice. It's a matter of whether or not Shell has the mechanical capability to be able to comply with the exploration effort that had been approved by the government."

When the *Challenger* did finally get out into open waters in Puget Sound a month later to show inspectors from the Bureau of Safety and Environmental Enforcement what it could do, things went from bad to worse. "During the inspection, BSEE staff observed the absence of clear lines of authority on the vessel, and the operation was beset by problems such as the tangling of a remotely-operated vehicle in the dome's rigging, a loose connection on one of the winches, and a serious miscalculation of the amount of weight attached to the dome to keep it submerged," read a later Interior Department review. "The containment dome, which had been positioned at a depth of more than 100 feet, rose rapidly through the water and breached the surface. A few minutes later, the tanks providing buoyancy to the dome vented, and the dome quickly plunged. It sank too rapidly to allow for pressure equalization, and the upper chambers of the dome were crushed." The *Challenger* would not be leaving Puget Sound that season. Its vaunted oil containment dome was now basically a stomped-on soda can. Turns out Shell had a terrific Oil Spill Response Plan—really excellent paperwork—but no way to effect it.

By the time Shell's drillships finally completed the trip from Dutch Harbor to their final Arctic destination, their mission had been greatly circumscribed. The company had received official permission to complete "top holes" only. That meant Shell could drill down about fourteen hundred feet into the seafloor, to a depth where its engineers were in no danger of actually hitting oil or gas, just to install a few preliminary well necessities, cap the hole, and leave it in place for the next season.

The Shell execs and the crew on the Disco showed a brave face to the world in spite of the setback. Shell posted a video of a Disco drill bit ready to spin down into the Arctic seabed. And this was no ordinary spin of the drill. "This marks the culmination of more than six years of effort by Shell," shouted the website on September 9, 2012. "This is the first time a drill bit has touched the sea floor in the U.S. Chukchi Sea in more than two decades." Managers on-site in the Arctic, meanwhile, were starting to shout something else. Something more like *Get the hell out of there!* An ice floe thirty miles long and ten miles wide, with a keen Arctic gale at its back, was already bearing down on the Disco. Twelve hours after that historic touch of the drill bit, the Disco had to disconnect, draw up its heavy anchors, and boogie. The ice floe did pass by, and the Disco crew was able to get back to work to finish up its top hole. The mission even generated a little press, and not all of it bad. A *Wall Street Journal* reporter, Tom Fowler, choppered out to the Disco several weeks after operations recommenced. He spent a few days observing the goings-on and reported back to the mainland. "The rig's 124-person crew included a half-dozen wildlife spotters hired from native Alaskan firms," he wrote near the end of October. "While federal environmental laws don't require such spotters, Shell brought them on board to ease concerns among the Inupiat people, who worried about impacts on their annual whale harvest.

"Jennifer Scott, one of the biologists on watch, said there were some signs of life amid the empty expanse: in addition to humpback and bowhead whales, a polar bear swam by the vessel one day, and a snowy owl took up temporary residence above the bridge. The drilling crews on deck didn't have time to notice. They moved steel casing and pipes into place as the ice-slicked decks heaved with the waves, trying to make the most of the lowered drilling expectations. In a few weeks the area will be encased in sea ice again, blocking Shell's progress for another year."

At the end of the short drilling season that included dodging ice floes and Native Alaskans who would not allow their semiannual whale hunt to be impeded, Shell had little to show for its now $5 billion investment: one Disco-drilled top hole in the Chukchi, one *Kulluk*-drilled top hole in the Beaufort, a smattering of press. And there would be more of only one of those three things in the coming months.

The Disco was the first drillship to pull up anchor and head down to Dutch Harbor, the way station in its three-thousand-mile trip back to the Vigor shops in Seattle, for a tune-up and resupply in anticipation of the 2013 season. But as the Disco neared Dutch Harbor on November 6, vibrations in its propeller shaft became so violent the ship's main engine had to be shut down. The Disco was towed, sheepishly, back into Dutch Harbor again. Ten days later and still in the harbor, when the crew attempted to start the main engine, it detonated a backfire explosion powerful enough to be felt—not just heard, but felt—by people hundreds of yards away. The attempt also ignited the insulation in the engine room, leaving the crew racing to extinguish the flames. The Disco had to be dead towed to port in Seward, Alaska, for a full-on Coast Guard inspection—an inspection that brought to light all the Disco's dirty little secrets. Here were a few of the notable Coast Guard findings, beyond the drillship's ongoing and unseemly oil-laden bilge-water pukefests: "Objective evidence revealed systematic failure and lack of main engine preventive maintenance, which caused loss of main propulsion and exhaust system explosion. . . . Multiple fire screen doors throughout accommodation spaces that would not self-close. . . . Main engine piston cooling water is contaminated with sludge and oil. Crew skims the oil off with a ladle & bucket during rounds." What state-of-the-art multibillion-dollar project doesn't include a little ladle and bucket duty? "Exhaust system back-fires on a regular basis. Chief engineer suspects this is due to change to exhaust system in order to accommodate helicopter deck installation. . . . Current propulsion arrangement does not result in sufficient speed at sea to safely maneuver in all expected conditions. . . . Observed oil soaked structural fire protection insulation in way of exhaust. . . . No evidence of at least one monthly Emergency Evacuation Plan drill between September 23, 2012, and October 26, 2012. . . . Observed multiple dead end wires and improper wire splices throughout main engine room."

The Coast Guard took the unusual step of placing the Disco under port state detention, the maritime equivalent of double secret probation, which raised the Disco immediately into the top 1 percent of safety violators. Coast Guard officials were also inspired to take the even more rare action of making a criminal referral to the Department of Justice, which resulted in Noble Corporation eventually copping a plea to eight separate environmental and maritime felonies. Noble forked over $12.2 million in criminal fines and community service payments, and this was in addition to the $710,000 in civil fines Shell paid for the Disco's twenty-three separate violations of its Clean Air Act permits. Apparently, the Disco's actual noxious emissions were considerably north of negligible or nonexistent. Shell chalked up its "excessive hourly nitrous-oxide emissions" to what its president had called "new learnings revealed." "Following a season of operations," a Shell spokesman said as the company made out the check for its civil fine, "we now better understand how emissions control equipment actually functions in Arctic conditions."

Shell's opportunities for new learnings about functioning in Arctic conditions had not been entirely extinguished at the end of that November, thanks to the Kulluk and its dedicated tugboat, the Aiviq. The Aiviq had by then hauled the Kulluk through the Slushee-like Beaufort Sea and back into manageable water near Dutch Harbor. Shell had the option of shoveling the snowdrifts from the Kulluk's deck and leaving the drillship parked safely at Dutch Harbor (its anchor system was far superior to the Disco's, and it had a customized rounded berth) until the new season opened up next summer. But the company was anxious to get the Kulluk back to Seattle for a couple reasons. First, the Arctic battering had left the ship in need of the expert ministrations of Vigor Marine. Second, Shell executives were hoping to outrun an oil-facilities tax levy from the State of Alaska. Shell was under the impression that if the Kulluk remained in the state past January 1, it would owe about $6 million to Alaska. "It's fair to say the current tax structure related to vessels of this type influenced the timing of our departure," a Shell spokesman wrote in an email to a local reporter in Dutch Harbor.

And so, the decision was made in early December to execute the two-thousand-mile trip back to Washington State before the Kulluk would turn around and come back up to try Alaska again next season. The trip would become one of the most documented sea voyages of the twenty-first century. The Department of the Interior, the U.S. Coast Guard, and the National Transportation Safety Board all investigated and weighed in with reports. The combined page count of the government reports and their investigation notebooks neared, if not exceeded, that of *Moby-Dick*. McKenzie Funk wrote a riveting ninety-two-hundred-word piece for *The New York Times Magazine* that detailed, among lots of other things, the weight of the eighteen crew members chosen to ride the *Kulluk* back to Seattle. (The smallest was about 235; many tipped the scales at over 300.) Observant marine and offshore drilling professionals called the voyage "a shambolic misadventure" and a "clown circus." Many, many new learnings were revealed.

There were things that should have given Shell pause about embarking on the towing operation in the first place. Shell's preferred marine-warranty survey company would not sign off on the tow plan. Too risky in an Arctic winter. So in order to keep its insurance in force, Shell had to scramble to get a different company to sign off, which the new company did, after a hasty and incomplete inspection of the *Aiviq*, the *Kulluk*, and the (always excellent) paperwork. The surveyor assigned to the inspection "did not conduct an independent assessment concerning the overall adequacy of the towing equipment," the Coast Guard report noted. "He stated that conducting this type of analysis was not in his scope of work as a warranty surveyor." Add to this that Shell did not send its tow plan to a single federal or state agency for review. Add to this that Shell's experienced operations manager chose that moment to go on holiday. His designated replacement, who gave final approval to the tow plan, was a new employee who, according to the Coast Guard, "had never reviewed a tow plan within Shell, and had not participated in any of the planning meetings . . . had not received training in the tow planning or review process, and had not received any specific instructions, de-brief or guidance from his supervisor on this process." Other than that, he was the perfect man for the job.

Consider a few other things that were ill-considered by the various decision makers. The conical design of the *Kulluk* complicated any towing operation. The 266-foot-high, twenty-eight-thousand-ton unit was likely to rock and spin in heavy seas, causing huge swings in the amount of tension on the tow chains. It was "like towing a large saucer for a tea cup," said a tugboat master who had actually tugged the *Kul-*

luk. "Like a buoy the size of a football field," said one coastguardsman. Then, too, there was the fact that the *Aiviq* would have to execute the entire two-thousand-mile tow by its lonesome, without a backup tug on hand. In its defense, the *Aiviq* was one of the most powerful ice-class tugboats on the water, and its crew had great confidence. "Do you have any major engineering issues?" the marine-warranty surveyor asked its chief engineer in their one brief meeting, on the day the towing operation embarked. "No," the *Aiviq*'s chief engineer answered. Okay, good enough!

But the truth was, the *Aiviq* was a little worse for wear on that day of departure, December 21, 2012. The tug's fuel injectors had been on the fritz for nearly four months, which caused occasional losses of propulsion. One of its thrusters was unusable; a fuel tank cracked; one of its generators occasionally failed, which diminished the tug's electrical output. The *Aiviq* had first suffered serious damage when it took on water while towing the *Kulluk* north in heavy seas at the end of August. Ten weeks after that, on the return trip from the Beaufort Sea to Dutch Harbor, one of its engines failed mid-tow, and the electrical system had gone completely dark. None of the *Aiviq*'s mechanical deficiencies was reported to the Coast Guard, even though notification was expressly required under the *Code of Federal Regulations*.

Still, the officers on the bridge of the *Aiviq* remained confident and confidence inspiring as they pulled the *Kulluk* out to sea on December 21. The seamen had proper licensing and training and, as far as the Coast Guard was concerned, "could have towed anything, anywhere in the world." But this was their first duty in Arctic waters in winter, and there was something of a learning curve. They had been warned to expect gales approaching fifty knots and dangerous, thirty-five-foot-high swells. "The Aleutian Low looms over the North Pacific as a climatic warning to mariners navigating the Alaskan waters," read the annual guidebook published by the National Oceanic and Atmospheric Administration. "This semi-permanent feature is made up of the day-to-day storms that traverse these seas in a seemingly endless procession. With these storms come the rain, sleet, snow, the howling winds, and the mountainous seas that make the northern Gulf of Alaska and the southern Bering Sea among the most treacherous winter waters in the Northern Hemisphere."

The second day into the three-week trip, the seas were already rocking, and the weather reports for the next three days promised much worse than the planners had anticipated. The captain probably wished he had been more adamant in his demands to raise the fuel vents on the soon-to-be water-slogged deck of his tug. He had certainly already begun to appreciate the drift of his near future. He wrote in an email to his cohort on the *Kulluk* that day, "To be blunt, I believe that this length of tow, at this time of year, in this location, with our current routing, guarantees an ass-kicking."

The full-on ass kicking commenced about seventy-two hours later, not long after the *Kulluk*'s eighteen-man crew finished its Christmas Day barbecue. "By midnight there were gale-force winds and swells the size of houses," McKenzie Funk wrote in his *New York Times Magazine* epic. "Rather than crash forward through the building swells, as other ships might, the *Kulluk* marked their passage like a giant metronome, pitching and rolling a stomach-churning five, then seven, then 10 degrees off vertical. Six hundred yards ahead, the same waves were bucking the *Aiviq,* but the two ships were out of sync. The towline between them was slack one moment, then crackling with tension, then slack again."

The winds continued to blow somewhere between twenty-five and fifty knots for the next day and a half. Swells fifteen to eighteen feet high crashed continuously over the decks of both ships. The big, buoy-like *Kulluk* continued its maritime version of the twist. The towline between the two vessels sagged and then shot tight. The captain of the *Aiviq* tried to alter course, but nothing much helped. From 5:30 to 11:30 on the morning of December 27, when the swells rose to over twenty feet, the "wire tensile strength overload" alarm sounded thirty-eight times. The bridge crew, exhausted from twelve-hour watches and from fighting the constant storms, did little to address the problem. Though "experienced in towing operations," read the Coast Guard's later report, "they possessed less experience in Gulf of Alaska waters, particularly during the wintertime. This specific lack of experience was displayed during the towing operations on December 27, where the crew took ineffective action to reduce extremes in towline tension during a period of nearly six hours."

At 11:35 that morning, the overtaxed towline between the *Aiviq* and the *Kulluk* snapped, and one 120-ton shackle dropped away to the ocean floor. The crews pulled off the heroic feat of attaching a new emergency towline in just three hours, but the *Aiviq* emerged from that operation badly damaged. The tug had executed a dangerous U-turn to get back to the *Kulluk* and taken on huge amounts of the sea in one spectacular roll. A giant steel hook fell from its housing and had to be welded to the deck for safety. Enormous "anchor balls," somebody told Funk, broke loose and careered around the deck. Even more dangerous, seawater sloshed into those unraised fuel vents. A few minutes before midnight, one of the *Aiviq*'s seawater-logged engines went down. By three o'clock the next morning, all four engines were drowned lifeless.

Coast Guard helicopters flew in replacement parts, and the *Aiviq* crew was able to retool and restart its engines. Over the next three days, various Coast Guard boats and a private tug, the *Alert*, were called in to take turns towing the *Kulluk* alone or in tandem with the hastily revived *Aiviq*. When the weather and the weight of the *Kulluk* weren't pulling these boats backward or toward shore, the tugs were able to hold steady or plow ahead at about one knot, which is the speed of a baby crawling. Or, more precisely perhaps, the speed of a baby learning to crawl. At Shell's request, a Coast Guard team executed a dangerous helicopter rescue of the men left stranded on the rocking *Kulluk*. Because of weight limits, it took three separate trips to get those eighteen trenchermen to safe ground. The upside: the men survived to work another season. The downside: the evacuation of all personnel also left the *Kulluk* incapable of dropping anchor.

As New Year's Eve approached, every boat but the *Alert* was out of commission, and the weather was taking another ugly turn. The winds gusted up to sixty knots that afternoon, and the swells rose to thirty-five feet, propelling the *Kulluk* toward shore. The captain of the *Alert* ordered its two engines cranked up to 100 percent capacity, using all of their 10,192 horses, just to keep the *Kulluk* stationary. And then the tug's onboard alarm began to wail. The exhaust manifold was overheating; the two engines were in danger of burning out. The captain of the *Alert* throttled down to 85 percent power and watched as the great, whale-pleasing blue and white hulk he was towing drifted toward shore. Finally, at 8:00 p.m. on New Year's Eve, Coast Guard officials ordered the *Alert* to release its hold on the *Kulluk* and save itself. The twenty-eight-thousand-ton drillship—unattached, unmanned, and carrying 143,000 gallons of diesel fuel, 1,000 gallons of aviation fuel, and 12,000 gallons of petroleum product varietals—ran aground on Sitkalidak Island about forty minutes later. The resting spot was about fourteen hundred miles short of Seattle. Thus ended the new learnings; on that remote, rocky shoreline, the great operational excellence demonstration that was the 2012 Arctic drilling season came to a close.

Shell announced a pause in its Arctic offshore drilling program in Alaska a few months later. The company did take another run at the well in the Chukchi Sea, in 2015, and pronounced it a dry hole. Shell would not be back to Arctic Alaska, it announced, "for the foreseeable future."

SEVENTEEN

SUCH A MAN IS BORN ONCE
EVERY FEW DECADES

ASPIRING TO RENEWED SUPERPOWER STATUS WAS A TALL order for the Putin government in 2013, and the day-to-day slog of doing what it took to keep the Russian banner flying high was wearing on everybody involved, all the way down the line into the lower ranks. Consider Viktor Podobnyy, a twenty-five-year-old agent in Russia's once-vaunted foreign intelligence service who was finding no great joy in his recent posting. Young Podobnyy was assigned to New York at the end of 2012 under the cover of official attaché to the Permanent Mission of the Russian Federation to the United Nations. Along with his undercover SVR cohort Igor Sporyshev, whose public face was as a Russian government trade representative working in the United States, Podobnyy had an agenda full to bursting. The pair had to do enough "clean" work at Russia's government offices in New York to avoid the suspicion of watchful American counterintelligence agents. (Sporyshev understood he was likely to draw the attention of the FBI because his father had been a career officer in the Soviet KGB.) Meanwhile, the duo was acting as point of contact for one of the few SVR deep-cover Illegals the U.S. government had not swept up in the 2010 dragnet.

Sporyshev and Podobnyy were also expected to trawl the city's universities and businesses for well-connected Americans who might be recruited as moles and informants. The chances of enticing a sympathetic professor or banker to turn against the United States were lately proving pretty much nonexistent. There was a slightly greater chance of getting sufficient dirt—*kompromat,* in SVR parlance—on some American to blackmail him or her to act as an agent for Russia. The more likely scenario was finding a bored and naive young academic or think tank supernumerary who would unwittingly spill useful information. The "useful idiot" seemed like the last great hope of Russian spydom in the United States in 2013.

The gestalt of the whole Russian spying industry in New York was tilting toward demoralized by the time fresh-faced Viktor Podobnyy got to town. It didn't take long for him to adopt the attitude, too. In the winter and early spring of 2013, Podobnyy and Sporyshev expended hours inside the top secret secure room of Russia's UN offices on East 67th Street in Manhattan, commiserating about the futility of the agency they dutifully served. Vladimir Putin could drape all the honors available around Anna Chapman and the other Illegals deported from the United States in 2010, but the arrests and public shaming in the West had badly dinged the reputation of the most capable department inside the SVR, Directorate S. No doubt the current batch of U.S.-based SVR agents was watching the first season of the popular new TV show *The Americans,* which had been inspired by the 2010 revelation of the Russian spy ring embedded in the nondescript suburbs of New Jersey and Massachusetts. The creators, however, had set their drama back in time, in the 1980s, when the stakes were much higher and the superpower competition more evenly matched.

Young Podobnyy occasionally defended the current state of Russia's premier espionage program. "First of all, Directorate S is the only intelligence that is real intelligence," he reminded Sporyshev in one of their safe-room bull sessions in April 2013.

"It *was,*" the older and more experienced agent reminded him. Not so much anymore. Sporyshev knew full well the lone Illegal he was running in New York City was good for little more than gathering the sort of business intelligence already available to a casual reader of *The Wall Street Journal.*

"Yeah, I don't know about now," Podobnyy relented, with no real fight. "Look, in the States even the S couldn't do anything. The [FBI] caught ten of them. . . . And then Putin even tried to justify that they weren't even tasked to work, that they were sleeper cells in case of martial law. They weren't doing shit here, you understand. . . . I agree that untraditional is more effective, but even the S cannot do anything here."

This defeatist attitude invited a certain sloppiness in SVR tradecraft among its New York team. In fact, it's only possible to quote Sporyshev and Podobnyy verbatim from that particular April 2013 safe-room conversation, along with many others, because those forlorn Russian spies—surprise!—were being recorded. Every time. Sporyshev and Podobnyy had usefully and idiotically and unwittingly carried FBI listening devices into their star chamber—literally into the supposed top secret, secure communications facility at the Russian UN mission. In fact, everything they did in New York, for years, was watched and recorded and pored over by the FBI, unbeknownst to the two spies.

The G-men who were listening in must have developed some sympathy for these two Russian sad sacks. They complained. A lot. Sporyshev, for instance, seemed tormented by his inability to recruit any useful American businesswomen. "There was a positive response without feelings of rejection," was about as good a report as he could make. "I have lots of ideas about such girls but these ideas are not actionable because they don't allow you to get close enough," he explained in the safe room one day.

Podobnyy took some time in that particular session to whine about his growing irritation with the most promising American contact he had made. Podobnyy had struck up a conversation three months earlier with a young, aspiring New York businessman at a symposium on the worldwide effects of the shale boom. The American, Carter Page, seemed heaven-sent to Podobnyy back on January 18, 2013. Here was a forty-one-year-old graduate of the U.S. Naval Academy who told people he had been a staff-level research fellow on the House Armed Services Committee in the early 1990s. He was also an avowed Russophile; he even spoke Russian, or tried to. His recent PhD dissertation focused on governance in the energy industry in oil-rich Central Asia's former Soviet states. New York University's Center for Global Affairs had signed up Page as an adjunct assistant professor. He was teaching a course there, he explained to Podobnyy, called "Energy in the World."

And the almost assistant professor was more than just an academic. His two passions, Page would say, were "business development and international relations." He had worked at the Moscow office of Merrill Lynch a decade earlier and had risen to the position of chief operating officer of its Energy and Power Investment Banking Group. He remained an avid follower of the Russian energy sector. His chief interest in early 2013 seemed to be the state-owned natural gas monopoly, Gazprom. "I was an adviser for them for many years," Carter Page liked to say.

Natural gas was Page's self-described obsession in the months around his impromptu meeting with the young attaché to the Russian mission in New York, and this new acquaintanceship with Podobnyy seemed to inspire him. On March 13, 2013, less than two months after meeting Podobnyy for the first time, Page reserved the name for a new company he was incorporating: Global Natural Gas Ventures LLC. He registered the company in Oklahoma several weeks later. Its official headquarters of record was, conveniently, just four miles down the road from the Chesapeake Energy campus. The idea of the venture, it seemed, was to promote natural gas as the clean fuel alternative of the future—just as Aubrey McClendon had been doing for years. That this idea was a tad stale by 2013 didn't shake Carter Page's resolve. The wheels in Page's head didn't turn with a great deal of velocity, but they exhibited real stamina. When he met again with Podobnyy over a Coca-Cola in New York that March, Page's chief interest was in making himself the point of contact between Russian and American natural gas interests. At least that's the way it sounded in Page's explanation to the House Permanent Select Committee on Intelligence member Mike Quigley during questioning in 2017.

"So you two talked about Gazprom?" Quigley asked.

"It definitely came up, yes," said Page. "It was me generally talking about some of the things I had been discussing with Chesapeake Energy."

This meeting with Podobnyy, Page told Quigley just by the by, also presented an excellent chance to practice his Russian-language skills with an actual Russian. "I told him that I had previously worked with [Gazprom] and that I know that they are similar to Chesapeake Energy in the United States. With the glut of natural gas that there is across

Texas, Oklahoma, and around the world, people such as Aubrey McClendon, who I knew at the time was the CEO and founder of Chesapeake Energy, they were looking for new ways to increase natural gas demand. And Russia, coincidentally, at the same time was also looking to do that and also had made objectives of increasing the use of natural gas in vehicles." Listening to Page talk to the congressman, one could imagine Podobnyy's frustration. Carter Page had a tendency to make a lot of words but rarely herded them toward any discernible meaning.

Page did appear to be going out of his way to attract the favor and attention of Russian energy bosses in the spring of 2013. As a fellow at the Center for National Policy, a U.S. national security think tank, Page wrote a blog post extolling the "leadership" of Igor Sechin in "build[ing] bridges" to Western oil companies such as Exxon. While calling out the Obama administration for imposing "excessive restrictions on Russian officials as seen in last year's Magnitsky Act which was reminiscent of the blacklists of the McCarthy era," he also lamented Sechin's uncharitable treatment at the hands of the American press. "The frequently unjustified maltreatment of Russia and its leaders in the US media further engrains long-standing tendencies toward misunderstanding, thereby offering a super-sized cover for equally large policy mistakes by the U.S. government."

There is no evidence that Page and Podobnyy kept up any serious face-to-face contact in the spring of 2013. They had a spotty email exchange, maybe a phone call or two. By his own account, Page mostly offered the Russian his personal outlook on the state of the global energy industry. This amounted to handing over lecture notes and reading materials Page was preparing for his NYU classes, "only at a much, much lower level. And his eyes were kind of glazing over, frankly," Page later explained. "My students in class that year were much more engaged and interested. He showed little to no interest at all."

Podobnyy was growing just as frustrated with Page by April 2013. The spy was sure that Page's eagerness to make big money in natural gas made him a vulnerable target—a target who might hand over something truly valuable or actionable. But it was also dawning on Podobnyy that calling Carter Page a "useful idiot" was only half-accurate. He wasn't proving very useful. "[He] wrote that he is sorry, he went to Moscow and forgot to check his inbox, but he wants to meet when he gets back," Podobnyy reported to Sporyshev on April 8, 2013. "I think he is an idiot and forgot who I am."

Sporyshev was mainly just listening, letting Podobnyy vent. "I like that he takes on everything," the younger spy continued. "I also promised him a lot: that I have connections in the Trade Representation, meaning you, that you can push contracts. I feed him empty promises."

"Shit," Sporyshev chimed in, clearly not happy about the prospect of getting roped into the Page operation, "then he will write to me."

Podobnyy told his accomplice not to fret. He wouldn't drag him into this particular abyss. But you kind of had to feel for these two Russian spies. The stupidities of the Carter Page operation were reminders of what felt like the relentless nothingness of their chosen occupation. They might as well be accountants or chemistry teachers. Two days later, Podobnyy and Sporyshev sounded like men headed for an existential crisis. *Good grief! Look at us! This is what it is to be a spy for one of the greatest countries on earth.* "I'm sitting with a cookie right now at . . . the chief enemy spot," Podobnyy complained to Sporyshev on April 10, 2013. "Fuck! Not one point of what I thought then [when I signed on], not even close. [I thought it would be a little like] movies about James Bond. Of course I wouldn't fly helicopters, but pretend to be someone else at minimum."

Sporyshev was in no mood to buck up his protégé. "I also thought at least I would go abroad with a different passport," he said with a sigh.

While Russia's supposedly elite spy agencies were boring their undercover agents half to death, and the FBI was all over their flaccid recruitment efforts in New York, there was another foreign spying effort under way in the United States. And this one was not only wildly successful; it also seemed like a hell of a lot of fun. The new mystery spy came on the scene in the first week of February 2013, sending stolen electronic correspondence and files, unsolicited, to a handful of outside-the-mainstream media organizations. The hacked files included screenshots of emails exchanged by the family of the former presidents George H. W. Bush and George W. Bush. "Puppets of the illuminati," the hacker called the Bushes—whatever that meant. There were also screen grabs of the fruits of W.'s newest hobby: he was trying his hand at painting. The hacker leaked a self-portrait of W. himself in the shower, and another of him sitting in his bathtub. Alongside its standard run of embarrassing mug-shot photos of disheveled newly arrested celebrities, the website the Smoking Gun wasted no time in uploading the paintings, along with photographs of George H. W. during his recent hospital stay and emails that revealed a few relatively innocuous family secrets.

The oil paintings accounted for most of the pickup in the wider media. "I gazed at the former president's legs and toes in the bathtub, overcome with relief that W. was now under the influence of Lucian Freud rather than Dick Cheney," *New York Times* columnist Maureen Dowd opined the next day. The *Times* art blog weighed in as well, with a semi-serious critique: "The forms are handled with care, but awkwardly, which is the source of their appeal. . . . Everything is honestly accounted for, not sharply realistic, certainly not finicky. . . . Whatever is going on psychologically, the paintings suggest a man, a painter, at ease with his body."

The whole thing seemed sort of like a good-time lark, right down to the strange watermark stamped across every item sent: "Guccifer."

Guccifer's hijinks took a darker turn a month later, when the hacker gained control of former secretary of state Colin Powell's electronic accounts. "You will burn in hell, Bush," read a new post on Powell's Facebook page. "Kill the illuminati! Tomorrow's world will be a world free of illuminati or will be no more!" Guccifer didn't stop at Powell's Facebook page. He sent dozens of news organizations an email from the former secretary of state's AOL account that read, "The 9/11 victim's blood is on my hands."

Three days later, a WikiLeaks-before-WikiLeaks site called Cryptome, along with the Smoking Gun and the state-owned Russian media company RT, received a new missive from Guccifer announcing the breach of the email account of Sidney Blumenthal, who had been a trusted senior adviser in the Clinton White House. "The online prankster known as 'Guccifer' has crossed party lines and hacked the AOL account of a former Bill Clinton aide," the New York *Daily News* reported. A few days later, scores of reporters, congressional staffers, and political operatives received an email blast that originated, inexplicably, from the AOL account of the wife of *Arrested Development* actor Jeffrey Tambor. *Mother of God!* Attached were four private and confidential memos Blumenthal sent to Hillary Clinton in the aftermath of the attack on the U.S. mission in Benghazi, Libya. Guccifer had modified the documents just a tad, but only in terms of their visual presentation. The memos were rendered in the hacker's preferred and decidedly creepy Comic Sans typeface, then set against a pink background.

The mere existence of the memos caused some real heartburn in the White House. Blumenthal had famously been denied a position in the State Department, because he was regarded as one of Hillary Clinton's most vicious hit men against Barack Obama during the 2008 primaries. The Obama brain trust was not happy to learn that Secretary of State Clinton had been regularly receiving information and advice from Blumenthal. The publication of these emails was likely to invite new questions from the rabid House Republicans about the tragic and deadly incident in Benghazi. Buried deep in the Smoking Gun's story was a strange fact, barely noted at the time. "Blumenthal's memos and emails to Clinton," the Smoking Gun reported, "were sent to her at a non-governmental email address through the Web domain 'clintonemail.com.'" The website Gawker had a sinister but decidedly narrow read on why Hillary Clinton would use a private email account to conduct semiofficial business: "There seems to be little reason to use a different account other than an attempt to shield her communications with Blumenthal from the prying eyes of [Freedom of Information Act] requesters."

The bosses at Russia's RT went with the Blumenthal story in a big way. Watchful editors at *Forbes* magazine ran a quick follow-up story about RT's coverage, which allowed them to report on the substance of the Blumenthal memos but at a comfortable remove. "RT, which is a propaganda arm of the Putin regime, . . . focuses on two of the four hacked emails, citing sensitive sources, on the attack on the U.S. consulate in Benghazi," said *Forbes* on March 19, 2013. "The reader should be warned that these are first and partial accounts of hacked emails that may be fabricated by someone with a hidden agenda. Time will tell whether they have any credence. The RT selection of excerpts appears to fit into Putin's agenda."

Guccifer was perhaps proving useful to Putin's RT propagandists, but no one in Russia or anywhere else knew who was actually behind these hacks or what his or her motivation was. One thing was clear, though: Guccifer was proving remarkably capable of flinging mud all across the American political map. It was one thing to steal documents from important people. Such stolen material could always be used for a ransom demand, or the files could be copied and handed over (or sold) to a spy service interested in foreign secrets. But stealing the materials and then making a public spectacle of their display—reformatting and repurposing the purloined material to inflict maximum humiliation and reputational damage on even the most elite public figures— that wasn't just mischievous and impressive; it was properly destructive. This was no longer Allen Funt's *Candid Camera*. This was a shot-to-the-groin compilation on *America's Funniest Home Videos*. Sure it was painful, but you can't look away! Russia's actual spies were eating cookies in an FBI-bugged, not-at-all-safe room, complaining that they couldn't get American women to talk to them, while this who-knows-who Guccifer character had successfully ripped off and then ripped open the private correspondence of the immediate former president, the current secretary of state, and the most revered figure in American national security, himself a former secretary of state and chairman of the Joint Chiefs of Staff. Nice work, whoever you are. And no FBI bugs anywhere to be seen.

Guccifer kept that mud flying fast and furious for the next four months, in what appeared to be a random and unconnected series of electronic thefts. The seemingly unaffiliated mystery agent hacked *Sex and the City* author Candace Bushnell and treated her fans to the first fifty unedited pages of her novel in progress; hacked a billionaire venture capitalist from a firm where Colin Powell had been a paid consultant; hacked famed Watergate journalist Carl Bernstein and offered up to chosen media outlets his stock portfolio balances and his private correspondence with the movie director Steven Soderbergh. When the Smoking Gun wrote to Guccifer and asked about his method of electronic thievery, the mysterious digital housebreaker waved it off: "These are irrelevant extraneous technical questions."

Wary news outlets that refused to traffic in the stolen goods Guccifer provided had to endure the hacker's scorn. "And last but not least I have a word for the Main Stream Zionist Media," Guccifer wrote. "You will fall like a house of cards!" He also embedded ongoing taunts aimed at the FBI and the Secret Service in his correspondence with the media: "i have an old game with the fucking bastards inside," Guccifer boasted. "this is just another chapter in the game. . . . i can figure out the feds have a finger up their ass; haha. . . . AND TELL THE FUCK-ING BASTARDS THAT . . . I NEVER STOP!"

At the end of July 2013, Guccifer circled back to Colin Powell, having successfully stolen into the email account of a Romanian politician who had sent the former secretary of state some slightly racy correspondence and some slightly racy photographs of herself in bikini-wear. "This hacker is driving everyone here crazy," Powell wrote to the Romanian woman. "Our security people have been chasing him for months." He advised her to delete any emails she had ever sent to him, but alas, by then it was too late. Guccifer uploaded the embarrassing correspondence and photographs of Powell and the Romanian pol to a Google Drive account. Then he used the hacked Facebook account of an air force general who had served with Powell on the Joint Chiefs of Staff to provide a link to the material. Powell must have known he had lost control of this story when five of General Merrill McPeak's Facebook friends "liked" the post. And he had certainly lost control of it after the *New York Post* published the bikini photograph. The popular, real-life American hero was forced to issue a public denial of any untoward relationship with the much younger Romanian woman. "Those types of emails ended a few years ago. There was no affair then and there is not one now," Powell said. "This was a friendship that electronically became very personal and then back to normal."

Guccifer remained committed to bipartisanship. In early December, the hacker released a set of doodles sketched by Bill Clinton on official papers from his White House years. One of the documents included Bubba's unfortunate but not altogether surprising "boner doodle." The one with the little happy-face guy, next to the delicious-looking chicken drumstick, next to the giant boner. Ah, good times.

All this Guccifer-spewed electronic detritus had caused plenty of heartache and embarrassment to some of the country's most celebrated private citizens. But what was really worrisome to U.S. law enforcement was Guccifer's reach into private email and Facebook accounts of men and women who were currently serving in national-security-related jobs, with security clearances. Guccifer had pilfered and disseminated private correspondence from a sitting U.S. senator, from the current chairman of the National Intelligence Council, and from the acting head of the National Nuclear Security Administration—the agency that, by official description, "works to ensure that the nation's stockpile of nuclear weapons is safe and secure."

"Good night America," Guccifer signed off on one of his emails to his media partners, "where ever you are."

The week before Christmas 2013, two websites Guccifer had come to count on, Cryptome and the Smoking Gun, received word from the hacker that law enforcement might finally be closing in. "I don't know what near future holds for me so i will schedule an email link for you . . . in case I disappear." The next day, as promised, he shipped them a link to the entirety of the "Guccifer Archive," which now resided in what the hacker called "the cloud of Infinite Justice."

The Smoking Gun wasted no time in reporting the contents. Seems Guccifer had been much more active than anybody had realized, and incredibly opportunistic, using hacked accounts' email directories to hop from one electronic lily pad to another—and another and another. The only real connection between the victims was fame. Modern-day illuminati you could call them, no matter how weak the flicker of renown. Guccifer had infiltrated the email accounts of the editor Tina Brown, the mean-girl biographer Kitty Kelley, the fitness guru Denise Austin, and the British actor Rupert Everett. He managed to hack the email of the *Downton Abbey* creator, Julian Fellowes, from which he stole the script for the finale of an upcoming season. (In an act of kindness, Guccifer had spared *Downton*'s millions of ardent viewers by keeping the script under wraps.)

And then, two weeks later, after nearly a full year of hacking mania, Guccifer was suddenly arrested, and his identity revealed. The revelation was kind of, well, unsatisfactory. Here was Marcel Lehel Lazar, a nondescript-looking forty-two-year-old wearing a pair of sunglasses and a tight-fitting "Authentic Vintage Clothing" T-shirt, being perp-walked to jail. Police had picked up the cyber pirate without incident at his modest little home in Sambateni, Romania, a remote village in the foothills of Transylvania, 350 miles from the capital city of Bucharest.

So Guccifer was unmasked, but as yet unexplained. Even the origins of his chosen cyber alias were shape-shifty. Lazar liked to add strange layers to the meaning of "Guccifer." It was a name meant to combine "the style of Gucci and the light of Lucifer," he once said. Lucifer was an angel who rebelled, one Romanian journalist pointed out. To which Lazar added, cryptically, that numerology was also at play: "Split Guccifer into numbers and you'll get 72, which is known as an absolute number of divinity. Google it." Lazar occasionally took off on rhetorical flights of vicious anti-Semitism and raging paranoia about the secret pact among leaders of the United States and Great Britain to rule the world. He claimed to have a very extensive tool kit with which he hoped to arrest the evil march of the Western illuminati: "I use any possible method to break electronic correspondence—including contact lists and metadata, like the NSA programs do, only that's artificial intelligence. I also use Kabbalah"—which seems strange for an avowed anti-Semite—"numerology, and the occult. Jung's archetypes."

The emerging biographical details didn't offer much help either, even those in a deeply researched and authorized profile by the Romanian-born journalist Matei Rosca. It seemed to stretch credulity past the breaking point to consider that this Lazar fellow was behind Guccifer's remarkably successful cyber attacks in America. He was high school educated and chronically unemployed—a former factory worker, a former paint salesman, and a sometimes taxi driver who had never received a minute of formal computer training. Even his wife, Gabriela, didn't really get it. She knew her husband spent an inordinate amount of time fiddling around on his laptop computer in the year before his arrest, but never thought it was a big deal. He always made time to look after and entertain their young daughter, she insisted, and remained diligent in his quest to keep their little backyard garden hoed and weeded.

Gabriela Lazar's first inkling that something strange might be afoot was in early January 2014, when she found her husband in the backyard with an ax in hand, smashing his laptop and cell phone to smithereens. She was only certain something was up when Romanian authorities showed up a few days later to take her husband off to jail. Later, while Marcel was serving his seven-year jail sentence in Romania, Gabriela was defensive. Her husband never took a dime from anybody, she insisted, though he clearly had the chance. "What did he steal?" she told Rosca. "He was just curious." Mrs. Lazar could also be defiant. "Such a man is born once every few decades," she said. "I'm proud I have a smart man."

Guccifer's actual motivation remained murky, too. "I was interested in the people, usually celebrities," he told investigators a few weeks after his arrest.

"Were you interested in something that would be the topic of news, or something that would put them in embarrassing situations?" the investigator asked.

"No, I was looking for something that would serve my interests."

The Romanian prosecutor who eventually secured Lazar's conviction theorized that he was a loner with an obsessive personality, way too much time on his hands, and a hero complex. "He is just a poor Romanian guy who wanted to be famous," the prosecutor said. "A compulsive need to be famous." The motivations were just too complicated, or too flighty, to really pin down.

Guccifer's operational methods, however, were not so hard to reckon. A *New York Times* reporter who got three hours with Lazar, as well as help from the Romanian prosecutor and the FBI, seemed to come away somewhat underwhelmed by the secret of Guccifer's success. "The answer," wrote Andrew Higgins, "turned out to be disappointingly banal: Mr. Lazar simply guessed the answers to security questions." Pet name. First car. Grade school attended. Street you grew up on. Mother's maiden name. All the standard stuff. Who doesn't use those? And all the answers are pretty easy to get if the person is a public figure. Many were available on *Wikipedia* and other public sites. Others might require the kind of down-the-rabbit-hole googling that can become addictive. Lazar was a stone-cold addict. At one point, he constructed a genealogy of the Colin Powell family four generations deep. He also spent days gathering and testing the street names near the grade school that Powell's Romanian lady friend had attended in her youth. And it worked. Security question answered. Bikini shot secured. Lazar never claimed any great genius. In fact, he once figured his success rate was somewhere south of 10 percent. But, hey, he had a lot of time on his hands. Lazar was, explained the Romanian prosecutor, "just a smart guy who was patient and persistent." And sometimes a hack was easy.

"Breaking into [Sidney Blumenthal's] email address book took me a few minutes."

Looking back on the Guccifer lark of 2013, with the remarkable cyber-shenanigans-filled political season of 2016 behind us, it's pretty clear that whatever was motivating that random Transylvanian, sitting at his kitchen table, patiently unraveling the online lives and habits of America's elite, it ended up being a beautiful test run for something way more destructive. Why throw good money after bad, shipping Cold War–style agents off to enemy territory to pretend to be bankers and trade attachés, so they could deal with wordy birds like Carter Page, when instead you could just steal everything you needed from the comforts of home? The Guccifer saga was a weird few months in the annals of criminal hacking, but apparently somebody in Vladimir Putin's Kremlin was paying very close attention. Why should some underemployed Romanian paint salesman be having all the fun in America?

EIGHTEEN

PUTIN ZASSAL

THIS WAS TO BE VLADIMIR PUTIN'S TRIUMPH—THE 2014 WINTER Olympics in Sochi. An event the Russian president had been working toward for almost a decade. Putin had flown to Guatemala back in 2007 to make a personal plea to the International Olympic Committee electors choosing the site of the 2014 Games. And it took some convincing. Sochi was not the obvious choice for an international winter sports festival, to say the least. The resort town on the Black Sea was a subtropical city with minuscule annual snowfall, doubtful utilities, and a dearth of lodging. The ski slopes were about thirty miles from the town center, and there was only one aged and crumbling highway from the seacoast to the slopes. This thoroughfare was entirely inadequate to handle the traffic the Olympics would bring. But Putin gave the committee his personal presidential guarantee. The Russian Federation would spend whatever money was required to remake Sochi into a worthy host city. The government had already set aside $12 billion for construction projects, a Winter Olympics world record and double the amount Canada was spending on the 2010 Games in Vancouver. Sochi would be ready, on time, to stage the most extravagant Winter Olympics the world had ever seen. President Putin could *make* it snow if he had to.

Putin carried the day in Guatemala. Sochi overtook the frontrunner, Pyeongchang, South Korea, and won a slim 51–47 majority in the second round of voting. "Russia has risen from its knees," exclaimed

Putin's economic development and trade minister on hearing the news. The Russian president, *The Guardian* later reported, had "wowed the International Olympic Committee in Guatemala with a speech in English and French."

Vladimir Putin kept his eye on the prize in the years of preparation that followed. "From the very beginning until this day the president controlled everything," the long-suffering mayor of Sochi told the *New York Times* reporter Steven Lee Myers a couple of months before the opening of the Games. "He follows the course of construction. He watches how all the state bodies, the financial organs, spend each ruble. . . . Personally, I am always very tense and nervous when I'm invited to present a report to the president. He sets the tasks, but he never says you did a good job. He always says simply that everything has to be finished."

There were plenty of serious public relations bumps in the new roads leading to the Sochi Games. Human rights groups around the world were calling foul on Putin's increasingly harsh crackdowns on political dissidents and his vicious new law criminalizing the advocacy of gay rights. His treatment of the homegrown Russian protest band Pussy Riot made for a particularly attention-getting example. Members of the band, renowned for performing in brightly colored minidresses, tights, and ski masks, had been arrested, fined, and let go in early 2012, after a badass rendition in Moscow's Red Square of their newest ditty— "Putin Zassal" (Putin Has Pissed Himself). But the Russian courts had shown less leniency after the band entered the Cathedral of Christ the Saviour of the Russian Orthodox Church later that year for the introductory performance of their original psalm begging the Virgin Mary to help them remove the evil Putin from power. The women were arrested and charged with "hooliganism motivated by religious hatred."

The Kremlin suspected the protest band was actually the tool of Western governments—hello, United States, hello, dreaded secretary of state Hillary Clinton—trying to tear down Putin. "Pussy Riot's act inside the Cathedral of Christ the Saviour is not the stupidity of young girls, but part of the global conspiracy against Russia and the Russian Orthodox Church," said the nationalist Russian pol and political scientist Sergey Markov. "Putin isn't obliged to just punish three idiots in a fatherly way, but also protect Russia from this conspiracy with all possible severity." Putin lived up to that obligation. For the song in the cathedral, three Pussy Riot members were convicted and sentenced to two years in prison. One band member's husband released to reporters their four-year-old daughter's most recent artwork—a vivid, Xena-like rescue scene. "For her it has been very emotional," said the father. "She breaks down the prison walls and helps [her mother] escape."

Putin's old friend Paul McCartney wrote a letter protesting the imprisonment. Other musicians including Sting, Pete Townshend, the Red Hot Chili Peppers, and Yoko Ono were busting Putin's balls, too. "I thank Pussy Riot for standing firmly in their belief of Freedom of Expression, and making women proud to be women," said Ono. In the months before the opening of Putin's Winter Olympics, the governments of Great Britain, Germany, and France let it be known they would not be sending any high-level officials to Sochi. President Barack Obama and the First Lady announced they would be sitting it out, as did Vice President Joe Biden and his wife, Jill.

On top of all that, a group of Putin's long-standing and most effective critics in Russia published a detailed report on Vladimir's spectacular profligacy during the preparations for Sochi. The main author of this report, Boris Nemtsov, was a brilliant Russian physicist and mathematician and a true believer in democracy and government transparency. He had been a rising political star in post-Soviet Russia—even appeared to be Yeltsin's heir apparent—until the economic crash in 1998 laid waste to the Kremlin hierarchy. Nemtsov watched the rise of Putin from the sidelines after that and was increasingly alarmed by the KGB-trained president's crackdown on the free press, by the extrajudicial way Putin and Sechin manhandled Yukos and Mikhail Khodorkovsky, among others, and by Putin's updated and upgraded Grabification 2.0. Nemtsov became one of the president's most vocal and most popular opponents, and a relentless burr under Putin's saddle. He co-authored a no-holds-barred study of the Kremlin's venality and mismanagement in its running of Gazprom in 2008. And in 2012, he publicly praised the Magnitsky Act, which permitted the U.S. Congress to mete out real economic punishment on specific individuals in Russia who committed gross human rights violations. Unlike Carter

Page, who decried the Magnitsky Act as latter-day McCarthyism, Nemtsov hailed it as the way to finally nick the "crooks and abusers" among Russian businessmen and officials.

But the newest report on Sochi, updated just two months before the opening of the Games, topped all of Nemtsov's previous broadsides against Putin. It was designed to hit when and where it would most hurt. The numbers were startling. Putin's record $12 billion Winter Games budget had ballooned to $50 billion, according to the report. This made the final price tag for Sochi the biggest ever for an Olympic Games, winter or summer. Almost ten times the cost of the immediately previous 2010 Vancouver Games. More than the cost of the previous twenty-one Winter Olympics *combined*. Nemtsov generously pointed out that major budgetary overruns are the rule in these projects. Vancouver's final bill, for instance, was a little more than double the original estimate. But that was nothing like what happened in Sochi. The cost of constructing the new thirty-mile highway and rail line leading from the Black Sea into the snowy mountains had run to more than three times the cost of the recent American space program to send a rover to the planet Mars (which is thirty-four million miles away). A new natural gas pipeline, built by the same Kremlin-favored Russian company that had built the inexplicably expensive Russian side of the Nord Stream pipeline, came in at five times the average cost of a European pipeline. This was an impressive feat, given that the Russian half of Nord Stream had been completed at only triple the cost of the European half—Putin was getting even better!

Labor costs did not account for any markups. Pay was lousy and spotty on every project. Workers who complained aloud were silenced with firings or even beatings. One worker sewed his lips together in a gruesome protest against unpaid wages, to no avail. Kremlin contractors simply imported foreigners who were willing to work eighty-hour weeks and didn't whine when their lousy, $2-an-hour wages were delayed or never paid.

Nemtsov reached a conclusion on the actual cause of the Sochi overruns. "This is a festival of corruption," he said. And, ever the scientist and mathematician, he produced the evidence to back it up. The report ran two distinct comparative analyses—budget overruns of Winter Olympics past and the actual costs of facilities at previous Olympics—and emerged with the same basic answer: Putin's builders had pocketed somewhere between $25 billion and $30 billion in "embezzlement and kickbacks." A few of the suspect, old Yeltsin-sponsored oligarchs had been strong-armed into investing in Sochi (at a loss), but more than 90 percent of the money spent on the Games came right out of the Russian Federation's government accounts. "The money stolen," read the report, "could have paid for 3,000 high-quality roads, housing for 800,000 people or thousands of ice palaces and soccer fields all over Russia."

State-owned Russian Railways—which mounted in its Sochi-area offices a framed portrait of the Soviet cosmonaut-hero Yuri Gagarin as a can-do morale booster—ripped off much of the $9.4 billion in Russian taxpayer money handed over to build that more-than-a-trip-to-Mars concrete and steel pathway into the mountains. Much of that money ended up in the pocket of the Russian Railways president, Vladimir Yakunin, one of Putin's St. Petersburg–bred *siloviki*. The most impressive takers, though, were Putin's old friends from his school days—the Rotenberg brothers. Arkady and Boris Rotenberg were Putin's youth judo partners, his current judo trainers, and fixtures in Putin's pickup hockey games. Imagine baseball-mad George W. Bush entrusting serious Department of Defense contracts to retired stars like Pete Rose and Jose Canseco. By about 2010, the Rotenbergs had amassed a billion-dollar fortune through Putin's good offices—much of it from the proceeds looted during construction of the Nord Stream gas pipeline.

But the Sochi Olympics put the Rotenbergs on a whole new level. Putin graced the brothers with twenty-one separate construction contracts, which paid out a total of more than $7 billion in the years leading up to the Games. They built a series of new bypass roadways and thoroughfares, a thermal electrical station, pipelines for natural gas, and the media center. They also upgraded the airport and the seaport. Along the way, the Rotenbergs slurped up rubles with athletic abandon. You couldn't call it reckless. The Rotenbergs, according to the Nemtsov report, "gained this profit while having their risk reduced to zero . . . because the facilities they are building will be turned over to the government." By showtime in Sochi, according to the annual *Forbes* list of richest humans, Arkady Rotenberg's net worth had tripled to $3.3 billion. "Friendship," Arkady Rotenberg once admitted, "never hurt anyone."

The Nemtsov report got a lot of pickup in the Western press in the weeks leading up to the Games and offered energetic journalists plenty of new leads. According to *Vanity Fair*'s Brett Forrest—who had earlier chased the Illegals heartthrob Anna Chapman through a series of Moscow nightclubs—the flow of goods and cash into Sochi set off a full-on organized crime war that left a trail of dead gangsters. Oh, and Russian Railways' boss, Yakunin, had siphoned off sufficient cash to construct a triple-château, 170-acre estate that had, among other things, an "immense" refrigerated room dedicated to the care and comfort of the family's fur coats. Putin was the proud owner of a new compound as well, this one in the mountains outside Sochi. "It is called Lunnaya Polyana, or Moon Field, a reference to the barren landscape upon which it sits," wrote Forrest. "It is protected by some of the 30,000 Spetsnaz special-forces troops that Russian military has dispersed into the mountains, there to live in tents until the Olympics are over. Putin has built himself two massive chalets, two helipads, a power station, and two ski lifts, servicing surrounding peaks." Smack in the middle of what was supposed to be a protected national park, "the Russian state built a private dacha on a UNESCO site under the guise of conducting meteorological research."

The Telegraph, out of London, reported that the few locals in Sochi who had tried to call out the corruption and the environmental damage—toxic sludge flowing into the mountain river—were "likely to find themselves de-housed, dragged through the courts, or even arrested."

If Putin and his government were at all bothered by the international press sniggering at their alleged and well-documented corruption, they were careful not to show it. Putin did not lash out at Nemtsov. His famously combative foreign minister Sergei Lavrov gave a lengthy interview to the editor in chief of *Foreign Policy,* the veteran U.S. journalist Susan B. Glasser. He told her, "As for the changes in the Russian foreign policy, yes, we have more domestic strength, if you wish. . . .

And we feel the change. And Russia feels more assertive—not aggressive, but assertive. . . . And of course we can now pay more attention to looking after our legitimate interests in the areas where we were absent for quite some time after the demise of the Soviet Union." To Glasser, it was an echo—"clear, if chilling"—of one of Lavrov's nineteenth-century predecessors: *Russia is not sulking, she is composing herself.* The Sochi Olympics would be a coming-out party for that newly assertive Russia. However snooty and dismissive the world press liked to be about Putin and whatever it was he was building in this post-Soviet gangster kleptocracy, it was time for the world to respect the reemergence of a confident Russia intent on recapturing its old Soviet superpower mojo.

Part of that confidence was Putin's own growing sense of self. He was Russia personified, with no checks on his power or person. And in the run-up to the Sochi Olympics, Putin—and by extension Russia—appeared confident enough to ramp up the project of rapport building with its historic enemies and current antagonists. President Putin had just that previous summer bestowed the Russian Order of Friendship on his new bestie from the West, the American who was going to help him conquer the Arctic and keep afloat the one-export, one-industry Russian petro-economy: Rex Tillerson. Putin was also granting ExxonMobil a hefty (though not majority!) 49 percent stake in another brand-new partnership with Rosneft—this one to frack shale deposits in western Siberia. "This ushers in a new era of cooperation," said Putin, just before pinning the handsome new medal on Rex's lapel. In November 2013, Putin even gifted a traditional miniature lacquered box to an oddball American businessman who brought the Miss Universe pageant to Moscow that year. What could it hurt? This guy Trump might prove useful.

As the Sochi opening ceremonies drew near, Russia's third-term president appeared committed to playing the good host on the world stage. In fact, he appeared near magnanimous. About six weeks before the Games kicked off, Putin's government issued a surprise announcement. It had decided to release the sacrilegious Pussy Riot "hooligans" from prison. A few days later a newly sprung Mikhail Khodorkovsky stepped off a charter flight in Germany, a man blinking in the new light of freedom for the first time in ten years. Putin had granted the former Yukos boss's long-standing plea for release from prison just a few days before Christmas. "He committed a very serious crime but he has served a very serious sentence for it," the Kremlin spokesman explained of Khodorkovsky. The spokesman also asserted, somewhat laughably, that President Putin had acted "on humanitarian grounds."

The whole magnanimous humanitarian vibe seemed to work, too. Putin appeared vaguely content with his current standing in the world when the Sochi Games opened on February 7, 2014. The big machers of the Western governments could steer clear of the Sochi Games if they so chose; this just cleared more room on the stage for Putin to shine. The 2014 Winter Olympics were every bit the triumph Russia had imagined. First off, Putin's security forces made sure the Games were incident-free. Drones armed with surveillance cameras whirred overhead; warships patrolled the Black Sea nearby; surface-to-air missile batteries were locked and loaded; 100,000 soldiers and police officers secured a generous perimeter. The feared terrorist attacks—from Chechens or Georgians or ISIS—never materialized. And Russia turned out to be the big winner in the various pricey sports arenas its taxpayers had financed. Putin's countrymen dominated the glamorous figure-skating competitions and took home the most medals overall, including the most golds. The doping scandals and the unceremonious medal stripping would come later, but the short-term glory was, well, glorious.

The only hitch in President Putin's giddy-up happened in the waning days of Sochi, well off-site, in the main square of Kyiv, Ukraine. Putin's longtime man in Ukraine, President Viktor Yanukovych, was losing control. A tense three-month standoff between pro-democracy protesters and Yanukovych's armed security forces had escalated from rock throwing and potshots into a murderous forty-eight-hour festival of violence. By the end of February 20, 2014—the day Canada's women were beating the pants off the Swedes in the curling final in Sochi—more than a hundred people were dead in the streets near Kyiv's Maidan Square. Hundreds more were wounded. Many of the dead had been gunned down by Yanukovych's rooftop snipers. Parts of the city were aflame, and angry Ukrainian citizens appeared ready to breach the manned barricades surrounding Yanukovych's presidential offices.

Putin's triumph in Sochi was suddenly drenched in Ukrainian blood. And vociferous condemnation from the West.

The Russian president remained silent at first as diplomats from Germany, France, and Poland raced to Kyiv to find some plausible way out of the unfolding disaster. When the Ukrainian president called Putin to explain the deal he was willing to make with the international envoys, it sounded to Putin like full-on capitulation. Yanukovych was prepared to call for a new election and to step down from office in the interim. He was even ready to tell his security force (including the snipers) to stand down.

Putin nearly pissed himself.

He was sure this entire protest in Kyiv was instigated and fueled by the United States. This Kremlin party line seeped well down into the Russian government and even into Russophile defenders in the West. "The U.S. government, particularly [Assistant Secretary of State] Victoria Nuland, who is in close affiliation with Mrs. Clinton as well. You talk about influence on the democratic process over there," Carter Page was still saying four years after the fact. "She's in the streets during this big revolution, kind of encouraging the protesters, the revolutionaries. Handing out cookies. Which started this big chaos in the country to begin with." The cookies started this chaos?

The question of U.S. involvement was front and center at the Kremlin and the Russian Federation security services: Had the Obama administration carefully orchestrated this violent convulsion in the Maidan for the express purpose of embarrassing Putin at the height of his Sochi triumph? Not gonna happen, said Vlad. Russia was done sulking. So his man in Ukraine was done sulking too. Putin told Yanukovych to stand firm. He warned him, "You will have anarchy [if you show weakness]."

NINETEEN

ALL HAIL THE MERCENARIES

U KRAINE HAS BEEN A COLORFUL BUT TATTERED RIBBON IN THE middle of a long tug-of-war between Russia and the West since sometime back around World War I. And a century into the tug, neither side has ever been willing to let go of its end of the rope. Vladimir Putin, for one, had expended a lot of time and money and energy (literally energy) to keep Ukraine within the Russian sphere of influence. He did not mean to let all that effort go to waste. "No Russian leader," the Pussy Riot paranoid Sergey Markov once said, "wanted to go down in history as the one who lost Ukraine."

Ukraine had been a founding member of the Union of Soviet Socialist Republics in the early twentieth century, but a conflicted one. The citizenry's sense of itself as a separate and sovereign nation was never extinguished, and when it finally got the chance in 1991, the industrialized nation of fifty million chose independence, with an exclamation point. Nine in ten Ukrainians voted "yes" in the world-changing Act of Independence referendum that year. Even in Ukraine's largely Russian-speaking oblasts on the Russian border like Luhansk, Donetsk, and Crimea, voters overwhelmingly picked independence.

Three years later, the new Ukrainian government traded in its nuclear arsenal—the third largest in the world behind the United States and Russia at the time—for "security assurances." The United States, the United Kingdom, and Russia signed on to the Budapest Memorandum in December 1994. Ukraine handed over its 176 long-range missiles and its nearly 2,000 nuclear warheads, and in return the other major nuclear powers agreed to respect Ukraine's existing borders and its sovereignty. And maybe also do a little extra for the fledgling democracy. Even as an independent and sovereign nation, the former Soviet Socialist Republic of Ukraine was in need of help. The West chipped in with a large aid package. Cash-poor Russia promised what it could, and what it could promise was a robust and ongoing supply of cheap energy.

Understandably, Ukraine had eyes for both suitors. The oblasts in western Ukraine tended to be more culturally European, keen on Ukrainian autonomy, and attached to the Ukrainian language. The eastern oblasts, with their large Russian-speaking populations, maintained greater affinity for all things Russian. So the national allegiance was always sort of in the middle. Ukrainians were hot to get in on Western Europe's free-market capitalism, but in their wobbly, brand-new democracy they ended up entrusting their political leadership in Kyiv to the old Soviet apparatchiks. The president they elected in 1994 was a former boss of Soviet industry and a longtime chieftain in the Communist Party, Leonid Kuchma.

Things went about as you'd expect with Kuchma in charge. The president tied Ukraine's future and fortunes closer to Russia and then stuck pretty close to the old Soviet playbook. When Putin ran for election in 2000, after being designated successor to Boris Yeltsin, President Kuchma forked over $56 million to the presidential campaign. And when Putin's victory earned him the keys to the Kremlin cash vault, he quickly returned the favor by sending $250 million to Kyiv. The thank-you check was ostensibly to pay off Ukraine's growing debt to Russia. Energy from Russia was cheap, but not that cheap. In actuality, Ukrainian oligarchs pocketed the bonanza of rubles.

When Kuchma's second presidential term was coming to an end in 2004, he selected as his successor another old Soviet hand, Viktor Yanukovych. Kuchma had appointed Yanukovych to the governorship of the Russia-friendly Donetsk oblast in Ukraine's far southeast back in 1997. And Yanukovych turned out to be a perfect match for Donetsk and its ways of governance. He was "a Communist Party apparatchik who prefers centralized authority," one of Yanukovych's allies explained. "He knows if he gives a little here, he can take a little there." Yanukovych was reputedly taking a little from everywhere. No operation was too small or too tawdry—including an illegal chicken-smuggling racket that ultimately became a gross-out international scandal and corruption case study. "One ton of bad meat is mixed in with three tons of normal meat," a worker explained to reporters from a German television station. A German microbiologist assigned to look at the resultant product said, "We have found a lot of microbes—especially intestinal bacteria. We have found things that can make us sick."

When Yanukovych had first announced his campaign for the presidency of Ukraine in 2004, Vladimir Putin did all he could to ensure Yanukovych's ascendance. Putin sent money to Yanukovych's Party of Regions. He made personal appearances with Yanukovych in the weeks before the final runoff. He is also widely suspected to have engineered a vicious assault against Yanukovych's chief rival, the Western-friendly Ukrainian democrat Viktor Yushchenko. Yushchenko got extremely and mysteriously sick early in the campaign season, his movie-star-handsome face suddenly pocked with disfiguring lesions. The diagnosis was sinister: dioxin poisoning. Russian officials have always denied involvement in the poisoning. When Yushchenko was asked if he thought Putin gave the order, he offered cryptically: "I have an answer, but I cannot voice it." Despite the monstrous and advancing effects of the poisoning, Yushchenko would not be intimidated or forced out of the race. He muscled through to the final two-man runoff against Yanukovych, a contest in which Putin's operatives helped orchestrate miraculous voter turnout in the Russophile regions in eastern Ukraine. Putin's crew was becoming quite accomplished at a certain sort of democracy. Yanukovych-friendly precincts boasted a turnout of up to 127 percent, according to impartial observers from the European Network of Election Monitoring Organizations. This miracle no doubt helped Yanukovych eke out a slim victory over Yushchenko.

International election observers cried foul even before the final votes were counted. One man on the ground, Chairman Richard Lugar of the U.S. Senate Foreign Relations Committee, decried a "concerted and forceful program of election day fraud and abuse." Somewhere near 100,000 protesters jammed into the central square in Kyiv—the

Maidan—in the days and weeks that followed, in what became known as the Orange Revolution. (The Orange team leaned democratically West. The Blue team leaned autocratically toward Russia.) The Supreme Court of Ukraine took a hard look at the election shenanigans, declared the results invalid, and ordered a new vote. Yushchenko won the rerun going away and was sworn in to the presidency on January 23, 2005.

Putin was a very unhappy camper after that election, but he was also a more educated camper. Yanukovych's flameout was a painful lesson and reminder that politicians were never a sure bet. There was always the possibility they could get tangled up in ideologies, or ideals, or pleasing the voters, or even that voters might just not like them. Better to put your eggs in a few different baskets, Putin figured, including some outside the square four corners of politics. The Kremlin settled on a number of key industry titans and organized crime bosses in Ukraine who could be counted on to do Putin's bidding in exchange for just cash: the oligarchs. No democracy needed, no international observers, no talkback. Nobody quite fit the bill for such an effort as well as Dmitry Firtash, a forty-year-old self-proclaimed multibillionaire who had succeeded precisely because of his thoroughgoing cynicism. Like Guccifer, only with ambition. And connections.

Dmitry Firtash—according to the story he told diplomats from the West and reporters from Ukraine—grew up a nondescript boy in a nondescript family in a nondescript rural town in Soviet Ukraine. His father taught drivers' education ("aim high in steering"); his mother worked in a sugar factory. The greatest portion of Dmitry's meager inheritance was a disdain for the ruling Communist Party. Firtash relented to membership in the communist youth movement, he once said, only "after being locked in a party member's office for two days without food or water." Without pull to get a place at university, or one of those coveted party jobs that Mikhail Khodorkovsky had wangled, Firtash served a short stint (drafted, of course) in the Soviet army. He had plans to become a fireman, up until the Soviet Union collapsed in 1991. What followed in Ukraine after the collapse was a strange but oddly heady time, if one could keep one's head. The way Firtash saw it, he was a young man "between two countries—one that had ended and one that was beginning." But Firtash flourished in this strange twilight zone of lawlessness and wide-open possibility. He made his first fortune exporting canned goods and dry milk into Uzbekistan and other former Soviet republics, then moved into the much more lucrative field of brokering natural gas sales.

There was a pile of money to be made in natural gas in Ukraine, so there were plenty of very interested parties. Firtash had to be able to deal with bankers, pols, and, most important, organized crime bosses. All of them well armed. All of them locked in a dangerous and uneasy partnership that sometimes proved fatal for the unluckiest. Firtash knew certain dinner invitations could come with a side order of assassination. Even into the early years of the twenty-first century, the natural gas business was still operating by "the law of the streets," Firtash explained to the U.S. ambassador to Ukraine. "It was impossible to approach a government official for any reason without also meeting with an organized crime member," Firtash said. He did what he had to do.

Particularly helpful to Firtash was his relationship with Semion Mogilevich, believed to be the "boss of bosses" of the Russian mob syndicate—worldwide. Mogilevich had a degree in economics from a university in Lviv, the largest city in western Ukraine, and a special talent for stock frauds of the bonanza size. He also enjoyed more traditional mob-like pursuits. So active was Mogilevich around the globe, he eventually landed on the FBI's "Ten Most Wanted" list. His greatest criminal hits, according to the bureau, included "weapons trafficking, contract murders, extortion, drug trafficking, and prostitution on an international scale." When asked about his ties to Boss Mogilevich, Firtash explained to American diplomats in Kyiv that he simply didn't have the luxury of choosing his benefactors in Ukraine. Without Mogilevich's help, he later explained, he would never have been able to build his business. His $5 billion business! Well, if you were Vladimir Putin, it was pretty plain to see Firtash's potential utility. Here was a man who could be counted on to do what must be done. Here was a man, also, who sat at the nexus of fuel and corruption, which were, by 2006, fast becoming the future of Russian power and influence everywhere. And the exact means by which Putin would reassert Russian control in Ukraine.

Ukraine had a mammoth appetite for gas—for Russian gas. The

country consumed more fuel as a percentage of its GDP than any nation in the world, and its fuel of choice was natural gas. The country bought three-quarters of its supply through Russia's state-controlled monopoly, Gazprom; it also made money transiting Russian gas through pipelines to Gazprom customers in Europe. So even after the Orange Revolution and the election of Yushchenko, Russia still managed to keep a hold on the reins of Ukraine's economy, and its politics—which was perfect, as far as Putin was concerned. The infinitely corruptible energy business allowed Putin to pick and choose who would be rich and who would be powerful in Ukraine. He had learned this system well in St. Petersburg and then in Moscow, and it fast became Putin's strategy for projecting Russian power beyond its borders. The biggest threat he had to keep at bay was the prospect of strong, rich, stable, Western-oriented democracies in Russia's near abroad. That sort of thing could not only challenge or constrain Russia's regional power; it could conceivably—the horror—inspire the Russian people themselves, leading them to demand a democratic say in their own government as well.

The solution was simple: use Russian natural gas and oil not only to make money for the Russian state but also to keep neighboring countries corrupt and dependent. It solved so many problems. It reduced expectations for democratic governance and the rule of law in those countries. It created a corruptly empowered political class invested in preserving the Russia-dependent system that enriched its practitioners and their families. It also created comfortable space for organized crime to flourish. The Russian government, under Putin's control, has steadily become more integrated with all kinds of transnational organized crime in the former Soviet sphere—and not just because Putin has tended to attract the kinds of broken-nosed toughs who would otherwise be called "henchmen" if Putin hadn't made them so rich. The beauty of Putin's ever-deepening kinship with the mob was that it gave him a whole other set of levers with which to settle problems—and to make problematic people go away—whenever it might be unseemly to wield the overt powers of the state.

Putin's team in the Kremlin was delighted to utilize a man with Dmitry Firtash's special skills and talents to shape Ukraine to its liking, to turn it from its increasingly worrying flirtation with the West, with the European Union, with—oh, God—maybe even NATO. They cut Firtash a sweetheart deal in Ukraine before the first year of Yushchenko's presidency was over. Firtash's new company, RosUkrEnergo, was given the exclusive right to buy gas from Russia to sell to Ukraine. At a very large profit. About $800 million clear profit in 2007 alone. Firtash's company wasn't making anything. It wasn't even necessarily *moving* anything. It wasn't really doing anything at all except getting paid. Ukraine could just as easily have bought the gas with no middleman and no markup, but Putin wanted both the middleman *and* the markup; Dmitry would turn out to be handy! And so would the assurance of fantastical corruption at the very heart of the Ukrainian state, and so would the prospect of all the richest and most powerful and influential people in Ukraine being dependent on Russia's every whim. It cost Gazprom a pretty penny—straight out of Russian government coffers—but it was worth it. Firtash (as well as some of Putin's other Ukrainian oligarchs) would have plenty of cash to spread around to shape their country in ways that Putin would appreciate. Some of that cash went back to Moscow as tribute. Even more of it went to prop up Yanukovych's Party of Regions, which meant a whole bunch of it passed through or ended up in the offshore bank accounts of the mercenary American political operative Paul Manafort, who was always available to help his friend Yanukovych, for a price. The price ended up being about $75 million over the course of a decade.

Manafort was clearly quite taken with Dmitry Firtash, the source of much of that cash. He went so far as to set up a handful of business entities designed to help folks like Dmitry, and most particularly Dmitry, get money out of Eastern Europe and Central Asia and into U.S. or international real estate holdings. "The advantages of a single investor," wrote Manafort, "include less exposure, more flexibility, less reporting requirements and the ability to organize off-shore to maximize the return of the investor." These companies, such as CMZ Ventures LLC, founded in 2008, were managed by an ex-con named Brad Zackson who had learned the New York real estate business at the feet of a master, a Queens-based mogul named Fred Trump. Manafort drew up a vision statement for the fund, just as the world's economy was collapsing and real estate was becoming really affordable: "to take immediate advantage of the distressed nature of the US property market . . . where sponsors are getting caught in the credit squeeze, creating a pressure to refinance or shed assets." Manafort also envisioned buying on the international market, to "provide optimal flexibility to our investors." Attorneys who took a good look at CMZ's early deals suspected that "optimal flexibility" included the opportunity for Firtash to launder more than $100 million of questionable overseas profits on one real estate deal alone—a very suspect move to buy the site of the recently demolished Drake Hotel on Park Avenue in Manhattan.

Manafort never actually closed any of the supposedly blockbuster real estate deals he conjured in order to spin-cycle those overseas millions. But he did successfully establish his worth as an oligarch's helper and a political operative in Ukraine. He helped the Moscow-friendly Party of Regions win a solid plurality in the 2006 parliamentary elections, and he spent the next few years dinging Ukraine's strongest Orange Party leaders, President Viktor Yushchenko and Prime Minister Yulia Tymoshenko. Tymoshenko was a particular threat to Moscow's influence in Ukraine. She had made herself the front-runner in the 2010 presidential election by seizing on Firtash's sweetheart gas deal and promising to end it. She made a good case: Why on earth should RosUkrEnergo be allowed to siphon off $800 million in a single year by playing a middleman nobody needed?

Manafort and his team went at Prime Minister Tymoshenko with full force and helped to drive her approval ratings down to 20 percent six months before the 2010 election. Even her renegotiation of the Russia-Ukraine natural gas deal in 2009—no more Firtash—wasn't enough to sway a majority of voters to her. The onetime rotten chicken smuggler and Party of Regions leader Viktor Yanukovych squeezed by her and into the presidency, finally, in February 2010. Manafort received much credit for the Yanukovych victory and a rich new contract as the new Ukrainian president's off-site political adviser.

One of Yanukovych's first acts as president was to sic a rabid state prosecutor on Yulia Tymoshenko. Lock her up! Yanukovych's prosecutor charged Tymoshenko with the crime of abusing her official powers by "illegally" arranging the new Firtash-free gas deal with Russia without the required bureaucratic sign-offs. Tymoshenko had a lot of sympathy in the United States and Europe, so Manafort got right to work on the public relations front. According to reporting by Luke

Harding in *The Guardian*—later corroborated in legal filings by Robert Mueller's special prosecution team—Manafort engaged a sleazy PR firm run by American expats to draw up an energetic media operation to smear Tymoshenko. FBC Media said it could execute all the old standards like feeding reporters dirt on Tymoshenko and ghostwriting demeaning op-eds. Plus the everybody-does-it blast emails to key opinion makers in the West. But they were ready to play the new fields too. How about strategic messages hostile to Tymoshenko planted for exponential growth in the increasingly ugly Twitter universe? How about "Wikipedia page modification to highlight [her] corruption"? FBC said it could use these e-spaces to paint her as "reckless," "unstatesmanlike," and "at worst malicious, defamatory and antisemitic." It could create an entire website dedicated to her ignominy: the Tymoshenko Files. Maybe even create anonymous online videos that would make her seem like a drunk-and-slurring-his-words-era Boris Yeltsin. "The social media space offers great opportunities for guilt by association," FBC explained. Manafort secured FBC a six-month contract at $250,000 a month and the promise of a one-year rollover for work well done and on budget.

Despite FBC's best efforts, Tymoshenko's conviction in October 2011—she was sentenced to seven years in prison, ordered to pay $194 million in restitution, and barred from running in the next presidential election—was seen in government offices across the West for what it was: a hit job by Yanukovych on his most able political opponent. So Manafort's dirty trickster public relations team kept at it. They got excellent help from emerging alt-right media sites like Breitbart News, which tossed a guilt-by-association anti-Semitism spray grenade: "One prominent Jewish leader, who asked to remain unnamed, says that [Hillary] Clinton's *New York Times* op-ed ripping the current Ukrainian administration [Yanukovych] has 'created a neo-Nazi Frankenstein by issuing a de facto endorsement of Mrs. Tymoshenko and her choices.'" A twofer. Tymoshenko *and* Clinton! "Gentleman, Here is the first part of a series of articles that will be coming as we continue to build this effort," Manafort's business partner Rick Gates wrote in an email forwarding the Breitbart piece to Alan Friedman, the former *Wall Street Journal* reporter who helmed the slime shop FBC. "Alan, you get full credit for the Frankenstein comment."

Manafort also got some backup from more mainstream and burnished quarters, though this help was a bit pricier. He arranged for a respected American law firm to produce an "independent" report on the Tymoshenko legal proceedings. That firm—Skadden, Arps, Slate, Meagher & Flom—didn't appear to rush to judgment. The three-hundred-page report (with eleven separate appendixes, including a helpful dramatis personae) was not released until December 2012, more than a year after the completion of the trial and more than a year into Tymoshenko's prison term.

Turns out, according to the Skadden legal eagles, the Tymoshenko prosecution had been on the up and up. There were certain irregularities that might be frowned upon in Western courts, the report found, but the conviction itself was solid. "The trial court based its finding of Tymoshenko's guilt on factual determinations that had evidentiary support in the trial record," said the report. It also made this straight-ahead assertion: "Based on the record, Tymoshenko has not provided clear and specific evidence of political motivation that would be sufficient to overturn her conviction under American standards." Ukraine's Ministry of Justice, which had officially commissioned the report, the *independent* report, pronounced itself "grateful . . . for this professional analysis that unconditionally lays out the facts of the matter."

According to ministry officials back in Kyiv, Skadden had done all this expert legal work on a more or less pro bono basis—how nice! Ukraine claimed to have paid the firm a meager $12,000 fee for the report. The lead attorney on the report—Obama's first White House counsel, Greg Craig—refused to divulge how much or how little his fancy rich-guy law firm had actually been paid. But it would turn out that Skadden had the same mercenary tendencies as Firtash and the rest. Thanks to an arrangement fixed up by Paul Manafort, Skadden received from private sources in Kyiv $4,657,568.91 (accounted for by federal prosecutors right down to the last penny!). Oh, and: "In addition to being retained to write the report," read one of Special Counsel Mueller's legal filings, "[Skadden] was retained to represent Ukraine itself, including in connection with the Tymoshenko case and to provide training to the trial team prosecuting Tymoshenko." So much for the idea that Skadden was supposed to be an impartial observer of these proceedings.

While the firm's official report stated that the trial court's finding of Tymoshenko's guilt "had evidentiary support," the report left out one of the American law firm's own conclusions—a conclusion that Attorney Craig had written into a private "Memorandum to File"—that in fact evidence of any criminal intent by Tymoshenko was "virtually non-existent." Documents hidden by the Yanukovych government would later show that an early draft of the Skadden report had been handily annotated by Ukrainian government officials in an effort to make the report "more sympathetic" to the Tymoshenko prosecutors. Skadden claims to have held the line on the most egregious suggestions, but it did let Manafort know that "tweaks have been made."

Anyway, corruption-wise, things were going along pretty swimmingly in Ukraine. With Tymoshenko stashed in prison, trashed by American PR firms and law firms and anything else Manafort could cook up, Russia's man in Ukraine—Dmitry Firtash—got back into the gas deal, which was better than ever. His company's operating profit for the years 2012 and 2013 added up to nearly $4 *billion*. With that kind of money available for corrupting any actual governance in the interests of the people in Ukraine, Putin's natural gas supplier monopoly hovered over the heads of the Ukrainian people like a sword.

Putin could tell things were going well when Yanukovych reneged on his campaign promise (hey, he had to get elected, didn't he?) to move Ukraine toward greater cooperation with, and perhaps even membership in, the European Union. Putin knew that wouldn't—that couldn't—ever happen. The problem was the Ukrainian people appeared to really like the idea. Even when Putin promised $15 billion worth of new aid to Ukraine, while the EU couldn't even come up with $1 billion, the will of the Ukrainian people was clear. They wanted the EU, no matter Putin's largesse. The Orange side revolted again, and what started on November 21, 2013, as a small demonstration in the Maidan grew in just a few days to another 100,000-person protest. The demonstrators took over the Maidan and refused to leave. A violent crackdown by police in the last days of November didn't quell the enthusiasm. In the face of Yanukovych's armed and ready-to-fire security forces, determined Don Quixote–like protesters strapped on pots and pans as makeshift armor and took to the streets. The crowds kept on coming. And growing.

Putin thought the cold Kyiv January would break the crowd if the security forces could not. He was wrong. In February, as the Sochi Olympics kicked off, they were still there. By the tens of thousands, wearing their makeshift twenty-first-century defensive kitchenware, huddled for warmth around trash can fires. The protest had morphed from a demonstration about the EU question into a demonstration about democracy itself—the will of the governed. Ukrainians were calling it the Revolution of Dignity. The demonstrators in Kyiv were gaining courage in numbers. On February 18, 2014, they armed themselves with rocks and bats and slingshots and braved a gauntlet of Yanukovych's brutal security forces—many of them hired thugs with billy clubs, tear gas, and guns—to march on the Ukrainian parliament, the Rada. When Yanukovych's security forces started killing protesters that afternoon, the crowds retreated to their barricades in the Maidan and remained there through a terrifying night, protected by a ring of fire. Yanukovych's security forces broke out machine guns and scrambled more rooftop snipers the next day, and the civilian casualty list just kept growing. "We are not afraid to die for freedom," yelled one defiant protester, standing behind a makeshift shield, wearing a plastic helmet and a surgical mask. "Freedom is for us. Freedom is ours. We will win, and Ukraine will be part of Europe, and Ukraine will be part of the free world! And we'll never be slaves. We will be free." Putin watched it all with a growing sense of dread and a growing sense of anger. Here, at his doorstep, was the Western conspiracy! America was the cause of all this mess. He was sure.

He was also very much aware of other reports lately coming out of Ukraine—very disturbing news on the energy front. Ukrainian companies were ratcheting up their own production in the country's oil and gas fields, signing production deals with the major Western oil companies. They could frack, too! Ukraine had almost 400 million barrels of proven oil reserves, and God only knew how much natural gas once the serious fracking got going. Ukrainian officials were already talking about being able to produce every cubic meter of natural gas the country needed, *inside* the country. And to be able to export gas to Europe at a profit. This was revolting to Putin, whose lifeblood income came from Russia's natural gas sales in Europe and whose gravitational pull over countries in his orbit was the control, corruption, and cash that energy supplies afforded him. Putin could at least manage Ukraine's fractious and corruptible lurches at political independence. He could not countenance the idea of Ukraine's *energy* independence, which would certainly lead to Ukraine's actual independence. Woe be unto the Russian leader who loses control of Ukraine. Especially now.

Then it happened. On the eve of the final day of the Sochi Olympics. Yanukovych lost his nerve, called off his security forces, turned tail, and ran. He gave over Kyiv and the federal government to the Orange revolutionaries. The Ukrainian parliament met in an emergency session; legislators voted Yanukovych out of office in absentia. The Rada ordered the immediate release of Yulia Tymoshenko. And it voted to refer Yanukovych and his henchmen to the International Criminal Court to answer for "crimes against humanity." Members of the Rada even introduced a new law making Ukrainian the official language of the country. No more Russian.

The Russian cause wasn't helped when regular Ukrainian citizens raided Yanukovych's lakeside presidential retreat outside Kyiv. They emerged with photographs of his zoo full of peacocks and ostriches and wild boars, expensive wines, gilded clocks and toilets, a gold bar in the shape of a life-sized loaf of bread, a sauna, dozens of vintage cars, fake ruins (they tried to appear to be Ionic), an eighteen-hole golf course, and a floating replica of a Spanish galleon that served as the president's private restaurant. Beats chicken smuggling in the provinces.

Yanukovych resurfaced a few days later in the city of Kharkiv, a Party of Regions stronghold in the Russia-friendly eastern part of the country, and reminded everyone that whatever happened in Kyiv, he remained "the legitimately elected president." But he ran into protests even there. Thousands of his countrymen faced him down right there on his home streets, chanting, "Ukraine is not Russia! Ukraine is not Russia! Ukraine is not Russia!" Yanukovych fled to Moscow.

Putin was done trying to make nice. He had had it with the United States meddling on his turf. He figured the United States had put $5 billion into moving Ukraine into the Western win column. Vice

President Joseph R. Biden had been in and out of Kyiv for years, insisting the Obama administration would protect Ukraine from Russian aggression. "We do not recognize—and I want to reiterate it—*any* sphere of influence," Biden reminded. And he followed that up with what sounded like an insult: "[The Russians have] a shrinking population base. They have a withering economy. They have a banking sector and structure that is not likely to be able to withstand the next fifteen years. They're in a situation where the world is changing before them and they're clinging to something in the past that is not sustainable." Privately, American officials were even tougher on Russia's decline—pointing to the increasing death rates among the country's younger set, its rampant alcoholism, its military's decline into second-tier status, and its rampant corruption. Hey, just saying, it can't be easy being a *former* superpower.

Putin sort of took it personally—on behalf of himself and on behalf of Russia, which were pretty much one and the same in his mind. And by 2014, in spite of his iron hold on the Russian presidency, Putin was very, very wary. All political opposition in Russia and in the near abroad, in Putin's mind, sprang from an aggressive, zero-sum U.S. foreign policy game—one that would ultimately put him in its crosshairs. "He is said to have watched the video of [the Libyan leader Muammar Qaddafi's gruesome lynching] over and over," Julia Ioffe later reported in *The Atlantic*. As one of Obama's key foreign policy advisers explained to Ioffe, the pro-Western revolt in Ukraine seemed to take Putin's paranoia to a new level. "Ukraine was such a part of Russia that he took it as an assault on him," said Ben Rhodes. "Putin had always been an antagonist, and aggressive. But he went on offense after the Maidan. The gloves were off, in a way."

The ukases from the Kremlin in the days after Yanukovych's embarrassing flight were swift, and swiftly executed. Some were clearly symbolic. Boris Nemtsov and the recently released Pussy Riot ladies were arrested and jailed again. The most important move was intended to project Russia's revivified superpower power. *We're done sulking.* Putin dispatched a Russian military force (sans uniforms) into Crimea, Ukraine's southernmost landmass, to take it for Mother Russia, while sending his spokesmen out to deny the presence of any regular Russian soldiers in the area. This was all an impromptu campaign by separatists in Crimea, Kremlin officials explained, who were prodded to action by the terrifying events of the Maidan. Whatever aid came from Moscow was simply to avoid a humanitarian crisis and a slaughter of innocent Russian-speaking people in Crimea by the crazed neo-Nazi Ukrainian nationalists. Startled Western leaders warned the newly formed Ukrainian government not to fight back in Crimea, for fear Russia would use it as an excuse to invade the entire country.

In less than three weeks, Putin ripped Crimea from Ukraine and took it for Russia. The "exit of Crimea from Ukraine," the Kremlin claimed, was the result of "complex international processes." It was the first time since World War II that one country had rewritten another's borders by force and seized an entire landmass and its people for itself. Putin had blatantly violated Russia's vow to respect Ukrainian sovereignty, and he didn't seem content to stop at Crimea. He was already moving his forces toward other oblasts in the east of Ukraine, which also happened to be the oblasts with promising fields of oil and gas.

The move left Western leaders in a pickle; they were clearly shaken and uncertain of the proper response. The wrong move could easily tip into regional or even global disaster. Europe was hugely dependent on Gazprom's natural gas. "There is *no sensible alternative* to Russian gas to meet Europe's energy needs," Germany's economy minister, Sigmar Gabriel, said at the time. "Many people acted as if there [were] plenty of other sources from which Europe could draw its gas, but this is not the case."

President Barack Obama, meanwhile, was wary of punching back too hard and possibly inviting an escalation of the fighting. He believed the biggest foreign policy blunders of the postwar world were almost always the outcome of too little restraint, not too much. He did not want to go down in history as the U.S. president who allowed a dispute over Crimea to spiral into a serious military conflict. But Western leaders feared Putin would be emboldened if they allowed him to perpetrate international thievery without serious consequences. They settled on middle ground—a new and pointed set of economic sanctions against Russia. Or, more to the point, against Putin. The United States and the European Union drew up a list of Russian oligarchs and Kremlin officials, froze their assets in the West, and declared them off-limits for American and European businesses. The people on the list had one thing in common: they were Putin's most trusted consiglieri. Among them were Arkady and Boris Rotenberg, Russian Railways' president, Vladimir Yakunin. And Igor Sechin.

This is when the Big Dog came out of the American Mercenary Pound. Rex Tillerson had too much at stake. Like potentially hundreds of billions of dollars of deals with Putin's favorite oil company. ExxonMobil and Rosneft—Igor Sechin's Rosneft—were just a few months away from spudding their first well in the Russian Arctic. The take there had the potential to fill ExxonMobil's treasury and its reserves for decades to come. And that's not even counting Exxon's cut in all that oil and gas hiding in the untapped shale in western Siberia. Rex still had details of the still expanding partnership to finalize with Igor Sechin, no matter his new standing as an officially designated international pariah.

CEO Tillerson really had only one lens through which to see this problem. ExxonMobil stockholders didn't care about the Helsinki Accords of 1975, or the Budapest Memorandum of 1994, or any other geostrategic niceties, let alone the rooftop government snipers shooting people trying to defend themselves with pots and pans. They cared about their return on investment. This blinkered way of looking at things might have encouraged a certain lack of self-awareness within the corporation, but on the plus side it really simplified the equation. ExxonMobil had its own foreign policy to serve its own specific interests. And that corporate foreign policy only sometimes overlapped with the foreign policy of the United States. "I'm not a U.S. company," Tillerson's predecessor, Lee Raymond, once said, "and I don't make decisions based on what's good for the U.S." ExxonMobil had never been shy about calling on the U.S. State Department when it was having trouble with some foreign government (costing the corporation money!), but ExxonMobil's leaders felt no obligation to return the favor.

In fact, the ExxonMobil brain trust seemed to exhibit few qualms about pursuing corporate and shareholder interests even at the cost of America's most dearly held foreign policy imperatives. Tillerson was pursuing a multibillion-dollar deal with the Iraqi Kurds in 2013 and

2014, for instance, to develop their oil fields and ensure the royalties flowed straight into Kurdish bank accounts and not into the central Iraqi government in Baghdad. The Obama administration asked ExxonMobil point-blank not to do that deal, and it was no idle request. Exxon's exclusive pact with the Kurds was an existential threat to the already shaky coalition of Shia, Sunni, and Kurd in Iraq. More than four thousand American men and women had already died trying to stand up a sovereign, democratic, and *united* government in Iraq. And Americans were still dying there for that cause. "In [the Iraqi prime minister Nuri al-] Maliki's view," Dexter Filkins wrote in a 2017 profile of Tillerson in *The New Yorker,* "giving the Kurds their own revenue source would hasten the breakup of the country." Maliki confronted Tillerson at a meeting at the Willard hotel across from the White House while the deal was being discussed. "Maliki argued bluntly, 'You're dividing the country. You're undermining our constitution!'" Filkins wrote. "But Tillerson held firm. . . . In the end, Exxon made the Kurdish deal."

"Was there any country in the world whose record of civil rights was so horrible, or whose conduct was so directly a threat to global security or U.S. national security interests, that Exxon wouldn't do business with it?" Rex was asked during an official U.S. Senate investigation. "The standard that is applied is, first, 'Is it legal?'" he replied. "Does it violate any of the laws of the United States to conduct business with that particular country? Then, beyond that, it goes to the question of the country itself. Do they honor contract sanctity?" Contract sanctity, that's the top. Below that, it's all negotiable.

Even when it wasn't strictly legal to do business with a particular country or individual—like Igor Sechin, post-sanctions—there was always some wiggle room. There were always going to be lawyers willing to find, or create, an out (thinking of you, Skadden). Tillerson appeared to have an abiding faith that his attorneys could find a legally defensible path around American foreign policy and national security policy in the spring of 2014, because ExxonMobil signed eight separate agreements with Igor Sechin in the month after he hit the U.S. sanctions list. Exxon had decided, after much consultation with attorneys and compliance officers, that the company was barred from engaging with

Sechin only where his "personal assets" were involved. And so it just kept doing business with him when it came to Rosneft—to the potential tune of tens and hundreds of billions of dollars. It chose to set aside the well-known fact that Sechin owned a nice little piece of Rosneft and enjoyed an annual compensation from the company of tens of millions of dollars.

The last of the eight post-sanction agreements ExxonMobil signed with Sechin personally was inked on May 23, 2014, in St. Petersburg, Russia, at the same international economic forum where Rex had received his Order of Friendship medal from Putin a year earlier. Rex wasn't there in St. Petersburg to sign the new papers with Sechin, but he made a point to send ExxonMobil's head of exploration in his stead. This was in spite of requests from the Obama administration for businesses to steer clear of Putin's favorite forum that year. Pretty much every industry complied, even freaking Morgan Stanley. The exception was oil and gas. "Western energy bosses saved the St. Petersburg International Economic Forum from complete failure by effectively standing by Russia," explained a reporter from Reuters.

Tillerson's efforts on behalf of President Putin were not merely secondhand, or sotto voce. At a public forum that spring, Rex insisted rather churlishly that sanctions were rarely effective—because they were, as a rule, poorly implemented. Tillerson was apparently not at all concerned that he might be undermining a critical and very delicate U.S. foreign policy strategy, that threats of economic isolation from the U.S. government would not be quite so worrisome to Putin if the head of the biggest U.S. oil company was simultaneously jumping into his lap. He just kept jumping. Tillerson assured his shareholders at ExxonMobil's annual meeting that the upcoming drilling campaign in the Russian Arctic was still a go. "There has been no impact on any of our business activities in Russia to this point," he said. "Nor has there been any discernible impact on the relationship." He even made a personal trip to Moscow a few weeks later, over the express objections of the U.S. National Security Council, to join Igor Sechin in proselytizing the great glorious goodness of the Exxon-Rosneft partnership.

The thing was, Rex appeared to be comfortable in Russia. He was among friends who really *got* him, who understood what he was all about. "I've known [Putin] since 1999 and I have a very close relationship with him," Tillerson said in a talk at his alma mater a few years later. "I don't agree with everything Putin's doing. . . . But he understands that I'm a businessman. And I've invested a lot of money, our company has invested a lot of money, in Russia, very successfully. . . . And he knows us being there has caused good things to happen for them. We've been a positive force." For Russia.

....

TWENTY

HIS IDEA OF AMERICA

MARCH 4, 2014, LOOKED LIKE ONE OF THOSE NIGHTS AUBREY McClendon dreamed of when he helped bring the NBA to Oklahoma City. The Thunder had, as per usual, filled every seat in its downtown venue—now known as Chesapeake Energy Arena, thank you very much. Aubrey agreed to pay more than $3 million a year for the naming rights back in 2011, but he figured it was worth the cost. Couldn't beat it for advertising: "Chesapeake Energy" (with its enviro-friendly blue and green logo), in lights, on the hottest ticket in town. The Thunder's success in the five years since the move had been beyond all expectations, and not only in attendance figures. The team was the pride of the plains. Oklahoma's first-ever big-league professional franchise had willed its way into the playoffs in just its second season and had been back every year since. The team advanced all the way to the NBA Finals against King (LeBron) James and his Miami Heat in 2012. Top story on *SportsCenter*! Every night! The Thunder was back in the championship hunt in 2014, owners of the second-best record in the NBA. And on this particular night, with Kevin Durant on his way to a forty-two-point game and Russell Westbrook on his way to another triple-double, the Thunder held a comfortable sixteen-point halftime lead over the Philadelphia 76ers. Sure to extend this latest win streak. Thunder Up!

McClendon and his wife were there at the game for the world to see, in their regular courtside seats as always, even though Aubrey's reputation had taken some pretty serious hits in the past few years. His profligacy and his addiction to huge helpings of debt—which sounded nicer when you called it "leverage"—had finally caught up to him. And in a very public way. Activist shareholders, led by America's most aggressive and venal corporate raider, Carl Icahn, had torpedoed Chesapeake's founder and CEO, and it hadn't been particularly difficult. Aubrey had loaded the tube for them. McClendon wasn't a nutty, Teodorin Obiang–level spendthrift, but he had a hard time, for instance, explaining to his stockholders all that vacation travel he and his family (and their friends) had taken at Chesapeake's expense, flying around the globe on the company's private jets. Investors were not much impressed by the fact that he had paid some of the jet money back. They were also not happy that the company had paid Aubrey $12 million for his personal collection of antique maps. Or that while the price of natural gas hovered between $2 and $4 per BTU—way off that prerecession surge of $14 per BTU, and way off the price Chesapeake needed to turn an actual profit—Aubrey continued to insist that Chesapeake maintain its go-go drilling pace. With Aubrey at the helm, backed by his handpicked enablers on Chesapeake's board of directors, the company had leaned hard into headwinds that turned out to be more like a monsoon.

By the middle of 2012, Chesapeake stock had dipped below $15, which was only a quarter of its high-water mark. The company had spent $40 billion cash in two years alone, according to *Forbes,* and was swimming in red ink. Its bonds were rated junk, and the company had had to pay a massive vig for a multibillion-dollar emergency loan from the sharks at Goldman Sachs. It was starting to seem unavoidable. Aubrey had to go.

On April Fools' Day 2013, Aubrey McClendon was ushered off the corporate campus he had built in Oklahoma City. Right past the beautiful new Whole Foods store. He was no longer running Chesapeake Energy; in fact, he wasn't much welcome anywhere at the company he had founded.

But by the night of the Thunder's righteous spanking of the 76ers in March 2014, Aubrey being Aubrey, he was back in the game—bigtime. He had reportedly just raised more than $4 billion for a whole new oil and gas venture. This was no mean feat, given that his misdeeds at Chesapeake (real and alleged) still trailed him like unsightly toilet paper stuck to the heel of his tasseled loafer. The Department of Justice's criminal investigation into McClendon's alleged price-fixing in a Michigan land play was a poorly kept secret. ProPublica, meanwhile, was about to publish a lengthy investigative piece suggesting that Chesapeake—desperate for cash in Aubrey's final months at the company—appeared to have started a scheme to chisel landowners in Pennsylvania out of due royalties. All Chesapeake had to do was inflate its supposed expenses, deduct those expenses from the royalties it would otherwise pay to the landowners, and pocket the difference. Well, sure, when ProPublica put it that way, it sounded terrible.

And on top of all that, that March evening, rolling toward Aubrey along the bright blue Chesapeake Arena baseline like an orange-tinted bowling ball was Harold Hamm, the new brightest star of Oklahoma's legendary oil and gas firmament. The sixty-eight-year-old Hamm was founder and CEO of the Oklahoma City–based drilling powerhouse Continental Resources. Recently named one of *Time* magazine's hundred most influential people in the world (a year before Igor Sechin made that list), Hamm had been the very visible and primary energy adviser to the Republican presidential nominee, Mitt Romney. And even if the 2012 race hadn't worked out for his man Romney, a year and change after the election Hamm was still the most widely quoted, most widely sought-after, most visible spokesman for American energy. And if that wasn't annoying enough, Harold Hamm was now definitely Oklahoma's richest oilman, and by far the wealthiest person in the arena that night. He put Aubrey in the shade. Only twenty-three human beings in all of America topped Harold Hamm in 2014. Only sixty-seven on the entire planet, according to *Forbes* magazine's list of the five hundred wealthiest people in the world—just out that week. And, honestly, *Forbes* might even have lowballed Hamm when it ranked him at just $14.6 billion. He was probably worth more like $17 billion.

Right at Hamm's elbow as he cut down the NBA baseline was the ubiquitous *Forbes* energy industry reporter Christopher Helman, who was working up a lengthy profile of Hamm. Aubrey knew the reporter on sight. He had been writing about Aubrey for years. Helman had recently written about Chesapeake's improving prospects in the year since Aubrey had been deposed, now that the company was under new, stable, non-Aubrey leadership. And while Helman had lauded Aubrey's "feverish" effort to "orchestrate a comeback for the ages," he also took a serious shot at an oil and gas real estate fund Aubrey was going to manage. "As *Forbes* contributor Richard Finger and I have spelled out in detail," Helman wrote, "an investor would have to be stupid to buy into his blind pool trust." Kick a man while he's down, why dontcha? And even after Helman had accepted Aubrey's gift of a very pricey bottle of wine from his personal collection.

But now Aubrey would have to smile and act nice, because there were news photographers milling around the Chesapeake Energy Arena baseline too, ready to memorialize a rare public meeting of Oklahoma City's two most celebrated oil and gas titans.

Hamm appeared to be in a buoyant mood as he approached. The $17 billion man had already knocked back two scotch whiskeys, according to Helman, was basking in the Thunder's dominance of the Sixers, and was warmed by happy news he received earlier in the day: it was beginning to look as if he would only have to hand over a minuscule portion of his company stock in his impending divorce. His personal ownership interest in the oil company he had founded, Continental Resources, would still be up around 70 percent. This could fairly be counted a spectacular and lopsided victory in the financial bloodletting arena of Marital Combat.

So Hamm had plenty to smile about when he reached the McClendons and offered a firm, roughneck-like hand. "McClendon seems surprised—the two aren't friends," Helman wrote of that moment. "When Hamm begins small-talking McClendon's wife, McClendon himself leans over to a *Forbes* reporter in a fit of pique. 'I don't get it,' he whispers. 'You write all this bad stuff about me, while you hold up Harold Hamm as some paragon of virtue.'

"Paragon of virtue?" Helman's story continued. "Maybe, maybe not. But what's clear is that Hamm made money the old-fashioned way: He stuck with what he knew—and innovated. McClendon bet $13 billion in borrowed money that he could buy millions of acres of trendy shale gas fields and flip them at top dollar, but he nearly bankrupted Chesapeake (and soon thereafter lost his job) when prices collapsed from the oversupply he helped create. Hamm plodded along with a buy-and-hold plan for less glamorous oil."

So it was Harold Hamm, and not Aubrey McClendon, who graced the cover of *Forbes* several weeks later, in front of a sky-blue background. The cover line was in red and white, to make sure nobody could miss the patriotic point: "The Man Fueling America's Future."

Harold Hamm's greatest asset, beyond his ginormous stake in Continental Resources and his nose for oil, turned out to be his own story. He wasn't one of these smooth-talking corporate technocrats like the CEOs at ExxonMobil or Chevron or Shell or BP—the globe-trotting suits who were pulling down tens of millions a year for judiciously husbanding and growing Other People's Money. And he wasn't a financial whiz or a debt stuntman like the accounting minor Aubrey. Hamm was an independent, a wildcatter, with his own skin in the game. He knew the actual value of a dollar. "Fifteen hundred or two thousand dollars might not be a lot of money to you, Bubba," the multibillionaire would say. "That's a lot of money to me." If he had a wine cellar like Aubrey McClendon's—which he did not—he would not have been showboating it. When Hamm dined out, it was a hamburger at Sonic or steak and a double scotch at Applebee's. He certainly wasn't flying off to Bermuda in a company jet. His recreation was fishing at the Lake of the Ozarks or hunting pheasant up in North Dakota, where he could also keep close watch on his most crucial oil fields.

The Legend of Harold Hamm was a tale Oklahomans could be proud of, though Hamm didn't always see it that way. He'd only started telling people his whole history a few years earlier, when a consultant he'd brought on to help him lobby state and federal governments, Mike Cantrell, helped convince him that he should open up. It took some doing, too, because Hamm was not at ease talking about his past. Not sure he wanted to reveal the fact that he'd grown up the thirteenth child of sharecroppers who sometimes took young Harold out of grade school so he could pitch in picking cotton and tomatoes. "He'd never talked about growing up on a dirt floor," Cantrell recalled. "He'd never talked about not having a new pair of shoes until his house burned down and the Red Cross bought him a new pair of tennis shoes. He'd never talked about that because he was embarrassed." But once Hamm did start telling his story, he began to understand its power. It *was* a hell of a yarn, a spectacular tale of outsized success, a story that revealed the glories of the oil and gas industry—and of Oklahoma, and of America itself.

Hamm was born in 1945 on a small red clay farm in Lexington, Oklahoma, and spent his childhood in a two-bedroom house with no electricity and no running water. When Harold was a junior in high school, his parents moved the family to Enid, Oklahoma, 130 miles north, and changed the course of his life. "Enid was a company town for Champlin Petroleum, and there was an oil boom going on," Hamm wrote fifty years later. "The oil people there were different—charismatic, bigger than life." By the time he graduated from high school, Harold Hamm was set on being an oilman. "It just grabbed my imagination," he said, "that anybody could find this hidden, ancient wealth and it was yours."

He ran his own ad hoc apprenticeship in Enid, driving tank trucks to rig sites and hanging around to get impromptu tutorials from the well servicing pros and drilling foremen. In 1971, after five years of nosing around the business, twenty-five-year-old Hamm had a hunch about an area near a long-abandoned well—and took a flier. Cantrell still remembers the first time he heard Hamm tell the story, at a college up in North Dakota, almost forty years after the event. "One of the students asked him, tell us about how you got started," Cantrell recalls. "Harold said, 'Well, I was running a truck in Enid, Oklahoma. Bobtail truck. Cleaning tank bottles, which is the lowest of the lowest jobs, and I finally got myself enough money together to drill two wells. First one was a dry hole.'

"Harold said, 'I had enough money to do the second well. Second well came in at thirty barrels an hour.' And then he said, 'If I hadn't a had enough money to drill two wells . . .' and this is the key—he said, 'Nobody woulda ever known my name.'"

For Harold Hamm, this represented his true origin story, as well as the razor's edge that separated a shoeless sharecropper's son from a young man with a shot at fortune. "Think about that," Cantrell says. "I mean I always knew I was somebody. My parents raised me to feel like I could do anything. I never needed anybody to know my name. But it was important to him to be known as somebody. And by God, he's done it."

From his storefront office in Enid, Hamm rode out the next thirty-five years of boom-bust cycles in the oil business, and always on his own hook. He never sold out to the majors and never ceded controlling interest in his business. He once dug seventeen dry holes in a row—"busted a pick"—but never lost faith in his ability to sniff out oil. "I'm a geologist," Hamm liked to say, pronouncing it "joll-gest"—or "an explorationist," which sounded like Indiana Jones with a land map and a divining rod. Hamm's first big discovery was just twenty miles from his office door in Enid, where he tapped seventeen million barrels of oil in a prehistoric meteor crater nine thousand feet beneath the earth's surface. That find made him a rich man, but it wasn't enough for Hamm. Money wasn't exactly his endgame, those closest to him suspected. What he really seemed to want was to be known as the man who found more oil than anybody else in America, ever. He had plenty of his own money to risk on the venture and made a big move in the first years of the twenty-first century.

Hamm was convinced hydraulic fracking and horizontal drilling could do for oil what they were doing for gas. He bet the ranch on that conviction, up in the Bakken oil field in Montana and North Dakota, and it paid. Made him fabulously rich. Seventeen billion dollars rich! Rich enough to fork over almost a million dollars to Mitt Romney's super PAC in 2012. And it made him famous. Glossy business magazine pinup famous! Romney himself held up Harold Hamm as the gold standard of American enterprise during the 2012 campaign. "This is how the founders envisioned America," Romney said. "They didn't want to have a country that was dominated by, driven by, guided by a government; instead they wanted to have a country that was driven by free people pursuing their dreams."

Hamm's growing wealth and fame made him uncompromisingly certain of his own vision of the national destiny. As Romney's hand-picked energy guru, he refused to abide any nay-saying whatsoever about the prospects for American oil and gas. The sharecropper's son need only point to his own company's numbers in North Dakota. "We've doubled our oil output in the last five years," he said in 2012.

"We'll double it again in the next five." He estimated a future take of 24 billion barrels of oil in the Bakken field alone, "maybe more." And what about Texas and Pennsylvania and Colorado? "America's endowed with 163 billion barrels of recoverable oil," Hamm said. "Enough to replace Persian Gulf imports for the next fifty years." The mother lode of all that ancient wealth was finally within America's grasp, see—so long as the anti-fracking paranoiacs and climate change alarmists and green energy missionaries and overreaching government regulators didn't louse things up. The United States "could be completely energy independent by the end of the decade," Hamm said. "We can be the Saudi Arabia of oil and natural gas in the 21st century." And just in the nick of time. As Christopher Helman had put it in his red-white-and-crude *Forbes* paean to Hamm, "Sure, there remain legitimate concerns about the environmental impact of fracking. But you wouldn't want to see what the American economy would look like without it."

Hamm didn't understand how anybody could argue against him—why anybody would *want to* argue against him. The collateral effects of his success had been truly and unexpectedly salutary, in part because a lot of wildcatters had followed his treasure map. North Dakota had jumped California and Alaska and trailed only Texas as the biggest oil-producing state in the country—increasing its output from just 29 million barrels of oil in 2003 to 395 million in 2014. The engines of the shale boom, hydraulic fracturing and horizontal drilling, had nearly doubled America's overall daily oil production in just five years. That meant wealth creation. That meant jobs. Harold Hamm figured the Great Shale Boom (along with those ancient and helpful tax breaks) was good for about sixty thousand "direct, indirect and induced jobs." That last kind must have been like "inducing" somebody to grill enough hamburgers at the new McDonald's to feed the itinerant petroleum engineers and drilling crews roaming the cold plains of North Dakota. Or to repair the state highways and county roads torn up by the heavy drilling machinery necessary to grow oil production in the state by a factor of ten. Or to dispose of the environmentally hazardous "filter socks"—two feet long, eight inches in diameter—stuffed with TENORM (*technically enhanced* naturally occurring radioactive material) that frackers had illegally strewn around roadside gullies and Indian reservations and empty buildings in North Dakota. These haphazard disposal episodes included one in which more than two hundred bulging, fifty-five-gallon trash bags full of toxic tube socks were tossed into an abandoned auto shop in the town of Noonan. That's nearly two giant plastic bags of steaming, radioactive socks per resident. "They were piled waist deep or higher," according to the local chief sheriff's deputy, who probably ended up with some oil-industry- "induced" (but taxpayer-funded) overtime pay.

Whatever. Industrial capitalism is not for the faint of heart. Gotta break a few eggs to make an omelet, right? Worried that burning hundreds of billions of newfound barrels of oil over the next fifty years might not be altogether sanguine for the general health of the planet? Harold Hamm wasn't. "I don't believe the scientific evidence of global warming is settled," he explained to Senator John Kerry. "There are multiple conflicting studies on this subject." There are not, actually. But as far as Hamm was concerned, these worrywart politicians and activists and scientists were looking at it all wrong. What really mattered was this: the oil industry had single-handedly hauled the country out of the long torpor of recession that followed the 2008 financial crash. Like *Forbes* said, you wouldn't want to see what the American economy would look like without it.

What bothered Hamm, more than anything, was that oil and gas hadn't got its proper due; the story of the boom hadn't got the traction it should. For all his good press, his magazine covers, his nice warm seat at the friendly stock-hyping business TV shows, all the private invitations from Republican Party leaders—in 2014, what Republican pol *wasn't* preparing to run for president?—despite all that, Harold Hamm felt mighty underappreciated. On behalf of himself. On behalf of his industry. On behalf of all the misunderstood true believers in the beauty and power of the free—and he meant *free*—market. "There shouldn't be any limits," said Hamm.

He could not see why the Obama administration was handing out big fat cheap loans and tax incentives to wind and solar and the other green energy sectors. "Green whatever is not creating a lot of jobs," Hamm asserted. And he could not see why, year after year, Team Obama kept threatening to construct federal environmental regulations for fracking (they hadn't yet, thank God) or to water down the array of federal tax breaks the oil and gas industry had enjoyed for more than a century. Hamm made a rare trip to Capitol Hill to testify before the U.S. Senate committee that was considering muting the tax givebacks for oil and gas. Better think hard on this, Hamm told them, because losing those tax advantages might *induce* him to cut back his own production by as much as a third. "The unintended consequences, if we are not careful, of changing these rules could be devastating," he said in his testimony. "We could stop this energy renaissance." Nice little economy you got going on here; shame if something happened to it. There goes energy independence. *Poof.* There goes your precious economic recovery. *Poof.* There goes free enterprise in the last truly free country on earth. *Poof.* "When Hamm looks at Washington, at regulation and at the antifracktivists," Helman wrote in that *Forbes* profile, "he sees them as simply out of step with his idea of America."

TWENTY-ONE

BECACAUSE THEY COULD

....

HAROLD HAMM WAS FIGHTING BATTLES ON MULTIPLE FRONTS in the spring of 2014. There was the biomass-solar-wind-green-*whatever*-loving, tax-and-spend Obama administration to contend with. And his wife's divorce attorneys clawing at his bank accounts. And damn it all, if the twenty-five thousand people protesting outside the state capitol in Oklahoma were any indication, his own home state was after a pound of his flesh too. Oklahoma was staring down the barrel of a budget crisis, and the crisis was growing. Annual tax revenues were shrinking so precipitously that the state was close to declaring a "revenue failure." Rainy-day funds were drying up, with little hope to raise money for basics like schools and cops and roads. But Oklahomans were still, as a rule, crouched in a rigid antigovernment posture; the voters there had made it clear they didn't trust lawmakers to spend their money wisely. And they had gone out of their way—at the ballot box—to amend the Oklahoma Constitution to make sure their elected officials couldn't reach too deeply into anyone's pockets. The constitutional amendment passed more than twenty years earlier by referendum had created a nearly insurmountable hurdle for the state to raise any new money through taxation; any proposed tax raise had to get 75 percent approval in both houses of the Oklahoma state legislature. And that wasn't going to happen. So more budget cuts were coming, wrapped in the same inane bumper sticker arguments. "We don't have a revenue problem," Republican lawmakers insisted. "We have a spending problem."

Problem was, in 2014, there wasn't much more spending to cut. Oklahoma schools were becoming a point of shame. Spending per student in public schools was down by almost 25 percent in less than ten years; the state ranked forty-ninth in the nation in that category. Oklahoma's public school teachers were among the worst paid in the country, edging out only South Dakota, Mississippi, and sometimes Idaho.

News reports of Oklahoma teachers forced to work second jobs running cash registers at Walmart or waiting tables at Chinese restaurants were bad enough. But consider this long unfixed problem: In May 2013, in the Oklahoma City suburb of Moore, seven schoolkids were killed when 210-mile-an-hour winds from an EF5 tornado blew apart their elementary school. "A child is pulled from the rubble of the Plaza Towers Elementary" is a caption from photos in the morning newspaper that you can't unsee. There had been no room in the school strong enough to shelter the children from the fatal fury of that storm. In Tornado Alley. And it's not as if there hadn't been plenty of early warning. Really early warning. Oklahoma averaged fifty-seven tornadoes a year, and a deadly F5 had taken pretty much the same path into Moore back in 1999. F4 tornadoes had ripped through Moore again in 2003 and 2010. A study that followed the child-killing 2013 disaster found that only 15 percent of Oklahoma's public schools had suitable shelters statewide, which left half a million teachers, staff, and schoolchildren vulnerable to the next inevitable, recurring terrifying weather event. But remedying even that kind of a simple problem was considered a nonstarter, budget-wise. Pay up to put safe rooms in those schools? How about, instead, just praying storms don't come back. That's free.

Ultimately, over time, that kind of decision making tends toward a reckoning. Or at least if things are working right, it ought to. In Oklahoma, this looked as if it might be happening on the last Monday in March 2014, when twenty-five thousand Oklahomans showed up at the capitol with homemade T-shirts and poster boards scrawled with slogans ("We Will Not Be Silent!"). They were there to protest the lack of funding for public schools. And the educators who had taken a personal day to attend the rally weren't there just to scream about bigger paychecks for themselves. "Sure, I would love another couple of bucks in my pocket," a teacher from Midwest City told a reporter. "But my students would really like technology in the classroom, adequate supplies, textbooks, all of that."

This determined rally suggested a very serious and growing desire among Oklahomans to raise the money from those who could afford it. Where to find the who-could-afford-it crowd was pretty clear. Oklahoma-based oil and gas companies had been enjoying a fabulous windfall. The price of crude oil had been hovering near or above $100 a barrel for more than three years. Oklahoma energy companies were banking record profits. A nice portion of those profits owed to the huge jump in drilling *inside* Oklahoma's state borders. Crude oil production was up by almost 25 percent in the last year alone. The oil and gas industry had accounted for about 8 percent of the gross state product in pre-boom 2003; it accounted for 18.4 percent in 2014.

Funny thing was, the state government of Oklahoma had managed to starve itself of the benefits of this incredible rise in economic activity inside its borders. The state's signature industry was booming, but the state's treasury was bare. From 2008 to 2013, tax revenues from oil and gas production had actually dropped from $1.14 billion to $529 million. More stark was this fact: at the height of the last big boom in 1982, oil and gas taxes accounted for 27.4 percent of all state tax revenues; at the height of the new boom, oil and gas taxes accounted for just 3.9 percent. And it's not like Oklahoma had built up a lot of other hugely remunerative new industries in the meantime. It was still oil and gas all the way; it's just that oil and gas (and the pets they fed and watered in the state legislature) decided they were done paying anything, anymore, that would support the state in which they operated, or the government that supposedly regulated them as an industry. Other shale boom states, like North Dakota and Wyoming, had seen their treasuries grow so rapidly they were able to sock away surpluses to hedge against the next (certain) downturn in oil and gas prices. But not Oklahoma.

Part of the way they pulled it off in the Sooner State—much to the lasting detriment of Oklahoma's schools, roads, and every other thing even a small, conservative government is supposed to provide for—was something that began as a very sensible and forward-looking temporary tax incentive. It then grew into a suckhole of taxpayer money big enough to see from space.

Horizontal drilling was a promising new technology back in 1994, but it was unproven and expensive. To mitigate the downside risk and encourage more drillers to give it a go, the legislature in Oklahoma offered a big tax giveback for anybody willing to invest in horizontal drilling. All drillers would continue to pay the normal tax of 7 percent on the market price of all the crude oil and natural gas they took out of the ground. But if they got that oil or gas from a newly drilled horizontal well, they got a rebate of six-sevenths of the tax they had just paid. That made the tax rate on a new horizontal well just 1 percent—but only for the first two years the well produced, or until its profits paid back the up-front expenses. Whichever came first. The cost to the state of this giveback wasn't much to speak of at first—maybe a few million dollars a year—but it didn't prove particularly effective as an incentive, either. By 2002, eight years into the experiment, horizontal wells were still only about 5 percent of the total wells drilled in Oklahoma. That year, by unanimous vote, the legislature extended the 1 percent tax gimmick from two years to four years, or until payback. Still a sensible and inexpensive way to incentivize horizontal drilling.

Then they decided that the "until payback" part was maybe still a little miserly toward the oil and gas companies. In 2010, the legislature decreed that horizontal drillers would get their 1 percent tax rate for four years no matter what—forget the part where that sweet deal ended when the well's profits had finally earned back the cost of drilling. They didn't even bother calling it a "rebate" anymore, and told drillers they no longer had to write the up-front checks. Legislators reminded their constituents that this further giveaway to the industry was still subject to a "sunset" review, which would allow them to end the big tax break a few years down the road. And by 2014, many Oklahomans were glad they had given themselves that out, because by then it was clear that the combination of hydraulic fracturing and horizontal drilling had taken off, and there was no longer need to sweet-talk anyone into drilling horizontally. The expense of drilling a horizontal well had come way down, and drillers found that unlike regular vertical wells a horizontal well rarely came up dry. At the high point of the shale boom, almost nine in every ten new wells drilled in Oklahoma were horizontal. Thanks to what started as that little temporary tax incentive back in 1994, the boom in horizontal drilling became one of the most expensive things the government of Oklahoma paid for. In 2014 alone, the state was on its way to shoveling nearly $300 million to the oil and gas companies drilling in the state. That's $300 million, to companies that really didn't need it. Whereas horizontal drillers paid 11.7 percent in production taxes in Wyoming, 11.5 percent in North Dakota, and 6.7 percent in Texas, horizontal drillers in Oklahoma paid an effective total rate of somewhere around just 3 percent. Check the school budgets to see how that works out in the end.

The brightest light at the end of the tunnel for Oklahoma's worsening fiscal crisis was that the great horizontal drilling tax dodge was finally going to sunset, as most of the state's citizens thought it should. An April 2014 poll found that only 28 percent of Oklahoma voters were in favor of extending the horizontal drilling tax break past 2015. Sixty-four percent favored simply letting the tax break expire "in order to provide more funding for education, public safety, highways and other state needs." For Harold Hamm and the other bosses in the oil and gas industry, this was a problem. They said the poll's results were a "myth"; this was a Democratic poll, after all, conducted by an outfit from up in New York City. The industry girded for a fight. At Hamm's Continental Resources, the vice president for public relations explained the company's guiding ethic at the Governor's Energy Conference in 2014. "A gentleman was in our office late last year, and he was just talking about courage," VP Kristin Thomas said. "He said, 'Just like cowardice is contagious, so is courage.' I wrote that down that day. And that is sort of our theme for the year. . . . We try to apply courage in everything that we do every day. Be courageous and proud of the message we have to tell."

Continental and its friends came out swinging, courageously, to save their epic and ruinous tax break. The industry commissioned its own poll, a Sooner Survey, run by homegrown Republicans, and found that 70 percent of Oklahomans were actually opposed to any such "tax increase." Yeah, when you asked it that way, you might get that answer. What was due to happen wasn't actually a "tax increase"; after all, a tax increase would require an affirmative vote from three-quarters of both the house and the senate, which was still absolutely, positively never gonna happen. What was actually on its way was the preplanned expiration of a huge, outdated, long-running program, which began with the state actually sending big fat checks to the oil and gas companies every year, to the tune of hundreds of millions of dollars. And those companies would call it a tax hike, or Martha in the morning, or Scooby Dooby Doo—anything—if they felt that would help them hold on to that deal.

Lobbyists patrolled the capitol corridors while the legislature was in session that spring, courageously telling the story of oil and gas. Ending the tax break "will definitely mean fewer wells drilled in the state," was how *The Wall Street Journal* quoted Continental's vice president of government and regulatory affairs, Blu Hulsey. Devon Energy's PR team concurred: "While some may think that raising taxes on the oil and gas industry could provide additional funding for education, drilling less wells in the state will end up decreasing total revenue traditionally designated for education in the long-run." To make that point in person, Devon shuttled a score of Oklahoma state legislators over to its mammoth new office tower, which looked down on the dowdy state capitol in the distance.

The drillers even staged a counterdemonstration on the steps of the capitol, the Rally for the Rigs, with its own signs: "Don't Be a Fracking Idiot!" A thousand people rallied for oil and gas, including hundreds of Continental Resources employees Hamm had bused over from his downtown Oklahoma City office tower. (Frugal as always, he had taken over Devon Energy's old headquarters when he moved Continental's home office from Enid a few years earlier. *Already set up for an oil company. Haven't had to change a thing.*)

Hamm's former government affairs pro, Mike "Bubba" Cantrell, came out of retirement to headline the rally. Cantrell was as close a thing as there is to a quintessential independent Oklahoma oilman. He was the third generation from his family in oil and gas, and his own son had followed suit. Cantrell loved the oil business, he loved Oklahoma, and he loved politics. He was also no ordinary Bubba but a kind of poet-philosopher of the southern plains. Cantrell was born and raised in Ada, and when he finished his undergrad degree at East Central State College at the top of his class, he thought he was on his way to a PhD and a career in research psychology. But Bubba and his brother decided to put to use all they'd learned working in their dad's oil business while they were growing up. What had felt like a forced march when they were kids turned out to be pretty damn useful. They borrowed money to buy out another driller and started punching holes in the ground. As soon as his first well hit, Mike was captured. He is not a traditionally religious man, but he speaks with godly reverence of his original successful well—of climbing up on the tanks and watching, for the first time, as *his* oil flowed in. He can still remember how it smelled.

Cantrell also made sure to remember that success in the oil business did not put him above his fellow Oklahomans, but wove him that much tighter into the warp and weft of their lives. At the moments in his forty-year career when the industry has been in bad odor in the state, Cantrell tried to do something about it—like starting an association of independent oil producers that has funded the cleanup of more than fifteen thousand abandoned well sites. "We're not a bunch of altruists out here trying to be Greek gods or something," Cantrell says. "We're trying to make money and we're trying to do it in a way that our kids and our grandkids and their kids can be okay.

"We're the small producers. It's our business. We're not representing some big company. [We're] not some New York money or some private equity money or some Korean stockholders' money. It's our money. So we have a longer-term view. The private equity funding model is the five-year model. You make your money. And you're out. But we live in these communities. Seminole. Ada. Ardmore. Duncan. Almost every community in the state we've got members. We send our kids to public school. We don't send our kids to private school. We don't fly in on corporate jets from Houston and influence public policy. We call our neighbor down the street and say, 'Hey, Joe, we need you to vote for this.'

"If you're gonna live here—if you're embedded in the culture—it's only smart to play nice with everybody. Our mantra is we'll never ask for anything from our state that's not good for our state. We might have a difference of opinion on what that means, but that is sure the standard that we try to hold ourselves to."

And as a dyed-in-the-oilcloth independent, Cantrell stood in particular awe of Harold Hamm. "He's 68 percent of Continental," Cantrell says. "He isn't using everybody else's money. He's using his money. You can see why he's a hero." When Hamm asked for Cantrell's help to fight the expiration of the favorable horizontal drilling tax rate, Cantrell answered the call. He knew there weren't actually that many Oklahoma drillers benefiting from the big horizontal rebates; he could cite statistics, chapter and verse, about the enormous percentage of small-business, independent, wildcatter, regular old vertical drillers just like him who were paying *seven times* the tax rate as the big machers like Continental and Chesapeake and Devon. He didn't appreciate being "lumped together as one big monolith called Big Oil." But he was a true believer in the American oil and gas industry; mindful of the benefits it had bestowed upon his state and the world at large. And he was, withal, a team player.

Cantrell had already made his rounds and used the goodwill he'd built up over more than forty years of politicking in the state. He made a call on Governor Mary Fallin and on the senate president pro tem and on the chairmen of the energy committees in both the senate and the house. What he proposed to them seemed like a reasonable solution: say a 5 percent gross production tax rate across the board for both horizontal and vertical drillers. Everybody's happy, because it's still less than half the tax on new wells in hot shale-play states like North Dakota and Wyoming. Doesn't encourage the sort of production that leads to a glut in reserves and a precipitous fall in prices—look at Aubrey McClendon and the natural gas problem. And it would actually add revenue to the state. Cantrell's wife had been a teacher for almost forty years. The dwindling school budgets were serious conversation at his own dinner table.

Cantrell was a little uncomfortable with the tone of some of the other speakers at the Rally for the Rigs; they brought a sharp edge of anger to the podium. There were threats of walking away from new drilling—walking away from the state—if the legislature let the tax break go away. There were plenty of other shale plays to go after outside Oklahoma, right? And here's that implicit gangster-style threat again: nice little industry you got going on here; shame if something happened to it.

When it was Cantrell's turn to speak, he turned down the heat.

There was no state in the Union that had done more to promote the oil and gas industry, as far as Cantrell was concerned. "Oklahoma's got a long history of doing what is best for the oil and gas industry because they realize that's what's best for Oklahoma," he said. "We're not here to protest anything. We're not mad about anything. We're just here to remind our legislative friends, as they take up policies, of how important our industry is.

"We want to make sure they don't create any unintended harm with what they do. . . . Our job is merely to tell them our story."

The story of oil and gas in Oklahoma is pretty much the story of modern Oklahoma. As to the chicken and the egg question, there is little doubt—energy came first. Oil was discovered in Oklahoma long before it was a state and still trumps government and governance. This much is clear when you walk the capitol grounds in Oklahoma City, which sit smack in the middle of a long-productive oil field. The most renowned producer on the capitol grounds, Petunia No. 1, a slant-drilled (quasi-horizontal) well that angled from a neatly tended flower bed (hence the name) to right under the capitol itself, was completed in 1941. The dome of the capitol, by way of comparison, was not completed until sixty years later. Petunia No. 1 had been capped by then, but not before producing 1.5 million barrels of oil. And it wasn't just Petunia No. 1: there was a time when two dozen wells simultaneously pumped oil and gas out of the state-owned grounds; gushers were said to have shot oil onto the walls of the white capitol.

Though the capitol grounds have now gone pretty much dry, you can still visit Petunia No. 1, and defunct derricks and pump jacks still dot the surrounding grasslands as outdoor museum pieces. The past is the present in Oklahoma City. And the future, too. Raise your eyes up to the horizon, and you can see above all else the sleek, new, 845-foot-high, Gotham-like tower that the oil and gas behemoth Devon Energy built on the recent shale boom.

As much as the oil and gas industry has defined the economy of the state, it has also helped to define the personality of the state and its citizens. There is a gamblers' aspect to life in Oklahoma, both in its promise of unexpected windfall and in its inherent fatalism. Thousands of families in the state receive "mailbox money" for leasing the mineral rights on their land. These royalty checks from oil and gas drillers arrive on a regular and ongoing basis, sometimes for decades. It's always somebody else, of course, who hits the big money, the millions-that-change-lives money. (That's part of the fatalism vibe; it's always somebody else who hits big.) Most of the actual luck is on the scratch-off lotto card scale—the sort of meager bonus that adds a welcome little percentage to the monthly paycheck or Social Security payment.

There is even a gamblers' approach to Oklahoma-style religion. The state's wealthiest and most famous man of the cloth was Ada-born Oral Roberts, who grew up in dust bowl privation and just escaped being felled by tuberculosis when he was seventeen years old. An itinerant preacher with no real prospects, Roberts earned a reputation as a miracle maker by laying on hands to heal the halt and the lame at tent revivals. He also promised to deliver true believers from poverty (if that's what they desired), preaching what he called "seed faith" in the 1940s, long before today's ubiquitous "prosperity gospel" took hold. Roberts called on his followers to do what he had done—ante up some cash to God (through the Oral Roberts Ministry, of course) and shorten the odds on receiving a fair share of earthly treasure. His pitch was a lot like what you might hear from the oil and gas salesmen. Make that investment, whatever you could afford, and Pastor Roberts will do the gospel drilling for you. And everybody knew somebody, or knew somebody who knew somebody, who had hit—in the spirit, or the flesh, or the wallet. Which means that message has had staying power in Oklahoma. Almost seventy years later, his son and inheritor is still singing that song. "God has a plan for your needs to be met," the Reverend Richard Roberts exhorts. "You can talk to God about your specific need, as you give." Like any lotto, ya gotta be in it to win it.

The whole casino feel of living in an oil- and gas-dominated state also maps neatly onto the only other vital industry in Oklahoma. "Farming is capital intensive," a wheat grower from the Oklahoma Panhandle explains. "A new John Deere tractor might be a half million dollars. By the time you get all the add-ons and equipment you need you could spend a million. No local bank is big enough, or stupid enough, to take the risk, because after you've made the investment, everything depends on the weather. The weather is the thing. And the weather is beyond your control. I've been doing it for forty years, and I'll tell you what farming in Oklahoma is. It's a gamble. Farming in Oklahoma is like going to Vegas every year."

That beyond-anybody's-control attitude—you try stoppin' a tornado—is part of what made the low rumble of a real citizen pushback against the oil industry in early 2014 such a big deal. Generally speaking, Oklahomans hadn't got much worked up when the state budget would bust for the nth year in a row. You figure you're playing against the house, as always. The fix is in. The lobbyists hold sway. Most years, when the good-governance pros and academics and lefty do-gooders make all the reasonable, data-rich arguments for why Oklahoma needed to shore up its tax revenue by making the oil and gas drillers chip in their fair share, voters shrug and let it pass. But 2014 was different, judging by those twenty-five thousand citizens (who were not bused in by their bosses) who showed up at the capitol to shout for school funding in March 2014, with T-shirts and slogans and homemade poster board signs. You could also tell 2014 was different by the fact that near the end of the legislative session, after handing plenty of money out to plenty of lawmakers, the oil and gas industry had not yet won the day.

But that just meant Harold Hamm had to lean in a bit more than usual. Courage!

On April 29, 2014, with just three weeks to go in the session and the horizontal drilling issue still hanging fire, Governor Mary Fallin's budget director, Preston Doerflinger, hosted a meeting at his boss's official residence in Oklahoma City. The main agenda item was deciding what was the right thing to do about the horizontal drilling tax break. The attendees, besides Doerflinger, were the heads of the three biggest oil and gas companies in Oklahoma City: Harold Hamm of Continental Resources, Larry Nichols of Devon Energy, and Aubrey McClendon's replacement at Chesapeake Energy, Robert D. "Doug" Lawler. This made Doerflinger the fourth most powerful man in the room, and it wasn't even close. And that meant he was really just there to listen. The Oklahoma energy bosses had come to dictate terms. Their terms were these: a flat rate of 2 percent on all new wells, horizontal and vertical, for four years. So the horizontal drillers would essentially maintain a tax rebate of 71.4 percent, down from 86 percent. The vertical drillers would get their own new 71.4 percent rebate.

Then the trio went as a team to the big local media outlets in Oklahoma City to announce the generous "compromise" they had offered. The oilmen's assurance that the plan would be revenue neutral, even in the worst case, met with a bit of skepticism, even among other Oklahoma oilmen. The state was in "desperate financial circumstances," according to the Tulsa oil billionaire George Kaiser, and most of the financial benefit of the proposed "compromise" would accrue to investors outside the state, while teachers and students in Oklahoma sucked fumes. "I have lived here for more than two-thirds of the life of this state," Kaiser said. "I see what's happening to the state. Something has to give. I'm prepared to pay my fair share." The implication was that all the other rich-guy oilmen should be willing to do the same. Some agreed. Most did not. And so George Kaiser of the Kaiser-Francis Oil Company, and later the Bank of Oklahoma, became a bogeyman: the George Soros of the Sooner State, a pinko who just wanted to grow the government into a monster. He was invested in solar energy, for gawdsakes! He was one of Obama's key fund-raisers. Sure, maybe he was from Tulsa, but they morphed him into an American heretic, without proper appreciation of free-market capitalism's meritocracy. "I recognized early on that my good fortune was not due to superior personal character or initiative so much as it was to dumb luck," was a Kaiser quotation his critics liked to trot out. How about that for being out of step with the idea of America?

Turns out the critics didn't need to blow that hard at Kaiser's house. The Continental-Devon-Chesapeake proposal was quite warmly received by the state's bureaucrats and legislators. The budget director, Doerflinger, who a year earlier had advised Oklahoma legislators to think long and hard before they extended the horizontal drilling rebate—"It's not responsible for government to give money away as an incentive if no incentive is needed"—was now singing a new tune. "The governor is inclined to support the concept," he announced, "and thanks the industry and the Legislature for collaborating in the review process." The senate president pro tem, Brian Bingman, who had come out of his office to show his support at the Rally for the Rigs, expected the proposal to be "received very favorably" in his august body. "I think it's a very fair and reasonable proposal," said Bingman, who brought special insight to the issue, being in the oil business himself.

Two big legislative items came down to the wire in Oklahoma in 2014: tornado shelters for schools and the horizontal drilling tax rebates. The tornado shelter legislation had been drawn up in a way that it wouldn't cost a dime out of state coffers. Everyone knew there was no way the Republican-dominated legislature was going to raise the revenue (Taxes! Ack!) needed to build shelters in schools across the state. Instead, the proposed legislation, as described by one local reporter, simply "called for a statewide vote on allowing school districts, with local voter approval, to increase their bonding authority to build tornado shelters." Let the nearest and dearest decide whether it was worth their own hard-earned money to protect their children from storm-borne disaster. "The elegance of paying for shelters locally is that it allows school districts to decide whether they want a shelter and, if so, what it would look like and how much they will pay for it," the governor's spokesman explained. This solution, alas and alack, was not elegant enough for Oklahoma lawmakers, who voted the bill down on their way out of town.

But they did pass the horizontal drilling "compromise" and almost exactly as Hamm and friends had proposed it: a 2 percent tax for every driller for the first three years. (A good bit over half of the oil and gas produced by a typical horizontal well is captured, and thus taxed, in the first three years.) The measure passed both houses of the legislature by comfortable margins. "Oil and gas has a ton of weight, and by darn they wanted their credit," said one of a handful of Republican lawmakers who voted against. "By golly they got their credit."

The only surprise at the end of the day was that the industry lobbyists managed to get this new tax break made *permanent*. No sunset, no pretending that at some point the teachers and tornado-shelter-less schoolkids of Oklahoma might get to end their "incentivizing" the drilling of oil and gas in their state. The measure to make permanent the 2 percent deal squeezed through by only one vote; Fallin's lieutenant governor had to rush over to the senate to cast the tiebreaker. But the tax break that Harold Hamm and the other oil pooh-bahs wrote for themselves was forever. No backsies. A few legislators tried to joke it away. "Nothing is permanent in this building," the house Speaker, Jeff Hickman, said during the floor debate on the bill. "I firmly believe if Elvis had died in this building he would be alive today." But good luck getting the 75 percent vote needed to raise the taxes on drillers, ever again.

The head of government and regulatory affairs at Continental Resources started calling friends in the business as soon as he got the good news. "You're not gonna believe this," he told one former coworker. "We got this thing permanent."

"Harold [Hamm] can't pay you enough for what that's worth," the friend answered.

When Mike Cantrell looked back a few years later, as the consequences of oil and gas's big win in the legislature had become clear, when the hole in the state budget had ballooned up to nearly $1 billion, he felt real regret. But he also looked back with a twenty-twenty understanding of how easy it had been, of how money, as he would say, most always trumps merit in politics. Of how much brute power the industry has over the people elected to keep it in check. "Do you remember what Bill Clinton said when he got caught [having an affair with Monica Lewinsky] and had to apologize on national television?" Cantrell said. "I've never forgotten this. He said, 'I did it for the worst possible reason. I did it because I could.' And that's why they did that. Because they could."

....

TWENTY-TWO

"WE GREATLY VALUE OUR RELATIONSHIP"

THE CAMERAMAN HELD THE SHOT TIGHT ON VLADIMIR PUTIN AS the Russian president began to speak. The muted tone of the brown drapes behind him set off bold splashes of color in the Russian Federation flags that rested at the edges of the frame, over each of Putin's shoulders. To camera left was the simple republican flag of single broad stripes of red, blue, and white. To camera right was that same flag but with a gilded Russian crest overlaid at its center, which added tsar-like imperial flair. "Good afternoon, friends, I am very pleased to see all of you. We are about to take another major step in the development of promising oil and gas fields in the Arctic," Putin began, his hands resting comfortably on the desktop, his fingers interlaced. "Practice shows that it is nearly impossible, or least very difficult, to implement alone such large high-tech projects, projects of global scale and significance. Today commercial success is determined by effective international cooperation."

Here was Putin, on long-distance video linkup, trying once again to invoke that popular Russian poet: *Let us join hands my dear friends. We won't get lost if we're together.*

Widen out from that tight frame, though, take a look at the room from which this linkup was originating, and the scene seemed at cross-purposes with Putin's message of friendship. The Russian president was a small man in one of the many cavernous voids of salons within his private residence in Sochi, sitting alone, behind two oddly configured blond-wood desks. These desks, which looked as if they had been delivered by Ikea that morning and assembled on the spot, were the only pieces of furniture in the high-ceilinged cream-colored room— save for a television monitor mounted on a long metal leg. Behind the monitor were a handful of state-approved photographers invited to memorialize the occasion. The small screen bore images from the other end of the video linkup, a live feed from atop a mammoth drilling rig in the Russian Arctic, as far north as a commercial oil rig had ever been planted. That was where the real action was, more than two thousand miles away from this antiseptic room in Putin's Sochi manor.

That day, August 9, 2014, marked the spudding of a crucial new well in the Russian Arctic, a well whose success might ultimately tilt the balance of the world's energy supply for generations. Cracking the Arctic would of course also bring the world one big step closer to the brink of irrevocable catastrophe. Here sit more than one-fifth of the world's oil reserves, and if you were looking for a do-or-die climate question, the most apt might be whether the Arctic would keep its huge store of fossil fuels or have it extracted and burned. But that kind of thinking was for sissies. The geopolitical and economic advantage that these guys sought would be earned in the short run, not on some distant horizon.

Putin was glad to have an ally who thought the same way. That August video link was a celebration of a new level of partnership (perhaps we could even say *trust*) between two great international powers—the Russian Federation and the ExxonMobil Corporation. Putin was not your natural warm-and-fuzzy type, but he was making an effort that day. He appreciated how the leadership at ExxonMobil stuck with Rosneft, its partner in this Arctic project, even after Putin had horrified the rest of the free world with his theft of Crimea and even after Russia's biggest oil company had been added to the growing U.S. sanctions list. "In spite of the difficult current political situation, pragmatism and common sense still have the upper hand, and that is very gratifying," Putin said from behind his Ikea-ish desks. "Once again, I stress, ExxonMobil is our old reliable partner, and we greatly value our relationship."

The ExxonMobil bosses were much less voluble that day. Rex Tillerson was not on hand for the Arctic rig festivities. Not even by remote video hookup. Which was understandable. It might make good business sense to defy the wishes and interests of the U.S. government and partner with Putin to drill the Russian Arctic, but maybe Exxon didn't want to call attention to it. Tillerson instead sent to the Kara Sea drilling platform his top executive on the ground in Russia, Glenn Waller, to represent Exxon management. Waller was prowling the deck of the rig with Rosneft's chieftain, Igor Sechin, that day, but he too shied at the invitation to make a big speech. Waller made brief remarks instead, in his characteristically fluent Russian, but with uncharacteristic wariness. He spoke briefly of long-term future cooperation—"We see big benefits here"—but his main message seemed to be environmental. "We think it is very important to protect the natural beauty of the Russian Arctic," he said. Rrrriiiiiight.

Rosneft (a.k.a. the Russian Federation) and Exxon (a.k.a. Exxon management and shareholders) needed each other just then. The fracking boom in America had reset the worldwide energy field, and these two corporate beings were scrambling to reassert primacy. The United States was beginning to look like it might be capable of overtaking Russia to become the world leader in oil production. All glory to the frackers (and all apologies to the cows, and the neighbors, and the future prospects for their drinking water). But America's largest oil company, ExxonMobil, had been late to the game on the big shale plays in Texas and North Dakota and Pennsylvania, and frustratingly low natural gas prices had rendered its $30 billion (and also late) acquisition of the natural gas fracking company XTO Energy something of a bust. That said, ExxonMobil's revenues and profits hadn't suffered much yet. Exxon's biggest oil and gas fields were outside North America. Brent crude oil was still priced at well over $100 a barrel on the international market and had been consistently over that mark the previous three years. Revenue was not the problem. But Exxon's metrics of success did not stop at annual profits; its long-term survival depended on growing its reserves. In blunt terms, it needed to produce more oil and gas than it sold each year. The corporation operated like a shark, constantly on the move, constantly on the hunt for sustenance. By that summer of

2014, the shark was a little bit skinny. Exxon's annual hydrocarbon production was slipping, and its annual growth rate in reserves was a tad meager for comfort.

Vladimir Putin and Igor Sechin felt Rex's pain. Sechin had grown Kremlin-controlled Rosneft into one of the largest and most valuable oil companies in the world, but he had done it in large part through smashing and grabbing any smaller company that smacked of competition or real skill in the field. That kind of gangster ethos can only get you so far. When you reward achievement with extortion, and technological advancement with theft and threat, eventually you no longer have great businesses in that sector.

That outcome was a near certainty, because Putin had decided that Russia would be a petro-state—choosing an economic future for his country that best served his own needs. Oil and gas could be wielded as an international cudgel to force other countries to respect and deal with Russia no matter anything else Russia did. The industry also—bonus!—trailed enough easy cash to generate almost instant, almost limitless corruption wherever needed. And when you have those kinds of goals in mind for your one indispensable industry, and you run that industry like a Mafia chop shop with less *omertà*, eventually the actual business side of your dark little authoritarian scheme is going to suffer. Both financially and in its basic technical competence. And indeed, by 2014, the bright red star of Russian energy was dimming; Rosneft was running on fumes. The company's production was flat, and Sechin had just been forced to go to Putin hat in hand to ask for $42 billion from the government treasury to help him make ends meet. That alone tells you something about the skill and capability of Russian business under Putin, when even one of the biggest oil companies on earth, in one of the world's most oil-rich nations, with the price per barrel of crude bouncing along at spectacular highs, doesn't make money.

And Putin and Sechin were anticipating bigger trouble ahead. There was the short-term problem—at least they hoped it was short-term—of having made the Russian Federation an international pariah with its naked aggression in Ukraine. And there was the much more worrisome long-term problem: cheap and easy-to-produce oil and gas in mainland Russia might have been plentiful, but it had never been inexhaustible. The energy industry in Russia was draining the old Soviet-era oil fields in a hurry. Meanwhile, there were competitive threats arising in its very own neighborhood. Other countries in Eastern Europe—Poland, Romania, *Ukraine!*—were already in deals with technologically capable Western majors to help them frack their own territory for oil and gas. That said, there were always means of disrupting some of these contrary developments. The Kremlin had poured illicit cash and other resources into the Green Party and environmental activist groups in those countries to slow the march of fracking. But without serious course correction, the Kremlin was steaming toward big trouble.

Putin knew that all too well as he sat in his cream-hued salon on August 9, 2014, and gave the signal to begin drilling in the Russian Arctic. Time for a big breakthrough in the Russian energy sector was running out. The future was now. And that future rested about a mile and a half down into the Arctic seabed, in a straight line from the drilling rig where Igor Sechin was holding forth. "The start of exploratory drilling in the Kara Sea is the most important event of the year for the global oil and gas industry," said Sechin.

Industry experts in the West tended to back Igor's claim. "It's probably one of the most interesting wells in the global oil industry for many years," said a senior research fellow from the Oxford Institute for Energy Studies. News coverage that day backed Igor's claim as well, adding eye-popping detail to Sechin's boast: early surveys suggested this particular section of the Kara Sea, an underwater area roughly the size of Moscow, was harboring maybe nine billion barrels of oil . . . And this was only a tenth of the total oil and gas equivalent in the Rosneft-owned drilling sites in the nearby Arctic shelf. Sechin's team claimed the Kara Sea held more oil and gas "than the deposits of the Gulf of Mexico, the Brazilian shelf or the offshore potential north of Alaska and Canada." Eighty-seven *billion* barrels in all. Enough to satisfy the demands of the *entire* world for almost three full years, even if nobody else on the planet produced a single drop.

This might indeed be the game changer Putin and Sechin were counting on. And Tillerson too. When one of the Kremlin-funded television stations, RT, reported on the exciting new Arctic oil exploration effort being launched and lauded by President Putin, it interviewed a research fellow from a conservative free-market London-based think tank who summed it up rather drolly. "[ExxonMobil] could do with the oil," said Keith Boyfield. "They've already invested a considerable amount of money."

Exxon had in fact sunk a ton of money into this potentially globally transformational project. It could change Exxon's future, and Russia's, and the world's. One immediate problem it faced, though, was the weather in the Arctic. The Exxon-Rosneft team had a window of about seventy days to get 'er done before the ice floes closed in on the drilling platform. And other obstacles were heading their way, too, from the realm of geopolitics.

In the aftermath of his forcible annexation of Crimea, Putin was enjoying an enormous surge in popularity inside Russia. This first step in the advent of what he called *Novorossiya* (New Russia)—restoring the lost territory and the old glory of a faded empire—had caused Putin's personal approval ratings to jump into the mid-80s by the summer of 2014. The approval numbers among his long-standing base constituency of poor, rural, less-educated Russians had ticked up to around 90 percent. The approval numbers among the urban intelligentsia, meanwhile, soared from below 50 percent to 75 percent. Russians had suddenly decided—after ten years of saying otherwise—that they would rather be struggling citizens of a superpower nation with swagger than struggling citizens of a beat country. This was Fortress Russia, piping state-sanctioned, state-happy news to all those within the walls, which meant King Vladimir reigned imperial.

On the other side of those walls, support for Putin was thinning to wisps. The spring and summer had been a disaster for his standing in the rest of the world. The illegal annexation of Crimea was bad enough, but the international community was alarmed, if not outright horrified, that the Russian putsch hadn't stopped there. Putin's military had also massed soldiers, tanks, and artillery on the Ukrainian border as a sign of encouragement to separatists in the Donetsk and Luhansk oblasts, a region known as the Donbas. Somewhere between a quarter and a third of the population in those two oblasts had voiced support for annexation to Russia. Putin's commanders explained they had moved military assets to the border in case they were called to sweep in and protect the Russian-speaking population in these oblasts from the depredations of Ukrainian leaders who had taken charge of the federal government in Kyiv. Nobody in the West was buying that explanation. That Russia's overriding concern was humanitarian stretched credulity. Humanity was not Putin's strong suit. The Donbas was a heavily populated and productive manufacturing area, with Donetsk alone accounting for about 12 percent of Ukraine's gross domestic product. The area nearby also accounted for something near 90 percent of Ukraine's oil and gas production, and fracking technology promised to open new fields. Grabbing the Donbas was a twofer. Russia could cripple the teetering economy of Ukraine and scoop up a healthy supply of oil and gas. *Novorossiya!*

When well-armed separatists began taking over government buildings in major cities in the Donbas, not many close observers believed the Kremlin's assertion that it was homegrown revolutionaries at work. The townsfolk in Kharkiv, for instance, were pretty certain it was Russian soldiers (in mufti) who proclaimed the liberation of city hall, because local separatists would have known that what they had actually seized and liberated was not city hall but the city's main opera theater. Many supposedly local "separatists" manning checkpoints and roadblocks did not know the names of nearby villages. Which seemed a tad suspicious.

The Russian army plants and their separatist cohorts in the Donbas declared independence from Ukraine in early May 2014. Hello, Donetsk People's Republic! As Russian-military-backed rebels in the Donbas rolled up serious real estate, Putin increased his pressure on Ukraine's shaky economy and its fractious interim government. Gazprom briefly cut off the supply of natural gas to Ukraine (just a reminder).

The Russians also began to beta test another potentially powerful weapon in the federation's fight to take control of Ukraine and to wreak havoc in general. As the presidential election to replace the runaway Putin puppet Yanukovych neared, the Russian military and security services fed social media sites all across Ukraine false stories about how the Orange movement was led by neo-Nazis and anti-Semites and downright terrorists. A social media post by a "physician" in Odessa claimed that anti-Russian Ukrainians had beaten pro-Russian separatists and then *burned them alive* simply because of their political views. When the doctor rushed to aid the victims, he explained, the rabid Ukrainian nationalists held him back. "One rudely pushed me, promising that I and other Jews would suffer a similar fate," read the fake post from a fake account by a fake Ukrainian doctor. "In my city such things did not happen even during the worst of Nazi occupation. I wonder why the world is silent." Thank you, Facebook.

Ukraine looked as if it might fracture in the lead-up to the election. The death toll in the Donbas fight rose to nearly a thousand. Factories went dark. One coal mine in the city of Donetsk had to be shuttered after the pro-Russian rebels made off with most of its wiring, detonators, and explosive powder. And then a funny thing happened in the election. Despite all the Russian propaganda and disinformation and manipulation, Ukrainians overwhelmingly elected the straight-ahead, pro-EU, pro–Revolution of Dignity candidate as the country's new president. In a very crowded field, Petro Poroshenko surprised the country by winning an actual majority of the vote. Candidates from the neo-Nazi and anti-Semitic far-right parties that were supposedly so popular polled as asterisks, down around 1 and 2 percent.

With the new government in place in Kyiv by the end of June, and with a clear public mandate behind it, the newly inaugurated Poroshenko got to work on behalf of Ukrainians. One of his first acts as president was to sign the official Association Agreement with the European Union that his Russian-tool predecessor had tried to back out of. "This is a really historic date for Ukraine," Poroshenko said at the signing ceremony. He then further exasperated Putin by expressing his hopes that Ukraine would one day be a full member of the EU. Poroshenko also defied Putin in an even more aggressive way; he mounted a serious military counteroffensive in the Donbas, using the national army to reinforce the pro-Ukrainian militia groups who had formed in the long weeks of absence of help from Kyiv.

June and July turned out to be very, very bad months for President Putin. There was a surge in the number of dead Russian soldiers being shipped back home from the Donbas. The corpses arrived in Russia under the cover of secrecy, cryptically marked "Cargo 200." The Putin critic and political opponent Boris Nemtsov saw it happen and immediately began a campaign to catalog a name-by-name record of the casualties for public release. Whatever the popular sentiment for *Novorossiya,* Nemtsov understood there was a limit to how many husbands, wives, sons, daughters, brothers, and sisters Russians were willing to sacrifice for another chunk of Ukraine. Officials in the Kremlin and the Russian military understood that too. Survivors of the dead received terse and pointed messages that suggested they keep their grief concerning these "volunteer" soldiers confined to the family circle. "You are an adult," a Russian Federation official explained to the wife of one casualty. "Russia is not conducting an organized military action. Your husband voluntarily went to the street where shots were being fired."

The Ukrainian regular army and its partners in the east, meanwhile, rolled up one pro-Russian separatist stronghold after another in Donetsk and Luhansk. By mid-July, Poroshenko's national government claimed control of two-thirds of the Donbas region and most of the major road crossings at the Russian border. The government in Kyiv reported that it had reduced the number of separatist fighters by more than half, from fifty thousand to twenty thousand, and drawn a circle around those that remained. "Every day our containment belt around the territories that unfortunately are still held by the terrorists will become tighter and tighter," Poroshenko's defense secretary said. "Every day, more cities are coming under Ukrainian control."

On July 16, 2014, with Putin showing no signs of backing down in the face of Ukraine's assertion of its sovereignty and the defense of its borders, the United States announced another round of sanctions. This new set, for the first time, included Rosneft. American companies were given license to go ahead with existing projects, but in the future there could be no new deals with Russia's oil giant. European Union leaders were wary about supporting the United States on the new sanctions, because they were scared of backing the volatile Putin into a corner. Not only did EU countries do ten times more trade with Russia than did the United States, but they were dependent on Russia for much of their energy.

That pragmatic reluctance held sway only a few days longer, until a Malaysia Airlines jet flying from Amsterdam to Kuala Lumpur was shot down as it passed over a corner of the Donbas. There were almost three hundred people aboard the flight, and more than two hundred were citizens of the EU. Bodies of a few of the victims, including a teenage boy, had landed amid a grove of fruit trees on the grounds of a Ukrainian orphanage. "I want to know why that boy died," one of the terrorized resident orphans told Anna Nemtsova, a Moscow-based reporter for *The Daily Beast*.

When the team from the Organization for Security and Co-operation in Europe arrived to sift for clues to help answer that question, Nemtsova reported, they were blocked from the crash site by soldiers wearing balaclavas and carrying Kalashnikov rifles. The inspectors could see hundreds of charred bodies and body parts being loaded into plastic bags. "You cannot go to that territory," they were told by the Russian/separatist soldiers. "Our investigators have not completed their work."

The international team that did finally conduct the delayed criminal investigation was careful and deliberate. Almost four years later, inspectors from Malaysia, Australia, Belgium, the Netherlands ("grieving nations" who had lost citizens in the disaster), and Ukraine were still working to uncover the absolute and verified specifics of the matter, which were these: The civilian passenger jet was shot down with a missile fired by a Russian-manufactured anti-aircraft weapon. The anti-aircraft system had been ferried across the border from Russia and then more than two hundred miles into Ukraine several weeks earlier on a lowboy trailer, hauled by a white Volvo truck, accompanied by a convoy of vehicles carrying armed men. That particular launcher proved to be property of the Russian army's Fifty-third Anti-aircraft Missile brigade, whose soldiers had fired the missile from a remote field about 150 miles north of the crucial separatist-controlled city of Donetsk. The spotters in the Russian brigade likely mistook the jet for a Ukrainian military plane. (The Russians had been shooting Ukrainian jets and helicopters out of the sky, with abandon, for well over a month by then.) Markings on the fatal projectile identified it as a missile produced in 1986 at the Dolgoprudny Research and Manufacturing Enterprise in Moscow. The anti-aircraft launcher that fired the missile into the cockpit of the Boeing 777 had been spirited back across the border into Russia within hours of the fatal launch.

Incriminating new information was still emerging in 2019. But even in the first few days after the tragedy, it was pretty clear who was to blame. Prime Minister David Cameron, who had lost ten British citizens in the shootdown, wrote an op-ed titled "This Is an Outrage Made in Moscow." One of the British tabloids called it, simply, "Putin's

Missile." The Kremlin denied responsibility, to little effect. Western Europe finally swung into Ukraine's corner.

Within two weeks, the EU had joined with the United States to take an even bigger bite out of Putin's hide, and from the part he actually cared about. The new sanctions would specifically bar the sale or transfer of advanced engineering systems that Russia needed to drill new oil fields. "In the energy sector, new precision-guided restrictions will make it difficult for Russia to access the technology and equipment needed to produce oil from deep water, Arctic or shale deposits," explained Jason Bordoff, who had just left his job as staff director in charge of energy and climate change at the National Security Council, and Elizabeth Rosenberg, a former senior sanctions adviser at the Treasury Department. "These are precisely the complex, challenging projects that Russia will have difficulty achieving without the technology of Western energy firms. The measures are designed to make it more difficult and costly for Russian energy companies to invest in replacing declining conventional oil output and meeting future production goals."

So this was the sticky wicket Rosneft and ExxonMobil faced as their jointly held drill bits powered down into the Arctic seabed that August. They knew already that they would need to hurry the drilling ahead of the on-marching ice floes. But now they would also need to take heed of these on-marching international sanctions, targeted at exactly the kind of high-tech, envelope-pushing drilling they were trying to pull off in the Kara Sea. That said, for all the international Sturm und Drang about these tough new sanctions, Putin himself didn't seem all that worried. Russia now had a partner, after all, and he was pretty sure that a company like ExxonMobil could do as it pleased, no matter the wishes of the current U.S. government. He had seen presidential administrations come and go in the United States, but ExxonMobil abided. "We're not going anywhere," Tillerson claimed he had once told Putin. "We've been around a hundred and thirty years. . . . We just have to comply with the law."

....

TWENTY-THREE

POBEDA!

AS FAR AS EXXONMOBIL LEADERSHIP WAS CONCERNED IN AU-gust 2014, the company still had a lot of wiggle room out in the Russian Arctic—even with the new sanctions against its partner, Rosneft. The joint Rosneft-Exxon Kara Sea project was already under way when the latest sanctions hit, so it was exempt as an ongoing operation. The sheer size of the drilling rig also seemed to suggest, well, inevitability. The West Alpha rig, leased from a Norwegian company, was a monster. Its derrick towered 350 feet above the main deck, which measured 230 by 216 feet. The thirty-one-thousand-ton rig stood sturdy, 155 miles off the Russian coast, against rough and rocking Arctic waters. It held fast by design: "an 8-anchor positioning system, which provides advanced stability," Rosneft boasted. "Most of the platform is outside the reach of waves, which are no impediment for the rig's operations."

Outside the reach of waves, real or geopolitical. That's sort of the way Vladimir Putin was feeling in August 2014, inside Fortress Russia, with reliable old ExxonMobil standing firm at his side. Screw the rest of the world and their carping about Crimea and Donbas and the shootdown and anything else. Together he and Exxon would make their strike in the Arctic, and the West would be at Russia's energy teat for another generation.

In Steven Lee Myers's fascinating and psychologically rich 2015 biography of Putin, *The New Tsar,* we get a clear view of Putin's me-against-the-world sense of self at that crucial time in his presidency. Separate and apart from the increasingly aggressive sanctions against Russia, and the widening international consensus behind them, Putin was convinced that almost all of Russia's biggest problems were the product of a global conspiracy against his country. He thought, for example, that the new downtick in oil prices in 2014 was a deliberate plot hatched by the United States and Saudi Arabia to weaken the Russian Federation. He was also incensed by news from the international arbitration court in The Hague, which had chosen this particular moment to issue its verdict on Rosneft's disputed grab of Yukos a dozen years earlier. The court ordered that Russia owed $50 billion in recompense and damages to Yukos shareholders and named Putin himself as a bad actor in the scheme. "Each step against Russia he [Putin] now believed to be a cynical, calculated attack against him," Myers writes in *The New Tsar.* "He simply no longer cared how the West would respond. The change in Putin's demeanor became acute after the downing of Flight 17, according to his old friend Sergei Roldugin. 'I noticed that the more he is being teased the tougher he becomes. . . . He has become more—I don't want to say aggressive—but more indifferent. . . . He does not want to compromise anymore.'"

Roldugin was maybe selling soft soap, because Putin's indifference and unwillingness to compromise turned pretty damn aggressive, pretty damn fast. Staging areas on Russia's western border filled with more than forty thousand Russian soldiers and weapons (including land mines, mortars, rocket launchers, surface-to-air missiles, 152-millimeter howitzers, anti-tank guided missiles, and actual battle tanks). Russian soldiers were ordered to scrub all insignia and identifying markings from their uniforms and equipment and vehicles, hand over their cell phones, and head west into eastern Ukraine. "They didn't say anything, just march 70 kilometers," one Russian paratrooper later said of his vague orders. "I guessed it, but I didn't know [we were in Ukraine] until they started shelling us."

Most of the Russian soldiers who crossed the border were not rabid partisans for Putin's fight, according to reporters on the ground from *The Guardian.* Typical among them was a recent recruit who signed up because there were no other paying jobs to be had in his town. Or an underemployed locksmith and reservist who, all things equal, according to his wife, would rather be home reading fantasy novels or playing *War Thunder, World of Warplanes, World of Tanks,* or his other favorite video games.

Even so, the Ukrainian regular army and militia units were no real match for even poorly motivated Russian artillery and tank units. The former president Yanukovych had pretty well hollowed out the Ukrainian military while in office. The Russians killed more than a thousand Ukrainian fighters in the early stages of their new offensive and began winning back substantial chunks of the Donbas. Locals cowered in their basements in cities and towns across the Donetsk and Luhansk, without electricity or clean water, while mortars and rockets whirred overhead. "We don't support anybody," one shell-shocked husband and father told the reporter Anna Nemtsova. "All we want is to stay alive. Please make the world understand that." One Ukrainian militia group that had successfully fought the Russians for more than four months was blasted by devastating heavy artillery fire in what had been considered a stronghold a few days earlier. The men and women of the recently formed Donbas Battalion had never before encountered a weapon that could fire three dozen incendiary rockets simultaneously. The Russians then invited survivors of the encircled and defeated battalion to flee through the "humanitarian corridor" they were holding open—and then killed a hundred of them in what was supposed to be their route for safe passage.

Putin hailed the "separatist" victories as if they were the result of pro-Russian homegrown Ukrainians carrying out operations inside their own country. The Russian military, he insisted, had nothing to do with it. As did Lavrov, his foreign minister, who had made a habit of hurt and angry denial, even when presented with the half a dozen regular Russian soldiers captured *in* Ukraine, or with satellite images of Russian troops and weapons on the march in the Donbas. These were, he lied, "just images from computer games."

The Western democracies were not going to escalate the fight by sending their own troops to defend Ukrainian sovereignty. Nobody was looking to invite World War III. But they did what they could. In the waning days of summer, European leaders pleaded with Putin for a cease-fire in Ukraine; he professed a willingness to let things simmer in place. The Russia-invented Donetsk People's Republic was already preparing a victory parade in the region's most important city. And Russian armor had nearly encircled the region's most important port.

The United States, meanwhile, unleashed a very specific new sanction it had been threatening for months. The wiggle room allowed for dealing with Rosneft and the rest of the Russian oil industry was officially closed. Prior deal or no, the Obama administration declared that all American companies had to cease operations in Russia. Even ongoing operations. No more grandfather clause. On September 11, 2014, Exxon thought it had forty days or so left to find the big prize in the Russian Arctic, give or take the weather. On September 12, Exxon was officially informed by the U.S. government that the company was done for the season in Russia; its crew had two weeks to cap the well in progress and get the hell out of Dodge. The Exxon lobbying team whined and wheedled and managed to buy themselves an extra two weeks, to October 10, to close up shop in the Kara Sea. "The license [from the U.S. Treasury Department] recognizes the need to protect the safety of the individuals involved in these operations as well as the risk to the environment," ExxonMobil's communications team explained in a careful public statement. "All activities related to the wind down will proceed as safely and expeditiously as possible."

This special two-week waiver from the U.S. government was not about giving Exxon a little extra time to find all that Russian oil and gas, see. The special waiver was about safety. And the environment. Oh yeah.

ExxonMobil's partner in the operation—Rosneft—was limping even before this latest hit. Earlier sanctions had already made it difficult for the company to service its reportedly huge $39 billion debt. Less than a week after the *goodbye, ExxonMobil* sanctions went into place, Putin's deputy prime minister took pity on Rosneft and announced that Russia's national welfare fund would hand over at least a bit of the $42 billion in cash the company had been requesting. But Putin and Sechin had another trick up their sleeves—an oldie but a goodie. On the same day as the bailout announcement, September 16, 2014, a sixty-five-year-old Russian billionaire named Vladimir Yevtushenkov was placed under house arrest in his mansion outside Moscow. He was held on suspicion of money laundering related to Bashneft, an oil company in Bashkiria, a province in the southwest of Russia.

The alleged money laundering for which Yevtushenkov was charged had taken place nearly a decade earlier. But the actual malefaction that got him arrested was much more recent: Yevtushenkov and his privately owned oil company had become a source of great and ongoing embarrassment to Sechin. While Rosneft lumbered in place, bleeding cash, Bashneft was thriving, due almost entirely to Yevtushenkov's management. The Russian billionaire had first invested in Bashneft back in 2005, gained a controlling stake in the company in 2009, and then transformed the lazy old Soviet-era company into a juggernaut. By 2014, Yevtushenkov's company was a darling of the Western investment crowd—and for good reason. Bashneft was the fastest-growing private oil driller in Russia, increasing its production almost 10 percent in a single year and piling up reserves. The company's stock price had tripled in just four years, and when its chieftain had gone to London in June 2014 to roadshow an initial public offering on the stock exchange there, investors flocked to the $800-a-night Corinthia Hotel to hear his pitch. (This was particularly galling to Sechin, who put a serious offer on the table to acquire Bashneft the previous year and had been, as the *Financial Times* put it, "rebuffed.")

Imagine the gall—here was Yevtushenkov preparing to sell large stakes of this newly valuable and productive Russian corporation to Western investors in London, thus keeping this prized and productive asset from the grasp of Sechin and Rosneft and the Russian state.

It didn't take an oracle to see where this was headed. Yevtushenkov's arrest was widely reported as an unfolding remake of Sechin's earlier Yukos smash-and-grab thriller. Didn't even matter that Yevtushenkov, unlike Yukos's boss, Mikhail Khodorkovsky, had never uttered a syllable of challenge to Putin's political authority. This time around, it was simply about business or, more precisely, power. Here was a jewel of the Russian oil industry, and its principal owner, its *Russian* principal owner, seemed to be forgetting his company's first duty was to the Russian state and Vladimir Putin (and Igor Sechin). Especially now, when the future of the Russian Federation was in the balance. Bashneft, like Yukos and Lukoil and every other oil-producing company in Russia, was first and foremost a "strategic asset" of the state; Putin occasionally invoked his own barnyard adage, according to Steven Lee Myers, to clarify his thinking on the subject: "A chicken can exercise ownership of eggs, and it can get fed while it's sitting on the egg. But it's not really their egg." So metaphorically speaking, Bashneft's eggs belonged to the Russian state. And the Russian state was hungry just then. So Sechin and Putin raided yet another nest.

Mikhail Khodorkovsky, the Yukos boss who had been divested of his company and tossed into jail for a decade, was pretty sure this remake was going to end just as the original had ended. "This is the very same Igor Ivanovich [Sechin], who in 11 years has not got any wiser and has perhaps become even greedier," said Khodorkovsky, who was finally a free man, and thus free to keep his distance and speak his mind in Switzerland. "If Yevtushenkov can make a deal, then he should do it."

He maybe should, but they made sure he couldn't. Yevtushenkov was in a very poor bargaining position thanks to a little early twenty-first-century Russian-style justice. *For my friends, everything; for my enemies, the law.* The Kremlin's courts had frozen Yevtushenkov's stake in Bashneft back in July, not long after he emerged from those IPO meetings with eager Western investors. On the news of his arrest in September, shares in his holding company, Sistema, dropped 37 percent. Shares in Bashneft had dropped more than 20 percent. Yevtushenkov appealed for immediate release—or at least access to his computers and phones so he could go to work to restore the lost value of Sistema and Bashneft. This appeal seemed to fall on deaf ears. Probably didn't help that news out of Western Europe that week darkened the mood in the Kremlin. The new sanctions were starting to pinch where it hurt. Authorities in Italy—home to Putin's old friend Berlusconi, now sadly out of office—had seized title to $40 million worth of property in Rome and Sardinia, including apartments and villas and a hotel. They all belonged to Putin's judo pal and Winter Olympics klepto-contractor Arkady Rotenberg.

On September 25, 2014, nine days after Yevtushenkov's arrest, and on his sixty-sixth birthday, a judge in Moscow declined to grant the billionaire's request for release, conditional or otherwise. He was to face criminal charges that carried a seven-year prison sentence. Yevtushenkov was ordered to remain under house arrest, without access to phones or the internet or any visitor not approved by the court. The next day the court seized his shares in Bashneft. Shares in his holding company, Sistema, dropped to less than half their value the day before Yevtushenkov's arrest. Bashneft was down more than a third. There was talk of a fire sale.

"The assumption is that a deal [to sell Bashneft] has been struck," said one investment banker. "The question is what will be left of the carcass."

Well, good things sometimes happened in bunches, even to not-good people. The day after the Bashneft asset seizure, on September 27, 2014, Rosneft announced that the West Alpha rig had struck oil seven thousand feet beneath the floor of the Kara Sea. Imagine the luck! It happened right inside the window that the U.S. government had afforded ExxonMobil to pack up its things, close off the well, and make sure the environment was all safe and sound. Turns out, ExxonMobil had used the time to just keep drilling. The hydrocarbon trap Exxon drillers had tapped was believed to hold about a billion barrels of oil and oil equivalent. This represented one of the largest single finds in years, anywhere in the world. The Norwegian owners of the West Alpha rig boasted of the speed of the operation. So too did Rosneft. "The drilling was completed in record-breaking time—in one and a half months." Exxon remained fairly mum about the find, perhaps because it was not eager to invite attention from officials at the U.S. Department of the Treasury. Sechin had the most to say that day. He had already told the world he suspected there was a new Saudi Arabia worth of oil and gas to be discovered, beneath the Arctic waters, off the continental shelf of Russia. Owned by Russia! With the help of his friend and partner ExxonMobil (and not to forget Western oil service companies like North Atlantic Drilling, Schlumberger, Halliburton, Weatherford, Baker Hughes, Trendsetter, and FMC—that's a lot of sanction waivers), he was on his way to proving it true. The first oil extracted in the Kara Sea, Sechin noted, "is an astonishing sample of light oil."

Sechin also took the opportunity to christen the newly discovered field—which might soon be home to as many as forty wells.

He called it simply Pobeda.

Pobeda means "Victory."

But of course there were loose ends left to tie up. In December 2014, after more than three months under house arrest, Vladimir Yevtushenkov was released. Good news: Putin's prosecutors were dropping the money-laundering charges for lack of actual substantiation. Yevtushenkov "is now a free man who can work productively," said his lawyer. Bad news: the real reason he was being released was that the three months he spent under house arrest had accomplished their purpose for the Kremlin. While Yevtushenkov was in stir, remember, a judge in Moscow "nationalized" the billionaire's shares in Bashneft, which meant that his shares in his own company were handed over to the Russian state. In three months, Yevtushenkov had been robbed by Vladimir Putin and Igor Sechin to the tune of about $8 billion, the vast majority of his net worth. Not to mention, of course, control of the best-run and most remunerative oil company in one of the biggest oil-producing countries on earth. Yevtushenkov did apparently retain a good portion of his sense of humor, however. "If you like another [of my companies] tomorrow and want to take it, you are welcome," he told Putin.

Control of Bashneft eventually ended up in the hands of, you guessed it, Rosneft. At, you guessed it, a steep discount. Igor Sechin's Kremlin-assisted "purchase" of a majority stake of Bashneft was concluded on remarkably favorable terms—he got the company for a pittance. Then, for a little icing on the cake, he found a court in Russia that would force Yevtushenkov to *pay* Rosneft $1.7 billion, for supposedly stripping Bashneft of its assets. So Putin and Sechin took his company, and then they made him pay them for the trouble of taking it. Gangster-style.

One unexpected piece of collateral damage in Sechin's new crocodile act was the serious injury to the standing of the economic development minister at the Kremlin, Alexei Ulyukayev. Minister Ulyukayev had had the temerity to voice his opinion that Bashneft should go to the highest bidder on the open market. And Rosneft should stay out of it. *For my enemies* . . . Sechin invited Ulyukayev to his home and, truly gangster-style, presented him with a gift basket of his famous homemade sausages, some fine wine, and, unbeknownst to his guest, $2 million worth of rubles, in cash, stuffed into the bottom of the parcel. Sechin then had the minister arrested on the spot (the FSB gendarmes were conveniently there, at the ready) for soliciting and receiving a bribe. Ulyukayev was sentenced to eight years in prison and ordered to pay a $2.2 million fine. That takes care of him.

Arkady Rotenberg did not get his Italian hotel and villas back, but he and his brother got the consolation prize of a fat new construction contract. Four billion dollars to build the twelve-mile-long bridge linking the Russian mainland to its newest territorial acquisition—Crimea. *All hail Novorossiya!*

On a cold day in Moscow at the end of February 2015, while the battle for eastern Ukraine rumbled on, Boris Nemtsov, who had become the most fearless critic of Putin's illegal annexation of Crimea and his illegal war in the Donbas, sat for a long interview with the Polish edition of *Newsweek*. He was due to lead a massive antiwar demonstration in Moscow two days later. Nemtsov understood it was likely to take decades to chip away at Putin and authoritarian rule in Russia, but he wasn't giving up, and he was driven by a sense of urgency. "I have no doubt that the struggle for the revival of Russians will be tough," he told the *Newsweek* interviewer. Putin "implanted them with a virus of inferiority complex towards the West, the belief that the only thing we can do to amaze the world is use force, violence and aggression. . . . [Putin and his *siloviki*] operate in accordance with the simple principles of Joseph Goebbels: Play on the emotions; the bigger the lie, the better; lies should be repeated many times. . . . Unfortunately, it works. The hysteria reached unprecedented levels, hence the high level of support for Putin. We need to work as quickly as possible to show the Russians that there is an alternative. That Putin's policy leads to degradation and suicide of the state. There is less and less time to wake up. . . . You need an alternative vision, a different idea of Russia. Our idea is one of a democratic and open Russia. A country that is not applying bandits' methods to its own citizens and neighbors."

Later the next evening, walking home after a dinner out with his girlfriend, Nemtsov was gunned down on a suddenly and strangely traffic-less side of a bridge across the Moscow River, steps from the Kremlin grounds. The assassination appeared to have been meticulously planned and executed by a team of two or even three dozen people. The Kremlin fingered a group of Chechen terrorists and continues to block independent investigations into Boris Nemtsov's murder. One very dangerous, very consequential loose end, tied off forever.

And where was ExxonMobil's chieftain, Rex Tillerson, in all this? He was standing by, waiting for the unfortunate geopolitical cloud to disperse. Rex didn't agree with everything Putin was doing, presumably. But, hey, Putin and his guys understood Tillerson, who was, after all, just a businessman trying to do the best he could in trying times. "The first time I went over to see [Putin, Sechin, and the others] after the sanctions were in place, I was a little nervous," Rex explained to a group of curious college students early in 2016. "And it was interesting because the first question they asked me was, 'Well, how are you doing? Are you okay?'

"And I said, 'Well, yeah, I'm fine. Why do you ask?' They said, 'Well, we just wondered whether your government was coming after you because you've been doing business with us.' They were more worried about me. And so they understood."

TWENTY-FOUR

"YEAH THAT WAS CRAZY"

A USTIN HOLLAND'S DREAM JOB AT THE OKLAHOMA GEOLOGI-
cal Survey was turning out to be not all that dreamy. In fact,
being the head seismologist for Oklahoma had become
a kind of nightmare—an eighty-to-ninety-hour-a-week, never-see-
your-children, everybody-is-screaming-at-you nightmare. Holland had
plenty of sympathy among the scientific community both inside and
outside his adopted state. "You've got a tough job, guy," one former
employee of the OGS wrote, but only at the end of a long email suggesting how Holland might better do that job. "If Austin hasn't aged 20
years in the past 3 he's a better man than I," a colleague of Holland's
wrote to friends early in 2014. "We have a new geophysicist to help
Austin out, but it's not the science, it's the politics, and she (no one) will
be able to help him out on that account."

By the fall of 2014, though, people in the field—even the people
rooting for him—were finding it hard to forgive, or even explain, Austin Holland's continuing reticence about the probable causes of the
new, fairly terrifying earthquake swarms in Oklahoma. Historically
un-shaky Oklahoma had suddenly become the earthquake capital of
America. The year 2014 was shaping up like no other in recorded state
history. Landlocked, stable little Oklahoma had suffered triple the
number of earthquakes that runner-up California had. Not OK! The
only other categories where Oklahoma led the country were top-tier
college football, annual decreases in public school funding per stu-

dent, and the rate of female incarceration. But on seismic activity, the state's prowess really stood out: there were 16 magnitude 4.0 quakes in Oklahoma in the first six months of 2014 alone and 268 magnitude 3.0 or better. That's in a state that had averaged *fewer than two* 3.0-plus quakes annually for the sixty years before 2008. The cause seemed pretty clear to anybody paying attention: the increase in seismicity was concurrent with the increase in newfangled, "unconventional" oil and gas drilling in the state. Yes, correlation isn't causation, but it felt as though every dentist and barber and dry cleaner in the state was certain the problem was fracking.

The layman's diagnosis was partially true. But seismologists and petroleum geologists and hydrologists were beginning to reach a more nuanced understanding. Hydraulic fracturing itself—breaking oil and gas out of shale rock—might cause an earthquake in one in every ten or even one in every twenty fracked wells. But the bigger culprit appeared to be the way the drillers were disposing of the billions of gallons of used slickwater and produced water the earth vomited up once the drillers were done with the fracturing part. And, then too, there was another fracking-era unconventional production process at play: something called dewatering, wherein Oklahoma drillers would vacuum up more millions of gallons of ancient, briny underground fluid, separate out the oil and gas, and then reinject the extracted fluid back into the depths of the earth. All this appeared to be playing havoc with the pressures and stresses on long-quiet faults down in the basement rock, just beneath what the business calls the "economically interesting strata," where the oil and gas is.

Academic papers had started to draw links between the earthquakes and the extraction and injection of increasing quantities of this underground goo. But there were so many unanswered questions about how much was too much: At what volume did you risk triggering quakes? Were there rates and depths of injection that were less dangerous than others? Could you fiddle with the timing to make the process safer?

Austin Holland had remained cautious as well, perhaps to a fault. He knew he was privy to a field of data that could really upset people, especially all the folks in Oklahoma who made their money in the oil and gas industry. (He'd been yelled at plenty by 2014.) But Holland also knew the data could provide real insight into this awe-inspiring new human capacity to alter the environment. The scientific term at issue would be "induced seismicity": man-made earthquakes. Imagine that. It's one thing to know we can visit Mars and invent the internet, but, seriously, human beings can make big earthquakes? Thousands of them? The meek may inherit the earth, but the bold could certainly screw it up in the interim.

From the time Austin Holland arrived in Oklahoma in 2010 through the first seismic swarms, and the record-breaking earthquake in Prague in 2011, and the exponential growth of felt quakes in his state, he remained determined to study induced seismicity the right way. Using all the new raw data. To make a real contribution to the scientific literature. But there was so much to keep up with now—ten or twelve magnitude 3.0 earthquakes *every week*. Each event produced useful new data points, which would help him be both accurate and confident in his conclusions. Holland meant those conclusions to be unassailable, so he tried as best he could to keep his head down and do his work, to do good science. He was also determined to produce a crucial tool the state lacked: a comprehensive and exquisitely detailed map of the faults that existed in the geologic strata that underlay the state. If Oklahoma was going to start shaking at this point in the twenty-first century, it was worth knowing where the shaking would most likely commence. But that kind of project would take time too, and he had so little time. He never seemed to have enough time.

All of this meant Holland did not feel comfortable enough, even in 2014, to make a definitive statement to the public at large about the precise perils of the oil and gas industry practice of wastewater injection. He had started to suggest the real possibility of oil and gas operations contributing to specific seismic events as early as 2011, but chiefly in peer-reviewed papers. He took pains not to incite undue public alarm, or to point toward any conclusions he couldn't prove from fact. "We clearly need to examine the issues and are actively working to understand them, but none of the discussion that is occurring within the popular media is at all helpful to the discussion or the science," Holland wrote to a fellow seismologist at the U.S. Geological Survey. "Every hour I spend talking to reporters is another two hours I really can't be doing the research that needs to be done." Holland was more open with his brethren at scientific conferences, but even there he seemed to hold back. Rivka Galchen from *The New Yorker* caught this interaction at an induced-seismicity conference outside Oklahoma City in November 2014: "Someone asked Holland about several earthquakes of greater than 4.0 magnitude which had occurred a few days earlier, across Oklahoma's northern border, in Kansas," Galchen wrote in a piece subtitled "The arrival of man-made earthquakes." "Holland joked, 'Well, the earthquakes aren't stopping at the state line, but my problems do.' There was a follow-up question: Why had there previously been no quakes in Kansas, and now for a year and a half there have been so many?

"As the question was asked, a couple of men wandered into the back of the room, where trays of beer and soda were set up. Holland called out, 'Well, Justin, what do you think of that question?'

"The U.S.G.S.'s Justin Rubinstein, one of the three organizers of the conference, said, 'Um, well, if you map the fluid-injection records and the earthquake records—there you go.' . . . Holland said, "Well, you heard it from him, not me."

Occasionally that fall, evidence of Holland's vexation seeped out. Like when a petroleum geologist who was certain that many of these earthquakes were unquestionably productions of the oil and gas industry buttonholed Holland after his presentation at the Osage Nation's annual oil and gas summit in Tulsa. "During Holland's question and answer session—and afterwards in the lobby—we had several exchanges. I pressed him hard," Bob Jackman wrote in *The Oklahoma Observer*. "Frustrated, he blurted out: 'You don't understand—Harold Hamm and others will not allow me to say certain things.'" Holland later claimed Jackman misquoted him. Jackman was sure of the quotation and said he wrote it down at the time: *Harold Hamm and others will not allow me to say certain things.*

Subsequent reporting certainly bolsters the fact of the matter, if not the actual quotation.

The way Harold Hamm saw it, folks just didn't understand what a dire threat all this earthquake talk posed. They didn't seem to appreciate what a ferocious multifront battle he was engaged in and how vigilant he had to be in controlling the narrative. It wasn't just the seismology crowd—the earthquake geeks. It was the politicians and the do-gooders. The entire Obama administration, he sometimes complained, was hostile to oil and gas. "The response by this Administration has been to put the foot on your neck," Hamm would say to his nodding cheerleaders on the business channels. There were people out there who wanted to tear him down, to tear down the idea at the heart of his America, to obstruct American progress. "Continued threats against business is not what makes your economy grow."

Hamm, the founder and chairman of Continental Resources, was working like hell to protect all that was great and good in the U.S. of A., which meant he had to keep telling his own story. And inspiring as it was, he felt the burden to keep improving on it. That wasn't easy, or cheap. Hamm and his wife, Sue Ann, had donated $20 million to the University of Oklahoma Health Sciences Center—the biggest gift in the history of the institution, several million more than they had just paid for a lovely sixty-four-hundred-acre cattle ranch in Carmel, California—to fight a disease that menaced more than 600,000 people in his home state. "The Harold Hamm Oklahoma Diabetes Center is on a mission to find a cure," OU's president, David Boren, said in announcing the donation in 2011. "While we work toward that goal, we are educating people about the challenges of living with diabetes, teaching them how to prevent the development of diabetes and its complications and providing the best possible diabetes care."

Hamm and his medical researchers might not ever beat the disease—he understood that—but write a check that size and not only do you generate a whole lot of goodwill but you control the story. Oklahomans should never forget: Harold Hamm had their best interests at heart.

Other menaces to the well-being of his fellow Oklahomans didn't give themselves over to simple check-writing solutions. These stories were much more difficult to control. Stories where other people might have something to say—in opposition. That's why it had required real time and effort and money to get Oklahoma's unpopular horizontal drilling oil and gas tax break extended into eternity. But Hamm had made it happen; that law was on the books by the fall of 2014. And now the whole man-made (read oil- and gas-made) earthquake problem threatened to tar the entire industry. This story line was shaping up as complicated and insidious, and Hamm had seen it coming. This unsubstantiated (by his lights) charge had been a thorn in his side for at least three years.

The issue first caught his interest when that damned scientist Austin Holland published a scientific paper in 2011, less than six months after Hamm's $20 million diabetes donation, suggesting that a series of mini-quakes around Elmore City might not be the "normal naturally occurring" event everyone suspected. The state's new and clearly more energetic seismologist had made a study of the data and found there was likely a correlation between the swarm of seismicity near Elmore City and the onset of fracking at a nearby well. "Our analysis showed that shortly after hydraulic fracturing began, small earthquakes started occurring, and more than 50 were identified, of which 43 were large enough to be located."

Holland's boss Larry Grillot, who was dean of the University of Oklahoma's Mewbourne College of Earth and Energy, had forwarded Holland's findings to the big Oklahoma City oil companies and the head of the Oklahoma Independent Petroleum Association as soon as he saw it. Grillot had been a longtime executive at Phillips Petroleum, and he figured the major frackers would want a heads-up. Oil companies like to get ahead of any potential public relations problem. The president of the OIPA immediately told Grillot it might be a good idea for the two of them to sit down with Austin Holland and, you know, explain things. Oh, and by the way, he told Grillot, one of his board members, Harold Hamm, was already setting a meeting with OU's president, David Boren, who also just happened to sit on the board of Hamm's company, Continental Resources. "I guess I'll just wait for my marching orders," Dean Grillot responded, "and it looks like this is starting to fall into the category of 'no good deed goes unpunished.'"

Hamm, it turns out, did have marching orders to issue, which went down the chain of command from the university president (Boren) to the dean (Grillot) to Austin Holland's direct boss, Randy Keller, head of the Oklahoma Geological Survey. As all of that rolled downhill onto him, Holland was encouraged, among other things, to revise his most recent public-facing PowerPoint presentation. His slide on earthquakes was scrubbed of any mention of "disposal," "recovery," or "fracturing"—anything that could be traced back to oil and gas. His conclusion that there was scientific evidence of a correlation between hydraulic fracturing and seismic events in Elmore City was diplomatically elided.

Holland really wasn't looking to pick a fight; he told his bosses he thought the edits from on high might "help [the OIPA] feel better about the presentation." So Hamm's intercession to keep the science at bay worked, for a while. The man-made earthquake question in Oklahoma remained a nonissue for the next few years. Which makes this a case study in what happens when a powerful industry thoroughly captures a state government. In theory, an industry's job is to make money—to serve its customers and provide for its employees and shareholders—while the government's job is to make sure the industry operates on a level playing field, that companies follow the law and don't endanger others. When government is no match for the power of the industry, it instead becomes an enabler, an apologist, and often a corrupt participant in the industry running roughshod. There's a reason why the oil derricks were built first and the state capitol dome was tacked on a while later.

And so, even upon the arrival of the most powerful earthquake in Oklahoma history—a huge 5.7-magnitude quake that hit the little town of Prague—the reputation of oil and gas was protected from any damaging political aftershocks. As Governor Mary Fallin's communications team considered the wisdom of the governor engaging questions on the quakes at an upcoming conference co-sponsored by the Oklahoma secretary of energy, her communications director wrote to the public relations squad, "Probably actually not a great topic. She could certainly say, 'yeah that was crazy.' The problem is, some people are trying to blame hydraulic fracturing (a necessary process for extracting natural gas) for causing earthquakes. This is an energy conference heralding natural gas as the energy source of the future . . . so you see the awkward position that puts us in. I would rather not have that debate."

But the beauty of being in the Fallin administration was that an awkward position like that was very easy to resolve; it took only one quick phone call to get everyone on the same page and to get a set of talking points to the governor in case she found herself in the emergency situation of being cornered by a curious (and, God forbid, well-informed) reporter. The helpful talking points missive came from one of the state's most active frackers—Devon Energy. "There is no current evidence that oil & gas operations had anything to do with the recent large earthquakes," read Devon's memo for the governor. "Such events are not uncommon in Oklahoma. . . . According to the OGS, the earthquake characteristics of both intensity and depth essentially rule out man-made causes." All of which turned out to be somewhere between premature, misleading, and outright bullpucky. But what was she going to do, tell Devon Energy to stuff it? Unimaginable. At least for that state at that time.

It should be noted, though, that Oklahoma's strategy wasn't the only way to approach this unusual new problem. Around the same time, the state of Ohio had also seen an uptick in earthquakes believed to be induced by industry. Rather than calling up the oil companies to give the governor talking points to deny it was happening, Ohio sent a very clear message to the fracking and dewatering pros by shutting down a disposal well near an active fault. We "won't hesitate to stop operation of disposal sites if we have concerns," said the director of Ohio's Department of Natural Resources. "And while our research doesn't point to a clear and direct correlation to drilling at this site and seismic activity, we will never gamble when safety is a factor." Oklahoma's state government, unsurprisingly, was more willing to roll the dice.

Which meant Austin Holland and the OGS were the flies in the petroleum-based ointment. Holland again irked the industry by going to a conference in Florida in January 2013 and pointing at large-volume injection wells as a possible trigger for the big Prague earthquake. One of Holland's colleagues at OU, the geophysicist Katie Keranen, was even more direct. "There's a compelling link between the zone of injection and the seismicity," she had been saying. And in March 2013 she backed up that statement with detailed evidence, in a peer-reviewed paper, using the readings from the Prague aftershocks to, literally, find fault. "If the geologists are right," noted Columbia University's Earth Institute, "it would mean that fault lines are far more sensitive to human activity than previously thought." Oklahoma's government was positively wired to do whatever the oil and gas industry wanted, no matter the cost, no matter the damage. And now here were these perky young scientists—employed by state institutions!—telling not just Oklahomans but the whole country that oil and gas were the bad guys here? And showing their work to prove it? No, not OK. Not OK at all.

Holland was forced to mouth an official OGS rebuttal of Keranen's paper as soon as it became public. He wrote up a detailed report for his bosses on just where the research stood and then saw it boiled down to a single page, which included statements best understood as either misdirection—"Some researchers have observed that the earthquake activity did not increase over time as injection increased, but rather occurred in a distinct 'swarm' more typical of a natural event"—or just total hooey: "The interpretation that best fits current data is that the Prague Earthquake Sequence was the result of natural causes." As if.

Holland would not soon forget subsequent meetings at the offices of New Dominion, owner and operator of the injection wells in question near the Prague site. New Dominion's VP of exploration, Jean Antonides, and his crew were on the attack against Keranen for having the gall to publish a peer-reviewed paper based on all the data the OGS and the USGS had gleaned from Prague. "We were told that they were looking at ways to file a lawsuit against her," Holland said in his 2017 deposition for a civil suit filed against New Dominion. "They just wanted to make things uncomfortable for her, is what they said." Dr. Keranen found herself another job about fifteen hundred miles away, at Cornell University, and was out of Oklahoma in a few months.

Austin Holland decided to soldier on at OGS because, despite the sound and fury from the industry, he believed the survey itself and its minders at OU were committed to doing good science. And for all the Harold Hamms and the New Dominions and their thug tactics, there were also a number of oil companies in the state that were happy to share data and were willing to exchange ideas in preparation for issuing an updated set of best practices for safe drilling and wastewater injection. The Oklahoma Corporation Commission, the state agency that regulated the oil and gas industry, was actually moving toward stricter rules for permitting. Holland kept telling himself he was making things better. He kept telling himself the fights were all about public relations and nothing to do with the actual science. "We have the academic freedoms necessary for university employees doing research," he insisted. But he must have been slightly chagrined when Antonides from New Dominion insisted that Holland chase down his asinine pet theory that the earthquakes were caused by the long drought, followed by periods of torrential rains, which filled up the underground aquifers too rapidly. It was bad enough that Antonides was out there flogging his stupid theory about how the heavy rains did it—were long droughts and heavy rains a new variable in Oklahoma?—but he was also disparaging anybody who linked the New Dominion injection wells with the Prague quake. "That's people watching too many Superman movies," Antonides told one reporter. "Some individuals pick only the data that serves their purpose." Antonides also tried a sort of backflip-handspring-triple-twist salesmanship trick when he made the case that the quakes were a good thing! States that *didn't* have them are the ones who should worry. To sell this particular idea, he called on a (false) theory that smaller earthquakes diminish the stress on faults and thus avert bigger quakes. "What happens if there had not been that release of energy?" he said. "They're kind of a savior. They help keep down the big ones." Sure, sure. That's a good one. It's one thing to just threaten and deride people and throw your weight around, but in a scientific battle the scientists were going to have an advantage over the guys talking about quake saviors and Superman and the rain.

By the fall of 2013, the OGS and the U.S. Geological Survey decided it was time to issue a joint statement on what was going on in Oklahoma. The statement, which Holland helped prepare, was hardly a barn burner. It simply announced that the two agencies were "conducting collaborative research quantifying the changes in earthquake rate in the Oklahoma City region, assessing the implications of this swarm for large-earthquake hazard, and evaluating possible links between these earthquakes and wastewater disposal related to oil and gas production activities in the region." The jump in earthquake rates "do[es] not seem to be due to typical, random fluctuations in natural seismicity rates," said the USGS's lead seismologist. "The analysis suggests that a contributing factor to the increase in earthquake triggers may be from activities such as wastewater disposal—a phenomenon known as injection-induced seismicity."

Tepid as the public pronouncement was, Harold Hamm took it hard. He decided he needed to get serious and start shutting this thing down. He dispatched his senior vice president for exploration, Jack Stark, to meet personally with Austin Holland at the offices of the Oklahoma Corporation Commission. Commissioner Patrice Douglas insisted to Holland at that meeting that she wanted to be able to make "data-driven" decisions that protected the safety of Oklahomans while also protecting the demonstrable economic rewards of the state's shale industry. Stark just wanted the whole thing kept quiet. "They are in denial phase that [induced seismicity] is a possibility," Holland reported to Dean Grillot and Director Keller after the meeting. Holland later explained that "it was clear that Continental did not want any discussions of induced seismicity in any shape or form."

For his part, Stark was apparently not satisfied with the outcome of the sit-down with Holland. The public information coordinator at the OGS got what felt to her like a very aggressive call on a Monday afternoon from a woman who said she was affiliated with Continental Resources. It was not clear exactly how she was affiliated, because the woman started barking questions right from the start of the conversation. She wanted to know if the OGS was connected with the U.S. Geological Survey and if OGS employees worked for the state. "She really kept asking about who pays us," the information officer, Connie G. Smith, reported in an email to Holland, Keller, and Grillot. "She kept asking who we work for and I kept saying 'We are a state agency and are part of the MCEE [Mewbourne College of Earth and Energy] at OU' and then she said 'Do you work for OU?' and I said we are paid and under the administration of the University of Oklahoma.

"She sounded like a lawyer because she was very brusque and was really grilling me and asking the same things over and over, and I immediately wanted to put my hand on a Bible . . . or on OGS Bulletin 40 at least!"

Holland emailed a reply to the rattled Smith an hour and a half later, with news that he had received his own grab-the-Bible call that same day: he had been invited to "coffee" with President David Boren and Harold Hamm. It would be a command performance, at the president's office. Just the three of them. "Gosh. I guess that's better than having Kool Aid with them," Smith wrote back, "I guess."

The meeting with President Boren, who was soon to get his own statue on campus, and Harold Hamm, the richest man in Oklahoma, was, as Holland would later deadpan, "just a little bit intimidating." Boren assured Holland at the top of the meeting that he had complete academic freedom (which right away was a pretty strong indication that he did not), but he told him that being a part of the OGS meant he had to listen to people within the oil and gas industry, too. So Holland listened, while Hamm filibustered. Harold Hamm presented himself as a man under siege, standing up for an industry under siege, and unfairly so. "[He] expressed to me that I had to be careful of the way in which I say things, that hydraulic fracturing is critical to the state's economy in Oklahoma, and that me publicly stating that earthquakes can be caused by hydraulic fracturing was—you know, could be misleading and that he was nervous about the war on fossil fuels at the time." That's a phrase that stuck with Holland—*the War on Fossil Fuels*. As if it were a war on America itself. Hamm even talked about the bad rap that coal was getting. But he circled back to fracking, and how maybe Holland had allowed a study on one well in Elmore City to bring him to "the wrong conclusion."

Holland sat quiet, even though the data and the science were clearly on his side. He didn't call Hamm's attention to the raft of recent peer-reviewed scientific literature about the connections between increased seismicity and hydraulic fracturing and, more important, between increased seismicity and wastewater disposal. He didn't call attention to the fact that his own recent paper on the topic had also been peer-reviewed. Holland had been around long enough to understand the futility of arguing with a successful Oklahoma oilman, especially the *most* successful Oklahoma oilman. "Honestly, it was nothing different than what I'd heard from those in the oil and gas industry since I basically showed up in Oklahoma. So it wasn't anything new. And I've been yelled at before; at least I wasn't getting yelled at."

Holland didn't feel much better after that meeting, but he hadn't gone in expecting to. Funny thing was, neither did Hamm, who clearly didn't feel that Holland had entirely taken to heart his concerns. He had doubts about this young scientist's willingness to Thunder Up for the oil and gas team. Hamm wanted all public comments out of OGS to henceforth come from the office of the university's longtime (and trusted) spokeswoman. And he was under the impression that Boren had made that happen. "I am glad you put Catherine Bishop in charge," Hamm wrote to Boren a few weeks after the delightful coffee meeting with Austin Holland. "This situation could spiral out of hand easily."

What did spiral out of hand soon after was the sheer number of earthquakes in Oklahoma. When the pace of quakes nearly tripled in 2014 from the year before, the USGS and the OGS put out another joint statement, updating their earlier one. "The likelihood of future, damaging earthquakes [in central and north-central Oklahoma] has increased as a result of the increased number of small and moderate shocks." So much for the idea that the little shakers kept the big ones at bay. "Building owners and government officials should have a special concern for older, unreinforced brick structures, which are vulnerable to serious damage during sufficient shaking," said Holland's counterpart at the USGS. *National Geographic* picked up the story of the growing problem and its by-now-clear association with unconventional drilling. "Underground disposal of wastewater from fracking may pose a much greater risk of causing dangerous earthquakes than previously believed" was the lede. "Worse yet, scientists are not yet able to predict which wastewater injection sites are likely to pose risks to buildings or critical structures such as power plants, and do not yet know what operators might do to mitigate the hazard."

So consider Harold Hamm at that moment, whose net worth had climbed up around $20 billion by the summer of 2014, with more and better wells coming on line all the time. His newest well in the Bakken was producing a record number of barrels per day. He had just won his signature victory in the Oklahoma state legislature: horizontal drilling tax breaks forever! But still he felt like Ayn Rand's John Galt, with all those envious small-minded bureaucrat number crunchers picking at him, these parochial, obstructionists putting limits on American business's God-given freedoms. How many lesser oil and gas and coal producers would be casualties of this War on Fossil Fuels? Well, he could play rough if he had to. And he would.

Holland got Hamm's rough treatment at a remove. When Austin or his new colleague Amberlee Darold popped up in public with a statement, or a paper, they were usually whack-a-moled back into their quiet hole by their bosses at OU and OGS. Holland felt as if Dean Grillot and Director Keller were looking over his shoulder more than ever. "They helped me with presentations, they'd take a look and change—for the public, change wording and that sort of thing," he explained in his 2017 deposition. "They would tell me that they had gotten a bunch of calls, complaints, after I'd given a news conference about some earthquake or something, and they'd say they had gotten a lot of complaints and that we need to really watch how we say things. . . . I also had points where the dean of the college asked to see my presentations to scientific meetings and would then wordsmith my presentations. . . . At one point I was asked to withdraw an abstract from a scientific meeting in Arkansas because the topic was earthquakes triggered by hydraulic fracture."

What Holland maybe didn't fully appreciate was the exact nature of the pressure that Grillot and Keller and Boren were getting and then passing on down to him. Hamm had not just written a $20 million check to the University of Oklahoma; hell, he was paying Boren around $350,000 in cash and stock that year alone to sit on the board of Continental Resources, which was about as much as Boren made as a full-time university president. When Harold Hamm spoke, everybody in the administration at OU felt more than obliged to hear him out. Like when Hamm called Grillot into a meeting at Continental Resources headquarters in downtown Oklahoma City on an unseasonably cool day in July 2014. Maybe Hamm was irked about what Amberlee Darold told a reporter from *Time* magazine for a story on the booming earthquake insurance industry in Oklahoma. "It's known that fracking can cause earthquakes and has caused earthquakes," was her quotation, in print, in a national magazine. "There's no question with fracking." Or maybe he was upset about Holland and Darold's recent public presentation, under the OU banner, which included these ditties: "Most seismologists believe the drastic rate change is NOT due to natural seismicity. . . . We do see earthquakes likely triggered by hydraulic fracturing . . . we do see some potential cases of induced seismicity from disposal wells . . . scientists generally agree that this triggered seismicity poses the greater risk (larger magnitudes)."

Whatever it was, Hamm was clearly itching to be heard that July day. When Grillot was waiting to be escorted up to Hamm's office, he saw President Boren on his way out. Grillot later made note in an email that Hamm would shortly be talking with Governor Fallin about putting the OGS under more reliable (industry-friendly) overseers than the academics at the University of Oklahoma. But when Grillot made his report of the meeting to OU's vice president for external relations and planning, the top-line item was much more, uh, sharply pointed. "Mr. Hamm is very upset at some of the earthquake reporting," Grillot wrote in an email a few hours after the meeting broke up, "to the point that he would like to see select OGS staff dismissed."

The university administration had the good sense to not immediately start axing employees explicitly because they refused to toe the oil and gas party line, but Harold Hamm still appeared to be in control of the bigger story. He dispatched his company's vice president for geology, Glen Brown, to mitigate the damage being caused by these reckless scientist loudmouths. The "natural swarm" of earthquakes, Brown explained, is "of very small magnitude and very small impact. Quite frankly, the way that people are talking about it is over-exaggerating what's going on." Brown was also running around Oklahoma City saying the swarms could very well have a global cause, that is, according to one reporter who heard his pitch, "major tectonic shifts in the earth's crust, triggered by earthquakes in Japan and Haiti." Okay, sure, Japan did it. And Haiti. Definitely nothing closer to home.

And Continental Resources didn't exactly have to roll the boulder up the mountain when it came to selling its self-exculpatory story in the state. When the Democratic candidate running against Mary Fallin for governor in 2014 suggested that the new science on induced seismicity was compelling and that state officials should be obligated "to make sure industries are applying safe practices," the editorial page of the state's largest paper—*The Oklahoman*—shot him down: "Most unacceptable is the notion that the science has been done. In fact the research is only beginning."

The Republican state representative from the earthquake-swarmed area around the town of Jones told *Newsweek* that the science was sure to find frackers and wastewater disposers innocent of any and all seismicity-inducing malfeasance. He was quite philosophical about it all. "The Earth, and the science of how everything works, is so big. We are so minute," said Representative Lewis Moore. "For us to think that we have so much to do with these things is almost ludicrous."

....

TWENTY-FIVE

ACTIVE APPRECIATION

THERE WERE SIGNS IN THE FALL OF 2014 THAT HAROLD HAMM might be losing his grip on his own story. An eagle-eyed set of reporters from Reuters caught on to an odd series of edits in Continental Resources' official literature. Deleted from the time line on Continental's website was an entry about Harold Hamm's critical *personal* role in striking oil in Oklahoma in 1974. Also gone was any mention of Continental's game-changing decision to make a big move into the Rocky Mountain region in 1993. The website now ceded partial credit to another company for a key discovery in the Bakken and scrubbed its brag about Continental being the first to complete a long horizontal multi-frack in North Dakota. Even more jarring was a deletion in Hamm's personal bio in Continental Resources' latest proxy statement: "As founder of the Company, Mr. Hamm is one of the driving forces behind the Company and its success to date. Over the course of the Company's history, Mr. Hamm has successfully grown the Company through his leadership skills and business judgment." All that crowing was there in 2013. Gone in 2014. The exercise in revision seemed like a planned campaign to minimize the previously mythic eminence of Harold Hamm. Which is exactly what it was. And it was all because, turns out, Harold didn't have a prenup.

The revisionist history about Harold Hamm's role in building Continental Resources was part of a carefully executed legal strategy that was designed to keep his soon-to-be-ex-wife from dipping too deeply into his trove of assets. The Reuters team made the discovery near the end of the nine-week trial of *Hamm v. Hamm,* which was taking place at the county courthouse in Oklahoma City. The journalists had plenty of free time to do enterprise reporting, because the judge had decided to close almost all of the divorce proceedings to the press and the public. Much of the evidence at trial involved proprietary information about the company's finances and operations. "There's no sense destroying a company over a divorce trial," the judge explained. And so, a sign was affixed to the door of courtroom 121: "Do Not Enter." This was disappointing to rubberneckers. Speculation outside the courthouse had been pretty frothy, even before the trial commenced—and not on account of the emotional matrimonial *mishegoss*. She said he was unfaithful; he said the marriage was loveless for years. Ho hum. It wasn't human drama driving interest in *Hamm v. Hamm;* it was epic financial drama. The numbers involved were just enormous.

The Hamms' combined net worth at the beginning of the trial in August 2014—with Continental stock prices at all-time highs and the price of West Texas crude still up around $100 a barrel—was estimated at $20 billion. If Sue Ann Hamm's attorneys managed to peel off a quarter of that for their client, it would be the biggest divorce settlement on record, anywhere, anytime. Other high-end divorce attorneys were panting about a payout to Sue Ann Hamm that could go as high as $6 billion or even $8 billion. Smarter money had it around $3 billion. "The question is," said one perhaps envious high-end divorce lawyer from neighboring Texas, "will Mrs. Hamm come out of this trial filthy rich, or filthy, filthy, filthy rich."

Harold Hamm had been worth a little more than $50 million when the couple married in 1988. By the time Sue Ann filed for divorce in May 2012, the couple's billions of dollars in assets were almost all in Continental Resources stock. That stock had appreciated in value 894 percent in just seven years. The financial outcome of the divorce, according to informed observers, would turn on "active appreciation of property" versus "passive appreciation of property." Active appreciation includes all of the asset appreciation due to the wit and genius and leadership skills and business judgment of one or both spouses. Mrs. Hamm was entitled to some of that. Passive appreciation is all of the asset appreciation that had accrued by the wheel-of-fortune method, beyond one's control—like other people's inventiveness, or the rise in real estate values, or the fluctuating price of oil. Mrs. Hamm had much less, if any, claim on the wealth that had accrued in this way. And so Harold was doing his ham-handed darndest to play down any of his own role in building up the share value of Continental Resources.

Mrs. Hamm was an attorney who had been an executive at Continental for years. She'd been active in the business, and she knew all about the operations and the value of the company. Her lawyers were said to be ready to present plenty of "active appreciation" expert testimony, attesting to her husband's business acumen and his nose for oil. Just read the glossies. Mrs. Hamm's main expert witness had this telling fact to proffer: energy companies had turned, on average, about a 700 percent return investment in the last twenty-five years; Hamm's Continental Resources had returned 44,000 percent. Gotta be genius! Mrs. Hamm's attorneys also promised to present as evidence that now-erased golden oldie from previous Continental proxy filings: *Mr. Hamm has successfully grown the company through his leadership skills and business judgment.*

Harold's attorneys would beg to differ. Even though the press was shut out of the courtroom, the quotable Texas divorce attorney was happy to explain to reporters the gist of Hamm's legal team's argument: "[Harold] didn't invent fracking or the new horizontal drilling technology or cause the price of oil to increase because of turmoil in the Middle East. These are all factors that Hamm's lawyers and experts are going to point to as being mostly responsible for the increase in the company's value."

In early November 2014, after more than nine weeks of trial testimony, all but three days of it closed to the public, the judge announced his decision. Sue Ann Arnall was not well pleased. She would definitely be appealing the judgment, her attorneys insisted. Harold Hamm, on the other hand, emerged from court a happy man. His divorce bill had come in at just under a single billion dollars. Just one! The judge ordered Hamm to hand over to Mrs. Hamm about $23 million in real property, including their sixty-four-hundred-acre ranch in California, and to write Sue Ann a check for $322 million by the end of 2014, and then to write her one $7 million check, minimum, every month, until the remaining $650 million was paid up. Oh thank God, is that all?

But then, the very week that judgment was handed down, the ground under Hamm's feet started getting seismically active, metaphorically speaking. The price of West Texas crude had been dropping, from $105 a barrel in July to down near $75 by mid-November. Hamm was misplaying the drop, in a very public way. He let it be known that he had sold all his hedges; he was all in on the future of oil. "We feel like we're at the bottom rung here on prices," he explained on a call to analysts in early November, "and we'll see them recover pretty drastically, pretty quick." What happened next went a long way toward proving the argument his own divorce attorneys made in court. Harold Hamm was wrong, on both counts. The price of crude continued its drop, pretty drastically, pretty quick, falling from $75 in mid-November to $66 at the beginning of December and then to $50 a barrel by January 5, 2015. Continental Resources' stock had dropped to $34.65 on January 5, which was less than half its value in the summer of 2014. Half of Harold Hamm's wealth had drained away in the four months following his billion-dollar divorce settlement.

On January 5, 2015, Harold decided that he wouldn't dribble out Sue Ann's settlement in $7 million increments, after all. She wasn't supposed to get anything at all while her appeal was pending, but he decided he would take one big swing at ending this thing once and for all. That day, he issued her a personal check, drawn from the Harold G. Hamm Trust, for the entire amount of the divorce settlement. It took two lines to hold the handwritten number: "Nine Hundred Seventy Four Million Seven Hundred Ninety Thousand Three Hundred Seventeen and 77/100—————." The offer was not received in the spirit Hamm had hoped. Sue Ann Arnall did cash the check, but issued a public statement: "Accepting the payment of less than 10 percent of our estate does not negate the principles at stake; my principles have not changed. I still believe the trial court's award was not fair and equitable. . . . I will not dismiss my appeal and do not feel that my right to appeal should be denied because I have accepted, in the interim, a small portion of the estate that we built over more than two decades."

Less than a month later, *The New York Times* pulled back the curtain just enough for a very unbecoming glimpse of what had really transpired in that Oklahoma County divorce court. (When an Oklahoma divorce makes the national section of *The New York Times,* it's never going to be good.) "Some in the courtroom started calling [Harold Hamm's] the 'Jed Clampett defense,' after the lead character in 'The Beverly Hillbillies' TV series who got rich after tapping a gusher in his swampland," wrote Robert Frank, who failed to note that Clampett had tapped that gusher with a rifle shot, quite by accident. *Then one day he was shootin' at some food, and up through the ground come a bubblin' crude.* "During his testimony, the typically commanding Mr. Hamm, who had been the face of the company for decades, said he couldn't recall certain decisions, didn't know much about the engineering aspects of oil drilling and didn't attend critical meetings." Harold's lawyers told the court that, by their calculation, "only five to ten percent of [Harold's] wealth came from his own effort, skill, management, or investment."

The hits on Harold Hamm kept coming. On March 3, 2015, *Energywire*'s Mike Soraghan began reporting out the fruits of a recent open records request. He had in hand, among other things, emails from the University of Oklahoma and the Oklahoma Geological Survey that revealed the meetings Hamm had demanded with the state scientists and the university faculty overseeing their work. Soraghan noted Hamm's gifts to the university and the director's fees Continental Resources paid to OU's president, David Boren. And made a pretty compelling case that Hamm had been strong-arming the OGS leadership and scientists. Boren declined comment when the first of the stories broke. Hamm demurred, too, through his previously courageous spokeswoman. "It is what it is," said Continental's VP Kristin Thomas, as Soraghan continued adding to the sordid story. "OGS is a public agency, paid for by taxpayers. They have hundreds of meetings. It is not a conspiracy."

The story got some more national pickup that spring, but Hamm remained fairly mum. He said nothing about it at *Forbes* magazine's Reinventing America Summit, where *Forbes* humbly billed him as "the Face of the American Dream."

All the press surrounding the OGS did draw out the head of New Dominion, who had been the chief architect and proponent of the "dewatering" process that occasioned so many injection wells in central and north-central Oklahoma. *Energywire*'s Soraghan reported on correspondence that made the very strong case that the founder and president of New Dominion, David Chernicky, had been alerted to the possibility of injection-well-induced earthquakes way back in 2007, after a magnitude 3.0 temblor hit near Tinker Air Force Base. The quake was very near where the company was injecting 100,000 barrels of wastewater a day back into its two injection wells, which were named Deep Throat and Sweetheart. "Speaking for myself, that earthquake hitting right next to the twinned disposal wells," an OGS staffer named Dan Boyd later wrote, "nailed the correlation." Boyd got a meeting with Chernicky, who was pleasant enough and agreed to give over some logs and pay for seismic monitoring at the site to study the correlation. But Boyd never forgot Chernicky's nonchalance. "He came in in a golf shirt and shorts, a John Boehner tan, and he brought three or four phones," Boyd said. "He would stop the meeting to get on the phone; he must've done that 15 times."

The heads-up from Boyd and the OGS didn't clip New Dominion's wings, not considering that a New Dominion injection well was among the most likely triggers of the magnitude 5.7 monster earthquake in Prague in 2011, a fact that was getting plenty of play by the spring of 2015, when Chernicky came out swinging in an interview with *Bloomberg*. He sang the praises of "dewatering," which had revived tired old abandoned oil fields. "I try to pick the ugly girl at the dance," Chernicky told the *Bloomberg* reporter. A charmer was Chernicky. He was even more colorful talking about the absurdity of "induced" seismicity. "The meager amount of science put forward is so flawed it can't even be considered science," Chernicky said. "It's emotion." He trotted out Jean Antonides and his horseshit theories about the rapid pressure changes in underground aquifers caused by the drought-monsoon cycles. And leaned on the equally horseshit theory about the tectonic shifts happening all over the globe—look at Japan and Haiti! When confronted with the notion that he was just kicking up dust so he wouldn't have to take any of the blame for the earthquakes, Chernicky bristled. "He insists nature's on his side," the *Bloomberg* profile concluded. "If humans can cause an earthquake," Chernicky said, "then they 'can probably fart and shift the orbit of the planet, too.'"

So, maybe not the most eloquent defender of the industry.

In the middle of all the press hoo-ha, Austin Holland stuck to his knitting. He had plenty to keep him busy. He was doing his research, working with the governor's new coordinating committee to help the Oklahoma Corporation Commission define safer volume limits on injection wells and better ways to monitor those wells. He was racing to complete a preliminary single map of faults in Oklahoma so both the drillers and the commission could try to make rational siting decisions. This was a killer job, which required Holland and his team to parse, as he remembered it, "sixty different versions of faults in some areas and work out some average aggregate for that area and try and decide, Okay, this is from 3D seismic. It's better than this fault that was mapped from well tops. So it was a lot of work to take all these different datasets and go through them, acre by acre, on my computer, and clean that up such that it was appropriate for publication."

He was proud of that early map, just as he was proud that the OCC's new "traffic-light" system he had helped develop was starting to come on line. The commission lacked the authority to institute any full-on moratorium on oil and gas activity, but it could now at least temporarily shut down operations within a specified distance of where any new seismicity occurred. That was actual progress.

Holland had become, withal, an incredible asset to the state of Oklahoma. Not just for his scientific contributions, but as an increasingly able and soothing explainer—for any audience. He could elucidate the process of "dewatering" and how injecting billions of barrels of ancient, brackish, salty, NORM-carrying, carcinogenic wastewater back into the ground *was* the safest way to dispose of it. "This is not water that we want pumped out onto the surface of the earth," he would say. He could describe how the Arbuckle formation, well below the water table, had fantastic permeability and could accept huge volumes of wastewater. But that there were limits, and wastewater could travel and have effect on faults quite far away from the well and over long periods of time. He could explain why operators needed to leave barriers between the Arbuckle and the strata directly below it, the basement. The basement was where most of the seismic activity actually happened. Any injection-well driller who punctured through to the basement had made a mistake. "We know that if you are actually injecting in the basement," he could explain to oil and gas pros, "you're much more likely to trigger seismicity."

After more than five years in Oklahoma, Holland had learned how to talk to the oil and gas crowd. He knew just how to urge them, gently, to be careful about the messes they left behind after the oil and gas was captured—because being careful was good business. "Really one of the things that can be incredibly useful is the same level of reservoir engineering and reservoir modeling that goes into your production environment may be just as warranted as for disposal wells," he told one group. "And that's an incredible rethinking. But there are now disposal wells that have been shut down within Oklahoma. So that's a lost investment. So by spending some investment up front you may help protect the investment of a disposal well and being able to use it within your production environment for the future."

In the end, his diplomacy, his thoroughgoing patience, and his diligence had won the day. He should have picked up *The New York Times* on April 22, 2015, and read these words as a triumph: "Abandoning years of official skepticism, Oklahoma's government on Tuesday embraced a scientific consensus that earthquakes rocking the state are largely caused by the underground disposal of billions of barrels of wastewater from oil and gas wells. . . . In a news release issued Tuesday, [Governor] Fallin called the Geological Survey's endorsement of that relationship significant, and said the state was dealing with the problem." The governor had come a long way from "Yeah that was crazy" and parroting Devon Energy talking points.

But by then, Austin Holland was going, going, gone. OU's spokeswoman Catherine Bishop handed reporters a copy of the letter Holland had written to his colleagues he was leaving behind. "The main reason for the move is to change my family dynamics," Holland wrote. "I have averaged 80 hours each week for the 5½ years I have been here. I want to change my work-life balance, and this opportunity is a good way to do that." The state's great explainer was leaving for a job with the U.S. Geological Survey in New Mexico, and he offered no further explanation at the time. He kept to himself the real reason he left, which was a dressing-down by Dean Grillot for publishing a peer-reviewed paper in *Science* titled "Coping with Earthquakes Induced by Fluid Injection."

Grillot has said he doesn't "recall" having reprimanded Holland that day, or ever having "put pressure on Dr. Holland to alter his research or conclusions." But Holland sure recalls getting the drift that his boss was not at all happy that the paper in *Science* made policy statements and offered policy recommendations. The dean seemed to be fixated on one particular passage, Holland later said: "For purposes of transparency and avoiding public distrust, it is important to put the results of these seismic network operations into the public domain in near real time. Even if a network is owned and operated by industry, regulators must ensure that seismic data are not withheld from the public. Similarly, making injection data—such as daily injection rates, wellhead pressures, depth of injection interval, and properties of the target information—publicly accessible can be invaluable for attaining a better understanding of fluid-induced earthquakes. Open sharing of data can benefit all stakeholders, including industry, by enabling the research needed to develop more effective techniques for reducing the seismic hazard." Did you say *open sharing of data*?

That was the offending statement that seems to have occasioned this meeting with the dean at OU—a meeting Holland later described as a "gut check" moment. He knew right then he was done. "I was just disappointed and devastated," he said. "I had taken the job at the Oklahoma Geological Survey because it was a perfect mix of what I wanted to do. Seismology is a field where you're studying something that has a direct impact on people's lives. . . . I'd spent my time, you know, working towards something, and I thought I was in my dream job, and then I couldn't be a scientist and do what scientists do, and that's publish with colleagues. That's the point at which I realized that for my scientific credibility, I had to leave the position I was in."

By the time Holland packed up his U-Haul and headed west for New Mexico, Harold Hamm was in serious damage-control mode. He had even given an exclusive interview to *Energywire*'s Mike Soraghan, the reporter who had ferreted out the news of Hamm's telling OU to shut Holland up. Hamm thought Soraghan's earlier coverage "kind of smacked of undue pressure and inappropriate behavior, and that's not what we're all about here at Continental." He wanted to, you know, set the record straight.

"Hamm says he wasn't trying to bully Oklahoma's state seismologist," Soraghan wrote in the first paragraph of his account of the interview. "We were in there because we are involved in fracture stimulation. We're the most active horizontal driller in Oklahoma," Hamm said, not exactly taking the question of bullying by the horns. He went on to explain what an "approachable" guy he was and how he always tries "to do the right thing. I don't try to push anybody around." (A few days later, *Bloomberg* would belie that statement by printing the Grillot email about his July 2014 meeting with Hamm: "Mr. Hamm is very upset at some of the earthquake reporting to the point that he would like to see select OGS staff dismissed.")

Hamm explained in the interview with Soraghan that he included the university president, David Boren—who also sat on Continental's board of directors—in the Austin Holland meeting because he was a peer (unlike Holland) and an all-around sensitive soul. "One thing about [Boren]: he's always been very, very concerned about other people's well-being," Hamm told Soraghan. "He doesn't want to see anybody trampled on and he's not going to do that." Boren, for his part, told *Energywire* that Hamm asked for the meeting because he wanted to hear "any information which might be helpful to producers in adopting best practices that would help any possible connection between drilling and seismic events." Uh-huh, sure he did.

But Hamm was still insisting Holland's conclusion about induced seismicity was flat wrong. And by Hamm's judgment, Holland was just a pawn in a much bigger fight. The War on Fossil Fuels, Hamm explained to Soraghan, was so much bigger than anybody understood, and so much more dangerous. "Hamm believes that the discussion of earthquakes and fracking plays into the hands of an active campaign to demonize the United States' oil and gas 'renaissance,'" Soraghan wrote. "That renaissance has been made possible by hydraulic fracturing and horizontal drilling. He sees the hand of petroleum-dependent Russia in the efforts to disparage it. . . .

"It all ties back," said Hamm. Which was nuts, of course. But it wasn't that much more nuts than the truth.

TWENTY-SIX

IT ALL TIES BACK

THE APPEARANCE OF THE MAN STANDING GUARD OUTSIDE THE Holiday Inn conference room door, in full snappy Cossack regalia—a fur hat perched nimbly atop his skull and a leather whip attached to his belt—was a pretty strong indication of strange happenings inside. For anyone who stepped through that door on March 22, 2015, and beheld the delegates of the first International Russian Conservative Forum, there was little doubt this conclave was full-on *Star Wars* bar scene. There was the odd lot of conferees in a mix of epaulet-fringed quasi-military uniforms and bargain-rack mufti; the buzz of new alliances being forged in a stew of suspected intergalactic jealousies, long-ago but unforgotten spites, and very current animosities; and the weird feeling that the Kremlin Death Star was endorsing and promoting all of it. The voices that rose above the din spoke in strident tones of all they knew to be right and good in the world: Western culture and tradition, Christianity, and the superiority of the white race—a race whose honored values faced the threat of extinction. "The West has been polluted by the virus of decadence, of liberalism, of homosexuality, of the destruction of the family," inveighed a delegate from a right-wing group in Scotland. Kris Roman, the lead delegate from Belgium, agreed. "Soon in the West it will be possible to marry a dog or a penguin," he said. "Children under five are taught how to play with themselves, and children over five are told that being gay is normal."

BuzzFeed News's Max Seddon reported that the delegates "railed, variously, against Freemasons; the corrupting influence of Hollywood; 'Nazi fascists in the EU'; a 'global cabal' of 'bloodsucking oligarchs'; non-white immigrants practicing 'alien traditions'; 'fags and dykes' and 'Zionist puppet filth.'" For all the apparent thrill of being able to say what they really felt, among friends, without fear of sanction—thank you, Cossack-suited guard, thank you, Kremlin-endorsed "free speech"—there was a sense of disappointment about the final attendance. Europe's bigger and better-financed right-wing nationalist political parties had ditched the conference. Apparently, the leading fascists in Europe didn't care to be associated with the self-declared neo-Nazis, and vice versa. Marine Le Pen, for instance, was happy to take big loans from a Russian bank to help finance the National Front in France, but she didn't want to be seen as too closely allied with this particular element right now, not with a national election on the horizon. The leading far-right nationalist parties in Austria, Hungary, and Serbia all begged off, too. Even the leader of the party that organized the conference, Russia's Rodina (Motherland) party, scuttled out of town at the last minute on what he claimed was important but unspecified business.

The folks who did show up at this multinational mind-meld didn't lack for ardor. The air in their conference room hung heavy with a desperate need to belong to . . . something. "What I'm looking for in Russia," said the Italian fascist Roberto Fiore, "is deep political and philosophical understanding." Alas, the community they managed to conjure felt a little thin that icy day in St. Petersburg. A Ukrainian academic who specializes in the rise of nationalist political movements in Europe described some of the conference's highlighted speakers. "Roberto Fiore . . . has almost forty years of experience of far-right activism," wrote Anton Shekhovtsov, "but in the most recent general election in Italy his party New Force obtained only 0.26% of the vote." Greece's Golden Dawn "has limited impact on Greek politics. The Belgian Kris Roman, whom the organizers proudly described as 'chairman of the Euro-Russia Research Center' is most likely the only member of this 'research center.' Nick Griffin, former leader of the British National Party who was expelled from this party in the autumn of 2014, represented the British Unity, a virtual party that largely exists on Facebook with four thousand 'likes.'"

The leading delegate from the United States, founding editor of the white supremacist online magazine *American Renaissance*, surveyed the room from his own spot at the dais and judged it wanting. "It's a bizarre lineup," Jared Taylor told *BuzzFeed News*. "The fringe of the fringe." This revelation did not dampen Taylor's hopes for this arid little seedbed of nationalist brotherhood. At least they had enemies to lash out at, together. "We are all united here in our opposition to globalization and in our love of traditional societies," Taylor told the room. "Tradition is under attack. One way is to replace the people who created traditions with an entirely different people. This is happening in the modern world through immigration. . . . Another way to destroy tradition is to try to undermine the traditions of a people and replace them with alien traditions. So there are two main ways by which tradition is destroyed: by replacing or diluting a people with foreigners, or by persuading a people to accept alien traditions." Taylor apologized for America's misguided embrace of "diversity," which he considered a form of national suicide. "We are all brothers and sisters, members of the same great family of Western Man. But we are a small minority on this planet. Our numbers are shrinking while those of every other group are growing. That is why we must have territories that are exclusively ours, which are for us alone and for our children forever. Without this, everything we love will be washed away."

One of the few rock stars at the event was a young rebel warrior just off the front lines in Donbas, where, he claimed, he was fighting the evil fascist government in Kyiv, which was out to exterminate all ethnic Russians in eastern Ukraine. (Even for the delegates, it was a dizzying exercise to keep track of just which fascists they were for and which they were against.) "I'm a nationalist," said Alexei Milchakov, who promised to return the Donbas to the warm bosom of Mother Russia. "I'm a patriot of my people. Right now in Europe there's an attempt to blur the lines, to mix everyone up."

Fellow attendees hurrahed this sentiment and railed against the United States and the EU for unjustly vilifying Vladimir Putin's ongoing attempts to bring back the pieces of Ukraine that rightfully belonged to the Russian people. Putin's nemeses in Russia came in for particular scorn at the conference, including Boris Nemtsov, who had been murdered steps from the Kremlin just three weeks earlier. "I know where they live," the Belgian Kris Roman said of Nemtsov and a number of other also recently deceased Putin critics. "They live in hell."

Even in absentia, Vladimir Putin, proud native of St. Petersburg, was the hero of the day. Conference literature bannered excerpts from one of his recent speeches. "We can see how many of the Euro-Atlantic countries are actually rejecting their roots, including the Christian values that constitute the basis of Western civilization. They are denying moral principles and all traditional identities: national, cultural, religious and even sexual. They are implementing policies that equate large families with same-sex partnerships, belief in God with the belief in Satan. . . . People in many European countries are embarrassed or afraid to talk about their religious affiliations. Holidays are abolished or even called something different; their essence is hidden away, as is their moral foundation. And people are aggressively trying to export this model all over the world. I am convinced that this opens a direct path to degradation and primitivism, resulting in a profound demographic and moral crisis."

Here was a true moral leader; this was the consensus of the first-ever International Russian Conservative Forum. "The salvation of my generation is the great Russian people, because Vladimir Putin understands that the rights of the majority should be put before the whims and perversions of the minority," exclaimed the Scottish delegate, beneath a photoshopped picture of a bare-chested Putin riding a bear. "Obama and America—they're like females. They're feminized men. You have been blessed by a man who is a man! And we envy that."

The image of Putin projected onto the whiteness of the low-ceilinged Holiday Inn conference room inspired feelings that might make a new bride blush. Here was the shirtless modern-day Nationalist Leonidas, riding his ursine mount, and the International Russian Conservative Forum delegates in that room were Sparta's three hundred bravest, there to hold back the hordes until the rest of the West could work up a sufficient appreciation of the dangers that lurked. The Russian journalist Ilya Azar sat in on the keynote speeches and couldn't quite believe their Putin worship: "Lenin died, Thatcher died,

Buddha died, Muhammad died, but Jesus lives! . . . God will save Russia! God will save the Russian people! God will save Vladimir Putin!" Azar described the culmination of that little riff as "quite unexpected."

The scene outside the hotel, however, betrayed the feebleness of the forum. The organization's website had basically begged for protesters—"enemies of Russia will not stop the International Russian Conservative Forum from taking place"—but these fringe creeps didn't even warrant a proper counterdemonstration. A dozen or so young men and women, easily outnumbered by police and Cossack guards, banged drums and pots, chanted, "Nazi fuck off! No to fascism!" and waved handmade signs: "Nazis licking Putin's ass. Omg. . . . We don't want foreign Nazis in St. Petersburg. We have enough of our own." The fascists in attendance complained about being called Nazis. The outright Nazis sporting swastika tattoos said they were a little hurt by that. A few of the loudest protesters were carted off to jail; one of the Cossack guards was wrist-slapped for ripping up a sign. Other than that, the only casualty seemed to be the hotel chain itself. "I will always spread information about how this hotel lets in neo-Nazis," one young man told Azar. "And of course I will never set foot in another Holiday Inn."

By the time a fake bomb threat broke up the conference—police suspected the call had actually come from one of the attendees, trying to drum up a little press—the first annual forum had been deemed by disinterested observers ineffectual and pathetic. "The flotsam and jetsam of right-wing fringe groups," Anna Nemtsova called the attendees in *The Daily Beast*. "This confab was for losers who can feel, in Russia, like they've found people who really understand and sympathize with them."

The whole scene invited more mockery than scorn, especially when it came to the sidebar participants, like Nathan Smith, the "foreign minister" of the Texas Nationalist Movement, a group advocating for the secession and reestablishment of an independent Republic of Texas. Smith made very little impression at the forum itself, his Texas-sized cowboy hat notwithstanding; he was not among the two dozen featured speakers. But he did take some time to explain to local reporters the ideals of this secession movement in Texas and how the U.S. government was "trying to artificially create the American identity."

"[Texans] need independence because . . . we have a completely different vision of the world and of politics, and we are not at all in agreement with the policy of the U.S. federal government," Smith was quoted in *Vzglyad*. "Today in power there are simply no people who represent the interests of the people of Texas. At the same time, we pay taxes that go up to Washington. Tell me, why do we need to belong to the United States?"

The Texas secessionists were a quarter-million strong, Smith insisted, and could point to comments by a recent governor of the state as more or less official proof that the movement was serious as a heart attack. "When we came in the union in 1845, one of the issues was that we would be able to leave if we decided to do that," Rick Perry had asserted, without benefit of factual underpinning. "You know, my hope is that America and Washington in particular pays attention. We've got a great union. There is absolutely no reason to dissolve it. But if Washington continues to thumb their nose at the American people, you know, who knows what may come out of that?" He had since walked that back a bit, but not exactly *all* the way. Most Americans might have understood that as Rick Perry being Rick Perry—flirting with Texas bad-boy chauvinism in the hopes of distracting people from the fact that he was about to attempt a run for president while under felony criminal indictment. Oops! But today's stupid political machismo stunt might become tomorrow's international flying wedge, and so Putin's government threw in with the wing-nut Texans. Russia likened their desire for independence—not to mention the wishes of separatists you could find in Hawaii, Puerto Rico, Northern Ireland, Scotland, and Catalonia to name a few—to that of the Russian speakers in Crimea, which Russia had heroically broken away from Ukraine, and in the Donbas, which Russia was trying to break away from Ukraine.

Almost nobody in the West took much notice of the sudden explosion in "Free Texas" tweets in the wake of that garrulous interview with the Republic of Texas's "foreign minister," Nathan Smith, in St. Petersburg in March 2015. *Politico*'s Casey Michel was on this story early, reporting the strange happenings in real time, but experts and Russia watchers in the West waved off all the Texit business as absurdist political theatrics from the Kremlin. "It's just another mischief-making gambit. Nothing seriously to be worried about," NYU professor Mark Galeotti explained to Michel. "Were the [Texas separatists] not both noisy and willing to play nice with Moscow, I doubt it would get much play. It's just another case of taking advantage of whichever 'useful idiots' happen to present themselves."

Maybe in an earlier age, but this was a different time—a moment when Vladimir Putin had growing, urgent (and increasingly hostile) geopolitical imperatives and when his intelligence apparatchiks were beginning to understand the power of certain new political tools at their disposal. Those "Free Texas" tweets were the first little pinholes that allowed a glimpse of a really weird future to come. To see how and where that future was being charted—to see how the freakish, the virulent, and the ugly were being weaponized for new uses—all you'd have to do is hail a cab under the portico of the St. Petersburg Holiday Inn that March day and ride ten miles north, to the squat four-story office building at 55 Savushkina, home of the Internet Research Agency.

The dark, heavy drapes were pulled tight on the windows day and night, so 55 Savushkina was a mystery even to people who lived and worked in the neighborhood—a subject of much gossip and speculation. There were suspicions that the Internet Research Agency was a seven-day-a-week, round-the-clock operation, but outsiders didn't know the half of it. There were only a few minutes a day when the hundreds of laptops in the warren of offices were idle. The bosses of the Internet Research Agency ran the operation on two separate twelve-hour shifts, which meant if you were in the area just before nine o'clock in the morning or just before nine o'clock at night, you could see small contingents of twentysomethings streaming in and out of 55 Savushkina. "They're so cool, like they're from New York," one observer told American reporter Adrian Chen. "Very hip clothing, very hip tattoos."

Many of these young professionals had been drawn to the Internet Research Agency by the ads that started appearing back in 2013. "Internet operators required! Task: posting comments on specialized Internet sites, writing thematic posts, blogs, social networks. Screenshots reports. FREE POWER SUPPLY!!! Learning is possible!" Setting aside the weirdness that in a country floating on gas and oil a FREE POWER SUPPLY at work is an advertisable perk, it's clear that jobs at Internet Research were coveted. Most of the hundreds of young people who worked at 55 Savushkina made around $700 a month; under the table, in cash. No need to report it to the tax authorities. This was very good money indeed for playing make-believe on your computer, twelve hours a day (two days on, two days off). The salary was equal to that of a full professor at a local university or close to that of "a journalist armed with legitimate facts and at considerable risk of being killed or imprisoned," noted Sam Zelitch in an essay for PEN America. "In the Russian workforce, there's as much money in chaos as there is in news."

Most all of the fun at Internet Research was in creating personas that could comment and blog and post and tweet and network with people anywhere in the world: a European fortune-teller who opined on dating, dieting, crystals, and feng shui; a young professional woman who unleashed bons mots about Kim Kardashian's latest nekkid selfie; a specialist in vintage automobile repair living on a sunny coast in Central America; a movie critic in Los Angeles. "It was an opportunity for them to live a life they always dreamed about and to pretend to be somebody else," explained Lyudmila Savchuk, who in March 2015 had only recently left the company. "They can be a gorgeous knock-out. They can be bodybuilders. They can live in any part of the globe. In America. They could live the life they've always wanted to live—through the internet."

Whatever the psychological benefits of the fantasy elements of the work, the physical work environment on Savushkina Street was no Silicon Valley start-up with foosball and craft beer and office dogs. Didn't matter if you were a member of the graphics team, the data analysis team, the department of commentators, the department of bloggers, the department of social networking professionals, or the rapid-response department. "They created such an atmosphere that people would understand they were doing something important and secretive," says Savchuk. "Humourless and draconian," was how a reporter from *The Guardian* described the outfit in a long investigative piece early in 2015. The Internet Research Agency was engaged in constant, rapid-response-driven information warfare. Speaking to co-workers was frowned upon. Talking about the work to anybody outside the building was forbidden. The nondisclosure form was the first thing a new employee signed. Show up late and you were docked pay. Fall short on the quota of work and you were docked pay. The folks on the social media teams were expected to produce five political posts, ten nonpolitical posts, and more than 150 comments every two days. Without fail.

The topics and tenor of the political content were decided at the top, every day. "We'd come in, turn on a proxy server to hide our real location and then read the technical tasks we had been sent," an Internet Research Agency employee explained to *The Guardian* in March 2015. Most of the technical tasks the previous year, as the agency was getting its sea legs, centered on Ukraine—looking for ways to justify Putin's invasion and takeover of Crimea and his ongoing military effort to do the same in the Donbas. Daily tasks called for savaging the new democratically elected, pro-EU, pro-U.S., anti-Russian government in Kyiv. They were fascists, anti-Semites, baby killers. Ukrainians fighting in their own country against out-of-uniform Russian soldiers and artillery and tanks were invariably described as "terrorists." The more shocking the fake stories about heinous atrocities committed by the Ukrainians against the Russian "freedom fighters" in the Donbas, the better.

In the first days of March 2015, immediately following the assassination of the Putin critic Boris Nemtsov, technical task orders spurred hundreds of posts and tweets pointing fingers at Ukraine for the murder. It wasn't Putin but the government in Kyiv that had killed Nemtsov! How does that even remotely make sense? Oh, follow along, why don't you. See, the Ukrainians killed him as an exercise in reverse psychology. Shooting Nemtsov on the night before his big antiwar march was *designed to stir up anti-Putin opposition in Russia*! Killing an anti-Putin leader—that's obviously a plot against Putin. "The murder is pure provocation. . . . The state is doing everything to catch Nemtsov's murderers. . . . [Putin's] best specialists have been sent to fulfill this goal." There was no evidence, no hint of corroboration, to back up this nonsensical claim. Which means you just have to make it more loudly and more frequently. The Internet Research Agency ops counted on a sentiment that had been invoked by one of the white nationalist speakers at that galactic freak-show International Russian Conservative Forum across town: "One hundred repetitions make one truth. The defenders of the truth can be overwhelmed by repeated lies." No lie was too outlandish, as long as it could at least plausibly confuse the real news, and as long as it increased anti-Ukraine, anti-Western online traffic and noise. The analytics department at 55 Savushkina tracked the metrics—how many comments, how often shared or forwarded or re-tweeted—and fed all that information to the technical taskmasters for message refinement.

And it wasn't just about shaping the response to real events that people would normally be talking about. The Internet Research Agency spread word of stories and ideas and characters that would otherwise not get a second glance if it weren't for the artificial hype its employees were churning out on a twenty-four-hour no-rest double-shift schedule. The morning after Foreign Minister Nathan Smith (Texas National Movement) gave his interview across town in St. Petersburg, Internet Research trolls were tasked to weigh in on the momentous secession crisis facing the Lone Star State. Dozens of tweets and social media posts started popping up, ready to be shared and retweeted, all across America. And in not particularly bad English. Some linked to what appeared to be earnest editorials, such as this ditty: "Perhaps nowhere else in the United States have local people discussed the topic of the annexation of Crimea to Russia, as in the state of Texas. The reason for the keen interest of the Texans to this problem is that the history of Crimea has much in common with the history of their own state." Sure, that's what Texas separatists were all about—solidarity with Russian-speaking Crimeans in the Ukraine. In the hands of Putin's internet trolls, any secessionist movement anywhere—however lame and parochial—could be adopted, mislabeled, and harnessed to help run down the West. And the social media fakery didn't end there, either. Internet Research soon set up its own Facebook page promoting secession—and it was a hit! "Heart of Texas" drew followers by the tens of thousands, all of whom could be spoon-fed content devised by Russian agents in St. Petersburg and in turn pass it on to who knows how many Facebook friends and Twitter followers. "Heart of Texas" was one of scores of separate IRA-controlled Facebook pages—not to mention thousands more social media identities and accounts operating on Twitter, Instagram, and YouTube—all created at 55 Savushkina.

By early 2015, when the St. Petersburg Holiday Inn was spinning its international lazy Susan of Nazis and fringe separatists, the Internet Research Agency's secret drive to expand the malevolent presence of covert Russian trolls in Americans' online lives was already a busy and expanding operation. The United States was the key and crucial target; Putin's Kremlin was committed to the mission of mucking with American democracy in general and the 2016 election in particular. And committed to a very modern method. The days of depending on hapless Illegals and mopey spies at the UN mission in New York were over. The return on investment had been too paltry. But the American virtual world was wide open and fertile with new possibility. It was also a fraction of the cost of active and actual human intelligence operations. Think of the Internet Research Agency's English-language department as a team of four hundred Guccifers, only with quality control engineers to fix up cultural references, usage, and grammar, and data analytics specialists, and IT specialists, and an endless array of protected virtual private networks behind them.

The heart of Putin's cynical play was information warfare, featuring cyber nuisances like trolling, and cybercrimes like identity theft, email hacking, and outright stealing. Putin's military intelligence and his foreign service pros were handling the most daring cybercrimes. The savvy well-paid kids at Internet Research were handling the rest, which meant the English-language department at 55 Savushkina had already become the favored elite in the building. They were the highest-paid crew at 55 Savushkina, and the hardest working. Even those with the best English-language skills had to master new areas of expertise. *Learning is possible!* They had to know how to use stolen identities to set up fake American-sounding accounts on Facebook and Twitter and Instagram. They had to study up on information provided by fellow agents recently returned from intelligence- and contacts-gathering trips in (the actual) Nevada, California, New Mexico, Illinois, Michigan, Georgia, New York, and Texas. They had to know where the most damage could be done. (A guy in Texas had told Russia's agent on tour it was the "purple states," but what exactly were those?) They had to discern which politically connected figures and follower-heavy celebrities sprinkled internet traffic magic dust that might just rub off on anybody who engaged them. And they had to be schooled in how to engage those mighty influencers. *National Rifle Association's Wayne LaPierre, we're looking at you. E! Entertainment's Kim Kardashian, we're looking at you, too?*

They had to get up to speed on American culture and politics, and specifically the most contentious and divisive issues of the day—immigration, gun laws, race, the Confederate flag. They had to spend hours screening one slightly cartoonish but very popular political series on Netflix. "At first we were forced to watch the 'House of Cards' in English," said one of the trolls who worked at IRA in 2015. "It was necessary to know all the main problems of the United States of America. Tax problems, the problem of gays, sexual minorities, weapons. Our goal wasn't to turn Americans toward Russia. Our goal was to set Americans against their own government. To provoke unrest, provoke dissatisfaction."

....

TWENTY-SEVEN

"ALL THEY HAVE IS THIS"

AFTER TWO YEARS OF INVESTIGATION BY THE FBI AND THE OFfice of Special Counsel, and more investigation by a handful of congressional committees, not to mention the relentless digging by dozens of able and talented professional reporters, we pretty much know *how* the Russians did it. How they mucked with our electioneering in 2016 in what the special counsel's final report called "sweeping and systematic fashion." We know that agents inside Unit 26165 and Unit 74455 of Russia's Main Intelligence Directorate of the General Staff (GRU) "used a variety of means to hack the email accounts" of the Hillary Clinton for President Campaign and its chairman, and to infiltrate—and then monitor and infect—the computer networks of the Democratic Congressional Campaign Committee and the Democratic National Committee. We know from federal indictments they were able to "capture keystrokes entered by" Democratic Party officials and employees and to take screenshots from their computers. We know Russian military intelligence officers released tens of thousands of stolen emails and documents through online entities they created, like "DCLeaks" and—as homage to that lonely but inspiring Romanian hacker—"Guccifer 2.0." (The GRU-controlled Guccifer 2.0 claimed falsely to be just another lone wolf operative who had stolen all the goods from a laptop on his kitchen table. "Fuck the illuminati and their conspiracies!!!!!!")

We know that Russian military intelligence agents used fictitious

American-sounding, American-seeming personas such as "Alice Donovan," "Jason Scott," and "Richard Gingrey" to drive traffic to the leaked material. We know the Russians handed over tens of thousands more pilfered emails and documents to WikiLeaks to ensure a wider distribution. We know that WikiLeaks released the first set of emails stolen from Hillary Clinton's campaign chairman on a day her opponent really needed a distraction from his own troubles.

We also know that the Kremlin-run trolls at the Internet Research Agency were actively spewing incendiary provocations and content designed to promote Donald Trump leading up to, and all the way through, the 2016 general election campaign, and then through the start of the Trump administration. Content created by the Internet Research Agency and its brethren is known to have reached well over a hundred million Americans in the election season. The IRA greatest hits Facebook pages were "Stop A.I." (meaning "All Invaders," complete with many graphics of scary-looking Muslims), "Being Patriotic," "Blacktivist," and "Heart of Texas." Each of those pages got more than eleven million discrete engagements. Heart of Texas, that original chestnut created way back in January 2015, had 200,000 followers by the time the election season was over, more than five million "likes," and almost five million shares. The scary anti-immigrant Invaders page got even more. These engagements were dwarfed by the total interactions with the most popular IRA-invented Instagram accounts, all created with the sole purpose of ripping at divisions in the American electorate. One of the IRA's fake American personas, Jenna Abrams (70,000 followers), started out trolling Kim Kardashian and then graduated to trolling people who thought the Confederate flags and monuments in the American South should come down. "Did you know that the flag and the war wasn't about slavery," Ms. Abrams scolded, "it was all about money."

The Internet Research Agency and its data analyzers paid Facebook for ads and "boosted posts" to stir resentments after police killed young unarmed African Americans in St. Louis, Baltimore, and Cleveland. And after a white supremacist gunman murdered eight African Americans at the Mother Emanuel AME Church in Charleston, South Carolina. "Another level of hate. Unfortunately, American tolerance is not what we think it is," read the ad for which Facebook pocketed $20 from the St. Petersburg troll farm. "What if America is still a deeply racist country? What if the church is not a safe place anymore?"

When not forcing their dirty fingernails into our various national open wounds, the Savushkina Street trolls pummeled the Democratic nominee with paid advertisements, writ ugly: "JOIN our #HillaryClintonForPrison2016"; "Hillary Clinton Doesn't Deserve the Black Vote"; "Ohio Wants Hillary 4 Prison"; "Hillary is Satan, and her crimes and lies had proved just how evil she is." African American voters—the bread and butter of the Democratic base vote—appear to have been targeted more aggressively than any other demographic, to turn them against Clinton or to dissuade them from voting altogether. "A particular hype and hatred for Trump is misleading the people and forcing Blacks to vote Killary," said the IRA-invented Woke Blacks. "We cannot resort to the lesser of two devils. Then we'd surely be better off without voting AT ALL." The IRA-created United Muslims of America posted an ad that read, "American Muslim voters refuse to vote for Hillary Clinton because she wants to continue war on Muslims in the middle east and voted yes for invading Iraq."

An official-sounding but fake "TEN_GOP" account—often assumed to be registered to the Republicans' state party in Tennessee—shouted out a make-believe story about the election board in Broward County illegally counting tens of thousands of fraudulent mail-in ballots marked for Hillary. #VoterFraud!!! "Heart of Texas" was also actively corrosive. Its ads decried the "Islamization" of Texans' once great republic and urged God-fearing Christians in Texas to protest the Islamic Da'wah Center in Houston, which had opened its doors more than a decade earlier as a center for worship, education, and outreach to the wider community. The "Heart of Texas" post in the spring of 2016 called the Islamic center a "shrine of hatred" and suggested that protesters "feel free to bring along your firearms, concealed or not!" American anti-Muslim protesters in fact turned out, holding white power symbols and Confederate flags, denouncing the Da'wah Center, at the time and place directed by "Heart of Texas." Houston police had a volatile situation on their hands when a separate and opposing group of protesters—there to support Muslims in general and the Da'wah Center in particular—showed up on the same day, at the same time, across the street. Turns out they'd been unwittingly summoned from St. Petersburg, too, by a separate Russian-controlled fake American entity called United Muslims of America.

As the election neared, the Internet Research Agency pros turned both rhetorical barrels on Hillary Clinton. If the Democratic nominee won the presidency, a "Heart of Texas" Facebook ad screamed two weeks before the election, there would be no choice but to secede. Because another Clinton in the White House would mean "higher taxes to feed undocumented aliens. More refugees, mosques, and terrorist attacks. Banned guns. Continuing economic depression."

We know the outcome of all this, too. We're still living it. Americans can and do argue whether, absent the big Russian push against the Democratic presidential nominee and for the Republican, Trump would have won his narrow Electoral College victory in 2016. And Americans can and do argue whether the Trump campaign's many open acts of boosting the efforts of Putin and his military intelligence cybercriminals and his army of Guccifer-descendant trolls at 55 Savushkina Street were provably criminal, or merely contemptible. But what is undeniably true is that Putin succeeded, probably beyond his wildest imaginings, in his highest real aim. The "goal seems to be not domination but chaos," longtime Moscow correspondent Susan B. Glasser succinctly explained in an essay in *Politico* a year after the 2016 election. "The objective is not to destroy us, but to weaken and confuse us."

Putin and his techno-warriors figured out what differences and disagreements and prejudices were corroding the health and cohesion of American society. They found the most ragged faults and fissures in our democracy: immigration, race, religion, economic injustice, mass shootings. Then they poured infectious waste into them. They used traditional media, social media, and disinformation to try to make citizens of differing experiences and viewpoints hate and distrust each other as much as possible; made public discourse and discussion as evil and mean-spirited and alienating as possible; created miserable expectations for coarseness and cruelty and blatant dishonesty in politics and civic life.

The Russian operation pushed American politicians and political parties to more and more extreme positions; it celebrated all manner of fringe, splinter, and radical politics and demonized centrists, moderates, and anybody on any point of the ideological spectrum who actually believed the levers of government could be harnessed for anything useful at all. And his achievement came cheap. A thousand—*ten* thousand—highly trained Illegals chatting up middle managers at conferences and dead dropping their expense forms could never have pulled off something this high-impact. This new type of operation was infinitely more effective, and bargain-basement affordable, and, because it worked, the blowback has been minimal. At basically zero cost, Putin succeeded in his biggest aim: he corrupted and polluted our most treasured possession, our democracy. *Pobeda!*

Even with an understanding of how he did it and how well it worked, what has not really been answered in any satisfying way is the question of *why* Putin went out of his way to muck around in our democracy. There are plenty of plausible explanations floating around out there. The most widespread is that Putin really did revile Hillary Clinton and blamed her for roiling the political dissent against him—inside Russia!—while she was secretary of state. She had been so eager and so aggressive in criticizing Russia's Kabuki theater democracy. So when Hillary Clinton seemed very likely to win the U.S. presidency in 2016, Putin figured he could at least rough her up pretty good, turn as many Americans against her as possible, and make it that much more difficult for her to govern effectively. Maybe even cast doubt on the legitimacy of her election, the way she had cast such withering doubt on the legitimacy of the Russian elections in 2011 and 2012, when she kept piping up about all the irregularities and stuffed ballot boxes that Putin really didn't want to have to explain, especially not to her. All that was true enough. But not exactly a full and compelling explanation.

Go back further than that, back to the root of the thing, back to when Vladimir Putin first became president of the Russian Federation, when it still had the makings of a potential superpower revival. Whatever its hard knocks on the way out of communism, this was the largest country on the face of the earth, with the only nuclear arsenal to match the United States of America. This was the country that gave us Tolstoy and Bolshoi and Pavlov. This was the country that launched the first man-made satellite into space. Launched the first *man* into space! And Russia, at the beginning of our century, also had the most impressive reserves of the most prized and remunerative commodities on earth—oil and natural gas. It was the sort of inheritance that, husbanded wisely and well, could have funded a border-to-border revival: education, infrastructure, health services, even fair elections. Could have financed new industry and technological advances. Could have provided a rich and loamy bed in which a modern republic capable of serving the general welfare of the Russian people would grow. Russia had the wherewithal to remake itself, again, into one of the most influential and powerful nations on the planet. A free, first-world Russia would have been a fearsome and worthy competitor in commercial and international affairs.

President Putin chose a different path, not least because establishing a diversified economy in post-Soviet Russia would have been really hard, requiring Russia to build and sustain a lot of things it hadn't ever had on a national scale: a reasonable expectation of the impartial rule of law, a reasonably competent government responsive to its people, reasonable public investment in the kind of physical and financial infrastructure that allows businesses to get established and grow, reasonable prospects for upward mobility and maybe even getting rich if you had talent and gumption and a little good luck. Results may vary as to what counts as "reasonable" in any one time and place. But a few things were certain: building that kind of a Russia would take a ton of work. And it would provide no guarantee of a lifetime leadership job for any one ruler—no matter how good he looked shirtless on a bear.

Putin opted for a shorter and easier path, which solved two problems: it gave him permanent job security, and it saved Russia the pain in the butt of actually building itself a modern twenty-first-century economy and government. Putin's most fateful decision for his country was that oil and gas wouldn't just be the profitable crown jewel in Russia's diversified economic array; it would be Russia's everything. And Putin would exercise almost complete control over it and use it in whatever way he saw fit.

It turns out to have been a colossal mistake, with grotesque consequences. For Russia, for the United States, for pretty much everyone except the oil and gas industry, and maybe Putin himself.

Now in his twentieth year running the show, Vladimir Putin presides over a metaphysical unforced error: the tragic scuppering of one of the potentially great nations in the world. Russia has been assiduously engineered into a sclerotic dictatorship; its economy wholly dependent on its one indispensable industry, which is by design almost solely monopolized by its big, lousy, noncompetitive state-controlled oil and gas companies, which are all run by spies or thugs or judo guys, and almost exclusively for the benefit of Vladimir Putin and his global aims. Their companies are not exactly soaring on the strength of their R&D prowess. And there's a good reason for that. No one, in any major Russian enterprise, has been allowed to succeed or prosper legitimately and on his own terms. Anyone who rose to any station must owe that ascent to Putin, and answer to him for it. That has been doubly true in the energy sector, which has been Putin's crucial lever of power. No one in that industry held on to money or power or property except with his say-so and on his ugly terms. If you were trying to become a clean businessman, running a capable and profitable energy company outside the control of the Kremlin, you were going to lose that business. Goodbye, Yukos. And maybe do a prison term. Hello, Mikhail Khodorkovsky. Alternatively, if you were a businessman or a crony who played along and served a useful purpose, you'd be rewarded with stolen goods. And you'd better stay loyal or you could do a prison term, too—look, you've got stolen goods!

That's how Russia's premier natural gas company, Gazprom, earned its reputation as "the worst managed company on the planet." And that's how the most Putin-loyal yes-man in Russia, Igor Sechin, became one of the most powerful figures in Russia. And how his company, Rosneft, became the behemoth of the country's oil industry—the Death Destroyer of Worlds, eating Yukos and Bashneft and any other cash-making morsels. It is not incidental that as an oil company Rosneft sucks. It wasn't as if it got big and powerful by streamlining its supply chains and inventing stuff. Rosneft sucks all the time, but especially lately, when—because of sanctions against Russia for its terrible international behavior—it no longer has access to all that nifty Western Arctic- and shale-drilling technology it needs to reap that increasingly hard-to-get Russian oil.

The country, meanwhile, has eroded into a stultifying economic sinkhole for average Russians. "Despite receiving $1.6 *trillion* from oil and gas exports from 2000 to 2011, Russia was not able to build a single multi-lane highway during this time. There is still no interstate highway linking Moscow to the Far East," Karen Dawisha wrote in her richly detailed 2014 book, *Putin's Kleptocracy*. "The inability of well-trained young graduates to succeed as entrepreneurs and innovators in Russia has stimulated emigration and plans to emigrate." Dawisha went on to quote a pollster in Moscow on the plight of young Russians: "They have nowhere to go, nothing to do, and nothing to hope for."

"The lack of adequate medical care produces five times more deaths from cardiovascular disease among women in Russia than in Europe," the professor wrote. "More Russian women die annually from domestic violence than the number of soldiers the USSR lost in the entire Afghan war. For Russian men, the situation is even grimmer. Poor workplace and road safety standards, plus high rates of suicide and homicide combine with the negative health effects of high alcohol consumption to make life especially precarious. . . . According to the World Health Organization, the life expectancy of a fifteen-year-old male is three years lower in Russia than in Haiti."

Let that sink in for a second: if you're a fifteen-year-old boy, your life expectancy is three years *longer* if you are in Haiti than in Russia.

Russia under Putin has become warped and stunted—a gigantic multi-continental country of 150 million souls, living on an economy considerably smaller than Italy's, with male life expectancy so low that you might think the national pastime really was Russian roulette.

This is a manifestation of a recognizable and widespread phenomenon—the Resource Curse—which has happened over and over again, with varying degrees of despair, from the Gulf of Guinea to the southern Great Plains. But Russia added a whole new twist to the Curse, a twist that helps explain the international order of things right now—or the lack thereof. When the Resource Curse takes hold in a country as big and influential and aggressive as twenty-first-century Russia, it turns out to be the entire world's problem. What has happened to Russia is like when a faraway humanitarian concern morphs from a charity cause into an international terrorism threat. Russia's Resource Curse has become a malignant tumor spreading through the rest of the world.

Unlike Soviet-era Russia, which used its oil and gas to provide for its own energy needs and the needs of its worldwide communist satellites, modern petro-state Russia has to sell its fuel on the global market without the benefit of a separate Soviet checkout lane. Which went pretty okay for a while. As recently as the George W. Bush administration, there were those in the United States who thought that Putin might be the great hope for a new Middle East–free global energy supply line. But as Putin's Russian Federation revealed itself to be a robustly corrupt, authoritarian regime happily committed to securing its own survival by force, it repeatedly and increasingly put itself into rogue state territory, and that ultimately screwed up its ability to play in the global markets as if it were some kind of normal country. Putin's best-known exports list has lately comprised the most dreaded organized crime syndicates on earth, money laundering on such a massive industrial scale that it can bring down whole national cornerstone banks in any part of the globe, exotic assassinations, rogue-state-friendly weapons systems, illegal out-of-uniform military incursions, and the first seizure of another country's territory in Europe since World War II. That sort of activity can get in the way of a country's global business operations, on the odd chance that there's anyone on the face of the globe who sees it as their responsibility to punish and isolate the kinds of international bad actors that invade their neighbors, shoot down civilian airliners, and send intelligence officers armed with nerve agent to assassinate their exiles in British cathedral towns.

Russia's way out of this existential conundrum has had two components: one business, one pleasure. The business part is tidy. With the broken-nosed, no-necked ex-spies perched atop the management structure of Rosneft and Gazprom, Russia's not exactly running a world-class operation when it comes to the production of its one indispensable commodity. Russia's economic future therefore depends on Putin making deals with major international oil and gas companies who can be counted on to understand his imperatives and to not care at all about ethics and governance and geopolitical consequences of their cozying up to the Kremlin. Those kinds of deals aren't just beneficial to the Russian economy; they're critical necessities for Putin's one-track plan for twenty-first-century Russia. And it turns out that as long as Putin is honoring the "sanctity of contract" and implementing friendly tax laws, industry leaders from the West have shown little hesitation in making those deals. That's the business part.

The pleasure part is less tidy, but presumably way more fun for its practitioners: if the problem is that Russia's behavior is too outré to be accepted in the global economy, then change the expectations for what counts as outré. Be the leveler. Corrupt other countries. Gain control over the former Soviet states in the near abroad by owning their politicians, by controlling the range of possibilities their people are allowed to choose for themselves. Ruin exemplars of governance and responsive democracy. Support separatism and the dissolution of bonds and treaties and Western norms wherever they're vulnerable. Become internationally powerful through force (when you can muster it) or sabotage. Cheating is now Russia's most viable avenue in world affairs.

And you can mark the precise time when all other avenues were sealed off: the immediate aftermath of Putin's shocking seizure of Crimea and his drive to forcibly annex much of resource-rich eastern Ukraine. Back in 2014, there was still enough U.S.-led traditional Western governance in the world to punish him with seriously harsh economic sanctions. Even those European countries Putin believed were so dependent on his natural gas supplies agreed he'd gone too far and it was time to say no in a meaningful way.

Those economic sanctions look like a pretty simple crime-and-punishment story from our vantage point, but from the Russian perspective the sanctions were much more gravely threatening. All of a sudden Putin and his *siloviki* had been stripped of Western oil and gas technology they desperately needed. All of a sudden they were unable to simply buy the fast-developing industry expertise required to stay competitive in the all-shook-up well-fracked new world order. Russia was literally barred by law from tapping that expertise. Even Putin's friends at ExxonMobil, who had aided Rosneft in making that tantalizing discovery of potentially billions of barrels of oil and oil equivalents off Russia's Arctic shelf, in the Kara Sea, couldn't help.

This is the vexing predicament facing the Kremlin: Putin's thug dream of resurgent Russian dominance—fueled by oil and gas—is one that can't come true without international help to make his one indispensable industry capable of competing in the global market. And he can't *get* that international help as long as he's recognized as a gangster and treated like one.

Putin and his lieutenants had been defiant when the sanctions first began to bite and ExxonMobil had been forced to pull up stakes in the Arctic. Russians could create their own Arctic-busting technology, they claimed, and promised to fund state-owned oil services companies to match any in the West. "We will do it on our own," Igor Sechin told reporters back in 2014. "We'll continue drilling here [in the Kara Sea] next year and the years after that."

Six months later, sanctions still in place, Sechin was forced to admit Rosneft lacked the equipment and technology to drill in the Arctic in the 2015 season. Six months after that, the Russian Energy Ministry said Rosneft would be lucky to return to a drilling platform in the Kara Sea before 2021. ExxonMobil, through it all, kept signaling to Putin and Sechin that it stood ready and willing to do the drilling for them. Just as soon as those sanctions were lifted.

But until then, the Putin-run oil and gas industry—the single engine powering the Russian economy—would be left to sputter. The country would stagnate and ultimately economically recede as the rest of the world drilled and fracked gas and oil that Russia could only make big, dumb moon eyes at.

So as of 2015, Putin faced a rapidly diminishing ability to use oil and gas as a substitute for legitimate global power, and no way forward without some kind of move—any move, no matter how nutty—to get those sanctions lifted and to relieve Russia of the burden of U.S.-led opprobrium and global Western leadership. It was worth trying almost anything.

As Special Counsel Mueller and reporters throughout Europe and America have made clear, the Russian Federation ultimately embarked on a deliberate and aggressive campaign to tear apart Western alliances, to rot democracy, and to piss in the punch bowl of free elections all over the civilized world. It continues to this day. And Putin isn't doing this because of Russia's strength. Not according to people who have watched the action up close. Russia "gives the impression that I am a lion who walks through the world hitting France with one paw, with the other Britain and America," says Romanian security expert Dan Dungaciu. "But it is not a lion. It is rather in the role of a hyena, which senses a crisis and goes there and plays on the crisis." The leaders of actually strong countries who have pushed back against Putin understand too. "I understand why he has to do this—to prove he's a man," Germany's chancellor, Angela Merkel, has said. "He's afraid of his own weakness. Russia has nothing, no successful politics or economy. All they have is this."

Putin has no one to blame but himself. He chose a future for Russia in which neither the economy nor the polity would be free. And that choice made Russia a weakling, a second-rate, second-world piker. Russia competes by shoveling toxic matter into the rest of the world's proverbial food supply, hoping to make everyone else as sick as possible, or at least as sick as it is. When the people of Ukraine stand up and make a rational decision for themselves, and toss out the fantastically corrupt Viktor Yanukovych and Putin's other henchman in Kyiv, the natural gas middleman Dmitry Firtash, all Putin knows to do is turn to a different type of corruption. He attacks with lies and disinformation, because those are the only cards he has to play to prevent the Ukrainian people from making rational decisions in their own national interest. Russian-speaking Ukrainians are being lynched, Putin's lying internet trolls scream, and so they're only rising up to defend themselves. Ukraine's Orange revolutionaries are neo-Nazis. Yulia Tymoshenko is the real natural gas swindler. Don't you agree, U.S. public relations firms, U.S. political consultants, U.S. banks, U.S. white shoe law firms? If the price is right, would you agree?

If that kind of corrupting is your best card, if that is your only real shot at international influence, or at least meting out some sort of punishment for the debilitating sanctions regime that followed the grab in Ukraine, then get hacking. It's cheap. It's doable, and it doesn't require making anybody think better of Russia. The agents of the Kremlin just have to tell the lies often enough and loud enough to sow doubt and dissension, to prove that leaders and governments and institutions in the United States are just as crappy as Russia's. And if Putin learned anything observing the winning-is-all oil and gas executives at ExxonMobil and BP and Chevron, or enablers at Morgan Stanley, or Davis Manafort Partners International, or Skadden, he learned that there are plenty of folks in the West who are happy to be part of it, happy to pitch in. Useful idiots can be found.

They're not even particularly hard to find, judging from a couple little emails that Vladimir Putin or any other sentient person on the planet could google and read at his leisure today. "[Russian pop singer] Emin [Agalarov] just called and asked me to contact you with something very interesting," an entertainment publicist had written to Donald Trump Jr. on June 3, 2016, when Putin's disinformation campaign in the United States was well under way. "The Crown prosecutor of Russia met with his father Aras this morning and in their meeting offered to provide the Trump campaign with some official documents and information that would incriminate Hillary and her dealings with Russia and would be very useful to your father."

"If it's what you say," Trump junior replied, a mere seventeen minutes later, "I love it."

....

TWENTY-EIGHT

"CONSTITUENCY TRUMPS EVERYTHING"

ON THE INCONGRUOUSLY SUN-SPLASHED LATE WINTER MORN-ing of March 2, 2016, on a remote strip of roadway north of Oklahoma City, the charred body of Aubrey McClendon was pulled lifeless from the driver's seat of his 2013 Chevy Tahoe. There were no skid marks to suggest McClendon had bothered to hit the brakes as he piloted his SUV across the traffic-less oncoming lane and into a concrete bridge abutment—at seventy-eight miles per hour. "He pretty much drove straight into the wall," Captain Paco Balderrama of the Oklahoma City Police Department explained. "There was plenty of opportunity to correct or go back to the roadway. That didn't occur."

The medical examiner determined that McClendon was likely killed on impact as a result of "multiple blunt force trauma." The death, as per the ME report, was ruled an accident. The extenuating circumstances, though, were strongly suggestive of suicide by automobile. The afternoon before McClendon's fatal crash, a grand jury in Oklahoma City's federal courthouse had weighed in on the quality of the evidence turned up in a long and intense investigation into Aubrey's business practices. "Beginning at least as early as December 2007 and continuing until at least as late as March 2012," read the fresh criminal indictment, "the defendant, Aubrey K. McClendon, and his co-conspirators knowingly entered into and engaged in a combination and conspiracy to suppress and eliminate competition by rigging bids for certain leasehold interests and producing properties." The Feds were trying to hang on Aubrey what they hung on John D. Rockefeller, a violation of the Sherman Antitrust Act. Aubrey began his defense that evening, and defiantly: "I am proud of my track record in this industry and I will fight to prove my innocence and clear my name." He was bolstered by some of the best legal counsel money can buy. "The prosecutors have wrongfully singled out Aubrey McClendon and have wrongly charged an innocent man," said his attorneys Abbe Lowell (who would go on to front for the Trump administration crown prince Jared Kushner in his various legal snarls) and Emmet Flood (who would sign on to protect President Trump himself from legal jeopardy arising from the special counsel's probe). "Starting today, Aubrey gets his day in court where we will show that this prosecutorial overreach was completely unjustified."

The next morning, shortly after receiving word that the biggest investor in his new oil and gas venture was not going to be putting another dime into the enterprise, McClendon got into his SUV and drove, alone, into eternity.

Thousands paid their respects in the days that followed; the encomiums were widespread and heartfelt. "The quality of life we have come to enjoy in Oklahoma City is due in no small part to his vision and generosity," said the chairman of the city's chamber of commerce. Aubrey was chiefly remembered, in public anyway, as the spur and the engine that had pushed OKC to finally, after decades of effort, realize its major-league aspirations. There were the boathouses on the Oklahoma River to point to, the dorms and athletic facilities at OU, the world-beating cancer treatment center, the beautiful Chesapeake Energy campus, the Whole Foods. And, of course, the large and happy NBA crowds at Chesapeake Energy Arena. Kevin Durant and his teammates were thundering up to the playoffs once again.

And all of it was true. But the dark side of Aubrey McClendon's career was not easily elided. The apologists referred to Aubrey as "embattled"; others less charitable called him "disgraced." There was that federal criminal indictment for starters and a raft of civil suits left to his estate to defend. His new oil and gas venture shuttered in a matter of weeks after his death—more than a hundred people out of work. The company he had founded and run for two decades was still staggering three years after his forced departure, unable to dig itself out from McClendon-led financial shenanigans. Chesapeake Energy had shed two-thirds of its employees in the previous five years, and its stock had recently sunk to $1.59 per share—capping a spectacular swoon from $70 a share at the height of the natural gas bubble. *Bloomberg Businessweek*'s ominously titled postmortem on McClendon, "The Shale Reckoning Comes to Oklahoma," noted that Standard & Poor's had downgraded Chesapeake's credit rating "for the fourth time since October, calling its $9.8 billion debt load 'unsustainable.'" Word on the street was that Chesapeake was headed toward bankruptcy. Analysts were beginning to ask this head-scratching question: For all the Aubrey-led hype and excitement about the wonders of natural gas in the fracking age, had anyone actually proved it out as a profitable venture? Aubrey McClendon certainly hadn't. The "better, brighter and more prosperous future" he conjured had turned out to be a mirage.

By 2016, Oklahomans were awake to the obvious and continuing costs of the last decade's oil and gas production frenzy and to their state government's willingness to give big companies like Chesapeake and Continental and Devon and New Dominion something approaching free rein. In 2016, as America prepared to vote in what would turn out to be its strangest presidential election ever, as the shale era—having reordered international geopolitics and driven Russia to the brink and pushed the environmental envelope so hard it scared even some of its pioneers, notably George Mitchell—wended deeper into its second decade, Oklahomans found themselves headed for trouble. Between the man-made seismic activity literally rattling the state and the barren state coffers that could no longer be dismissed as just an ideological talking point, Oklahoma was barreling toward a dangerous slick in the state's glorious, oil-soaked history.

There were more than a hundred magnitude 3.0 or above earthquakes in Oklahoma in February 2016 alone, which followed on the state's annual record of nine hundred in 2015. Oklahoma was outpacing California for seismic activity by a multiple of six. Anybody who still suggested the increased seismicity in Oklahoma was a naturally occurring phenomenon was either a fool or a paid liar. Meanwhile, thanks largely to the ongoing cash giveaways to horizontal drillers, the state's accounts were so depleted that Moody's rated it as among the three states in the Union least capable of riding out a recession. Expenditures on public education had further shriveled. Reuters reporters Luc Cohen and Joshua Schneyer were already digging into the ugly numbers in the winter and spring of 2016. In May 2016, they noted that while North Dakota, the other great shale boom state, had increased its spending per student by 26 percent in the previous eight years, Oklahoma had gone in the opposite direction in that same period—down by a nation-leading 24 percent. "Among the hardship measures being implemented, according to recent school surveys: bigger class sizes, teacher pay cuts and hiring freezes, cutbacks in arts, athletics and foreign language instruction, fewer offerings for special needs and gifted students, and a moratorium on field trips," wrote Cohen and Schneyer, right before noting this telling fact: "The Oklahoma oil industry is publicizing the role energy taxes play in helping fund schools. In March, a poster in the lobby of driller Continental Resources' headquarters featured a smiling boy and read, 'Oklahoma oil & gas produces my education.'" Yeah, you bet it does. They then quoted the spokeswoman for Harold Hamm's Continental Resources, who gets no points for originality but plenty for consistency and team spirit. "We don't have a revenue problem in Oklahoma," she said. "We have a spending problem."

More and more underpaid teachers in Oklahoma were spending their own pocket money on classroom supplies while taking second and third jobs to make ends meet. Dozens of districts across the state had cut back to a four-day school week, because that's all they could afford. The prospect of ever building safe tornado shelters in public schools appeared worse than unlikely, more like dead in its tracks.

But then something happened in Oklahoma. What happened was democracy. "In politics, money most always trumps merit," says Mike Cantrell, the independent Oklahoma oilman who finally got fed up with the lousy funding in education and bucked Big Oil in his state. "But constituency trumps everything." After years of killing cuts, the constituency finally started to kick up enough of a fuss that pols started to worry about the damage to their elective selves if they stuck to the status quo. Starting in early 2018, months of walkouts, strikes, and rallies by students, teachers, and parents across the state finally gave Oklahomans in elective office enough courage to punch the bully in the nose. Or at least to be seen *trying* to throw that punch if they wanted to keep their seats.

In the spring of 2018, the legislature approved a series of tax raises (with the needed three-quarters majority in both houses) to increase funding in public education, including a teacher pay raise of close to 15 percent, across the board. Key was a hike in the energy production tax from 2 percent to 5 percent. And then, miracle of miracles, the doomsday Oklahoma's big horizontal drillers warned of did not come to pass. The minimal tax increase did not depress the economy. Drillers did not flee the state for more tax-friendly environs. The November 2018 revenue from gross production taxes, according to the Oklahoma state treasurer's report, was 125 percent higher than in the previous November. The overall receipts for the previous twelve months represented an all-time record. School districts were expecting another bump in funding. The state had yet to diversify its economy in any significant way, which meant it still has to ride out the ups and downs of oil and natural gas pricing. But Oklahoma now appeared to have resources enough to cushion the hardest blows—a projected budget *surplus* of $612 million.

And how about this for a statistical trend? Magnitude 3.0 earthquakes in Oklahoma have dropped from that all-time high of 900 in 2015, to 623 in 2016, to 302 in 2017, to 196 in 2018. Interested observers have not chalked this up to Governor Mary Fallin's statewide all-faiths-welcome Oilfield Prayer Day. It happened because the constituency in Oklahoma—of all faiths—was pretty damn restless. Town halls on the earthquake problem were punctuated by chants of "*Moratorium now!*" "I am scared to death, and I think that echoes the sentiment of many in this room," one woman explained to Representative Lewis "the Science of How Everything Works Is So Big" Moore, at a town hall in Edmond, just outside the capital city. "Until there is a comprehensive, implementable, affordable plan to deal with this water, why do you not support a moratorium?" she asked. Moore fumfered out a nonanswer and was cut off by his constituent. "This is an issue that will turn a red state blue. And every one of you who needs to get reelected needs to take that very closely to heart. This is a state where the legislature, the government, and the Oklahoma Corporation Commission and David Boren—everyone down there at OU—have put the interests of the oil companies in front of that of the constituency and the electorate."

Ultimately, even Governor Mary Fallin heard their civic prayer, if only because the shift in the political winds was too real and too strong to resist. Once she finally acknowledged, after years of foot-dragging, that drilling operations were triggering earthquakes, she empowered the Oklahoma Corporation Commission to take active steps to try to fix the problem. The governor also got the commission a little seed money of $1.4 million to start the job. Since 2015, the commission has compelled operators to prove that they are not injecting wastewater into the basement rocks, where added pressure is likely to increase the danger of triggering earthquakes. The commission can—and does—issue orders to operators near active faults, or "Areas in Interest," to shut down injection wells or prescribe volume limits for the amount of gunk they're shooting back down into the earth. When an earthquake does happen, the OCC is authorized (and expected) to shut down all the injection wells in the surrounding area.

The commission also published new guidelines for monitoring and controlling fracking operations in areas of particular concern in the state. Drillers are now required to notify the OCC of their hydraulic fracturing schedules and to allow for real-time monitoring of pressure, flow rates, and volumes of sand injected at each separate stage along a horizontal well. The OCC has the authority to shut down any hydraulic fracturing operation in the case of induced seismicity (a.k.a. a frack-quake), which studies now suggest happens in a little more than one in every twenty fracking jobs. The drillers, even the biggest ones, with the most money and the most sway, are no longer actively resisting every tough regulatory action in dark red Oklahoma. "The earthquake issue is serious enough that it has captured the public's attention, so there is a heavy pressure from the public," says Jake Walter, who is Austin Holland's replacement as the Oklahoma state seismologist. The industry is "more willing," says Dr. Walter, to bow to public safety concerns. "Nobody wants to be having their name stained by being associated with a particular earthquake."

. . .

It's comforting to hear that the oil and gas industry has a sense of shame. But the truth is, it probably doesn't. Counting on the industry's sense of human responsibility—counting on it to act responsibly simply on its own recognizance—has proven to be a losing proposition. Oil and gas are valuable everywhere in the world, but with only a few exceptions the industry that produces them has shaped nations and states in ways that serve itself while screwing pretty much everybody else. As if its life depended on it, the industry has argued that it needs government off its back, it needs freedom and space to operate as it sees fit, and only the industry itself has the technological know-how to set the boundaries and expectations for how it behaves. And yes, energy exploration and production require some high-tech science and know-how, but it is not some freaking mission to Mars. Despite its gee-whiz nerds-R-us advertising and its self-proclaimed technical genius, this is an industry that can barely launch a mission to Alaska, one that still uses paper towels and dish soap as its highest-tech and most effective cleanup tools when something goes wrong.

The real genius of the oil and gas industry is the magic trick it does—again and again—in which it uses the hugely remunerative prospect of oil and gas profits to hypnotize otherwise sentient landowners and lawmakers and even whole countries into plighting their troth to the drillers. (Remember, the U.S. government willingly supplied the industry with a small arsenal of nuclear bombs at one point.)

That's how we get the twin engines of petroleum-powered governance, which suck the life out of democracies everywhere: corruption, in which the industry effectively owns politicians; and capture, in which the industry effectively owns the whole government. The result is everything the oil and gas producers need to get by and cash in—predictable government that responds to the industry and not to any other stakeholders that might get in its way. And one size doesn't necessarily fit all; the industry can work as happily with a weak and feckless government as it can with a dictatorial authoritarian regime, as long as it's at least in cahoots with (if not fully driving) government decisions. This isn't to say that the oil and gas industry is hell-bent on bad government for some ideological reason; it's just practical business sense. Democratically responsive government not only turns over whenever its people want change; it also creates the prospect of all these too-hard-to-plan-for X factors, like independent, non-industry-friendly regulations, or a legislature deciding to calculate the full publicly borne costs of oil and gas exploration and production, or a government even deciding to take the expanding costs of global warming out of the hide of the industry that brought it down upon us. The industry will be sure to stop that kind of government activity in its tracks. Oil and gas producers will spare no expense in that enterprise. As long as they've got the power to do it.

It's easy to work up some proper indignation over the damage wrought by America's biggest producers of oil and gas. They've managed to stunt developing countries on almost every continent and to prop up authoritarian thieves and killers all along the number line from Obiang to Putin. They've fouled oceans, gulfs, lakes, rivers, and streams around the world. They've induced man-made earthquakes; strewn radioactive waste about the landscape; killed off family pets and farm animals; sickened schoolchildren; turned state governments into impotent little quisling servants that rip off their own people to make sure the industry gets everything it wants, and more. And that's not even to consider the Big One: they are the chief drivers of the global climate catastrophe. While fueling that catastrophe—literally—they have also funded a decades-long campaign of denial that ensures the climate problem will get worse and that any solutions to it are seen as politically and economically impossible.

But ask yourself this: What is the point of outrage at oil and gas producers? What good can possibly come of it? It's like being indignant when a lion takes down and eats a gazelle. You can't really blame the lion. It's who she is; it's in her nature.

The nature of Big Oil and Gas hasn't much changed since its inception at the end of the nineteenth century. The entire point, and therefore the controlling instinct and the base ethos, is to make money—as much money as possible. That's true in theory for every industry, but the amount of money potentially at hand for producers of oil and gas sets these particular products apart from every other low-tech filthy widget in the world. Combine that with the inherently destructive and polluting nature of production, and you end up in a relentlessly, recklessly driven cost-cutting environment in which it's probably mathematically worth it to try to get away with almost anything. In the most profit-making industry on earth, there is still no meaningful R&D investment in cleanup technology, nor has there ever been any measurable slowdown in the pace or number of disasters that need cleaning up. That applies both to unseen accidents and missteps that happen almost every day and to epic media-frenzy disasters like the Deepwater Horizon oil spill. Consider also this remarkable fact: the Deepwater Horizon is about to lose its place as the largest known oil spill in U.S. history—to another spill *in the Gulf of Mexico.* Turns out an oil rig toppled by Hurricane Ivan in 2004 has been leaking, twelve miles off the coast of Louisiana, every day since then. The spill remained a secret until 2010, when environmental scientists spotted an entirely separate oil slick during the Deepwater Horizon great paper towel cleanup. An analysis by an independent geoscientist in October 2018 found that the rig was still leaking as much as seven hundred barrels of oil into the Gulf every single day, which means, after nearly fifteen years, the record was in its sights.

When *The Washington Post* first reported this story in 2018, it noted for context the overall offshore drilling statistics compiled by the federal government's Bureau of Safety and Environmental Enforcement. "For every 1,000 wells in state and federal waters, there's an average of 20 uncontrolled releases—or blowouts—every year. A fire erupts offshore every three days, on average, and hundreds of workers are injured annually." But the *Post* also noted statistics that the oil and gas producers found much more compelling. The Gulf of Mexico, said the *Post,* is "expected to yield more than 600 million barrels this year alone, nearly 20 percent of the total U.S. oil production. Another 40 billion barrels rest underground, waiting to be recovered, government analysts say."

And it is in the nature of the beast to go get those barrels, so long as there is money to be made. In fact, the breakthrough technologies of hydraulic fracking and horizontal drilling in the last generation have made the industry more energetically predatory than ever before. And even more delusional. "Every time we can't drill a well in America, terrorism is being funded," Harold Hamm said at the 2016 Republican National Convention. "Every onerous regulation puts American lives at risk." This is an industry that has demanded and received special treatment for more than a century and regards this private right as its due. But even if "energy independence" is our international relations insurance policy and the safety of our energy supply is a core national security issue, why are oil and gas the only energy sources to which those imperatives redound? Why are oil and gas the only energy sources seen as appropriate tools to reach these two national goals? Heaven forbid the government instead offers breaks and incentives to, say, renewable energy. Then suddenly the industry becomes the champion of the free market. *Government should not be in the business of picking winners!*

The oil and gas industry, as ever, is wholly incapable of any real self-examination, or of policing or reforming itself. Might as well ask the lions to take up a plant-based diet. If we want the most powerful and consequential industry on our planet to operate safely, and rationally, and with actual accountability, well, make it. It's not mission-to-Mars complicated either, but it works.

TWENTY-NINE

CONTAINMENT

ELECTIONS HAVE CONSEQUENCES, POLS FROM BOTH OF AMERICA'S major parties like to say. Especially after they win. And this adage has proved demonstrably true, even when the winners have encouraged and accepted illegal aid from the military intelligence services of a sworn enemy of the United States. Take, for instance, the first fruits of the most unlikely electoral victory in modern U.S. history, harvested just a few weeks into the presidential administration of Donald J. Trump and tucked into a gift basket presented to the American oil and gas industry: "Resolved by the Senate and House of Representatives of the United States of America in Congress assembled, That Congress disapproves the rule submitted by the Securities and Exchange Commission relating to 'Disclosure of Payments by Resource Extraction Issuers' and such rule shall have no force or effect." Oklahoma's senior senator, James Inhofe, had already put his own headline on the resolution, in plain language, and resolutely. "Overturning this SEC rule," he wrote, "is another important step to ending the Obama Administration's war on fossil fuels."

In U.S. election cycles from 2012 to 2016, the oil and gas industry upped its already considerable spending on candidates protective of its prerogatives, while loudly decrying that so-called Obama war: the industry contributed $152 million to Republican candidates, as compared with $21 million for Democrats. Nine of every ten campaign dollars from the ExxonMobil PAC went to Republican candidates in

2016. And investments like that tend to pay off, both well and quickly. For Harold Hamm, the 2016 election cycle was like winning the daily double. First, his ex-wife Sue Ann lost her appeal of their billion-dollar divorce settlement. And then, jackpot, a Republican administration rode back into the White House. Donald Trump would surely strip away all those nettlesome Obama-era regulations. Trump "absolutely gets it," Hamm explained. "He believes in American energy for America's future." Whether or not Donald Trump absolutely got that or anything, it says something about the industry's mad skillz that the first legislation out of the new session was its baby. Its seemingly arcane but absolutely beautiful baby.

Rex Tillerson was confirmed as secretary of state on the day the "end the war on fossil fuels" resolution passed the House. He issued no public statement, even after Trump signed the bill into law on Valentine's Day 2017. But if anybody was due a victory lap, if only around his new government-issue desk at Foggy Bottom, it was longtime ExxonMobil CEO Tillerson. The quiet little, below-the-radar, technical-seeming resolution was narrowly targeted to steamroll the one speed bump Congress had finally come up with to try to slow the ability of the most powerful industry on earth to warp nations in its own interests, to eat governance for breakfast so it could poop out royalties by lunchtime. That quiet little boring measure that so thrilled Senator Inhofe—the curtain-raising legislation of the 115th Congress—nullified a provision in the 2010 Dodd-Frank Wall Street reform law that required oil and gas companies listed on the American stock exchange to publicly report all taxes, royalties, licensing fees, dividends, and bonuses paid to foreign governments or foreign government officials with whom they were doing business. This provision in Dodd-Frank, Section 1504, was designed to induce financial transparency for oil and gas industry operations in developing countries like Nigeria, Liberia, Guyana, Azerbaijan, and, Exhibit A, Equatorial Guinea. They were all Resource Curse case studies by then—revenues from oil and gas enriching the lucky few at the tippy-top of the government pyramid structure while the rest of their countrymen festered in worsening indigence and privation.

Section 1504 had been a first step toward the U.S. government finally taking responsibility for the role of American companies in those corruption disasters, by at least forcing them to disclose whom they were paying and how much. How does the GDP of a country rise by more than 5,000 percent but the poverty rate doesn't drop and the infant mortality rate actually gets worse in that time? Equatoguineans might want to know. Specifically. Section 1504 would give them—and all of us—real data to work with to figure it out.

It's worth repeating what the late Republican senator Richard Lugar wrote when he sponsored the measure: "When oil revenue in a producing country can be easily tracked, that nation's elite are more likely to use revenues for the vital needs of their citizens and less likely to squander newfound wealth for self-aggrandizing projects." Lugar had also been clear-eyed about the cost to the United States of allowing corrupt government actors in those countries to consistently fail their own citizens. The Resource Curse, Lugar wrote, "exacerbates global poverty which can be a seedbed for terrorism, it dulls the effect of our foreign assistance, it empowers autocrats and dictators, and it can crimp the world petroleum supplies by breeding instability."

Rex Tillerson had begged to differ, rather vociferously, back in 2009 and 2010, when Section 1504 was heading toward becoming law. That was when the ExxonMobil chief had thrown his uncharacteristic fit of red-faced apoplexy over the provision in a personal meeting with Senator Lugar—at least according to Lugar's staff. This sort of enforced reporting requirement would disadvantage American companies against competitors from the world's other major oil-producing nations, Tillerson had argued. And continued to argue. For the next six years. Why should the United States go all goody-two-shoes when oil- and gas-producing titans in Saudi Arabia and Venezuela and China and wherever else weren't compelled to do the same? And so no, ExxonMobil did not want to explain, exactly, how it was that it managed to secure twenty years' worth of oil rights in Nigeria despite reportedly being outbid by a Chinese-led consortium by more than double—by more than *$2.25 billion.* Is it possible that there was a little sweetener there for someone in a decision-making capacity over that contract? Maybe? Anyone want to check the books? Did every Nigerian official who looked at that potential deal just independently—and for the good of his or her country—decide to give away $2.25 billion?

How about the details of the production agreement ExxonMobil had negotiated with Guyana, which included an $18 million "signing bonus" to the Guyanese government (anyone in the Guyanese government looking to buy some Michael Jackson memorabilia?). No, ExxonMobil would not be disclosing the amazing footwork that must have led to those improbable deals. "We are a commercial enterprise and we have competitors," Exxon's Man in Guyana explained. "And learning bits of information about how other negotiations have worked or how our negotiations work—the things that we value—provide kind of intellectual property to competitors."

KFC has its secret herbs and spices, fracking companies have their proprietary slickwater goo, and apparently Exxon has its secret special menu of which exact government officials or proxies an American oil company must pay off—and how well—in order to secure the right to profit from a country's natural resources. Without hassle from said government.

In the six-plus years that Section 1504 languished in the murky purgatory of lobbying, lawsuits, and regulatory rollout, if anything, the daily lives of the First Family of Equatorial Guinea, the Obiangs, had continued to improve. Teodoro Obiang was by 2017 the longest-serving president on the planet and without opposition on any front, having just "won" the latest "election" with 93.7 percent of the vote. President Obiang had just completed construction of a new capital city—the country's third. Unlike the other two working seats of government, the new capital was much nearer Obiang's home village, and well inland, away from the gulf coast. President Obiang had chosen this site because he had grown especially wary of maritime coup attempts. (Even the corporate American mercenary force that he had agreed to pay hundreds of millions of dollars had not filled him with sufficient confidence.) But carving a modern new city out of the jungle was a costly proposition, which meant a good chunk of the oil revenue from ExxonMobil and Hess and Marathon and others went into its construction. The International Monetary Fund reported that Obiang's government appropriated more than a quarter of Equatorial Guinea's total 2011–2015 infrastructure budget for the building of the third new capital city. In 2016, the year of completion, that number jumped to half.

How much of that was spent actually constructing the new capital and how much was simply pocketed by Obiang's family and his loyal government ministers remain matters of conjecture. This was like Putin's Sochi Olympics construction project, only with a smaller circle of judo partners and cronies in play. Much of the construction money was funneled through a privately owned enterprise called Abayak SA. Abayak was a busy little shell company, and the largest in the country; aside from owning a 15 percent cut of ExxonMobil's oil distribution business in Equatorial Guinea, Abayak enjoyed a monopoly on importing cement into the country, which proved mighty valuable when Obiang determined to make his new city in the jungle. Who benefited from Abayak's supremely well-positioned market share? President Teodoro himself owned 75 percent of Abayak shares, his favored wife owned 15 percent, and the final 10 percent ownership stake belonged to Teodoro's eldest son, the Michael Jackson glove–loving international playboy and driving menace, Teodorin Obiang. Teodorin, who had ascended from minister of forestry to vice president in the summer of 2016, had brand-new tankfuls of cash in the form of new construction contracts and subcontracts, from which he could siphon off tens of millions more dollars.

When one of Teodorin's "construction company" partners discovered the impressive amplitude of his plunder, the First Son had the man tossed into one of Equatorial Guinea's storied prisons, for fear he might blab to criminal investigators in the United States and France who had Teodorin in their sights. Roberto Berardi spent more than two years behind Equatoguinean bars and emerged seventy pounds lighter and much scarred. "True terror was when they tortured my neighbors in the cell next to me," Berardi, an Italian national, said after his release in 2015. "Hearing those cries and blows every night was terrible. It destroys you psychologically. It was more frightening than when I was beaten myself. . . . The prisons are full of innocent people who are tortured, as well as foreigners, who are exposed to the worst violence. . . . What I saw in prison was like a horror movie."

The everyday Equatoguineans who steered clear of President Obiang's notorious penal system weren't exactly flourishing, in spite of the extra $25 billion or so in oil and gas revenue that had poured into the country after 2010. "Equatorial Guinea ranks 138 out of 188 countries in the United Nations Development Programme's Human Development Index, a measure of social and economic development," noted a 2017 Human Rights Watch report. "Its score is almost identical to that of Ghana and Zambia, despite boasting a per capita income that is more than five times as high." Education was a shambles, and getting worse. Little more than 10 percent of Equatoguinean children made it to middle school, and almost half of those had fallen badly behind. It was not uncommon to find a teenager in the first grade.

The report noted that Equatoguineans' access to safe drinking water had not improved one whit in more than twenty years. One in four children suffered physical consequences from lack of sufficient food. Six in ten deaths were the result of malnutrition or easily eradicable communicable diseases. The country's vaccination rates for tuberculosis had actually dropped from 99 percent in 1997 down to 35 percent in 2015. The health-care system was no great help when someone did get sick. "If people [in critical condition] don't have money, they die," a doctor at a public hospital in one of the three capitals told researchers from Human Rights Watch.

Terrible to see it all laid out like that in black and white, sure, but it does conjure up what that ExxonMobil company spokesman had said around the time of the Riggs Bank hearings a decade earlier: "It is not our role to tell governments how to spend their money." And to be honest, ExxonMobil and other oil and gas drillers continued to benefit from presidential-level corruption in countries like Equatorial Guinea; it just simplified the process of doing business there. It was quite clear whom to pay, and no one in the country had enough of a death wish to try to get in the way of Obiang delivering on his promises to let the Western companies do what they wanted. So long as nasty, authoritarian strongmen like Teodoro Obiang didn't start making untoward new demands on oil and gas producers, and they honored ExxonMobil's bottom-line imperative—the "sanctity of contract"—all was cool.

Anyway, by the time the Human Rights Watch report on Equatorial Guinea surfaced in 2017, Big Oil had its hands around the neck of Section 1504. Republicans controlled the Senate, the House, and the presidency. They were seizing as much control as they could of the judiciary. And ExxonMobil's Tillerson had ascended to—of all things—U.S. secretary of state. Kind of a head-scratcher, if you had governance in mind, to give this job to a man with no government experience who had shown no interest in American foreign policy to date, had raised eyebrows, consternation, and even alarm among U.S. diplomats and national security specialists on both sides of the aisle. Not that Rex didn't have spirited defenders, especially on social media. "Attacks on Rex Tillerson implying he is in pocket of Russia are despicable. He's a distinguished American, with incredible accomplishments," said one tweet. And another: "RT if you are PROUD to have Rex Tillerson as the next Secretary of State!" Except, alas, as we would learn soon enough, both of those were from @TEN_GOP, one of the many splendid accounts secretly set up by Russians working at the Internet Research Agency in St. Petersburg. When @TEN_GOP got suspended by Twitter for being a Russian op, Russian-controlled @ELEVEN_GOP (get it?) took its place: "Trump to name Exxon Mobil CEO Rex Tillerson as Secretary of State! Good!"

Jane Mayer later reported in *The New Yorker* that, according to a dispatch from the British intelligence veteran Christopher Steele, senior Russian officials had boasted about successfully blocking the appointment of the vocally anti-Putin former Republican presidential nominee Mitt Romney. "The memo said that the Kremlin, through unspecified channels, had asked Trump to appoint someone who would be prepared to lift Ukraine-related sanctions, and who would cooperate on security issues of interest to Russia, such as the conflict in Syria," Mayer explained. "As fantastical as the memo sounds, subsequent events could be said to support it." The first of those events was the rejection of Romney. In early 2018, *The Wall Street Journal* did an analysis of since-deleted Russian social media accounts that tried to steer the secretary of state appointment: "Weeks after Donald Trump was elected president, Russia-backed online 'trolls' flooded social media to try to block Mitt Romney from securing a top job in the incoming administration. . . . The operatives called [Romney] a 'two headed snake' and a 'globalist puppet,' promoted a rally outside Trump Tower and spread a petition to block Mr. Romney's appointment to the top diplomatic job." And it made an impression. In all the right places: "Around that time, Trump senior adviser Kellyanne Conway said Mr. Romney had been 'nothing but awful' to Mr. Trump during the campaign, and tweeted that she was getting a 'deluge' of negative comments about him from Trump loyalists." Trump loyalists, at least some of whom were writing from Savushkina Street.

After humiliatingly courting and then dumping Romney, Trump switched horses to Rex "We Do Not Support Sanctions, Generally" Tillerson. "A surprise to most," Mayer wrote, "and a happy one in Moscow." The two men had never met before the meeting in which Trump offered him the position. The Kremlin certainly seemed to be delighted with the choice. "[Tillerson] fulfills his duties very professionally," said Putin's spokesman Dmitry Peskov on hearing the news. Rex was a very special kind of win-win. Good for Russia. Good for oil and gas.

But, in truth, it was *all* good for oil and gas at the dawn of Trump.

Just a few weeks after Trump and his Republican majorities got in the saddle, Section 1504 was toast. Senator Inhofe, sponsor of the legislation that strangled 1504, was still crowing a month later, when the new Republican president was considering an executive order to gut the Obama administration program designed to decrease carbon emissions by a third. Gone were the days when Inhofe had to be the self-styled "one-man truth squad" at international climate change symposia, proudly standing up to defend the helpless, damsel-in-distress, misunderstood energy industry. Lonely work but somebody had to do it, Inhofe would say. "We've endured eight years of an administration that buys into the alarmist mentality that the world is coming to an end, and it's due to man-made gases," Inhofe offered in his excoriation of the Clean Power Plan on the Senate floor on March 14, 2017. "That's what the hoax is."

With a Republican House and a Republican Senate and Trump now in a position to deliver his lifetime wish list, Inhofe pulled out all his greatest hits—a trifecta of conspiracy theory, bad science, and economic forecasts unsupported by fact. He explained how scientists from the National Oceanic and Atmospheric Administration had hidden data exculpatory to the greenhouse gases. "Just a few weeks ago, a whistleblower alleged that a June 2015 NOAA report manipulated data," he said. "Conveniently, the computer with the data suffered a complete failure and none of the data was saved." He enumerated the benefits of increased carbon dioxide emissions: "Many people still remind us, over and over again, that CO_2 is actually a fertilizer. It helps things grow." He ad-libbed make-believe statistics attributed to the energy-industry-backed National Black Chamber of Commerce, enumerating the damage certain to fall on "the most vulnerable people" if emissions were reduced. The Clean Power Plan "would increase black poverty by 23 percent, Hispanic poverty by 26 percent, reduce black jobs by 200,000 and Hispanic jobs by 300,000, with a cumulative job loss of 7 million for blacks and nearly 12 million for Hispanics by the year 2035."

When the new American president signed on the dotted line, Inhofe was in his glory. "This order is a clear sign to the country that Trump is serious about unleashing this country's energy dominance."

Some hope still remained on the transparency front, thanks to something called the Extractive Industries Transparency Initiative, which had gained a great deal of momentum in the previous few years. For all the same reasons that Lugar and Cardin had written Section 1504, for all the potential benefits that might flow from stopping the fire hose of corruption that the oil and gas industry sprayed into weak countries, more than fifty countries around the world had committed to public reporting of all money received, of all kinds, from oil and gas producers. The United States had been one of them, a leader by example. Until, suddenly, it wasn't. Just a few weeks after Congress knifed Section 1504, *The New Yorker*'s Adam Davidson reported, the Trump administration unilaterally canceled mandated, regularly scheduled meetings of the EITI stakeholders in the United States, which included representatives from the federal government, energy companies, trade organizations, and civil society groups like Global Witness and Oxfam America.

Industry watchers initially scratched their heads about the meaning of the United States canceling those meetings, but not for long. Before the end of the year, the United States announced its full withdrawal from the agreement. Forget transparent financial reporting in developing countries. Oil and gas companies wouldn't even need to report their tax expenditures here, inside the United States of America. "The argument for withdrawal, according to the formal letter from the Department of the Interior to the chair of the E.I.T.I. board, is that U.S. law simply doesn't allow for the kind of transparency that E.I.T.I. requires," wrote Davidson, who had been closely following the action. "This argument is hard to accept, since the U.S. played a central role in crafting the rules of E.I.T.I."

Senator Ben Cardin and Richard Lugar, who by then had been

forcibly retired by Indiana Republicans for his dastardly bipartisan proclivities, issued a joint statement on hearing the news. "The Department's justification for withdrawing from EITI—because the initiative contravenes the U.S. legal framework—is a front meant to mask Big Oil and Gas' money and influence," they said. "There is no U.S. law that prevents oil, gas or mining companies from voluntarily disclosing their federal tax payments to the American people. The Trump Administration's move today is a painful abdication of American leadership on transparency and good governance." EITI's founding voice Daniel Kaufman, writing in the *Financial Times,* pointed out the rich irony that even Russian and Chinese oil and gas companies were reporting their tax expenditures. It was just the American majors who didn't want to. "The US ones refuse to change their old habits," he said.

Jay Branegan, who had worked for Lugar in the Senate and witnessed Rex Tillerson's outburst about government-enforced transparency, wrote an incisive op-ed in the days after the American withdrawal from EITI. "The US action is a stab in the back to the activists in poor countries around the world who have been struggling to expose corruption by their countries' leaders," Branegan wrote. "It's probably not too strong to say that for the past several years, the major US oil companies duped the public and their shareholders about their commitment to good governance and corporate responsibility. Last week, when their fraud was exposed, the Trump administration colluded with them to try to cover it up. The timing of the pullout—as Congress is preparing unprecedented corporate tax cuts and new 'Paradise Papers' revelations about the widespread use of offshore corporate tax avoidance schemes—led many to ask, 'Just what are ExxonMobil and Chevron and the others trying to hide?'"

As I was finishing the manuscript for this book, the Justice Department released most of Special Counsel Robert Mueller's report on Russia's election interference: "The investigation established that the Russian government perceived it would benefit from a Trump presidency and worked to secure that outcome, and that the [Trump] Campaign expected it would benefit electorally from information stolen and released through Russian efforts." The unspooling story of Russia's election attack—and its care and feeding of the Trump campaign—has been told through Mueller's indictments and through the pages of his report and in episodic bursts from America's major dailies. But in the big picture, the trails between Trump and Russia turned out to be not only myriad, but surprisingly, well, greasy.

The Tweedledum and Tweedledee of the Trump campaign foreign policy team, Carter Page and George Papadopoulos, were both self-styled energy experts when they were plucked from obscurity and in-stalled on Team Trump. Papadopoulos was introduced to the nation by Donald Trump as "an oil and energy consultant" and "an excellent guy" and then put on display at the all-for-the-cameras show Trump captioned "Meeting with my national security team" on his Instagram feed. Eventually, it would be Papadopoulos's advance-notice bragging about Russia's hacking of the Democrats that would spur the FBI to open its initial investigation into what the hell was going on between the Russians and Trump.

As for Carter Page, proprietor of Global Energy Capital LLC—wow, that sounds big—Mueller reported that Page's July 2016 trip to Moscow while he was a Trump campaign adviser included a meeting with Andrey Baranov, an old Gazprom hand who had become the head of investor relations at Rosneft. ("Page believed he and Baranov discussed Rosneft president Igor Sechin, and he thought Baranov might have mentioned the possibility of a sale of a stake in Rosneft in passing.") Page told Mueller that on that same trip to Moscow his meeting with another Russian oil company, Tatneft, included a discussion of him potentially becoming a consultant for the firm. The Kremlin must have been especially eager to keep Page in the clover, this nonentity who miraculously got himself named one of only five key foreign policy advisers to Trump after he sent the campaign co-chair and deputy campaign manager emails in early 2016 slagging the U.S. sanctions on Russia.

Mueller also makes nearly four dozen mentions in his report of Robert Foresman, one of the U.S. bankers who helped smear some in-ternational validation onto Putin's Yukos heist back in the day. Fores-man had acted as a sort of character witness for Igor Sechin as early as 2008, telling U.S. State Department officials that the Rosneft boss was smart, hardworking, patriotic, and "exceptionally courteous." In

Mueller's telling, Foresman was back and forth between Moscow and the United States during and after the 2016 presidential election, seeing off Putin emissaries on their way to a meeting with Jared Kushner, and helping to identify the best Kremlin communication channels for Trump national security adviser Mike Flynn. In conveying a Kremlin invitation for Trump to attend a Russian economic forum, Foresman referenced "an approach he received from 'senior Kremlin officials' about the candidate." Foresman also requested a meeting with Trump himself to discuss "concrete things" that cannot be communicated over "unsecure email"; when that didn't happen, he asked for a meeting with Donald junior, maybe. Or Eric? Is Eric available? Among the "concrete things" he wanted to discuss were "details of a Ukraine plan."

Foresman is one of many characters in the Trump-Russia drama who shopped the Trump camp some plan or other for lifting U.S. sanctions on Russia. Former Ukrainian president Viktor Yanukovych, still cosseted in Moscow, was hot to get Paul Manafort to use his influence with Trump to push a drop-sanctions "peace plan." "All that is required to start the process is a very minor 'wink' (or slight push) from [Donald Trump]," one of Manafort's key contacts in Ukraine wrote in an email. "The email," wrote Mueller, "also stated that if Manafort were designated as the U.S. representative and started the process, Yanukovych would ensure his reception in Russia 'at the very top level.'"

Dropping sanctions was also the whole point of the visit of all those Russians to Trump Tower in June 2016, the meeting that President Trump memorably summarized as being about "Russian adoptions." The ban on American families adopting Russian orphans was Vladimir Putin's retaliatory measure against the U.S. sanctions regime. Dropping the sanctions would mean dropping the adoption ban, so that meeting really was just another Russian effort to scheme against sanctions. Only this time they also got an American president to put out a press statement boosting Putin's anti-sanctions propaganda effort that leveraged sympathy for poor Russian orphans.

Still another drop-sanctions effort was a "peace plan" shopped to the incoming Trump administration via Michael Cohen and Felix Sater, who had been working on Trump's secret Moscow real estate deal all through the 2016 primary season. In truth, a critical subtext of the Moscow Trump Tower project—which Mueller assessed could have been worth hundreds of millions of dollars to Trump—was dropping U.S. sanctions on Russia. In Mueller's sketch of the contours of the deal, potential financing would have been through Genbank, which may or may not have been working on the potential deal with a larger Russian bank, VTB. In either case, both are sanctioned entities, so no deal could have happened through them as long as sanctions remained in place. In one memorable telling after Mueller's report was released, Felix Sater explained to *Forbes* that maybe the deal wouldn't have been financed by any banks at all—maybe it would have been financed directly by the Rotenberg brothers, the judo guys, Putin's construction goons. OK, maybe, but they too are under U.S. sanctions. The point is that all of the potential financing entities described in conjunction with the Trump Tower Moscow deal were under sanctions. With sanctions in place, such a deal could never happen. Lift the sanctions, though, and, hey, now maybe we could start to envision the Ivanka spa atop the old pencil-factory site.

Sanctions, again and again, are the core issue—the boring, insistent thing—at the center of all these otherwise intriguing and/or laughable contacts and overtures that everyone in Trump's orbit tried to keep so secret during Russia's extraordinary intervention in the 2016 election and beyond. Russia wants what it wants. But what it needed right then—like a junkie long past his last hit—was sanctions relief. With an economy completely dependent on oil and gas, and an oil and gas industry completely dependent on someone else's expertise, the sanctions that preclude Russia from getting that expertise were like a tourniquet around the neck. Sanctions were the entire ballgame for the Russians, and they had made that abundantly clear to Team Trump by the time it entered the White House.

Investigative journalist Michael Isikoff was the reporter who first ferreted out that Trump hit the ground running with a day-one concerted effort to try to unilaterally get rid of the sanctions. "Unknown to the public at the time, top Trump administration officials, almost as soon as they took office, tasked State Department staffers with developing proposals for the lifting of economic sanctions, the return of diplomatic compounds, and other steps to relieve tensions with Moscow," reported Isikoff for Yahoo News. State Department veteran Dan Fried told him that in the first few weeks after Trump was inaugurated, he received "panicky" calls from officials who told him they had been "directed to develop a sanctions-lifting package and imploring him, 'Please, my God, can't you stop this?'"

He could, actually. Fried and Tom Malinowski and other State Department old hands broke the emergency glass and sounded the alarm on both sides of the aisle in Congress that the Russia sanctions needed to be made statutorily binding—stat. Incredibly, it worked. With Democrat Cardin and Republican John McCain in the lead in the Senate, Congress moved with uncharacteristic agility and swiftness to pass legislation to codify the sanctions and make it harder for Trump to undo them on his own say-so. The national legislature did it at lightning speed, even after Tillerson begged members to soft-peddle the new law. "I would urge allowing the president the flexibility to adjust sanctions to meet the need in what is always an evolving diplomatic situation," the secretary of state said as the bill was hurtling toward passage. Trump squeaked like an unoiled hinge over how much he hated the legislation and didn't want to sign it. It was only when his hand was effectively forced by a veto-proof majority (98–2 in the Senate, 419–3 in the House) that he finally relented. The C-SPAN feed of the vote wasn't as cinematic as the red-shirted teachers sitting-in under their state's capitol dome, but in its own way, that early behind-the-scenes fight to save sanctions was the same small-*d* democratic power at work.

To the extent that Congress and civil servants watchdogged the issue of sanctions, it seemed to drive the Kremlin and the Trump administration nuts in equal measure. The bipartisan tenacity on this issue should, however, give the rest of us cause for hope. Behold the mercies of non-unitary government authority, and a free press, too. But when it comes to those sanctions in particular, and the constraining influence of democratic accountability in general, there is also—in these United States—another daunting political counterforce at work. And it's not the headline-grabbing titans of the digital global era. Sure, big tech and big finance are the talk of the chattering classes, revered and reviled in equal measure as masters of the universe that play an outsize and often malign role in social and political outcomes. But the oil and gas industry has been remaking the world in its favored image for generations. And it's not finished with us yet. Climate disaster has put a spotlight on the need for human society to evolve beyond dependence on petroleum, but our very capacity to decide on that—or anything—remains at risk as long as the industry is still ranging like a ravenous predator on the field of democracy.

The oil and gas industry—left to its own devices—will mindlessly follow its own nature. It will make tons of money. It will corrode and corrupt and sabotage democratic governance. It will screw up and—in the end—fatally injure the whole freaking planet. And yes, it will also provide oil and gas along the way! And jobs for the workers who produce those things for it. The end-times battle that we're engaged in now is to figure out how to get along *without* oil and gas—and we're plugging away but still a ways off from that—and, in the meantime, commit to a whole new level of constraint and regulatory protection against this singularly destructive industry to minimize its potential harms.

This is a doable, winnable fight here at home—ironically, or perhaps sadly—because the industry has been cut so much slack for so long, particularly in the last two decades of bipartisan cheerleading for "energy independence." America really is swimming in oil and gas—rah rah rah, sis boom bah. But meanwhile, American oil and gas companies have been allowed to wreak geopolitical and environmental havoc both at home and the world over. Which means the menu for starting to fix it is pretty darn straightforward, and features a lot of low-hanging fruit.

As a start, they should be making full public disclosures of all their payments to governments and government actors. Even the half-on-the-take U.S. Congress believed that as recently as 2016. When U.S. oil and gas companies undermine U.S. foreign policy objectives abroad—by drilling Russia's Arctic for it after the seizure of Crimea, or single-handedly funding rapacious dictators-for-life in central Africa, or negotiating independent deals with Iraqi Kurdistan to break up the unified national Iraqi government that U.S. soldiers were (at that moment!) dying to hold together—they should face severe punitive consequences at home. If it were a rival, rogue country tear-assing across the globe screwing things up in these ways, a normal U.S. government would be at the least sanctioning it, if not leading global efforts to roll back those actions. When it's not a country doing it but instead U.S.-based multinational oil corporations, the United States, at a minimum, should punish those companies, or even block them outright in a process tuned to ensure that U.S. oil doesn't run a second U.S. foreign policy that our own military and intelligence agencies and foreign service have to pay for, potentially with their lives. And this wouldn't be reinventing the wheel. When foreign companies and countries want to buy assets in the United States that have potential strategic value to us as a country, those potential purchases are run through a fairly rigorous, high-level review by something called the Committee on Foreign Investment in the United States. Foreign deals by U.S. oil majors could be subject to a parallel process, for parallel reasons. If they're going to have their own foreign policies that are indifferent or even hostile to American national interests, and if they're going to take actions that have profound effects on foreign governments, their deals should be subject to the kind of rigorous review to which we subject foreign countries.

Most of all, the point is that it's time for the most lucrative and reckless and destructive industry on earth to pay for what it does. Here at the end of the world, with the climate crisis bearing down like Godzilla over downtown Tokyo, U.S. taxpayer subsidies for oil and gas drilling are now almost literally insane. As is the in-kind-donation equivalent of letting companies drill on federal land. What, there aren't enough private farms to kill the cows on and screw the landowners? You need to drill national monuments, too?

Coal is dead. As dead as whale oil and kerosene and every other fuel source we once believed we couldn't live without. Oil and gas are dead, too—only they just don't look sick yet. Jobs in those industries must and will become jobs in other industries, which will undoubtedly be a painful adjustment. But that pain will be less than the damage wreaked by letting them continue to run their own course. With the accelerating pace of sea level rise and global warming, the worst silver lining in the history of silver linings is that new jobs and new industries may derive from the need to clean up the messes of the industry thus far, to sandbag us against the worst damage it has already done.

Oil and gas industry incentives are accelerating us toward destruction on multiple levels—geopolitical balance, governance, environmental injury, and climate apocalypse. Democratic accountability and government action to countermand and control the industry's actions are the ways to beat that—the only ways. Democracy is still, as always, our last best hope. Which means, more than ever, we need to preserve and protect our democracies from the influence of the industry, and from the rogue-state anti-democracy behemoth it has fueled in Russia, and from the malign self-preservation instincts that kick in when things get unstable and chaos swirls.

And yes, there are superheroes among us who spice up the plot and inspire us and show us that what we never thought was possible can actually be done. In this case, it's Oklahoma schoolteachers—lots of them Republican voters—who came to such a roiling boil they rattled the lid off the most industry-captured state government in the United States. When they chanted "This is what democracy looks like," they were writing a caption for the rest of us, to understand and underscore the global importance of what they did in their state. It's the transparency activists—the technocratic anticorruption nerds who have figured out that following the money doesn't just unravel criminal schemes but traces corruption and grand-theft kleptocracy to its origins. It's all the reporters around the world who are doing the difficult and dangerous work of telling the story of corruption and oil and gas depredations. It's the opposition activists like Alexei Navalny and the martyred Boris Nemtsov who haven't just opposed Putin's government; they have exposed his government's secret wealth, the massive rip-off of the Russian people that has made Putin likely the richest man on earth and has made his gangsterism a ravening global menace.

Containment is the small-c conservative answer to the problem at hand—democratically supported, government-enforced active and aggressive containment. It's the only way to fight against the industry's reliance on corruption and capture. The question isn't whether it's doable; it is. It's just whether we'll have the focus and the persistence to actually do it. Powerful enemies make for big, difficult fights. But you can't win if you don't play, and in this fight it's the stakes that should motivate us: Democracy either wins this one or disappears. It oughtta be a blowout.

ACKNOWLEDGMENTS

THANK YOU TO THE GREAT AND GOOD MARK ZWONITZER, WITHOUT whom this book would not exist. Thanks to Laurie Liss for talking me into it, against my better judgment. Thanks to everyone at Crown, especially Rachel Klayman, Gillian Blake, Zachary Phillips, David Drake, Penny Simon, Melissa Esner, and Annsley Rosner. Something more than thanks is due the excellent staff of *The Rachel Maddow Show,* and Cory Gnazzo and Kelsey Desiderio in particular, for their limitless patience with me. I swear I will not do this again.

ACKNOWLEDGMENTS

NOTES ON SOURCES

I HAVE NOTED WITHIN THE TEXT MANY OF THE AUTHORS, REPORTERS, academics, government officials, historians, and oil and gas operatives who informed my own understanding of this story. But there are other sources that deserve recognition. What follows is meant not to be an all-encompassing list but to give you an understanding of where I went hunting for statistics, scholarship, expert analysis, official inquiry, and reportage, where I found the most treasure, and where you might do your own digging to learn more.

One general note that applies to every chapter: For all the numbers cited throughout this book concerning production, consumption, imports, exports, and pricing of crude oil and natural gas at any given time, both domestically and around the world, I have relied on the official statistics provided by the U.S. Energy Information Administration. These, and much more, are accessible at eia.gov.

INTRODUCTION

Details of Vladimir Putin's visit to New York City in 2003, including his schedule, transcripts of his speeches, and remarks, are available at the official English-language website of the Russian Federation presidency, en.kremlin.ru. This site also includes photographs and footage of public events. Aside from news reports on the history of Lukoil and its move into the U.S. market (including reporting in *The Moscow Times*), there is very useful information in the company's annual reports and financial statements. Also helpful was the 2007 study "Lukoil: Russia's Largest Oil Company," sponsored by the James A. Baker III Institute for Public Policy at

Rice University and the Japan Petroleum Energy Center and authored by the *Financial Times* Moscow correspondent and longtime petroleum industry watcher Isabel Gorst.

Putin's visit to the Lukoil station grand opening in Manhattan, including the lead-up and the aftermath, was covered in detail by the two New York tabloids—the *Post* and the *Daily News*. There is footage of the visit itself in the NBC News archives. Thomas Beller provided some of the richest and most telling detail of the Lukoil station grand opening at his slice-of-life New York City website Mr. Beller's Neighborhood.

Michael McFaul's testimony about Putin and Russia is from a hearing before the U.S. House of Representatives Committee on International Relations' Subcommittee on Europe. The transcript of the hearing, "Russia's Transition to Democracy and U.S.-Russia Relations: Unfinished Business," is available, among other places, at the Carnegie Endowment for International Peace website at carnegieendowment.org.

CHAPTER ONE

For information on the beginnings of the oil industry in America and on John D. Rockefeller's place in it, I have relied on Daniel Yergin's *Prize: The Epic Quest for Oil, Money, and Power;* Ron Chernow's *Titan: The Life of John D. Rockefeller Sr.,* as well as Brian Lamb's interview of Chernow on C-SPAN; and H. W. Brands's *American Colossus: The Triumph of Capitalism, 1865–1900.* Also helpful were contemporaneous accounts of Rockefeller such as Ida Tarbell's *History of the Standard Oil Company,* Samuel Milton Jones's *New Right,* and Charles W. Eliot's 1915 essay in *The Atlantic Monthly,* "National Efficiency Best Developed Under Free Governments."

Information and text from the decision in the case of *Standard Oil Co. of New Jersey v. United States* is readily available. The Legal Information Institute at Cornell University provides quick and easy access at www.law.cornell.edu.

CHAPTER TWO

Project Rulison (and Project Plowshares generally) were remarkably well documented in official U.S. government documents, studies, and investigations. Almost all of these are accessible at the Department of Energy's Office of Legacy Management website, www.lm.doe.gov/Rulison. Among the most comprehensive and most useful are the Atomic Energy Commission's Project Rulison Manager's Report from April 1973 and a remarkable 1970 paper titled "Economics of Nuclear Gas Stimulation," whose lead author was G. W. Frank of the Austral Oil Company. Also helpful were accounts of the longtime head of the Atomic Energy Commission, Glenn Seaborg, including a collection of his speeches, *Science, Man, and Change;* a book co-authored with Benjamin S. Loeb, *The Atomic Energy Commission Under Nixon: Adjusting to Troubled Times;* and his recollections of interactions with President Richard M. Nixon and his staff available at the Department of Energy's Lawrence Berkeley National Lab website: www2.lbl.gov/Publications/Seaborg/NatService.htm.

Especially helpful in understanding some of the concern about the various nonmilitary nuclear projects undertaken by the Atomic Energy Commission was a 1994 oral history of Seaborg's longtime colleague John W. Gofman, conducted by staff of the Berkeley Lab and the U.S. Department of Energy's Office of Human Radiation Experiments, as well as Aileen Alfandary's 1979 interview of Gofman for Pacifica Radio.

I am hugely thankful for Chester McQueary's rollicking 1994 essay in *High Country News* recalling his experiences on the day of the underground nuclear detonation.

Excellent secondary sources on Project Rulison and similar undertakings include Scott Kaufman's *Project Plowshares: The Peaceful Use of Nuclear Explosives in Cold War America* and Russell Gold's *Boom: How Fracking Ignited the American Energy Revolution and Changed the World.*

George Mitchell's life and his long quest for utile fracking technology and Nick Steinsberger's breakthrough in slickwater are well covered in Gold's *Boom,* Gregory Zuckerman's *Frackers: The Outrageous Inside Story of the New Billionaire Wildcatters,* and Lawrence Wright's 2017 *New Yorker* article "The Dark Bounty of Texas Oil."

CHAPTER THREE

The story of Mikhail Khodorkovsky's rise and his demise was well covered as it was happening, jumping from the business pages to the front pages. But Masha Gessen's 2012 article in *Vanity Fair* "The Wrath of Putin" is an excellent primer. For his colorful rendering of Khodorkovsky, Yukos, and especially Joe Mach, I am indebted to Thane Gustafson for his book *Wheel of Fortune: The Battle for Oil and Power in Russia* and for the many excellent talks he gave in promoting the same. Sabrina Tavernise of *The New York Times* did some of the best reporting about early twenty-first-century Russia, and her 2001 interview of Joe Mach is a treat. I was also greatly helped by "The Yukos Case: The New Dimension in Money Laundering Cases," a 2008 doctoral thesis by the Russian corporate lawyer turned academic Dmitry Gololobov; it's available online at the website of the University of London. While Boris Yeltsin's tragic fumble in his attempt to reform the Russian economy and polity was also well covered in real time by journalists in Moscow, Gololobov's thesis is an instructive guide from somebody who saw it happen from within.

The U.S. senator Ben Cardin's 2018 report for the Senate Foreign Relations Committee, "Putin's Asymmetric Assault on Democracy in Russia and Europe: Implications for U.S. National Security," includes some very good backstory on the Yeltsin era and Putin's ascension.

Karen Dawisha's *Putin's Kleptocracy: Who Owns Russia?* provides, among many, many other things, insight and detail on Putin's rise from KGB apparatchik to Russian Federation president. I am especially indebted to the translation of *Reform of the Administration of the President of the Russian Federation* at the Miami (Ohio) University's Havighurst Center for Russian and Post-Soviet Studies, where Dawisha was the longtime director. Professor Dawisha died while I was working on this book. Her intellect and her insight about modern Russia are already missed.

It is worth repeating here that the best reporting on the story of Morgan Stanley in Russia—and particularly its aid for Rosneft—is from Ian Katz, Jesse Drucker, Irina Reznik, and Ron Bousso in *Bloomberg* in the summer of 2014.

It's not always simple, but I was able to access transcripts, footage, and photographs of the 2009 International Investment Forum in Sochi at the "Archive of the Official Site of the 2008–2012 Prime Minister of the Russian Federation Vladimir Putin," which has exactly that awkward title and is (loosely) kept up by the Russian government.

CHAPTER FOUR

Aubrey McClendon spent a lot of time and energy drawing attention to himself and his business. There were dozens of long newspaper and magazine profiles of him over a twenty-year period, each with gold to mine. The following were the most helpful to me: Terzah Ewing, "Chesapeake Energy Is a Gusher," *Wall Street Journal*, February 27, 1997; Jerry Shottenkirk, "Hard Work, Luck Make Billions for Oklahoma Executive," *Oklahoma City Journal Record*, August 13, 2007; David Whitford, "Meet Mr. Gas: Aubrey McClendon," *Fortune*, May 12, 2008; Grant Slater, "Chesapeake's Aubrey McClendon Aims to Cement Legacy with Sprawling Campus," *Oklahoma Gazette*, August 6, 2009; Christopher Helman, "The Two Sides of Aubrey McClendon, America's Most Reckless Billionaire," *Forbes*, October 5, 2011; Christopher Helman, "In His Own Words: Chesapeake's Aubrey McClendon Answers Our 25 Questions," *Forbes*, October 5, 2011; Jeff Goodell, "The Big Fracking Bubble: The Scam Behind Aubrey McClendon's Gas Boom," *Rolling Stone*, March 1, 2012; John Shiffman, Anna Driver, and Brian Grow, "The Lavish and Leveraged Life of Aubrey McClendon," Reuters, June 7, 2012; Maureen Farrell, "Aubrey McClendon: Pioneer of the U.S. Shale Boom," *Wall Street Journal*, March 2, 2016. These profiles and reportage were helpful in this and the later chapters about McClendon and Chesapeake.

Chesapeake Energy's annual reports and proxy statements are also a pretty good way to see just how McClendon and his team told the company story, as well as the state of its production, growth, and finances at any given time.

CHAPTER FIVE

Oklahoma City's long, strange (and ultimately successful) quest for major-league status is a well-documented saga. But there are a few specific sources that stood out. Sara Rogers-Dewberry's 2013 interview with author and politician David Holt, for SB Nation, had gems throughout. The occasion for the interview was the publication of Holt's book, *Big League City: Oklahoma City's Rise to the NBA*. The work of the local journalists Mary Jo Nelson and Steve Lackmeyer was a great help in understanding the history and material consequences of the Pei Plan. *The Oklahoman*, however one might feel about its sometimes astonishing editorial page, was and remains a great news organization full of able reporters who cover local business and politics with real savvy. The contemporaneous promotional film *Growing with Pride*, produced by the Oklahoma City Urban Renewal Authority, is worth a watch—even if just for the theme song. You can find it on YouTube.

Former Oklahoma City mayor Ron Norick's wide-ranging and comprehensive 2009 interview with the Voices of Oklahoma oral history project added much behind-the-scenes color to the story of Oklahoma City's capital improvement plan that began back in 1993 and continues today. The audio and transcript can be found at www.voicesofoklahoma.com.

The bombing of the Alfred P. Murrah Federal Building was among the most covered news events of 1995 and well documented by the FBI. But if you haven't yet visited the Oklahoma City National Memorial & Museum, you should. It's crucial to understanding the weight of that tragedy on the city and its citizens; it's also just something that every American should see and take in.

CHAPTER SIX

There was a slew of really good reportage on Rex Tillerson—both his biography and his tenure at ExxonMobil—that came out in the weeks and months after his more-than-surprising nomination to be U.S. secretary of state. Among the best was by the team at *The New York Times,* which included Clifford Krauss, John Schwartz, David E. Sanger, Ben Hubbard, Dionne Searcy, and Nicholas Casey. Also great was Dexter Filkins's 2017 profile in *The New Yorker,* "Rex Tillerson at the Breaking Point." The 2008 interview of Tillerson by *Scouting,* the official publication of the Boy Scouts of America, was surprisingly revealing. But the national treasure of a resource when it comes to understanding Tillerson, the ways he was shaped by Exxon, and the ways he helped shape ExxonMobil is Steve Coll's *Private Empire: ExxonMobil and American Power.* Coll's book is also the best resource for understanding the standard operating procedures and the central mission of ExxonMobil. Anybody who has written about the company and its leaders in the years since the publication of *Private Empire* owes a big debt to Coll. And that now includes me.

In terms of ranking annual net profits of international energy corporations, I have not included entities wholly owned by governments and not publicly traded, such as Saudi Aramco. It is worth noting that when Aramco, in 2019, divulged its net profits for the first time, the stated figure was $110 billion. ExxonMobil's net profits that year were about $21 billion. Something to be said for state-owned enterprises in a totalitarian state. Especially in that particular totalitarian state.

A most excellent resource for statistics on how much ExxonMobil (and any other corporate entity) spend on lobbying is the database at OpenSecrets.org, the website of the Center for Responsive Politics. CRP, founded in 1983 by two former U.S. senators, one Republican and one Democrat, is a bipartisan, not-for-profit research group that aims to shine a light on money in politics. It hits that mark. In my day job, and for this book, CRP and its OpenSecrets.org website are invaluable transparency resources.

The full transcript of the U.S. House of Representatives Subcommittee on Energy and Environment of the Committee on Energy and Commerce hearing, "The ExxonMobil-XTO Merger: Impact on U.S. Energy Markets," is available, among other places, at www.govinfo.gov/content/pkg/CHRG-111hhrg76003/pdf/CHRG-111hhrg76003.pdf.

CHAPTER SEVEN

The background and specifics of the Jones Award come from the World Affairs Council of Greater Houston's official website. The awards banquet honoring Tillerson was covered by publications such as *Oil & Gas Journal, Offshore Engineer,* and *The Houston Chronicle.* ExxonMobil's various transgressions against the Migratory Bird Treaty Act and the Clean Air Act, as well as the underpayment of royalties from American Indian and federal lands, are spelled out in releases from the U.S. Department of Justice Office of Public Affairs.

For the details of the Deepwater Horizon disaster, its lead-up, and its long, unhappy aftermath, I relied chiefly on the following sources: "Deepwater: The Gulf Oil Disaster and the Future of Offshore Drilling," which is the report to the president by the National Commission on the BP Deepwater Horizon Oil Spill and Offshore Drilling; the *Regional Oil Spill Response Plan—Gulf of Mexico,* revised and filed by BP in June 2009; a review of the causes of the actual blowout by the U.S. Chemical Safety and Hazard Investigation Board; the EPA Newsroom for information on the dispersants; and "The Ongoing Administration-Wide Response to the Deepwater BP Oil Spill" available at obamawhitehouse.archives.gov.

The full transcript of the June 15, 2010, U.S. House of Representatives Subcommittee on Energy and the Environment of the Committee on Energy and Commerce is available at www.govinfo.gov/content/pkg /CHRG-111hhrg77911/html/CHRG-111hhrg77911.htm. The hearing is also available to watch at C-SPAN.org.

The May 1, 2010, rupture of the ExxonMobil pipeline in Akwa Ibom (and the weeks-long uninterrupted leak that followed) were first reported in the West by John Vidal, the environmental editor of *The Guardian.*

CHAPTER EIGHT

Like the rest of the world, I am indebted to Ken Silverstein for his dogged reporting on Teodorin Obiang and Equatorial Guinea. A number of congressional investigations added detail to the story of the Obiang family and its plunder of Equatorial Guinea. These include "Keeping Foreign Corruption Out of the United States: Four Case Histories," a majority and minority staff report of the U.S. Senate Permanent Subcommittee on Investigations, released in conjunction with its 2010 hearing on the same subject, and "The Petroleum and Poverty Paradox: Assessing U.S. and International Community Efforts to Fight the Resource Curse," a 2008 report to the U.S. Senate Committee on Foreign Relations by its ranking member, Richard Lugar.

Peter Maass was once again in the right place at the right time, doing excellent reporting in Equatorial Guinea, this time for *Mother Jones.* Thanks also to Global Witness, which has been uncovering the debacle in Equatorial Guinea for nearly two decades now. Human Rights Watch's July 2009 report "Well Oiled: Oil and Human Rights in Equatorial Guinea" was another great resource. And the forty-four-page 2011 affidavit filed by the U.S. Attorney in the federal district court in California in the forfeiture case against Teodorin is an astonishing read, right down to the details and pricing of his auction house shopping spree in late 2010 and early 2011.

Details of Qorvis's contract work for Equatorial Guinea and the Obiang family are searchable at the Department of Justice's Foreign Agents Registration Act website (www.justice.gov/nsd-fara).

CHAPTER NINE

There are plenty of general sources like the CIA's *World Factbook,* Human Rights Watch, and Global Witness for the postcolonial history of Equatorial Guinea, but I am particularly indebted to reporting by Silverstein and Maass, as well as Sunday Dare's 2012 report for the International Consortium of Investigative Journalists, "Making a Killing: The Curious Bonds of Oil Diplomacy." Alexander Smoltczyk's 2006 series in *Spiegel,* "Torture and Poverty in Equatorial Guinea," also has excellent detail about the recent history of Equatorial Guinea, as well President Obiang and his corporate suitors from the West. The 1991 interview of the former ambassador Frank S. Ruddy for the Oral History Project at the Association for Diplomatic Studies and Training was also very interesting.

"Money Laundering and Foreign Corruption: Enforcement and Effectiveness of the Patriot Act, Case Study Involving Riggs Bank," the 2004 report of the minority staff of the U.S. Senate Permanent Subcommittee on Investigations (as well as the transcript of the committee hearings into same) is a fascinating look into the way U.S. oil companies and banks have operated in Equatorial Guinea. And of course, Steve Coll added to the understanding of ExxonMobil in Equatorial Guinea in *Private Empire.*

I was particularly helped in understanding the history, the benefits, and the difficulties of Section 1504 by a transcript of the Brookings Institution's 2014 symposium "Transparency and Natural Resources: How the U.S. Can Regain Its Leadership."

CHAPTER TEN

The story of the Russian "Illegals" and their arrest and aftermath was reported with an eye to detail by Philip Read and Judy Peet for the Newark *Star-Ledger,* Toby Harnden in *The Telegraph* (London), and Manny Fernandez and Fernanda Santos for *The New York Times.* The *New York Post* and the New York *Daily News* each brought their own notable styles to the coverage. *Spies: The Rise and Fall of the KGB in America,* by John Earl Haynes, Harvey Klehr, and Alexander Vassiliev provides a nice primer on the history and methods of the Illegals program (Vassiliev is a former KGB man himself). Brett Forrest's career through Moscow in his 2012

Politico story "The Big Russian Life of Anna Chapman, Ex-spy" is both fun and informative. Anna Chapman's online presence is still there for all to see. But the best sources for the Illegals in early twenty-first-century America (including the fruits of the fine FBI counterintelligence work, thank you, Peter Strzok and others) are the two criminal complaints filed against them in the U.S. District Court for the Southern District of New York.

CHAPTERS ELEVEN AND TWELVE

The Oklahoma Geological Survey is the record keeper for all seismic activity in that state and I have relied on its data. Thanks also to Oklahoma's current state seismologist, Jake Walter, who provided slides and data from the OGS's 2018 presentation, "The Past and Future Seismic Hazard in Oklahoma," as well as his professional insight into the geology of Oklahoma.

Walter's predecessor at OGS, Austin Holland, is really the centerpiece of this and later chapters about induced seismicity in Oklahoma. Holland, as a matter of popular demand, made many public statements concerning the "earthquake swarm" that plagued Oklahoma throughout his tenure at OGS. But for what he was seeing and thinking and feeling at a given time, there is one indispensable source—a deposition he gave, under oath, on October 11, 2017, in the case of *Jennifer Lin Cooper v. New Dominion LLC, Spess Oil Company, and John Does 1–25*. This was six and a half hours of sworn testimony in a case concerning the earthquake in Prague, Oklahoma, in 2011. Holland's deposition that day was both wide-ranging and deep. He spoke not just to the science of seismicity but to his own personal history and motivations and to his own experiences and feelings about his work in Oklahoma—all under oath. It reveals a true public servant wrestling with big issues, an excellent and devout scientist thrown into the lion's den of politics. This testimony forms the basis of my portrait of Holland. The entire document is worth a read if you have the time. It can be accessed, among other places, at www.news9.com/story/36778039/new-details-revealed-in-state-earthquake-hearings.

The information about Aubrey McClendon's travel, salary, bonuses, perks, and so on comes from his employment agreement, detailed in Chesapeake Energy's Definitive Proxy Statement from 2010, from legal filings in a 2012 lawsuit filed by former employee Debra Boggs, "individually on behalf of all other similarly situated persons" against Chesapeake Energy and McClendon, and from reporting for Reuters by John Schiff, Anna Driver, and Brian Grow.

For the deleterious effects of the fracking process, as you can tell by the text of this book, I am much indebted to Michelle Bamberger (a veterinarian) and Robert E. Oswald (a professor of molecular medicine) for their study "Impacts of Gas Drilling on Human and Animal Health" and for their follow-up book, *The Real Cost of Fracking: How America's Shale Gas Boom Is Threatening Our Families, Pets, and Food.*

The unfolding story of the fatally poisoned cows was best covered by Vickie Welborn and Kelsey McKinney at the *Shreveport Times*. DeSmogBlog is another energetic string gatherer in the ongoing safety lapses in fracking all over the country, including the 2010 ExxonMobil/XTO waterfouling spill in Lycoming County, Pennsylvania. Specifics of that Lycoming spill are also laid out in the settlement with XTO Energy announced by the Environmental Protection Agency and the Department of Justice on July 18, 2013.

Aside from benefiting from Russell Gold's book *Boom,* I was greatly helped by his deep dive published in *The Wall Street Journal* in 2014, "Energy Boom Puts Wells in America's Backyards." Gold and a colleague turned up the notable fact that in that year, as he said, "15.3 million Americans lived within a single mile of a well that has been drilled since 2000. That is more people than live in Michigan or New York City."

George P. Mitchell's op-ed co-authored with Michael R. Bloomberg appeared in *The Washington Post* on August 23, 2012.

The admission that way back in 1967 the U.S. Army Corps of Engineers and the U.S. Geological Survey had determined that "significant seismic events in the vicinity of Denver, Colorado," were caused by the "deep, hazardous waste disposal at the Rocky Mountain Arsenal" was buried on page 9 of the Environmental Protection Agency's eighty-one-page report, "Technical Program Overview: Underground Injection Control Regulations," published in December 2002.

The full text of the OGS statement on the Prague earthquake sequence of 2011, sent out on March 22, 2013, can be accessed at the survey's website: ogs.ou.edu/earthquakes/OGS_PragueStatement201303.pdf.

CHAPTER THIRTEEN

The Atlantic has an excellent photo essay on the building of the Sochi Olympics, and a transcript of remarks from Putin's meeting with Tillerson at Sochi is accessible at archive.premier.gov.ru. Steve Coll also detailed that meeting in *Private Empire*. Contemporaneous reporting by Andrew Kramer at *The New York Times* and Douglas Busvine at Reuters provided context and texture to the Sochi meeting. The state of ExxonMobil in the summer of 2011, as perceived and heralded by ExxonMobil, can be found in contemporaneous press releases available on the corporate website. I very much appreciated the neutral take on the Russian oil and gas industry in "The Analysis of Russian Oil and Gas Reserves," by Yulia Grama, at the Department of Diplomacy, National Chengchi University, Taiwan, which was published in the *International Journal of Energy Economics and Policy.*

The New Yorker's Connie Bruck did some of the best reporting on BP's Bob Dudley's dangerous slalom through Moscow and the Russian oil and gas industry.

CHAPTERS FOURTEEN AND FIFTEEN

The following were key sources for biographical information and color on Igor Sechin: his bio page at Rosneft.com; Dawisha's aforementioned *Putin's Kleptocracy;* "Factbox: Russia's Energy Tsar: Who Is Igor Sechin?," Reuters, June 2010; "Igor Sechin: Rosneft's Kremlin Hard Man Comes out of the Shadows," *The Guardian,* October 2012; a 2008 U.S. diplomatic cable titled "Russia: Bringing Sechin into Focus"; "Oil Boyar," *The Economist,* December 2016; Dexter Filkins's 2017 profile of Tillerson in *The New Yorker;* Mikhail Zygar's 2016 book, *All the Kremlin's Men: Inside the Court of Vladimir Putin;* and Alec Luhn's colorful February 2017 story in *Vox,* "The 'Darth Vader' of Russia: Meet Igor Sechin, Putin's Right-Hand Man."

The median household income data in various countries come from a Gallup study released in 2013. Aside from contemporaneous reporting, the outlines and specifics of the early Putin strategy and tactics for using Russia's oil and gas sector to further his political and geopolitical goals are described in detail by Zygar in *All the Kremlin's Men,* Dawisha's *Putin's Kleptocracy,* Senator Cardin's report "Putin's Asymmetric Assault on Democracy in Russia and Europe: Implications for U.S. National Security," and writings and lectures by former U.S. Energy Department official Leonard Coburn. "Putin and Gazprom: An Independent Expert Report," by Boris Nemtsov and Vladimir Milov, and translated by Dave Essel, is a cogent and early explanation of the consequences of Putin's use of Gazprom for state ends. And for the lay of the land in the Russian oil and gas sector circa 2012, I am indebted to Thane Gustafson for his book *Wheel of Fortune* and his various (and always entertaining and informative) public talks and lectures.

CHAPTER SIXTEEN

The assessment of oil and gas reserves in the Arctic comes from the U.S. Geological Survey's fact sheet "Circum-Arctic Resource Appraisal:

Estimates of Undiscovered Oil and Gas North of the Arctic Circle," announcing the results of the study completed in May 2008.

The tale of Royal Dutch Shell's mishaps in the Alaskan Arctic in the 2012 drilling season is laid out in official government postgame reports, including "Report to the Secretary of the Interior: Review of Shell's 2012 Alaska Offshore Oil and Gas Exploration Program" (March 2013); the U.S. Coast Guard's "Report of Investigation into the Circumstances Surrounding the Multiple Related Marine Casualties and Grounding of the MODU *Kulluk*" (December 2012); and the National Transportation Safety Board's Marine Accident Brief, "Grounding of Mobile Offshore Drilling Unit *Kulluk*" (December 2012). The various legal transgressions Shell and Noble were forced to cop to are detailed in official announcements by the Department of Justice (December 2014) and the Environmental Protection Agency (September 2013).

Besides McKenzie Funk's excellent "The Wreck of the Kulluk" in *The New York Times Magazine* in December 2014, I benefited from contemporaneous reporting in the *Anchorage Daily News* and *Marine Log*. The *Taranaki Daily News* provided great coverage of the Disco's brief, unhappy stay in New Zealand. Alaska-based reporter Jim Paulin first elicited the remarkable fact that Shell decided to make the ill-fated *Kulluk* tow, at least in part, to save on the fairly meager tax bill the corporation would have had to pay to the State of Alaska had it stayed put in Alaska that winter.

CHAPTER SEVENTEEN

The portrait of the two sad-sack Russian spies in New York (including contact with Carter Page) was laid out in telling detail in the twenty-six-page criminal complaint *United States of America v. Evgeny Buryakov a/k/a "Zhenya," Igor Sporyshev, and Victor Pobodnyy*. Garrett M. Graf's "Spy Who Added Me on LinkedIn" (*Bloomberg*, November 15, 2016) had additional color about the FBI's infiltration of the spies' supposedly secure quarters.

Thanks to Steve Horn, at DeSmogBlog, who turned up the registration papers Carter Page filed at the office of the Oklahoma secretary of state for the establishment of Global Natural Gas Ventures LLC in Oklahoma City—among other Page-related memorabilia. And thanks to Carter Page himself for his strange testimony before the U.S. House of Representatives Permanent Committee on Intelligence on November 2, 2017. The official record of those proceedings also includes Page's letters to then FBI director James Comey, and a number of Page's self-selected essays in which he lays out his feelings about Igor Sechin, the Magnitsky Act, and the unfair treatment of Russia and its government officials by the U.S. State Department in the Obama administration. It's not hard to see why the Russians thought there might be an especially Putin-friendly candidate in the hunt for the 2016 Republican presidential nomination after Donald Trump plucked Carter Page off the funny pages and named him one of his five key foreign policy advisers.

Aside from the postarrest reporting by Matei Rosca and Andrew Higgins, the sketch of Marcel Lehel Lazar ("Guccifer") is drawn from the criminal complaint, the plea agreement, the statement of facts, and the prosecutors' sentencing letter in the case of *United States of America v. Marcel Lehel Lazar* filed in the U.S. District Court for the Eastern District of Virginia. Oh, and the Guccifer Archive itself is still floating around out there in what Lazar called "the cloud of Infinite Justice."

"The Weird History of How the Hillary Clinton Email Story Was Broken—and Buried" by Callum Borchers (*The Washington Post,* July 5, 2016) is a nice little windup of how the Blumenthal-Clinton email exchange—and thus Hillary Clinton's use of a private email server while secretary of state—was uncovered by Guccifer first.

CHAPTER EIGHTEEN

The world owes its knowledge of Putin's corruption in the construction projects for the Sochi Olympics to the investigations done by Russian dissidents Boris Nemtsov and Alexey Navalny. Much of their work was published in English in *The Interpreter.* Many other journalists, as detailed in the text of the book, followed their lead and added to it. Human Rights Watch's February 2013 report, "Race to the Bottom," detailed life and pay, such as it was, for the locals and the migrants who served as the labor for the Sochi construction boom.

The official archive website of the Russian Federation presidency reveals a surprisingly frank rendering of Putin's reaction to what he perceived as Yanukovych's weakness in the face of the escalating Revolution of Dignity protest in Kyiv.

CHAPTER NINETEEN

The twenty-year-old Budapest Memorandum, in which Ukraine gave up its nuclear arsenal in exchange for security assurances from Russia, the United Kingdom, and the United States, was suddenly back in the news and much talked about after Putin's forcible annexation of Crimea in 2014. I was able to access text of the original agreement at the Security Council Report website (www.securitycouncilreport.org). SCR is a not-for-profit organization founded "to advance the transparency and effectiveness of the UN Security Council."

Details of Russia and Putin mucking around in the politics of Ukraine come from Karen Dawisha's *Putin's Kleptocracy;* Oleksander Andreyev's "Power and Money in Ukraine," at Open Democracy, February 2014; Senator Ben Cardin's "Putin's Asymmetric Assault on Democracy in Russia and Europe: Implications for U.S. National Security," 2018; and Mikhail Zygar's *All the Kremlin's Men.* The portrait of Dmitry Firtash is drawn in part from his wide-roaming talks with U.S. State Department officials in Kyiv. I was greatly aided in understanding the general structure of Ukraine's energy sector as well as its energy needs by Simon Pirani's 2007 analysis for the Oxford Institute for Energy Studies, "Ukraine's Gas Sector." Nemtsov and Milov, in "Putin and Gazprom: An Independent Expert Report" (2008), helped with the Ukrainian energy sector and Firtash's place in it. As did the brilliant "Comrade Capitalism" series published by Reuters. Firtash's general business practice and philosophy are also detailed in prosecutorial filings in *United States of America v. Dmitry Firtash et al.,* filed in the U.S. District Court for the Northern District of Illinois, Eastern Division.

Paul Manafort's work for, and compensation received from, the Putin-backed Party of Regions in Ukraine is spelled out in indictments, trial testimony and exhibits, statements of offenses, plea agreements, and sentencing memoranda in the recent federal criminal cases brought by the Office of Special Counsel against Manafort. So too is his energetic work tearing at the reputations of the Party of Regions' leading political opponents, including Yulia Tymoshenko. The exquisite details of Manafort's business relationship with Firtash bubble up in exhibits produced in various civil suits brought by Tymoshenko, as well as employees of CMZ LLC.

The mercenary activities of Skadden, Arps, Slate, Meagher & Flom are laid out in the settlement agreement reached between the firm and the National Security Division of the U.S. Department of Justice in January 2019. As this book was going to press, a further criminal complaint against the former Skadden attorney Greg Craig was pending.

For the final curtain of the Revolution of Dignity in Maidan, the ouster of Yanukovych, and the immediate consequences thereafter, I was greatly helped by Steven Lee Myers's 2015 book, *The New Tsar: The Rise and Reign of Vladimir Putin,* and by staff of the National Security Council at the Obama White House. For understanding both the hopes and the experiences of Ukrainians on the ground during the siege, the 2015 documentary film *Winter on Fire: Ukraine's Fight for Freedom,* directed by Evgeny Afineevsky (and available on Netflix), was a very helpful resource.

The Guardian produced a textual and photographic tone poem of Yanukovych's presidential palace soon after Putin's puppet fled Kyiv for safe haven in Russia. It is unforgettable.

If you want a little insight into how Rex Tillerson felt about Putin, check out his talk to the Undergraduate Business Council at the University of Texas on February 9, 2016. I accessed it at www.dallasnews.com/business/business/2016/12/13/exxon-ceo-rex-tillerson-words-favorite-ut-prof-became-engineer.

CHAPTER TWENTY

To understand the contours and the depth of the downward turn for Aubrey McClendon and Chesapeake Energy, I was especially helped by Russell Gold in *The Boom*, reporting by CNN's Maureen Farrell, *Forbes*'s Christopher Helman, and the Boggs lawsuit. Abrahm Lustgarten's reporting on Chesapeake Energy chiseling landowners due royalties, in ProPublica and *The Daily Beast* in 2014, was an eye-opener for many—including, apparently, the U.S. Department of Justice.

Details of Harold Hamm's history and personality and general philosophy come from Adam Wilmoth's "Q&A with Harold Hamm" in *The Oklahoman*, June 2007; Nathan Vardi's "Last American Wildcatter" in *Forbes*, January 2009; "Birth of a Wildcatter—How Harold Hamm Got His Start" in Hamm's own words (*Forbes*, December 2012); Josh Harkinson's December 2012 report in *Mother Jones*, "Who Fracked Mitt Romney?"; Hamm's own statements in his many appearances on the cable TV business channel chat-fests; and his occasional testimony on behalf of the oil and gas industry before Congress. But thanks especially to Mike Cantrell, in Oklahoma City, for his help in humanizing Hamm.

Thanks to James MacPherson of the Associated Press for his reporting on the radioactive oil filter socks strewn willy-nilly about the North Dakota landscape.

CHAPTER TWENTY-ONE

Data about the state of Oklahoma's economy and the ebb and flow of its tax receipts comes from the monthly reports from the office of the state treasurer, including the newsletter *Oklahoma Economic Report*. A number of organizations—left, right, and center—tracked revenue from oil and gas production and spending on education and other state needs in Oklahoma. The Oklahoma Policy Institute, and especially its founding director, Dave Blatt, were founts of information about Oklahoma politics and budgeting in this time period. I was also helped by the 2014 and 2017 studies—"Oklahoma's Oil and Natural Gas Industry: Economic Impact and Jobs Report"—commissioned by the Oklahoma Energy Resources Board, in conjunction with the Steven C. Agee Economic Research and Policy Institute at Oklahoma City University, and by the Oklahoma Academy for State Goals' 2018 report, "Aligning Oklahoma's Tax Code with Our 21st Century Economy." The National Education Association does a bang-up job of collecting data on school spending and student population in every state across the nation in its "Rankings & Estimates" publication.

The National Conference of State Legislatures, RegionTrack, and Headwaters Economics all compiled statistics that put Oklahoma's oil and gas tax revenues and state spending in context with other major oil- and gas-producing states. *The Oklahoman* (and its digital arm, NewsOK .com) and Matt Trotter at Public Radio Tulsa provided great coverage of the 2014 budget fight both on the inside and on the outside of the Oklahoma state legislature. Thanks to longtime legislative staffer, state legislator, and 2014 gubernatorial candidate Joe Dorman for taking the time to explain the intricacies of state government as it has been practiced in Oklahoma City in the late twentieth and early twenty-first centuries. Dorman was the best-versed parliamentarian in the state legislature until he lost his seat to term limits, a bumper-sticker-friendly but shortsighted provision in state law that has wiped away institutional memory and capability in the state's legislative bodies. (And same goes for every other state that tries it, too.) And thanks again to Mike Cantrell for his clear-eyed view on the varied and various constituencies in Oklahoma policy making.

The National Weather Service has a roundup and details of the biggest tornadoes in Oklahoma at www.weather.gov/oun/tornadodata-ok.

CHAPTERS TWENTY-TWO AND TWENTY-THREE

A transcript of Putin's remarks on the occasion of the initial drilling by ExxonMobil-Rosneft in the Kara Sea, along with photographs, was available at the official website of the Russian Federation presidency, en .kremlin.ru. You can also watch the RT feed of the video linkup at www .youtube.com/watch?v=AIi_14i8ACA. Glenn Waller's remarks were quoted in coverage by Reuters and later by *The Australian Financial Review* in Waller's home country.

Sam Greene, a sociologist at King's College London, and Graeme Robertson, a political scientist at the University of North Carolina at Chapel Hill, reported the Levada Center's polling numbers on Putin's popularity within Russia in the aftermath of the Crimea annexation in a guest post in *The Washington Post*. They also parsed, expertly, the reasons behind the post-annexation surge in popularity for Putin within Russia.

There has been a slew of excellent reporting and analysis surrounding the reasons for Putin's putsch in Crimea and the east of Ukraine, as well as the contours of the operation itself. Among the most helpful sources for understanding Putin's mind-set at the time were Myers's *New Tsar* and Zygar's *All the Kremlin's Men;* Julia Ioffe's 2018 piece in *The Atlantic,* "What Putin Really Wants"; Vladimir Sorokin's "Let the Past Collapse on Time!" (*New York Review of Books,* May 2014); and "Russia's Breakout from the Post–Cold War System: The Drivers of Putin's Course," by Dmitri Trenin, director of the Carnegie Moscow Center, in December 2014.

There has been a lot of great reporting on the ground in Ukraine, but once again a Boris Nemtsov–led investigation is critically helpful for understanding the view from the Russian side. It was Nemtsov's team that unearthed the story of "Cargo 200." You can access "Putin. War. An Independent Expert Report," which Nemtsov did not live to see finished, at www.4freerussia.org/putin.war/. "Hiding in Plain Sight: Putin's War in Ukraine," by experts at the Atlantic Council, is another valuable resource. The Atlantic Council in general stayed busy training a bright and unflattering light on Putin's activities in Ukraine from the beginning of the war there. Elena Kostyuchenko, graduate of Moscow State University, did remarkable reporting on the unhappy (and often fatal) experiences of Russian soldiers in Ukraine in *Novaya Gazeta.* Some of her best work was translated and published in part in *The Guardian.* Anna Nemtsova has done great reporting work inside Ukraine. And Alec Luhn's "Life in a War Zone" in *The Guardian* in July 2014 was a very human article about the very human cost of that war. As was his September 2014 piece in *Foreign Policy,* "Anatomy of a Bloodbath."

For specifics on the downing of the Malaysia Airlines jet over Ukraine, the best sources are the Joint Investigative Team reports, available at the official website of the Netherlands Public Prosecutor's Office (www.om.nl/onderwerpen/mh17-crash/).

There has been much investigation, official and journalistic, into Russian efforts to use social media to muck around in Ukraine's politics, which turned out to be something of a warm-up for the United States in 2016. Radio Free Europe was on the Ukraine case early, and so too was Paul Roderick Gregory, much of whose work on the subject was published by *Forbes.*

ExxonMobil, Rosneft, and Seadrill all have energetic public affairs teams that produced a steady stream of information through their respective official corporate websites. If you want to know their stated rationale for any given move, it's right there in black and white. Like ExxonMobil's successful drilling efforts in the Kara Sea, the undoing of Yevtushenkov and Bashneft, which was happening at the same time, was a well-covered event. But for Sechin's takedown of Russia's minister for economic development Alexei Ulyukaev, check out Karina Orlova's "Sechin's Sausages: A Glimpse of the Underbelly of Russia's Oil Industry" in *The American Interest,* September 2017.

The Tillerson quotations at the end of chapters 22 and 23 are from his aforementioned talk at the University of Texas in February 2016.

CHAPTERS TWENTY-FOUR AND TWENTY-FIVE

Austin Holland's 2017 sworn deposition notwithstanding, the deepest well of information about power and politics around the earthquake issue is the reporting of investigative journalist Mike Soraghan for *Energywire.* The documents he turned up, often pried away from government agencies using the Oklahoma Open Records Act, form the backbone of this part of the story. The *Bloomberg* reporter Ben Elgin unearthed some other notable emails about Harold Hamm and the pressure he was putting on OGS administrators. Rivka Galchen's "Weather Underground" (*The New Yorker,* April 6, 2015) provided a nice snapshot of both Holland and the seismicity issue in Oklahoma at the time.

Statements and papers from the U.S. Geological Survey and the OGS are available at their respective websites. Zoë Schlanger at *Newsweek* elicited the quotation from Representative Lewis Moore at the end of chapter 24.

The eagle-eyed reporters from Reuters who spotted and reported all the strange changes in Continental Resources were Joshua Schneyer, who also did yeoman's work on the Oklahoma school budget situation, and Brian Grow, who had earlier reported on some of Aubrey McClendon's slippery behavior.

CHAPTERS TWENTY-SIX AND TWENTY-SEVEN

There was a fantastically entertaining slew of reportage on that confab of nutty hard-right political groups in St. Petersburg, Russia, in March 2015. Great stuff was dug up by Max Seddon for *BuzzFeed News,* Anna Nemtsova for *The Daily Beast,* Ilay Azar for *Meduza* (an online newspaper out of Riga, Latvia), Paula Chertok for *Euromaidan Press,* and Neil MacFarquhar for *The New York Times.* A full transcript of the Putin speech at the Valdai Discussion Club in 2013, which was referenced in the conservative forum's literature, can be found at en.kremlin.ru/events/president/news /19243.

There is a lot of information about the inception, mission, management, and operations of the Internet Research Agency in the February 2018 and September 2018 indictments filed by the Office of Special Counsel in the U.S. District Court for the District of Columbia. But there was a lot of really good reporting being done in real time, long before the U.S. Department of Justice got involved. Reporters for the local St. Petersburg newspaper *My Region* kick-started this story. Shaun Walker at *The Guardian* and Adrian Chen at *The New York Times Magazine* both filed excellent, detailed reports on the firm in the spring of 2015. For a clear-eyed insider account of working at the Internet Research Agency, tune in to Lyudmila Savchuk's talk at the Atlantic Council's 2018 Transatlantic Forum on Strategic Communications (www.youtube.com/watch?v=klyhzAumPfU&t=1252s).

Both the two special counsel indictments of the Internet Research Agency and the separate indictment of members of the Russian Federation's GRU intelligence services (*United States of America v. Viktor Borisovich Netyksho et al.*) offer clear and straightforward accounts of Russian Federation government interference in the 2016 U.S. election. Statistics about how and how far those operations reached into the American polity are further spelled out in "The Tactics & Tropes of the Internet Research Agency," a report by New Knowledge, commissioned by the U.S. Senate Select Committee on Intelligence. You can find it at document cloud.org/documents/5632786-NewKnowledge-Disinformation-Report-Whitepaper.html.

The full complement of Donald Trump Jr.'s infamous "I love it" email exchange was published in *The New York Times* on July 11, 2017. Trump junior himself released them on Twitter when it became clear the *Times* had the goods. Many other publications followed suit. So they are there for the reading. And then blinking, and then reading again.

CHAPTER TWENTY-EIGHT

The specifics of Aubrey McClendon's death and the finding of cause come from the official reports from the Office of the Chief Medical Examiner in Oklahoma. You can access the full March 1, 2016, indictment of McClendon at www.forbes.com/sites/christopherhelman/2016/03/01/the-federal-indictment-of-aubrey-mcclendon/#37eeecd8574a.

The statement released by the attorneys Lowell and Flood on behalf of McClendon was quoted in *Forbes* and the *Oklahoman* website, among others.

The fiscal and economic situation in Oklahoma remained easily traceable in the state treasurer's monthly reports.

Footage of the town hall meeting featuring Lewis Moore in Edmond can be found at www.desmogblog.com/2016/01/19/fracking-industry-linked-earthquakes-oklahoma-crack-political-party-lines.

Jake Walter, the current state seismologist in Oklahoma, was especially helpful for understanding not only the science of seismicity but also how the political and regulatory steps taken in the governor's office and the Oklahoma Corporation Commission helped reverse the enormous ten-year rise in earthquakes. Mike Cantrell was also helpful with the politics and constraints of OCC.

Darryl Fears of *The Washington Post* deserves credit for alerting the wider public to the long, slow seep of an oil spill that was in the process of overtaking Deepwater Horizon as the biggest oil spill in the United States.

If you want to watch Harold Hamm's full speech to the 2016 Republican convention you can access it at www.youtube.com/watch?v= M6NmkiXMe0I.

CHAPTER TWENTY-NINE

The statistics about oil and gas industry election spending are compiled and analyzed at OpenSecrets.org. *The Guardian*, with an assist from Global Witness, did key reporting on ExxonMobil's dealings in Nigeria. Senator Sherrod Brown called it out on the Senate floor during the debate about Section 1504 at the beginning of 2017. The best stories about the "bonus" ExxonMobil paid to the Guyanese government, including quotations from the ExxonMobil exec there, were in local publications including *Caribbean360*, *The Gleaner*, and *IslandVibez*.

The current situation concerning the Obiang family and Equatorial Guinea is detailed in the June 2017 report by Human Rights Watch, "'Manna from Heaven'? How Health and Education Pay the Price for Self-Dealing in Equatorial Guinea." Philip Willan laid out the details of Roberto Berardi's imprisonment in a July 2015 story for *The Italian Insider*.

Jay Branegan's essay, "EITI Pull-Out: Another Blow to U.S. Leadership on Fighting Corruption," is worth reading in full (www.thelugarcenter .org/blog-eiti-pull-out).

INDEX

Read on for an excerpt from
Rachel Maddow's new book

CROWN
NEW YORK

Available wherever books are sold

....

"WHAT'S A SPIRO AGNEW?"

WHEN LYNDON JOHNSON REQUESTED AIRTIME ONE EVE-
ning at the end of March 1968, network television bosses
in the know assumed the president planned to address
the nation on the growing conflict in Vietnam. LBJ certainly had some
explaining to do on that front. He had campaigned for the presidency
four years earlier on a pledge to keep America from getting dragged
into a full-on war in Vietnam. He had promised that he would not send
thousands of young American men "to do what Asian boys ought to be
doing for themselves," that is, fighting off the Communists. But then
he had done just what he said he would not.

By the time the 1968 presidential primary season was in full cry,
with Johnson fighting off challenges from the peace-monger candidates in his own party, the war in Southeast Asia was not only raging
but escalating. Dozens of U.S. soldiers and marines died every single
day in Vietnam: every day, seven days a week. By that spring, many
of the American boys being killed over there were draftees, not volun-
teers. The Tet Offensive, launched by the North Vietnamese forces at
the end of January 1968, had spiked U.S. casualties on the battlefield.
And spiked the number of troops Johnson said he needed on the

ground in Vietnam. *More than half a million.* And all of that spiked doubt and frustration back home. After the surprise of Tet, the war suddenly seemed far from winnable anytime soon. More than a thousand American boys were dying every month, and nobody was sure this dear and bloody sacrifice would achieve anything worth having.

Johnson's nationally televised address on March 31, in prime time, unfurled—at the start—about as expected. While many Americans doubtless fumed about missing the new episode of *Bonanza* or *The Smothers Brothers Comedy Hour,* the president spent nearly three-quarters of an hour defending the war in Vietnam and restating its purpose. He granted the "pain [the war] has inflicted" and "the misgivings that it has aroused," but would not apologize for doing what he thought best. "What we are doing now, in Vietnam," he said, "is vital not only to the security of Southeast Asia, but it is vital to the security of every American." He was aiming for peace, and soon, he explained, but refused to give away the store to the Commies. "Our common resolve is unshakable," the president asserted, "and our common strength is invincible." He insisted that the enemy's recent campaign of attack was a failure. "[The Tet Offensive] did not collapse the elected government of South Vietnam or shatter its army—as the Communists had hoped," he said. "It did not produce a 'general uprising' among the people of the cities as they had predicted." But you could almost hear it in his hangdog voice; Johnson's own confidence seemed shaky.

And then, right at the end of his address, the president said something unthinkable, something nobody saw coming. "With America's sons in the fields far away, with America's future under challenge right here at home, with our hopes and the world's hopes for peace in the balance every day," he said, "I do not believe that I should devote an hour or a day of my time to any personal partisan causes or to any duties other than the awesome duties of the office—the Presidency of your country. Accordingly, I shall not seek, and I will not accept, the nomination of my party for another term as your President."

I shall not seek, and I will not accept. Good God.

A sitting president of the United States, constitutionally eligible to run for another term, decided—without warning to even his closest aides, without confiding completely in his own vice president—to call it quits.

That bombshell tossed into the middle of the presidential nominating process sent both Democrats and Republicans scrambling to recalculate their odds and their strategy. Each major party's nominating process had been a pretty wild political slalom that year. But now, with the incumbent's stunning announcement that he was leaving of his own accord and the race for the White House suddenly wide open, both the Democrats and the Republicans eventually decided to settle on tried-and-true figures for the top lines of their respective tickets: LBJ's incumbent vice president, Hubert Humphrey, would run for the Dems, and Eisenhower's old VP, Richard Nixon, would be the man for the Repubs. The only surprise on either slate turned out to be the man whom Nixon picked to be his running mate: a little-known first-term governor from a mid-Atlantic border state—a novice and novel political figure who would ultimately turn out to have far more impact on our national trajectory than most Americans have ever stopped to consider. His now-all-but-forgotten story has also turned out to be an odd historical doppelgänger, almost a premonition, for what the country would go through with the next Republican president who would face impeachment, after Nixon.

On paper, the Democrats' 1968 nominee—Humphrey—was a stolid, predictable, no-nonsense choice. Not only was he a household name for his long service as LBJ's vice president, but he had been a lion of the Senate, a brave and early champion of civil rights. A safe choice for the Dems. You might think. The optics of the Democrats' 1968 convention were considerably less reassuring. There were fits of pandemonium on the floor of the convention hall in Chicago, led by antiwar Democratic delegates who were sure that Humphrey was poised to continue the grinding, disastrous war that was ripping the country apart.

And the action inside the hall was nothing compared with the energetic and riotous activity that all but shut down the streets surrounding the site of the convention, Chicago's International Amphitheater. Those frantic scenes became the enduring images of the 1968 presidential election: outrage and antiwar protests laced by paroxysms of violence; Mayor Richard Daley's Chicago police, joined by National Guardsmen, clubbing the "agitators" first into submission and then into paddy wagons.

A young Republican political operative sent to monitor the Democratic convention surveyed the scene and reported back on his findings. "We should side with Daley and the cops," twenty-nine-year-old Patrick Buchanan told his boss, the party's newly minted presidential nominee, who really didn't need to be told. Law and order, that was his thing.

The Republicans had held their own convention a thousand miles south of Chicago, in sunny Miami Beach, Florida, a few weeks earlier. And while the action inside the hall made it appear, at least to those watching at home, to be a considerably more genteel affair, the goings-on outside were something akin to the chaos that would soon unfold in Chicago.

Just as Republicans from across the country were in the midst of coronating Richard Nixon as their nominee, a torrent of violence and unrest was erupting just across town, in one of Miami's predominantly African American neighborhoods. What began as a "Vote Power" rally organized by local black leaders quickly turned into a violent confrontation with police.

Miami's malignantly bigoted police chief, Walter Headley—who had famously proclaimed a year earlier that "when the looting starts, the shooting starts"—confidently assured the public that his officers "know what to do." Hundreds of Miami city police, county police, and, eventually, National Guardsmen met the protesters with a show of force that included armored military vehicles, bayonets, and "clouds of tear gas." When all was said and done, three people were dead. And dozens more were injured, including a five-month-old baby who was teargassed by police. The officer responsible said of the incident, "I'd do it again." Though he added, "I'm sorry the baby got gassed."

Inside the protected confines of the Miami Beach Convention Center, it was lawful and orderly, with about as much drama as a gathering in Mamie Eisenhower's drawing room. Which was exactly what the Republican pooh-bahs were hoping for. They needed their party to be the real safe choice in these roiling times.

The GOP had kicked around the idea of nominating for president the moderate, aristocratic governor of New York, Nelson Rockefeller. Or maybe the Michigan governor, George Romney. There was a late flurry of interest in a comely new California governor named Ronald

Reagan. Reagan had Barry Goldwater's hard-right politics, presented with a polish and sheen burnished on Hollywood's back lots. But Reagan was a novice. He'd run his first political race just two years earlier. Republicans instead settled on their own safer bet—a man with a big résumé, a reputation for political genius, and the tenacity of a rat terrier.

Richard Milhous Nixon was already, by then, a very familiar face in American politics. He was elected first to Congress in 1946, then to the Senate just four years later. He had been Dwight Eisenhower's vice president for two full terms, eight years dutifully serving at the shoulder of the most popular Republican president of the century to that point. Nixon had come within a whisker of the presidency himself in 1960, losing to John F. Kennedy in a race that was defined by Nixon flop-sweating his way through a debate with the slightly younger and much more telegenic senator from Massachusetts.

But even after that loss in 1960, even after an even more humiliating defeat in the race for governor in his home state of California two years later (even after he told the reporters who covered him, "Just think how much you're going to be missing. You don't have Nixon to kick around anymore"), he still refused to quit. He campaigned for Republicans across the country in the off-year election of 1966, earning due credit for helping Republicans rack up big gains in the House. And, cashing in those chits in the race for his party's presidential nomination, he handily dispatched all his rivals in 1968. He started as the front-runner, won almost every primary contest, easily batted down weak attempted challenges from Rockefeller on the left and Reagan on the right, and then won the nomination easily, on the first ballot of the convention in Miami.

Whatever else there is to be said about Richard Nixon, he was one hell of a political gamesman. Nixon understood that if he was to avoid losing the presidency—*again*—in what was sure to be another close race, he needed a number two on the ticket who added value, who shored him up where he was weakest. And so, the real business of the Miami Republican convention didn't happen on the floor, or even out in the streets beyond the convention hall. The real business of the convention happened in Richard Nixon's head and heart as he calculated his choice of a running mate.

There was plenty of buzz on the convention floor about the next veep nominee, on both sides of the party's political wings. The short list drawn up by the delegates and the network commentariat included that conservative up-and-comer from California, Ronald Reagan, as well as the moderate John Lindsay, the mayor of New York City. Nixon was reportedly agonizing over his pick; the press pack stalked the convention, in the sweltering August heat of Miami, hunting for word on the only real news to be had. Nixon pushed the decision later and later, until he finally made up his mind at the very last minute, on the last day of the convention.

At just before 12:30 that afternoon, with the hungry reporters duly alerted and assembled, Nixon finally emerged with the news they had been after. But first he teased, for drama's sake. "Our deliberations took place, for your information, throughout the night last night, except for one hour. I took that hour off for sleep," Nixon said. "They began again this morning at 9 o'clock and have continued until the present time." Then, finally, mercifully, Nixon came out with it. "I have now made a decision. I shall recommend to the convention that it nominate for vice president on the Republican ticket Governor Agnew of Maryland."

Governor Who? Of Where?

Even Governor Spiro Agnew himself was a bit taken aback, the way Nixon later told it. When a reporter on the convention floor asked how his running mate had reacted when he got the call, Nixon responded with a rare flicker of humor. "I think the best indication of surprise is when a lawyer has no words," he said. "Governor Agnew, as you know, is a lawyer and is a very articulate man. . . . I'd say there's about 20 seconds before he said a word!"

In a year of boldfaced political names like Lyndon Johnson, Hubert Humphrey, Bobby Kennedy, Ed Muskie, Nelson Rockefeller, and Richard Nixon, this newcomer just didn't seem to fit the bill. Who the heck was Spiro Agnew?

Or, as the joke went at the time, "*What's* a Spiro Agnew?"

The country, like most of the working press, could be forgiven its ignorance. Spiro Agnew, aged forty-nine, had been governor of Maryland only eighteen months, having won office largely because the competing Democratic machines in Baltimore accidentally blew up their own party's primary and let the nomination go to a kook perennial candidate segregationist who publicly accepted the no-longer-quite-so-coveted endorsement of the Ku Klux Klan. Agnew's gubernatorial victory certainly didn't owe to his long history in Maryland state politics. He had won exactly *one* race in his entire career to that point, serving as county executive, which is sort of like being mayor of Baltimore County, from 1962 to 1966. So of course nobody outside Maryland knew much about him. Really, nobody inside Maryland knew much about him. Spiro Agnew had gone from obscure local official, to fluke governor of Maryland, to the nominee for the vice presidency of the United States in less than six years.

The choice was a genuine surprise to everyone: to Agnew, to the Republican Party, to the national political press corps, to the rest of his fellow Americans, most of whom were just learning his name. And then puzzling out why exactly a guy with a Greek name was an Episcopalian.

The Nixon team, however, knew exactly who (and what) Spiro Agnew was, even without taking the time to learn much about him and even without bothering to vet him too awfully closely. For Nixon and his team, Spiro Agnew represented political expediency. What looked to outsiders like a roll of the dice, a dangerous gamble, was actually a result of Nixon's reading the political landscape from thirty thousand feet. Humphrey would be tough enough to beat on his own, and Nixon was already worried about a third-party challenge from the populist, racist former Alabama governor George Wallace—a potential shot to the heart of the Republicans' emerging southern strategy. Nixon had seen enough of Agnew to know he could help where it counted most.

Dueling narratives about the new vice presidential nominee emerged before the Republicans even broke camp in Miami. The GOP message gurus introduced Spiro T. Agnew—"Ted" to his friends—as a political figure best captured by the catchy radio jingle created when he ran for Maryland governor just a few years earlier, sung to the tune of Frank Sinatra's "My Kind of Town (Chicago Is)":

"My kind of man, Ted Agnew is!"

"My kind of man, Ted Agnew is! Our great new talent for! Governor! And what's more, he's your kind of man, Ted Agnew is! Taking your stand, Ted Agnew is!"

In the Republican telling, Agnew was a blue-collar, tell-it-like-it-is leader who could appeal to working-class voters because he was one of them. He was not a career politician but the son of Greek immigrants who put himself through law school after honorably serving the country in the military (including earning a Bronze Star for his service during the Battle of the Bulge). He was a political outsider, a straight shooter defined by straight-up American ideals: hard work, honesty, integrity. Agnew was that kind of man. "Well, I like him because he's honest," one supporter offered, "he's really honest."

The Dems wasted no time in constructing a Spiro Agnew counter-narrative, releasing their own TV ad highlighting Agnew's complete lack of experience on the national stage. It was, well, kind of mean-spirited when you get right down to it. The spot begins with a tight and inelegantly framed shot of a small corner of a television set, with its ungainly fat channel-changing knob as the focus. Then comes the sound of a man, off camera but apparently tuned into the set, beginning to chuckle. The camera slowly pulls out as the man's laughter grows louder and more insistent, to the point of hysteria, until the lettering on the television is revealed in full: "Agnew for Vice-President?" The laughing fit continues after a hard cut to the next screen, white lettering on a black background: "This would be funny if it weren't so serious." As the 1968 general election season got under way, the Democrats seemed intent on having sport with Spiro Agnew. They were going to make him a laughingstock. A national joke.

But a funny thing happened on the way to the White House that year. The Dems soon found out Spiro Agnew could give as good as he got. They learned that if you wanted to play nasty, Spiro Agnew was all in. He was blunt. He was vociferously politically incorrect. He was likely to answer any opposition jabs with a flurry of roundhouses and haymakers. And that made his campaign events a sensation the national news media could not ignore.

Agnew could be counted on to taunt antiwar protesters, East Coast "elites," and the unwashed "hippies" who, in his telling, contributed nothing useful to society. "I'll tell you this," Agnew said at a rally in York, Pennsylvania, "they can't run a bus, they can't serve in a governmental office, they can't run a lathe in a factory, all they can do is lay down in the park and sleep or kick policemen with razor blades!"

"Somewhere, somebody failed you," Agnew barked at a group of hecklers, while the cameras rolled. "Your churches must not have gotten through to you because you don't even know anything about the golden rule! . . . I'm frankly ashamed of you. And I think you ought to be ashamed of yourselves."

The crowds who came out to his rallies reveled in Agnew's unapologetic take-the-paint-off-the-walls partisanship. His increasingly confrontational taunts became a constant presence on the network newscasts. What news executive could pass on scenes like this?

Governor Agnew's lack of filter occasionally led him into controversy on issues of race and ethnicity that might have shamed other pols. Like his law-and-order insistence that petty looters ought to be shot by police. Sure, the cops should try to make an arrest first, but if that fails, "the officer should not hesitate to shoot him." After the collective horror generated by that position, Agnew clarified that he just meant that taking aim at a few looters "would be a tremendous deterrent." During one short stretch of the campaign, he was forced to apologize for crudely referring to Polish American voters as "Polacks," and then immediately thereafter for describing a Japanese American newspaper reporter as a "Fat Jap." Agnew promised that he meant no offense with the remarks, apologizing, he said, "if I have inadvertently offended anyone." But close observers began to get the feeling there was nothing *inadvertent* about it. Reporters covering him on the trail at the time said he was undaunted by the criticism, apology notwithstanding. They started calling the incident "the boo-boo in a muu-muu."

Spiro Agnew's political brand was built around the idea that he was an outsider who had never been a card-carrying member of the patrician establishment. It would have been off message, off brand, for him to start acting like a career pol either—careful, measured, mealy. And if he didn't actually appear to care whom he had offended, that became a feature of his candidacy, not a bug. Rather than hurting him, his "slip-ups" seemed to solidify his support with the Republican base.

"I guess by nature I'm a counter-puncher," he proudly told reporters. "You can't hit my team in the groin and expect me to stand here and smile about it."

Agnew counterpunched himself all the way to the White House, at the side of Richard Nixon. And he didn't stop once he settled in behind his new desk on Pennsylvania Avenue. "In Spiro Agnew," wrote that young Nixon political op, Pat Buchanan, "I found a fighting ally in the White House, a man with guts and humor, willing to give back as good as he got, who did not flinch from battle. He relished it."

Funny thing this, old habits die hard. And when the exercise of those habits has delivered fame and glory and raucous applause, they are unlikely to die at all. It is a rare man or woman who is ever really changed by ascension to high office, or tempered by the solemnity of the oaths they have sworn or by the national duties they have shouldered. And Spiro Agnew was certainly not among that rare breed.

Temperamentally, ethically, he was largely untouched by office. But the reverse is hardly true. Spiro Agnew left indelible marks on his office, on his party, on his government, and on his country.

And yet, for all his very real impact, Agnew's story is largely forgotten today. Even fairly assiduous students of America's modern political history can be forgiven for being a tad fuzzy on what exactly prompted Agnew's dramatic resignation from office in 1973. *It was some penny-ante tax evasion back in Maryland, right?*

Part of the reason for the lost history of Spiro Agnew is the simple factor of time. It's been more than fifty years since that 1968 campaign season, and nearly fifty since he resigned the vice presidency in disgrace. But time alone does not account for Agnew's obscurity. Agnew's downfall, of course, was also overwhelmed by the sheer epic sprawling disaster of Richard Nixon and the Watergate scandal—the only scandal in living memory to unseat a president.

But it's definitely worth stopping and considering Spiro Agnew and his crimes and misdeeds all on their own. Because Agnew's is a story of a scandal so brazen that, had it not occurred at the same time as Watergate, would likely be remembered as the most astonishing and sordid chapter visited upon a White House in modern times. Heck, in any times.

Agnew's is a tale of a thoroughly corrupt occupant of the White House whose crimes are discovered by his own Justice Department and who then clings to high office by using the power and prerogative of that same office to save himself.

And the playbook Agnew wrote to try to save himself has left its own long legacy. For the elected official who prides himself on busting through political norms—and insists on always punching back harder than hit—it's a pretty straightforward set of plays. And leaves no time to fret over the destruction you leave behind. If saving yourself means undermining the institutions of democracy—the Department of Justice and the free press, for starters—well, fire up the backhoe. Obstruct the investigations of your crimes; smear and threaten and demand investigations of the investigators; play the victim; indict the press; throw up a smoke screen of legal argument, no matter how bizarre or foundationless. *The vice president of the United States cannot be indicted while in office. Says so in the Constitution. Sort of.* And by all means convince your legion of supporters that the allegations against you are all vicious lies, that the evidence against you is conjured and concocted by enemies threatened by your overwhelming political strength. That it's all just a big witch hunt.

But there is another piece of the Agnew story also worth considering, one with a slightly happier tincture. Because the whole story of Agnew's crimes and his downfall and his descent, ultimately, into something between ignominy and obscurity is not all bad, or entirely dispiriting. This is also the story of faceless but faithful public servants doing their jobs with thoroughgoing integrity. It's the story of determined young federal prosecutors who uncovered the crimes of a politician at the very top, faced down a torrent of threats to their persons and to their investigation, and refused to stop until the truth emerged. It's also the story of their bosses at the Department of Justice who shielded them from the predations of Agnew and his partisans.

Terrible people doing terrible things is a (terrible) fact of life, but it doesn't ordinarily bring on a constitutional crisis; it's the reason we have law enforcement. But when the very worst people are at the top of American government, and willing to use the awesome powers of their office to stay there and thwart justice, the protection of the Constitution requires the very *best* people, also in office, willing to stand up and do what's right. This is that story, too.

And if any of this sounds familiar, it's because history really is here to help.

©2019 NBCUniversal Media, LLC™

ABOUT THE AUTHOR

Rachel Maddow is host of the Emmy Award–winning *Rachel Maddow Show* on MSNBC, as well as the author of *Drift: The Unmooring of American Military Power,* a #1 *New York Times* bestseller. Maddow received a bachelor's degree in public policy from Stanford University and earned her doctorate in political science at Oxford University. She lives in New York City and Massachusetts with her partner, artist Susan Mikula.